Attain Glorious Immortality

By following the footprints of the Master: Heaven Awaits!

A personal guide to finding and following the Narrow Way to eternal life of unending jubilation in the magnificent Kingdom of Heaven

By

J. William Lucky Lynde Goddard

Copyright © 2012 J. William Goddard

His true followers develop a faith or trust which perceives the invisible, accepts with absolute certainty the incredible, sometimes receives the unattainable, gains a peace beyond understanding and are truly content in the tranquility of blessed assurance.

Dedication

This manual is dedicated to our Lord Jesus Christ, Who suffered and died an agonizing death, in order to provide every member of the human race an opportunity to Attain Glorious Immortality.

Acknowledgements

Cover illustration by: Smart Art Studios, Tulsa, Oklahoma
Editors: Diane Bertone and Linda Stephens

Reviewers - Scriptural accuracy: Bob & Anne Green, William Corns, Vic Emerson, Harold Lasiter, Roy Miller, Charles Hammett, Dan Harris, Charles Dickinson, Kyle Buck, Kermit Buck, Charles Bailey, Darrell Blackman, Spud Barrett, Marvina & Gary Goddard, Ph.D. and the late Olen Campbell, a faithful Christian and friend, who at 85, passed shortly after completing his review

Challenge and Encouragement: Carol & Fred Albright, friend, All American and number 1 critic, Kim Hunter, D.O., an exceptional Physician and Healer, Vicky Troxell, Candy Elias, Dorothy Hall, James & Jamie Gilbert, Anna Miller, Johnny & Betty Wood, Chris Jones, M.L. Goddard, Sheri Kishen, Sandra Penner, David Million, H.D. & Patricia Ann Wilson, Amanda Kelly Cross, Jonathan & Babette Biddlecombe, Scott Frigard, N.L. Goddard, the late Patty Choat, a genuinely dedicated Christian lady, a victim of cancer, who was taken from us far too soon and the late Les Hall, a devoted and knowledgeable Christian, as well as, a faithful husband and friend.

All rights reserved. No part of this publication may be reproduced, stored in, a retrieval system or transmitted in any form or by any means – for example, electronic, photocopy, recording without the prior written permission of the publisher. The only exception is brief quotations in printed reviews.

Unless otherwise stated all Scripture references are taken from the King James Version (KJV)
Copyright © 2012 J. William Goddard
Printed in the United States of America, 2012 – First Edition
10 9 8 7 6 5 4 3 2 1

ISBN-13:978-0-615-62449 5 - Premier Literary Advisers
ISBN-10:0615624499

Published in association with Premier Literary Advisers

HIS TRUTH

Lake Eufaula, Oklahoma
HisTruth@gmx.com

Table of Contents

Preface	4
Foreword	5
General Prologue	7
Chapter I: Understanding our God	25
Chapter II: Guide to the Divine Format of the Bible	55
Chapter III: The Message of Christ	63
Chapter IV: The Authority of Christ	71
Chapter V: The Church that Jesus Built	75
Chapter VI: Preparing for your place in Heaven	89
Chapter VII: The Way of the Cross	105
Chapter VIII: Introduction to the Life of Christ	123
Chapter IX: The Life of Christ	127
Chapter X: Christ our ultimate Pattern	165
Chapter XI: Simplified Overview of the Old Testament	171
Chapter XII: Simplified Overview of the New Testament	181
Appendix 1: Quick Start Guide to Glorious Immortality	191
Appendix 2: Checklist to determine if a religious group is His Church	199
Appendix 3: Comparative Analysis – Do you attend His Church?	203
Appendix 4: Examples of unsupported teachings	211
Appendix 5: Comparative Analysis of selected religious organizations	217
Appendix 6: Summary of selected elements of the Divine Mosaic	223
Appendix 7: Words of Jesus, His Apostles and Disciples	233
Appendix 8: Selected Prayers and related Teachings of Jesus	245
Appendix 9: Significant Prayers of the Bible	247
Appendix 10: Relief for the anxious or troubled Mind and Spirit	249
Appendix 11: Message to new Christians	251
Appendix 12: Biblical Myths Misconceptions and Mysteries	255
Finale	265
Closing Comments - Suggested Outside References	269
References	270
Detailed Outline of Contents	271
Additional works coming soon	274

Preface

This guide was written for all those in search of answers:

Answers to questions regarding that pesky feeling that something is amiss; which sometimes changes into periods of unexplained dread, anxiety or guilt.

In many cases, this undefined yearning began early in the teen years and continues as an on-going intermittent irritation.

Some have described these sensations as a definite feeling that something just below surface is missing or as an ongoing feeling of quiet dissatisfaction that our life is incomplete.

The problem seems to be difficult to explain or put a finger on.

In order to gain relief some turn to the excessive use of mind numbing substances or riotous lifestyle.

After recuperating from an alcoholic or drug induced high, these underlying frustrations are often accompanied by a devastating sense of guilt, which usually results in the need for additional relief.

This type of behavior often leads to a downward spiral with almost certain negative consequences.

The cause and a simple, but effective cure are disclosed in Appendix 10.

Direct *answers* are provided for individuals who are active members of a church, perhaps for many years who honestly do not have an elementary understanding of the basic tenets of his or her faith, but have remained active, for the usual reasons.

These individuals may harbor a strong desire to understand the Message of Christ, but are heavily involved in work, school activities and social events with precious little time to study the dogma of their church and develop a clear understanding of the Teachings of Jesus and His Disciples. Unfortunately, a lack of knowledge often thwarts efforts to obtain a full understanding of the subjects and issues being discussed or taught in his or her church.

Answers are provided for long-term church members, who love and are making sincere efforts to serve God, but have weighty questions concerning the inconsistencies that exist between the doctrine being taught from the pulpit and the Teachings of the Bible.

The *answers* provided will assist the user in rapidly developing a greater understanding of our Creator, the Message of Christ, His Church, the Life, Death and Resurrection of Christ and His Holy Word.

For the student without training, this guide will open up the treasures of the Word. He or she will experience a special thrill in clearly defining Biblical Truths, which may not have otherwise been as easily accessible.

This guide will assist you in obtaining the answer(s) you seek.

In His Holy Name,

M.L. Main

M.L. Main
Associate Managing Director

Premier Literary Advisers

HIS TRUTH

Lake Eufaula, Oklahoma
HisTruth@gmx.com

God, our everlasting King, Lord, Creator and Savior is for evermore glorified and praised.... Heaven Awaits!

Foreword

This is possibly the most significant self-help book you will ever utilize, as it is a clear-cut instructive guide to the most essential, valuable and important volume, in your personal library.

The results of recent religious polls reveal the existence of substantial uncertainty throughout the world, regarding the basic Teachings of Jesus and His Disciples.

Research clearly indicates a widespread, misguided belief that God deeply loves and would never allow his children to suffer for all eternity. While it is true that God is Love, a study of the Bible will reveal that He is also a God of Wrath.

His sense of Divine Justice demands eternal reward for His faithful followers and everlasting punishment for all those, who choose to disregard His Will.

Each of us will enter the final phase of our existence either at the moment of death or somewhat prematurely upon the Second Coming of Christ.

The human body is mortal, but your soul is immortal!

The final segment of your life will be everlasting, either in marvelous contentment and elation or overwhelming anguish.

We are living in the end times.

All those living at time of the Second Coming, will be eyewitnesses to a spectacular exhibition of the unbelievably awesome Power of our Creator. At that very moment the words "paradise lost", will take on a whole new meaning for all those who failed to take advantage of their time on earth to follow the footsteps of the Master.

This terrorizing event will reveal itself in the form of titanic lightning flashes, immense flames and massive cloud formations, which will change from the normal distinctive sky of blue instantaneously into a unique, eerie, but strikingly regal fusion of white, orange and red.

Fright and terror or elation and overwhelming ecstasy will fill every living soul, upon hearing the thunderous shout of the archangel and deafening trumpet blast.

This spectacular panoramic view will be overshadowed by the awe-inspiring grandeur and glory of the Second Coming of the Lord, along mysterious disappearances; thousands rising to meet their Lord in the air, as well as, the dead and all those alive being transformed into eternal beings.

After all the worldly riches and achievements of man, along with all his hopes for building future splendor have been destroyed; and the final dream has faded away. After that wonderful, magnificent and dreaded Day of Judgment has past... and Lord Jesus has proclaimed His final irreversible verdict...

Now that every individual, above the age of accountability who ever dwelled on the face of the earth has learned his or her eternal destiny and is either joyfully looking forward to countless eons of boundless bliss, discovery, contentment, serenity and the loving eternal light of their Lord.

Or, the overwhelming majority desperately searching for relief, even for just a moment, from the nightmare of never-ending fires, brimstone, total darkness and the unrelenting chaos of Hell, with absolutely no hope of further appeal, release or escape. One can only feel compassion for all those who find themselves in such an appalling position, as they are completely defenseless and will be punished for all time, without end.

For all those interested in learning more about the end of the world and the fate of the unprepared, a projected account of the end of the world and the events following entitled **"The very first day of Eternity",** which is based upon the Words of Jesus and His Disciples has been included at the end of the General Prologue, which follows this section. This narrative will provide the reader with a vivid frame of reference and understanding of the reality of Hell, as well as, the fact that each of us has a choice as to where we spend our eternity.

The purpose, of course, is to focus attention directly on one critical question, which should be carefully considered, while we live in the relative safety and comfort of our temporary home here on earth.

Exactly how does one avoid the everlasting Wrath of God and properly prepare for a place of rest and joyfulness in the Glorious Kingdom of Heaven?

Naturally, we must attend to the requirements of everyday living, but we are also required to make an effort to gain the hope of Heaven, by sincerely seeking to live a full Christian life and actively preparing ourselves for a place in Heaven.

We do this by expressing our Love for the Lord, with enthusiastic praise, vigorously searching the Scriptures, carefully following the Patterns, Commandments, Instructions and Examples provided, as well as, regularly Worshiping our Lord in Spirit and in Truth.

It is a grave error to ignore the only process of being saved from the everlasting flames and darkness of Hell. Our Salvation is based solely on the perfect, sinless life and supreme sacrifice suffered by Jesus Christ. His Miraculous Resurrection not only confirmed His Divinity, but provided the Way (JOHN 14:6), which is our only Hope of gaining complete remission of sins and Glorious Immortality in the magnificent Paradise of the Kingdom of Heaven.

Disregard of His Words recorded in New Testament will absolutely guarantee eternal damnation and everlasting retribution.

Several years ago, our Lord impressed upon the mind of the author the necessity to make available specific information regarding the simple requirements to be saved from the fires of Hell, using mass communication methods. Rather than enjoying the material blessings of God and fruits of his labor during his retirement as planned, the author was humbled, felt duty-bound and compelled to create this manual. This manuscript is not inspired, but does contain numerous passages from the inspired Word of God, which provide direct support of each declaration of the author.

Consideration has also been given to those living a fast paced lifestyle and all others who wish to rapidly learn the specific Divine Will of God. A series of two quick start outlines are available in Appendix 1, which will provide a basic understanding of the Key Patterns, Examples, Instructions, and Commandments, presented in the New Testament, in just a few hours.

Recognition, appreciation, praise, honor and glory are offered to our God, for His love, guidance, and the talents, He so liberally endowed upon His servant. The author is well-known for his capacity to present complex and sometimes perplexing concepts in a simple, easy to understand manner. The writer was moved by and gives gratitude for spoken words, in countless sermons, and insightful writings of the many dedicated men of God, which provided the foundation of knowledge and understanding necessary for development of this volume.

This manual will assist you in discovering the answer(s) you seek

God be eternally Honored, Praised and Glorified…Heaven Awaits!

General Prologue

Contents

A. Introduction

B. Summary of Objectives

C. Overview of Appendixes

D. Detailed Outline of Contents

E. How to make the best use of this manual

F. The very first day of Eternity

G. Closing Comments

A. Introduction

The term General Prologue is employed in this volume to clearly indicate that the introductory remarks of the author are of much less importance than everlasting Divine Will of God. Wycliffe first used this expression of humility in his translation of the Bible, published in 1384.

It is suggested that this guide be used in conjunction with your personal Bible or New Testament.

This volume was produced in a large size, in order to gain the advantage of being relatively flat, when open.

These materials have been prepared in a modified outline format, in order to quickly convey comments, concepts and suggestions in a minimum number of words. Whenever possible, short phrases are used in lieu of complete sentences.

Capitalization, underline, italics and bold have been employed to emphasize key words or concepts.

In Addition, for purposes of clarity only, the author has added one or more words to various passages of Scripture, which are denoted by brackets.

In the process of your studies, the use of the educational concept of reinforcement or the use of recurring verses, definitions and comments will quickly become apparent.

In doing so, the author used the same method employed in the New Testament by our Lord, His Disciples and many Gospel Ministers today.

This ancient technique was employed to reduce confusion and in order to assist individuals new to the study of the Bible, in quickly gaining an understanding of the fundamentals.

Individuals learn at different rates, therefore once an understanding of the element(s) involved has been developed, *simply disregard the repetitive information.*

This manual is not just another analysis of the Bible, but rather a sincere effort to create an easy to understand academic and logical approach to gaining a clear understanding of the Message of Christ.

The information is presented in the form of a straightforward, unemotional, how-to guide to accomplishing *ultimate goal of finding and following the Narrow Way,* by learning, observing and conforming to the specific Teachings, Commandments, Patterns, Instructions and Examples provided by Jesus, His Apostles and Disciples.

MATTHEW 7:13-14
Enter ye in at the strait gate: for wide is the gate, and broad is the way, that leadeth to destruction, and many there be which go in there at: Because strait is the gate, and *narrow is the way, which leadeth unto [eternal] life, and few there be that find it.*

Make no mistake; you will not accidentally or unintentionally wind up in Heaven.

Jesus promised to prepare an eternal home in Glory (JOHN 14:2-3) for all serious minded people who are willing to study, comprehend and conform to the specific Divine Will of God, which with the aid of this volume is not difficult **and ...**

Then make a persistent, unwavering and **intentional** effort to carefully follow His simple Directives in order to prepare themselves for their everlasting place of joyfulness in the Glorious Kingdom of Heaven. (REVELATION 2:7).

Discerning the narrow winding path that leads to immortality should be the number one objective of every human being on earth!

This vital objective along with the **ultimate goal of being properly prepared** on that glorious Day of the Judgment will result in His faithful servants receiving permission to enter the magnificent Kingdom of Heaven, granted by the Grace of God.

It handbook was prepared for individuals in an academic setting, those being taught in training classes in their places of Worship and for everyone looking for the Narrow Way to Heaven in the maze of false teachings and blind alleys constructed by Satan and his disciples in our modern "anything goes" society.

The powers of darkness have increased significantly in their efforts to lead the vast majority to the horrors of Hell. In just the last fifty years, we have witnessed a steep decline in morals and acceptance of evils that had been unspeakable for centuries.

(1) The need for accurate open declarations of the specific Divine Will of God and the frightening results of disobedience has never been greater than today.

In the opinion of the author, most people have a longing for and an active interest in gaining complete understanding of the Will of their Creator, but are uncertain as to how to proceed.

(2) State of Uncertainty and Confusion

Jesus and His Disciples originally taught the specifics of his Divine Will, which was known, in the first century, as the **Gospel of Christ, the Truth** or the **Faith**, in order to develop belief, faith; trust in Jesus Christ and to explain His Divine Directives or the specific **Will of God, the Father**.

Reference: JOHN 12:49-50

In the opinion of the writer, the entire New Testament should be considered the Gospel of Christ. However, **confusion and uncertainty** exists regarding the **precise meaning of the term the Gospel of Christ,** which is discussed in Chapter III.

Therefore, the author determined it was necessary to make use of the alternate terms The Message of Christ or the specific Divine Will of God, in order to overcome confusion

The Divine Directives of Christ recorded in the four Gospels (Matthew, Mark Luke and John) were further clarified, amplified and added to in the remaining books of the New Testament.

Paul confirmed the Authority of His Disciples to make these additions to the **Message of Christ** or the **Divine Will of God** in 1 CORINTHIANS 14:37.

In essence, an essential purpose of this manual is to illuminate the elements of the *Gospel or Message of Christ,* which is also known, in the pages of the New Testament Bible, as the *Truth* or the *Faith*. The definition of each of these terms is: the complete, all important and specific, *Divine Will of God*.

(3) Another obstacle facing mankind is the immense, wicked Influence of Satan and his evil angels, which include:

(a) Distraction (the diversion of the mind of man from His Word, to the carnal attractions of this world) **(b) Delay** (the attempt to influence mankind to put off addressing spiritual concerns, until it is too late) **(c) Defeat** (the endeavor to create a feeling of failure to such extent that the individual loses his or her willingness to even attempt to obey) **(d) Doubt** (an evil effort to create doubt regarding their Creator, His Word and their personal ability to become His faithful follower) **(e) Discourage** (encourages mankind to focus on the negative aspect of this life and not on the positive aspects of working toward and attaining Glorious Immortality)

(4) Divine Format of the Scriptures.

It is the author's belief that one of the leading reasons why the vast majority has difficulty in understanding the Bible is due to a widespread failure to recognize that from the very beginning, the Scriptures were provided to mankind in a **Divine Format**.

The author has labeled and refers to this celestial system as the **Divine Mosaic**, due to its similarity to a very large and highly detailed mosaic, montage or tapestry.

An important personal objective of the author in publishing this handbook was the conversion of the significant elements of the **Divine Mosaic** into an arrangement of essential information in the form of lists, outlines or detailed explanations, which are easily understood.

The use of this manual will remove most of the effort involved in searching out and determining the elements of His Message.

An expanded explanation of the **Divine Mosaic** is provided in Chapter II and a *comprehensive summary of the significant elements* is presented in Appendix 6

B. Summary of Objectives

During the planning process, the author created a list of objectives to be achieved and the specific information to be included in this handbook.

The following is a summary of those objectives, in no particular order.

(1) Provide precise and complete information, concerning the Teachings of Christ and His Disciples.

In a clear, simple to understand format, based exclusively on the inspired Word of God, explaining how to fulfill His (Jesus Christ) Divine Purpose for mankind, which is for each individual to live a full, gratifying and fruitful Christian life as a faithful child of God.

(2) One of the main thrusts of the powers of darkness is to discredit the importance of the Holy Word of God.

An important objective of the author is to counter this massive wicked endeavor by Satan the evil prince of this world with a detailed explanation of the Message of Christ or the specific Divine Will of God.

(3) Provide the user with useful suggestions or methods of locating the Church, which Jesus built with his own hands, as described in the pages of the New Testament.

False teachings abound ranging from "believe and receive brand of religion" to devil worship.

A common expression, which only adds to the confusion, is the familiar phrase **"Attend the Church of your Choice"**.

While the people living in a democracy, such as the United States are free to choose any church or form of faith, many people are concerned and question how to choose the "right" church or the **"Church of His Choice"**.

In a perfect world, if everyone had listened to the Words of God, and if men had not introduced their own ideas, thoughts and traditions, there would still be only one Church today.

This world is not perfect and as a result of Satan encouraging men to add their personally conceived convictions and rituals to worship, we have the religious divisions of today.

By using this guide, his or her Bible, the suggested outside reference books and internet key-word searches, the reader will be empowered to readily identify His Church, by understanding its characteristics and using the process of elimination.

(4) Provide the knowledge and information, which will encourage and allow the user to rationally develop independent conclusions regarding finding and following the Narrow Way.

The intent is to provide every individual seeking eternal salvation a complete clear-cut understanding of the significant elements of Message Christ and His Disciples.

This approach should also assist the user in avoiding the blind alleys constructed by Satan and his followers.

Once the Way of Truth is determined, each individual must commit to following Jesus, which will require the denial of many worldly pleasures.

(a) In MATTHEW 7:13-14, Jesus warned that only a few will be willing to prove themselves during their earthly life or trial period.

For those who do, He promises a marvelous, everlasting gift!

REVELATION 2:10
Fear none of those things which thou shalt suffer: behold, the devil shall cast some of you into prison, that ye may be tried; and ye shall have tribulation ten days; **be thou faithful unto death, and I will give thee a crown of life.**

Be assured that gift of a Crown of Life is well worth the effort.

(5) Provide each user an opportunity and an organized method of examining his or her beliefs in the brilliant light of the Truth contained in God's Word.

Many people select the "church" they attend for the wrong reason or reasons. The family has always attended, most popular in the area, beauty of the building, location, fame of leader or for a worldly advantage in the political, business or social arenas.

Common reasons given for church selection include generalization such as; the "church" is filled with good people, does many good works, etc. These words of praise would apply to the vast majority of all religious organizations.

Religious surveys reveal that many have switched from one church to another for reasons other than a change in personal conviction.

Motivation may include the desire to please a spouse or family members or for business, political or social reasons.

Biblical scholars agree that from an ethical point of view, changes for such reasons can only be considered spiritual dishonesty.

A common pitfall is to base beliefs on feelings, personal judgment, or teachings of relatives, a prominent preacher or a human creed. To base beliefs upon such is to disregard the Word of God.

(a) Most shocking of all is the in-depth studies, which reveal the disturbing fact that millions have never examined the basis of their professed religious position nor have gained a clear understanding of the doctrine or beliefs of their church or faith.

(b) All churches teach contradictory doctrines.

For example, Baptists teach that baptism is by immersion only. Methodists believe that sprinkling, pouring, or immersion, according to personal convenience or preference, is acceptable to the Lord.

Baptists teach that once an individual is saved and becomes a child of God, he or she cannot fall from grace or be lost.

Methodists teach that a child of God can fall from grace and be lost.

(c) Of great concern is the very real possibility that millions of current faithful believers, who love and serve the Lord, are worshipping in vain. Regardless of the level of their faith, purity, righteousness and other Christ-like characteristics, they are all in danger of being eternally lost, if immediate steps are not taken to correct their fatal flaws.

(d) Therefore, for their eternal personal safety, regardless of current religious affiliation, it is recommended that each individual systematically, investigate and

test tenet of their faith, against the Words of Jesus and His inspired followers.

If the reader is a member of a specific faith, the author recommends he or she use Appendix 3 to quickly determine if personal beliefs and the tenets of their church are based solely upon the Word of God.

(e) This manual will also assist the user, in sorting out the Will of God and determining the Church of our Lord from the thousands of religious entities that exist in the twenty-first century.

This usually difficult and time-consuming task can be **easily and quickly accomplished** with the aid of Appendices 2, 3, 4, 5 and 6.

(6) Provide Scriptural support for each and every declaration regarding elements of the Faith.

(a) In Spiritual matters, the Bible is the ONLY source of trustworthy information.

It is the position of the writer that God, the Father has expressed His complete precise and explicit Will, through His Son Jesus and the Holy Spirit, who inspired the Disciples of Christ to write the books of the New Testament.

(b) Therefore each declaration made in this uninspired work of man is supported by one or more passages from His Holy Word to confirm its validity.

(7) Assist the reader in learning to effectively search the Scriptures and discovering the specific Divine Will of our Lord by utilizing the full counsel of God.

As the reader explores the Patterns and other elements of Divine Mosaic, he or she will discover that the Message of Christ and His Disciples is **quite specific**.

(a) While He did not provide a specific list, one of Christ's requirements is that each follower vigorously <u>search</u> the Scriptures

JOHN 5:39
Search the scriptures; for in them ye think ye have eternal life: and they are they *which testify of me."*

Paul adds this advice in 2 TIMOTHY 2:15 "Study to shew thyself approved unto God, a workman that needeth not to be ashamed, *Rightly [correctly] dividing the word of Truth."*

The user is provided with a simple technique of accurately dividing or determining the meaning of the specific Divine Will of God or test a wide range of religious briefs in Chapter II, Section C.

(b) The Command that His faithful followers utilize the entire counsel of God is recorded in ACTS 20:27 "For I have not shunned to declare unto you all the counsel of God."

It is simply not permissible to pick and choose the Patterns, Instructions, Examples or Commandments we wish to follow and disregard those which are not pleasing to us.

There are **<u>no</u>** unimportant Patterns, Instructions, Examples or Commands.

(c) Our Beliefs must be based upon clearly defined convictions.

These convictions must be based solely upon the Word of God, embracing His total counsel, while including only the Teachings, Patterns, Commandments, Instructions and Examples provided by Jesus, His Apostles and Disciples.

(8) To present a detailed guide to His everlasting Divine Will of God on a straight forward even handed basis, <u>without</u> bias or prejudice.

Without question, the author is a theologian who holds strong beliefs, theories and opinions; *many of which cannot be supported.* Therefore, he has intentionally placed all these **"on hold",** while writing this volume.

In order to make proper use of this manual, *the reader must also temporarily put all preconceived concepts, beliefs and opinions* **"on hold"** and search the scriptures with an open mind.

This step is necessary, in order *to rationally determine the specific requirements* of our

Lord and Savior, in order to be among the few that are allowed to enter the Gates of Heaven.

Every individual using this guide, including the author, who is honestly seeking the Narrow Way, approaches the topic with a bundle of beliefs formed in early childhood or from a variety of sources. Most may be true, but on the other hand, some may be erroneous or outright wishful thinking.

Therefore, it is in your absolute best interest to carefully examine each belief and compare them against the Words of Jesus and His Disciples or the **standard** by which we will be judged by our Lord on Judgment Day.

JOHN 12:48
He that rejecteth me, and receiveth not my words, hath one that judgeth him: *the word[s] that I have spoken, the same shall judge him in the last day.*

(9) Define a small fraction of the misinformation and false teachings, which have resulted from a major cultural shift.

Based upon the results of recent research, many scholars and religious leaders, who clearly understand the everlasting consequences, are alarmed at the downward trend in the level of Biblical knowledge.

While the United States is acknowledged as the most religious country of the industrialized nations, its citizens are profoundly ignorant regarding the teachings of the Bible.

Due to the post 1950 cultural shift, from print to video, America has slowly drifted away from reading His Word. According to surveys Bible study is not practiced in approximately 97% of all homes. Unfortunately, the Holy Scriptures, while highly revered, have become more of a decoration and symbol of Authority, than a book to read.

Those of us who were born prior to 1940 can remember a time, prior to this cultural shift, when life was lived at a much slower pace. During that time, most people read their Bibles on a regular basis, friends dropped in unannounced and passages from the Bible were among the topics of discussion.

Vacation Bible schools often ran between ten and fourteen days. Prayers, devotional Bible reading and morality training were encouraged in the public schools.

The decline in the study of the Bible was a gradual process. It now appears to have begun as more and more families obtained the new technology of television, which many believe marked the beginning of change. Regardless of the reasons, an immense cultural shift did occur.

The consequences of this shift are numerous, including the massive decline in the study of the Bible, which along with the deception of Satan, resulted in the **development of many generalization and misconceptions,** such as the following:

(a) Many believe all churches are basically the same.

It is simply **not possible** for all religions to be based on the specific **Divine Will of God**, since many teachings are completely opposite from one another.

Therefore, we can be absolutely certain, that all these churches **cannot** be totally consistent with the Message of Christ.

2 THESSALONIANS 2:12
That they all might be damned who believed not the truth, but had pleasure in unrighteousness

(b) Widely held misconception that many roads lead to salvation

The Words of Jesus in MATTHEW 7:13-14 reveal that there is **only one narrow path leading to Heaven** and **that few will find it.**

This manual is your complete guide to finding that Narrow Way and carefully following it, by observing and conforming to the specific Teachings, Commandments, Patterns, Instructions and Examples provided by Jesus, His Apostles and Disciples!

(c) Many people believe that members of numerous faiths, including non-Christian will be saved.

This is wishful thinking, which has concerned a multitude of religious leaders.

This concept is in direct opposition, to the clear declaration of Jesus.

JOHN 14:6
Jesus saith unto him, **I am the way,** the truth, and the life: no man cometh unto the Father, but by me.

(d) Many believe that it does not matter what you believe, just as long as you are sincere.

Yet another conviction without Biblical basis or support, which is in direct conflict with the Words of Jesus

MATTHEW 15:9
But in vain they do worship me, teaching for doctrines the commandments [traditions, teaching and convictions] of men.

As a result many individuals fall prey to false doctrines, due to the lack of knowledge of the Message of Christ.

(10) Combat the widespread problem of Biblical illiteracy.

Reviews of a recent book by Stephen Prothero, as well as other polls and surveys by respected organizations (Pew Forum on Religion and Public Life and the Harris Poll Religious Beliefs of Americans), have revealed a shocking lack of knowledge of basic Biblical details among Americans.

In **"Religious Literacy,"** Stephen Prothero, the chair of the religion department at Boston University, exposes the startling state of religious illiteracy in the United States.

Such ignorance is perilous because religion **"is the most volatile constituent of culture"** and, unfortunately, often **"one of the greatest forces for evil"** in the world, he writes.

For example, ninety percent of Americans claim to believe in God or a supreme Deity, but at the same time religious illiteracy is persistently demonstrated by the inability of the majority, including Christians to name even one of the four Gospels.

Even more surprising, the majority of Americans believe that Jesus was born in Jerusalem. (He was born in Bethlehem.)

"Being a Christian has become synonymous with having a born-again experience or opposing abortion and stem-cell research," he said. "American Christians focus on loving Jesus rather than learning what he taught. Prothero, further declares that **"faith without understanding is the standard"** and **"religious ignorance is bliss."**

To his credit, Mr. Prothero offers solid suggestions for including religious instruction in the public education system, while preserving First Amendment boundaries. It could take decades, in the current political environment, for these suggestions to begin to make a difference.

While the author whole-heartedly **agrees** with using an educational approach in the future, he believes that a **more immediate solution is required** to address the rapidly expanding dilemma of Biblical illiteracy; therefore this volume is dedicated to providing **a full range of Biblical information** including the following:

(a) To remove the mystery and eliminate uncertainty by providing a simplified clear-cut guidance to the basic unchanging eternal plan of our Creator that will actually assist those seeking clarity by providing an easily understood arrangement of the essential information and allowing the Bible to speak for itself!

Users will almost immediately realize that a substantial percentage of the information provided consists of passages of scripture copied directly from the King James Version of the Bible. This version was chosen because it is, by far, the most popular version of the Holy Scriptures.

It is recommended that this guide be used in conjunction with your personal Bible.

It is also suggested, if possible, that the user download the latest version of the Biblical computer software by eveningdew.com, free of charge.

The author has taken the liberty of highlighting key passages; however, the user is encouraged to carefully study the full passage in order to achieve complete understanding.

(b) Encourage and assist the reader in developing an expanded understanding and a much greater appreciation of their Creator.

(c) Assist the reader in expanding his or her vision of the greater Spiritual Realm, which has no limits and completely encompasses our massive universe of which the planet Earth is a very minuscule component.

(d) Provide examples of how our Creator made use of Patterns in Old Testament times and detailed explanation of the Patterns provided for all those living since the death of Christ or under the New Covenant.

(e) Spell out, in detail, His Pattern or Plan of Salvation, which is one of the key elements of the Message of Christ, required to successfully follow the Narrow Way.

(f) Reveal how we are directed to properly prepare ourselves for a place in the Kingdom of Heaven, by spreading His Word, our good works and faithfulness.

(g) Provide detailed information regarding; why our Savior came to earth, three days, which for all time, permanently altered the future course of the planet, the universal problem of sin, background and role of Satan, the evil prince of this world, as well as the Day of Judgment and more.

(h) Present a detailed outline of the Life of Christ, from His preexistence until today, which includes an overview of His Life, His role as our ultimate Pattern and the Divine Characteristics, His followers are instructed to pursue, as well as, His Divine functions today.

(i) Provide sweeping overviews of both the Old and New Testaments, including a brief summary of each book and listings of famous stories, estimated timelines, as well as significant, interesting and meaningful passages.

(j) Finally offer a Finale, which includes a brief analysis of the status of our society, a call for action and a stern reminder that there is absolutely no escape from the Realm of God.

C. Overview of Appendixes

Appendix 1: Quick Start Guide to Glorious Immortality

This Appendix was prepared for knowledgeable individuals or those living a fast paced lifestyle and all others who wish to **learn the fundamentals quickly**.

This is highly encouraged, because time is definitely of the essence, when a person is seriously considering becoming a Christian.

No man knows the time of his departure from this life, so it is only prudent to act as quick as possible once specific Divine Will of God is known and understood.

This material is presented in an outline form with verse references only, to provide each individual the advantage of uncovering the Truth, using his or her personal Bible or Biblical computer program.

(1) The purpose of this appendix is to guide the seeker of Truth to a clear understanding of the following basic fundamentals:

(a) Determining the modern name of His Church and developing a basic understanding of the New Testament Patterns, which governs certain aspects of the Church of our Lord.

The Holy Scriptures are the singular and absolute final authority in regards to the Divine Patterns of the functions of His Church.

The use of Appendix 2, 3, 4, 5 and 6, as well as the introductory information provided in Appendix 1, Suggested Outside References listed in the final section of this volume (books are available at most public libraries) or internet key-word searches should prove very useful in making a definitive determination of the only modern church, which replicates precisely and completely His Church of the first century.

This information is provides with full text verse references in Chapter V.

(b) Determining the steps required to conform to His Divine Pattern (Plan) of Salvation.

An expanded outline of the Pattern (Plan) of Salvation is provided in Chapter VI, with full text verse references.

Appendix 2: Checklist to determine if a religious group is His Church

This Appendix contains a checklist in the form of a series of questions to assist the user in determining if any religious group or organization under his or her personal review conforms precisely to the Scriptural Patterns and other requirements provided in the New Testament.

This is a very important determination. In order to be saved, Christians are required to conform, organize and harmonize their Worship of God in precise accord with the Patterns, Commandments, Examples and Instructions of Jesus and His Disciples without unauthorized additions or creative enhancements.

The Scriptural correct answer, without exception, to each and every question is yes.

(a) Appendix 2 & 3 are similar, but were designed for two completely different purposes.

Appendix 2 was designed to scripturally test the tenets of any church or faith.

Appendix 3 was developed to assist an individual in comparing the tenets of his or her personal church or faith against the Divine Pattern. Each statement of position includes supporting logic and/or verse reference(s).

In the long experience of the author, he has been able to identify only one of the well-known houses of Worship that conforms specifically to each and every element required by our Lord.

(b) The author would readily admit that it is possible that small lesser known churches exist somewhere in this world that also precisely conform His Will.

If you locate one or more, the writer would appreciate being advised of the name and address of each, at the address listed below.

If for any reason, after making your best efforts, you are unable to determine the identity of the Church of our Lord, drop a note to 131 W. Foley #1445, Eufaula, Oklahoma 74432. Or forward an e-mail to luckylynde@gmx.com

Upon receipt, the author will provide the names and addresses of congregations in your area, of the only church he is aware of that matches His Divine Will.

Appendix 3: Comparative Analysis – Do you attend His Church?

Do you attend His Church?

This is a question that every individual who loves our Lord Jesus should carefully and critically consider!

This significant question immediately leads to two other related questions, which are also of great importance.

(1) Are the members of my church or faith walking the Narrow Way that leads to eternal life?

(2) Do the members of my church or faith Worship God in Spirit and in Truth?

In the first century, there was only one Church, but as a result of Satan encouraging men to add their own thoughts and traditions to worship, we have the religious divisions of today.

In light of the grave warning in MATTHEW 7:13-14, it is strongly recommended that every follower of Christ compare and evaluate the beliefs, practices and traditions of their church or faith with the Commandments, Patterns, Instructions and Examples, provided by Jesus and His Disciples, in the pages of the New Testament.

To assist the user completing an in-depth examination, a series of yes or no and fill in the blank questions have been provided for their personal consideration

Each question is followed by a commentary, which either provides support or opposition based solely on the Word of God.

Appendix 4: Examples of unsupported teachings

The purpose of this appendix is to point out examples of teachings or practices of major churches, **which have no Scriptural support or are in direct opposition to the Message of Christ.**

It remains the sole objective of the author to uncover and highlight the Truth and not to offend, in any way, any person or religious organization.

In this section, we will delineate the various tactics Satan has used men to twisted the precious Words of the Lord Jesus and the eternal effects that inappropriate worship may have on the unsuspecting.

Appendix 5: Comparative Analysis of selected religious organizations

This analysis compares several popular forms of organized religion, with the Divine Pattern of His Church.

As you will note, with the exception of His Church, every church listed fails on one or more points to match the Divine Pattern, as will the overwhelming majority of all religious organizations.

Appendix 6: Summary of selected elements of the Divine Mosaic

A significant reason the vast majority has difficulty in understanding the Message of Christ is due to the reality that this vital information is provided to mankind in a Divine Format.

The comprehension of this single fact is a major step towards a greater understanding of His Holy Word.

This comprehensive overview will remove much of the uncertainty regarding the specific Divine Will of God.

Appendix 7: Words of Jesus, His Apostles and Disciples (with significant quotes from the Old Testament)

Those familiar with His Word know that it contains passages that address a full range of topics from Angels to finding solace when facing the tribulations of this life.

The purpose of this appendix is to quickly assist those who are not familiar with the Bible to tap into the ageless fund of knowledge provided by our Heavenly Father.

This is a sampling of the hundreds, possibly thousands of pearls of knowledge, found in the Scriptures, which will aid the user in living a more fulfilling life.

Appendix 8: Selected Prayers and related Teachings of Jesus

Much can be learned from the study of the content in the Prayers of our Master.

Christ provided each of us with a perfect Pattern for Prayer in MATTHEW 6:7-13, which is not intended to be recited, but to be used, as a Divine Pattern or Example to follow.

New Christians are encouraged to start with a careful review of the line-by-line analysis of this Glorious Example of Prayer, which is provided under the heading *Pattern of Prayer, our access to God, in Chapter VI.*

It is suggested that you take time to address your Heavenly Father with great humility and sincerity, before each meal.

You may pray at any time or place and if necessary, are permitted to pray silently, since He knows all your thoughts.

Appendix 9: Significant Prayers of the Bible

Few, if any Christians of today, have the ability to pray with the passion of Jesus Christ, the audacity of Abraham, the courage of Moses or the intensity of David.

Most could noticeably improve by simply studying their Patterns of Prayer.

This section has been included in order to provide the reader an understanding of the nature of prayers God has honored and answered.

Appendix 10: Relief for the anxious or troubled Mind and Spirit

This section is provided for the benefit primarily to those users who have not yet followed His Pattern of Salvation.

The specific cause and the time honored cure for that longing, which some call "a hole in the heart" is explained.

The balance of this appendix will discuss the Blessed Assurances of the Master, His Apostles and Disciples, which most will find helpful in **coping with a troubled spirit or heart.**

Appendix 11: Message to new Christians

At the very moment following baptism you have been greatly blessed, have taken on the responsibilities and accepted the limitations related to becoming a Christian.

The decision to turn away from a life of sin and become a follower of Christ is similar to an earthly marriage, which should never be entered into lightly, but with due consideration.

This Appendix provides the user with a basic sampling of the Blessings in Christ, a recommended course of immediate action and suggestions for avoiding sin and temptation.

Appendix 12: Biblical Myths, Misconceptions and Mysteries

Over the years, numerous myths, mysteries, misunderstandings, questions and misconceptions have developed regarding the Biblical account of various events.

The purpose of this appendix is to encourage the reader to use the **Bible as their primary reference and NOT to trust the words of men,** by providing answers and corrections to numerous misconceptions, myths, mysteries and questions

D. Detailed Outline of Contents

The inclusion of index was carefully considered, the huge number of references to certain keywords made the proposed index somewhat unwieldy. It was concluded that an expanded detailed outline of contents would be of much greater value to the majority of users.

E. How to make the best use of this manual

This handbook has been designed as a reference, which will meet the needs or requirements of a wide range of users, from the beginner to the very experienced, by providing a simple method of accurately determining the Will of God.

The author recommends that individuals with limited knowledge or those who prefer to learn, without the necessity of looking up each and every verse begin with Chapter 1 and simply study the material like a standard textbook.

The reading is easy. Key components of the Word have been presented in a modified outline format and supported by appropriate Biblical references, many of which include the entire text of the passage.

In order to gain the maximum benefit the user is encouraged to look up each verse reference-only passage, in order to enhance their understanding and his or her ability to make proficient use of their Bible or Biblical computer program.

On the other hand, an experienced user or those with limited time may wish to skip to the Appendix 1.

If this option is selected, the following outlines the recommended course of immediate action:

(1) Determine the name of the modern church, which is a mirror image of His Church or the original primitive church, which was organized shortly after His earthly death in the first century.

(2) Develop an understanding of His Pattern or Plan of Salvation.

(3) Seek the assistance from the Leaders of a local congregation of His Church and using the information provided; confirm that the Church selected is properly structured in accord with the ancient Patterns.

(4) Arrange for Baptism.

(5) Review the elements of Remaining Faithful and begin your journey.

The author firmly believes this handbook is a unique and distinctive approach to a complex multifaceted subject, which has the very real potential of assisting millions.

Comments, suggestions or corrections are always welcomed and appreciated. Please feel free to forward an e-mail message to luckylynde@gmx.com or drop a note to 131 W. Foley #1445, Eufaula, Oklahoma 74432.

If you have specific questions, please include your telephone number and the best time to call.

To follow is a fascinating account of the end of the world and the very first day of Eternity

Before beginning your study it is strongly suggested that the user read the fictional account of the very first day of Eternity

This story is intended to provide the reader with a vivid frame of reference and understanding of the reality of Hell and the fact that each individual has a choice of where he or she will spend their immortal lives.

F. The very first day of Eternity

This is the very first day of forever and Dr. Alan Smith is suffering in Hell, along with countless others, in a raging sea of lost souls. Everyone is now desperately attempting to adjust to living forever in total darkness, flames and intense pain, far removed from the light and love of God with simply no means of appeal for mercy or hope of release.

The Day of Judgment is now complete and the humbled, faithful and unfaithful servants of God have received their final judgment.

Only the very few who had been saved were privileged to enter the glorious pearly gates of Heaven.

The vast majority, of the billions of human beings who ever walked the face of the earth, are now here in this exceedingly unpleasant, ghastly and horrifying place, which was prepared for the devil and his angels.

Key Passage: MATTHEW 25:41

The day Christ returned to earth

The tragic saga of the former Dr. Smith began less than 24 hours ago. Before becoming a permanent prisoner of Hell, he had been a very successful physician, specializing in the treatment of cancer.

He had arisen to a beautiful day, and everything seemed to be right with God.

How could he have possibly known that within the next few hours that his world would be devastated in overwhelming flames and fury, or that time would end abruptly and eternity begin?

Reference: 1 THESSALONIANS 5:2-3

In his former life, Alan Smith had been doing quite well in most facets of his life.

Alan had a loving wife, two beautiful girls, a solid income and all the elements of the good life.

He and Susie had married immediately after graduation and begun a family.

The pair agreed upon almost everything, except their religious faith. Alan had been raised in the largest church in town, while Susie preferred a conservative congregation, which carefully followed the Teachings of Christ and His Disciples.

On many occasions, Alan recalled, Susie had attempted to convey the importance of testing the tenets of any religious faith against the Teachings found in the Bible, to no avail. Susie had regularly warned that she felt he was failing to Worship God as Commanded.

There would be no need for his skilled medical services in his present or future circumstance, since he and each of his fellow inmates had received new incorruptible bodies. These bodies were not physical, but spiritual and had been created to function perfectly for all eternity. (1 CORINTHIANS 15:52)

Essentially, the past 24 hours have been horrendous for Alan. First, his wife and angelic twin daughters, who were preparing to attend the first grade, simply disappeared while they were enjoying breakfast at their favorite coffee shop.

As he frantically searched for his family, he noticed that the waitress and cashier, who were always there to welcome guests, were also missing.

At that instant, the words of Jesus in LUKE 17:34-36, flashed in his mind - Alan immediately knew, but he told himself, "It cannot be the Second Coming of Christ; there must be some other answer".

Then suddenly, without warning, out of the blue, it all began with a startling, extremely powerful shout and trumpet blast that was not just heard around the world and to the depths of the oceans, but echoed throughout the entire universe.

No human had ever heard the voice of the archangel before, but there was no question when that mighty sound rocked each soul. The events that followed were nothing short of shocking, astonishing, marvelous and beyond belief.

Reference: 1 THESSALONIANS 4:16

Alan could now see literally thousands of people rising to meet Christ in the air.

Reference: 1 THESSALONIANS 4:17

For some unknown reason, Alan felt no upward pull; in fact he could feel nothing, except a growing feeling of fear and dread.

Alan was concerned, but told himself that some mistake must have been made. He would, without doubt, be assigned to his rightful place in Heaven.

From his youth, Alan had been a member of the church of his forefathers where many of the most important people in the area attended to worship God.

Alan attended church most weeks and tried to pray daily. He had given to the poor by providing no or low cost medical services, honored his father and mother, and in the past three years had earnestly tried to live a Christian life by carefully following the instructions of his pastor, Rev. Charles Wright, who had always reassured the members in his church that they would definitely be among the few given permission to enter His Glorious Kingdom.

In his sermon just last week, he taught that there are many paths to Heaven, and if an individual had truly accepted Jesus as Lord and maintained his or her faith in God, they would without any doubt be saved.

The turmoil continued with the blue-sky turning white and orange from dense clouds.

The sudden appearance of Jesus Christ, the Almighty Eternal King of Kings in all his glory, amidst gigantic lightning flashes and an astonishing intense inferno, commanded the immediate attention and focus of every living being on the face of the earth.

The Second Coming of Christ was unlike any event ever seen or even dreamed of by any member of mankind. An almost overwhelming feeling of apprehension and trepidation overtook Alan, as he viewed the amazingly terrorizing scene that had completely engulfed the sky above.

References: 2 THESSALONIANS 1:8, REVELATION 1:7

Bewilderment was coupled with high-pitched reverberation of desperate parents calling and then screaming the names of their children mixed with the resonance of wails, weeping and shrieking that surrounded him.

The dead then began to rise, not only from the cemeteries, but from many unexpected places.

Alan remembered that his late grandfather had once told him that the entire world was a gigantic graveyard, where the bodies of the billions of previous inhabitants were buried.

Reference: JOHN 5:28-29

The light of the sun was now rapidly fading to black. Stars, which were becoming visible during the middle of the day, appeared to be racing towards the earth, and the moon had taken on an eerie bloodlike shade of red.

The once stable universe appeared to be coming apart and the earth seemed to be spinning out of control. The ground was moving, quaking and rolling creating huge cracks, which caused the pavement to buckle, resulting in numerous accidents.

Huge sheets of glass were falling as large buildings twisted and strained against unseen forces. Structures, both large and small were crashing to the ground. Large trees and utility poles blocked the thoroughfares.

In the midst of all this chaos and uncontained reverberation, flaming volcanic matter from deep in the earth began to gush forth.

All-consuming firestorms, driven by hurricane force winds, had broken out all over the world.

In the distance, it sounded like a great battle was being waged in every direction. Many people were now in a state of frenzied panic, looking for loved ones and attempting to find a place, any place to hide.

Somehow, every one that was left behind knew exactly what was happening.

Reference: REVELATION 6:12-15

Christ had returned and this world would be no more!

Finally, there was the greatest blast ever heard and Alan blacked out. Thankfully, he had been spared the sight of the total destruction and annihilation of the planet earth.

Reference: 2 PETER 3:10

The Day of Judgment

When he revived, Alan found himself at a place he did not know in the midst of a enormous multitude of peoples from all nations.

In the distance he saw a new heaven and a new earth, as the first heaven and earth along with all the treasures of mankind had been totally destroyed.

Alan had another glimpse of Heaven when he saw the breathtaking, splendid, golden glory circled and elaborately jeweled throne of God, as well as, all the magnificent grandeur and brilliance that surrounded Him. The sight completely overwhelmed Alan, as well as every person in the multitude, which encircled him.

References: MATTHEW 25:31-34, ROMANS 14:10, 2 CORINTHIANS 5:10, HEBREWS 9:27

As a medical doctor, Alan and Susie had the financial resources to travel the world. The couple had visited many wonders of the world that had been built by mankind, but the finest things on earth they had seen were quite plain and ordinary in comparison.

Alan had always pictured the figure of Jesus as a man, as an individual who was somewhat frail, humble, with little interest in worldly goods or possessions, but very rich in grace and mercy.

Alan considered Him the perfect example for men to follow. Many elements of his analysis of our Lord would radically change, very shortly.

In time, as the monumental mass of humanity moved closer to the throne, Alan saw Susie and his twin daughters, who were standing on the right hand of Jesus.

Each had a brilliant radiance about them and they were smiling brightly, in a manner Alan had never seen before.

He attempted to make his way to their sides but was prevented and told firmly that he could not go to either the left or right until his judgment was pronounced.

Alan then looked to those who had already been judged, gathered on the left hand of Jesus and felt a deep compassion for each person as they stood silently with the face of doom that expressed intense regret and severe sadness.

Alan was becoming increasingly apprehensive as he heard the verdicts being announced.

The quotes from familiar passages "you failed to express your love of God by seeking first the Kingdom of God" (LUKE 10:27-28, MATTHEW 6:33) "you failed to search the scriptures" (JOHN 5:39), "you failed to consider the full counsel of God" (ACTS 20:27), "you failed to rightly divide the word of Truth" (2 TIMOTHY 2:15) or "you failed to worship in Spirit and in Truth" (JOHN 4:24) caused him to search his soul. His thoughts raced. Had he failed to do these? Had he not placed enough importance on his eternal life after death?

Judgment at the Throne of God

When Alan kneeled before Jesus, he felt quite insignificant and very small in the presence of the awesome grandeur and glory of the Son of God, his King, Jesus Christ.

His attitude was now one of profound and obvious humbleness, which was completely out of character for the highly educated, cultured, sophisticated doctor he had been, up until just moments before the disappearance of his wife and daughters.

In a twinkling of an eye, Jesus searched the Book of Life for Alan's name and judged him according to his works.

When He pronounced the judgment that Alan feared, a deep depression engulfed him and the nagging question: how could an intelligent, skilled individual be so successful and totally fail in the most significant aspect of his life?

Reference: REVELATION 20:12

He knew for certain, that he had no one to blame but himself, he had simply failed to personally put God first in his life, seek His Kingdom, and carefully search the Scriptures, as well as, Worshiping in Spirit and in Truth.

Those fatal errors resulted in the selection of an improper church, which conducted unacceptable forms of worship and a vast accumulation of unforgiven sins, over his lifetime.

Immediately, **Alan clearly understood that his name had never been written in the Book of Life** and that all the time he had invested in good works, prayer and worship had been absolutely in vain.

Reference: MATTHEW 15:9

After hearing the verdict of his Lord Jesus, Alan immediately cried out for mercy as many had before him and pleaded that he endeavored to live a good life.

Alan had in fact lived a good life, much better than most; however, he failed to study his Bible and therefore was unaware of the strict requirements of God.

In addition, he had never been able to accept the fact that a loving God could ever sentence His children, who had endeavored to serve him, to everlasting punishment.

In an instant he understood, that his God was absolutely just.

God had simply promised to reward the righteous and punish the disobedient.

Before he had the honor of standing before his Lord, Alan had not understood that he would be judged according to the Words of Jesus as recorded in the Bible.

Christ, the supreme and final Judge of mankind, simply could not accept his lack of understanding as an excuse for his failure to worship in Spirit and in Truth.

References: JOHN 4:23-24, JOHN 12:48, ROMANS 1:31

As he was being lead away, he looked over his shoulder, desperately searching for Susie and the girls, but they had already moved on to their reward of everlasting happiness in an indescribable state of ecstasy, exploring the boundless joys of Heaven.

All remembrance of lost souls they had known on the old earth had now completely vanished.

Reference: REVELATION 21:4.

On the other hand, Alan's reminiscences were crystal clear.

He suddenly understood that the memory of his loved ones, just as the rich man had remembered his brothers in LUKE 16:28, along with the total separation from God, were to be a part of his everlasting punishment.

When finally the last person to have ever walked the earth was judged and his fate determined, the multitude that gathered on the left of the Throne of God extended in every direction further than the eye could see.

As each condemned person stood silently reviewing their life on earth, suddenly without warning, the ground opened around them and they were all cast into the gigantic lake of fire that had been prepared for the devil and his angels by the immense and mighty hand of God

Back to the realty of everlasting punishment

Even the chaos and violent clamor that had occurred during the end of time on the old earth did not approach the uncontrolled pandemonium that rules this cavernous pit of total blackness.

It is filled with dense smoke, noxious odors and volcanic flames mixed with brimstone that erupts without warning, causing intense suffering.

Alan has been searching for a place to rest and escape this excruciating pain, even if only momentarily, to no avail.

Reference: REVELATION 14:11

During his lifetime Alan had a close friend named John Greene, who regularly attended a different denomination.

John believed that God in His mercy would never punish the lost souls for all eternity but rather would immediately annihilate sinners in the second death.

As he stood on the left hand of Jesus, prior to being thrown into these terrible flames, Alan hoped and prayed that John had been correct, that his punishment would be limited to a total separation from his God forever and he would be totally destroyed in an instant.

It has been several hours now, and Alan is beginning to believe his recollections of God's word.

First, he called to mind the story of Lazarus and the rich man (LUKE 16:19-31). Alan had studied this passage several times but had been unable to determine its exact meaning or application.

It was now clear, that the Words of Jesus had not been only a prophecy, but a graphic forewarning and preview of the future.

Alan then recalled the words of Jude "to whom is reserved the blackness of darkness" (JUDE 1:13) and the warnings of Jesus in (MATTHEW 13:42) "And shall cast them into a furnace of fire: there shall be wailing and gnashing of teeth." and (MARK 9:44) "Where their worm dieth not, and the fire is not quenched."

Alan had come upon his grandmother, Laura Jones, who had sorrowfully told him that she had seen his father, mother; her only child and their former pastor Rev. Charles Wright. She had attempted to reach them but was unable to break through the masses of lost souls.

Alan complained to his grandmother and indicated that he felt he had been treated unfairly. How could my God of love assign me, His loyal servant to this horrendously dreadful place with all of these appalling and repulsive individuals?

He then related to her details of several disagreeable encounters he experienced during the first couple of hours. There were mass murderers, serial rapists and others who committed unspeakable crimes during their lifetimes. One young man who had been privileged to be born into a family that attended His Church, but had drifted away, to follow his lust for life

Alan felt great sympathy for this grand lady, who worshipped at the same church he had attended and attempted to follow Christ all her life. Alan could plainly see that in addition to enduring the terrors of Hell, she was still in deep despair after hearing Jesus say, "You did not obey My Commandments, therefore, I never knew you."

Alan felt deep compassion not only for her, but the millions of others, like himself, who had been absolutely certain they would be among the saved, only to be shocked and surprised to find themselves among the condemned, simply because they had failed to worship in Spirit and Truth.

Alan's grandmother pointed out that just one unforgiven sin would prevent a person from entering the Gates of Heaven and seeing the face of God, the Father.

She explained that Christ had given His life for our sins and they had simply been found guilty of gross disobedience.

The final ruling of our Lord Jesus is supreme and absolutely without appeal whatsoever, as His Judgment is the highest of all.

In other words, we failed, during our time on earth, to carefully follow His Commandments and now must accept His Holy, final verdict of everlasting punishment in the Lake of Fire with the devil and his satanic angels.

This story, of course, is a fictionalized illustration, since Christ has not yet come for the second and final time.

It is, however, based upon *scriptural Truth and a keen familiarity* with expected reactions of human beings in distressing situations.

Conclusions

(1) Some of the elements in this narrative are conjecture, but the following are fundamental Biblical facts we do know, which are provided with supporting key passages:

(a) One day, when mankind least expects it, Jesus Christ will come in His Glory with His Holy Angels. (MATTHEW 25:13, MARK 13:32-33)

(b) That His coming could be at any time – day or night. (1 THESSALONIANS 5:2-3)

(c) That when He comes, the vast majority will NOT be ready. (MATTHEW 7:13-14)

(d) The earth and heavens, as we know them will be destroyed. (2 PETER 3:10)

(e) Someday each of us will die; this is an inescapable fact of life. (HEBREWS 9:27)

(f) There will definitely be a Day of Judgment. (2 CORINTHIANS 5:10, REVELATION 20:12)

(g) The vast majority will be punished for all eternity. (REVELATION 14:11)

(h) A Glorious place of abode will be prepared for His faithful followers. (JOHN 14:2-3)

(i) We shall have a new incorruptible spiritual body. (1 CORINTHIANS 15:50-54)

(j) For His faithful followers, death, sorrow, crying and pain shall be no more. (REVELATION 21:4)

(k) His faithful followers shall be like our Lord Jesus. (1 JOHN 3:2)

(l) The glory, joyfulness and unexpected surprises are far beyond our understanding or imagination. (1 CORINTHIANS 2:9, HEBREWS 12:22-23, 1 PETER 1:4, REVELATION 3:12, REVELATION 7:9, REVELATION 21:1-2, REVELATION 21:10, REVELATION 22:1-3)

The most important question is: Where will each individual dwell for all eternity?

If you fail to accept God's Grace and Love, by becoming His faithful servant and an active member of His Church, you have selected Hell and **to spend eternity as an angel of Satan, in everlasting Fire, by default.**

A similar choice was offered centuries ago to the children of Israel.

DEUTERONOMY 30:19
I call heaven and earth to record this day against you, that I have set before you life and death, blessing and cursing: *therefore choose life, that both thou and thy seed may live:*

Choose life!

G. Closing Comments

The user is expected to be pleased as they begin to understand the author's suggested method of gaining a comprehension of the Word of God and His Divine Will.

This technique allows the reader to quickly gain an understanding of His eternal Truths and the ability to come to his or her own independent rational conclusions.

The information provided not only removes much of the mystery often associated with the Bible, but also assists the user in recognizing and avoiding the blind alleys constructed by Satan and his disciples.

The writer anticipates that individuals trained in the study of the Bible, will find this manual to be a practical reference.

In addition, many of the millions of current members of His Church will find this volume a handy guide to the vast majority of the significant elements of the Faith

This volume should also prove to be very useful in the hands of the student who has little or no formal training in the study of the New Testament.

It will open up the treasures of the Word, and will likely provide the user the special thrill of having the ability to extract information from the Bible that may have been otherwise inaccessible.

Inexperienced users of other materials produced by the author have claimed to be pleasantly surprised at their increased level of understanding after only a few hours of use.

This guide is not comprehensive.

Additional volumes covering advanced spiritual concepts will be produced in the same format, if God wills and only through His gracious providence.

His true followers gain a peace beyond understanding and are truly content in the tranquility of blessed assurance... Heaven Awaits

Chapter I

Understanding our God

Chapter Contents

A. Introduction

B. Seek First the Kingdom Of God

C. Examples of what our Lord Jesus really wants from His followers

D. Support for an Absolute Belief in God

E. Fear of the Lord Is the Basis of All Knowledge, Wisdom and Understanding

F. The Godhead, a Divine Entity

G. Earthly Structures Similar To the Divine Composition

H. Understanding the Nature of the God of Heaven

I. The Interrelationship and Interaction of the Godhead

J. Attributes of the Godhead

K. Examples of the ferocious Wrath of God and His awesome power

L. The Wrath of God

M. The Love of God

N. The Grace of God

O. Patterns of God

P. Our God is a God of Patterns

Q. Examples of the Blueprints or Patterns of God

R. Patterns provided to Moses and the nation of Israel

S. Pattern of the Temple

T. God requires strict obedience to His Patterns and Commandments.

U. Examples of Disobedience to the Patterns of God

V. Final Comments

A. Introduction

(1) Significant Points to be addressed in this chapter

(a) To point out that the state of <u>confusion</u>, uncertainty or lack of understanding addressed in this guide has existed for at least three thousand years or a thousand years before the birth of Christ.

(b) Examples of what our Lord <u>really wants</u> from His followers.

(c) Assist the reader in expanding their <u>vision</u> and understanding of his or her Creator and the all engulfing, immeasurable Spiritual Realm of God.

This will be accomplished by asking the reader to consider a commandment from the Divine point of view and by providing detailed information, which reveals the factual reality of the Divine Spirit or our everlasting, all-powerful and boundless God, from various points of view.

(2) The problem of uncertainty, confusion or lack of understanding has existed for centuries

(a) Consider the plea of King David (This plea was made about 1000 years before the Birth of Jesus)

PSALMS 119:33-34
Teach me, O LORD, the way of thy statutes; and I shall keep it unto the end. *Give me understanding* and I shall keep thy law; yea, I shall observe it with my whole heart.

(b) Even His Apostles, before the indwelling of the Holy Spirit (ACTS 2:1-4), after spending many months listening to their Lord, did not have a clear understanding of His teachings.

MATTHEW 15:16
And Jesus said, *Are ye also yet <u>without</u> understanding?*

LUKE 24:45
Then <u>opened</u> he [Jesus] *their understanding, that they might understand the* [Old Testament] *Scriptures*

Please note: The opening of the understanding of His Disciples <u>did not occurred</u> until 40 days after the Resurrection of Jesus Christ, just before His Ascension to His Father in Heaven and ten days before the creation of His Church

(3) The Divine Point of View

The Divine Point of View is another approach, which may be useful to the user. It is suggested that in addition to considering the information provided in this handbook from his or her personal perspective that the reader endeavor to develop an expanded comprehension and greater understanding by attempting to look at the Patterns, Teachings and Commandments of our Lord and Savior from **His Point of View.**

In other words, a method of exercising our minds and increasing the range of our perception by attempting to logically determine the Divine Reasoning behind His Commands and Directives

The exercise is not to attempt to compete with God, which is not possible, but rather to logically determine the reason(s) why, for example, Jesus Commanded in MATTHEW 6:33 that we <u>first</u> seek the Kingdom of God.

There is almost universal agreement among experienced diplomats and successful sales professionals that the ability to look at a situation or issue from the point of view of the other individual(s) involved is an absolute requirement for long-term success in their chosen field. The same principle applies to each of us, who wish to expand or improve our understanding of our Creator.

(4) The boundless Spiritual Realm of our God has no limits and completely encompasses our massive universe of which the planet Earth is a minuscule component

(a) In order to know God, **we must understand that He is an invisible Spirit,** which is in constant attendance not only in all parts of the Earth and the Heavens, but throughout the entire universe and quite possibly far beyond.

(b) Each of us was born into hopefully a loving physical family. A detail often overlooked is that we are also the offspring of our devoted **Spiritual or Heavenly Father.**

Our Heavenly Father, who has always been, is now and will be forever, knew us long before our physical birth and is well aware of the future time, date and place of our ultimate demise.

Key Point to carefully consider

Just as there is no way to avoid physical death, it is **simply impossible to escape** from the infinite or unending Spiritual Realm of our Heavenly Father

(c) We all currently live in two realms of existence

The Physical Realm in which we all currently understand and the spiritual realm which we will all ultimately, fully comprehend

In addition, we will all reside in the Spiritual Realm forever, **either in glorious ecstasy or appalling anguish,** beginning at the moment of our death or upon the Second Coming of Christ.

B. Seek FIRST the Kingdom of God

MATTHEW 6:33
But seek ye first the kingdom of God, and his righteousness; **and all these things shall be added unto you.**

It is important to understand that this verse contains, not only a Commandment, **but also includes a very encouraging <u>Promise.</u>**

In order to seek the Kingdom, we must develop a general understanding of the Nature of God and a **very specific comprehension of His Divine Will.**

Fortunately, God has revealed numerous elements of His nature in the Scriptures, which are summarized from various perspectives in this chapter.

In addition, the widespread misconceptions regarding His physical nature and erroneous beliefs concerning the scope of the Wrath of God, which have developed in our society, will also be addressed.

C. Examples of what Lord Jesus really wants from His followers

(1) Lord Jesus requires complete OBEDIENCE to His Words in the New Testament. (MATTHEW 23:23, MARK 13:31, JOHN 14:23, JOHN 15:7)

Simply, that you live your life in *obedience* to the specifics of His Divine Message.

(2) His Commandments generally fall into three classes

(a) The first type relates to **His Divine Patterns** (Pattern of Salvation, forms of Worship in His Church, Prayer etc.), which are fully explained in this manual.

These Commandments should present no real difficulty in obeying as they are **simply, to be carefully followed.**

(b) The second type relate to **personal behavior.**

For example, the *most important Commands* are to Love your God and neighbor.

MARK 12:30-31
And thou shalt love the Lord thy God with all thy heart, and with all thy soul, and with all thy mind, and with all thy strength: this is the first commandment. And the second is like, namely this, Thou shalt love thy neighbor as thyself. There is none other commandment greater than these

Additional reference: LUKE 10:27-28

The Commandments of the Master were further illuminated, augmented and supplemented by His Apostles in the remaining books of the New Testament.

Paul confirms this role of the Apostles in 1 CORINTHIANS 14:37 "If any man think himself to be a prophet, or spiritual, let him acknowledge that the things that I write unto you are the *Commandments of the Lord."*

(c) The third type is of a **general nature.** .

(1) For example, we must believe in His existence

HEBREWS 11:6
But without faith it is impossible to please him: for he that cometh to God *must believe that he is,* and that he is a rewarder of them that diligently seek him.

The best evidence of existence of our God is the amazing universe in which we reside. A logical study of the universe and its size, complex design and origin will reveal that God exists, as well as, His immense Power and Divinity. (ROMANS 1:20)

Note: Support for unconditional belief in our Creator is provided in the section following.

(3) Christians are directed to circumvent and avoid <u>Sinfulness</u>

(a) *Jesus provided a Comprehensive list* (REVELATION 21:8)

(b) *The Great Apostle Paul provided two detailed summaries* (ROMANS 1:23-31 and 1 CORINTHIANS 6:9-11).

(4) Jesus requires that His followers make their own personal <u>determination</u> of how to find and follow the Narrow Way by searching the Holy Scriptures

JOHN 5:39
Search the Scriptures; for in them ye think ye have eternal life: and they are they which *testify of me.*

Additional reference: ACTS 17:11

Reminder: The purpose of this manual is to assist the user in completing their personal search, which includes the determination of the precise requirements to be among the few, who by their individual efforts will have properly prepared for their place in Heaven.

Important Point to consider

The general status of the religious world in the twenty-first century is a *state of absolute confusion, which almost always results in bewilderment and uncertainty* in the mind of the seeker of Truth.

It is the opinion of the author that God, the Father and His Son Jesus are definitely not pleased, but bear no responsibility for the current dilemma of mankind.

1 CORINTHIANS 14:33
For God is not the author of confusion, but of peace, as in all churches of the saints.

It is the firm belief of the author that the *answer to each and every question and dilemma of life* is provided in His Word.

Therefore, the only way to overcome this dilemma is to turn to the Bible, which contains the *only Divine message* that has ever been supplied to mankind and *is to be our sole source* of spiritual information.

2 TIMOTHY 3:16
All Scripture is given by inspiration of God, and is profitable for doctrine, for reproof, for correction, for instruction in righteousness:

JAMES 1:21
Wherefore lay apart all filthiness and superfluity of naughtiness, and receive with meekness the engrafted word, *which is able to save your souls.*

The following summarizes the benefits of diligence Bible study.

The Holy Word of God
an All-Sufficient Guide
author unknown

- ❖ The Bible contains the mind of God, the state of man, the way of salvation, the doom of sinners.
- ❖ Its doctrines are holy, its precepts are binding, and its histories are true and its insights unsurpassed.
- ❖ It is the traveler's map, the pilot's compass, and the builder's blueprint.
- ❖ It should fill the memory, rule the heart and be a guide unto the feet.
- ❖ It is the power of God, the work of the Holy Spirit and the glory of Christ.
- ❖ It contains light to direct, food to sustain, and peace to comfort you.
- ❖ It is our teacher now, our judge in the future and will be preserved forever.
- ❖ Its value beyond pure gold, its taste above fresh honey,
- ❖ Here paradise is restored, heaven is opened and the gates of Hell disclosed.
- ❖ Read to be wise, believe it to be safe and practice it to be holy.
- ❖ Study the Bible slowly, carefully, frequently... and prayerfully!

(5) His followers are required to make use of the complete counsel of God.

ACTS 20:27
For I have not shunned to declare unto you all the counsel of God.

(a) There are <u>no</u> unimportant Patterns, Instructions, Examples or Commands

It is simply not permissible to pick and choose the Instructions or Commandments we wish to follow and disregard those, which are not pleasing to us..

(6) Adding to or taking away from the Holy Scriptures are <u>condemned</u>, in both the Old and New Testaments.

(a) Each follower must also seriously consider and keep in mind the stern New Testament injunction against adding to or taking away from the Word of God.

DEUTERONOMY 4:2
Ye shall **not add** unto the word which I command you, **neither shall ye diminish ought from it,** that ye may keep the commandments of the Lord your God which I command you.

An additional warning is provided in PROVERBS 30:6 "**Add thou not** unto his words, lest he reprove thee, and thou be found a liar."

John clearly states in 2 JOHN 1:9 *"Whosoever transgresseth, and abideth not in the doctrine of Christ, hath not God.* He that abideth in the doctrine of Christ, he hath both the Father and the Son."

(b) And finally in the closing verses of the last book of the New Testament the meaning of this Commandment is made absolutely crystal clear.

REVELATION 22:18-19
For I testify unto every man that heareth the words of the prophecy of this book, If any man **shall add** unto these things, **God shall add unto him the plagues** that are written in this book: And if any man shall **take away** from the words of the book of this prophecy, **God shall take away his part out of the book of life,** and out of the holy city, and from the things which are written in this book.

(c) In addition, the forgoing verses (REVELATION 22:18-19) clearly indicates that God <u>has not and will not</u> provide mankind with any revelations other than those, which are included in the His Holy Word.

(7) Christians are directed to shun and reject False Teachers and Teachings

2 TIMOTHY 4:3-4
For the time will come when they will not endure sound doctrine; but after their own lusts shall they heap to themselves teachers, having itching ears; *And they shall <u>turn away</u> their ears from the <u>truth</u>,* and shall be *turned unto <u>fables</u>.*

Additional references: MATTHEW 24:11, MATTHEW 24:24, ACTS 20:29-30, 2 CORINTHIANS 11:13-15

D. Support for an Absolute Belief in God

Many have wondered if the God of Heaven really exists. Arguments associated to this and related topics fill hundreds of volumes.

The author will not attempt to prove the existence of God; only affirm his personal belief, based upon the statement in GENESIS 1:1 "In the beginning God [Elohim] created the heaven and the earth."

Elohim or Elohay is from the Hebrew root word meaning "strength" or "power", which has the **unusual attribute** of being plural in form, is found over 2000 times in the Old Testament. *Therefore, from the very beginning* [GENESIS 1:1] *this plural form for the name of God* was used *to describe the one true living God*

The creation or existence of God cannot be absolutely proven by quoting scriptures.

(1) The belief that God created all things, both seen and unseen, as well as, all life is a <u>fundamental</u> requirement of becoming a Christian.

It is important to note that the issue of the existence of God is not just a modern question, **but also existed during the first century.**

JOHN 10:38
But if I do, though ye believe not me, believe the works: that ye may know, and believe, that the Father is in me, and I in him.

JOHN 11:42
And I knew that thou hearest me always: but because of the people which stand by I said it, that they may believe that thou hast sent me.

Additional reference: 1 JOHN 5:13

(2) Statement of belief by King David

PSALMS 14:1
The fool hath said in his heart, There is no God.

(3) Statement of belief by the writer of the book of Hebrews

HEBREWS 3:4
For every house is builded by some man; but he that built all things is God.

(4) Logical reasons to believe in the existence of God

(a) The universal belief in God

Reference: ACTS 17:26-28

(b) The universal sense of morality

ROMANS 1:18-19
For the wrath of God is revealed from heaven against all ungodliness and unrighteousness of men, who hold the truth in unrighteousness; Because that which may be known of God is manifest in them; for God hath showed it unto them.

Additional reference: ROMANS 2:14-15

(c) The precise design of the universe

ROMANS 1:20
For the invisible things of him from the creation of the world are clearly seen, being understood by the things that are made, even his eternal power and Godhead; so that they are without excuse.

Additional references: PSALMS 19:1, PSALMS 97:6, ISAIAH 40:25-26

In summary, the universe in which we live reveals the results of a master plan devised by an Intelligent Designer, who possessed the power to execute the plan by creating the Heavens and Earth, then creating and breathing life into the first man.

(d) The order and design of the seasons

ACTS 14:17
Nevertheless he left not himself without witness, in that he did good, and gave us rain from heaven, and fruitful seasons, filling our hearts with food and gladness.

(e) The intricate design of the human body

Dedicated evolutionists are free to reject God, as the Creator and embrace Darwin's unproven theory as their personal belief system.

However, our society is quickly approaching the day when their claims that evolution is the absolute scientific standard, will not be blindly accepted, due to advancements in the study of the human genome. The discovery that life is encoded with an astonishing amount of information written in a distinctly comprehensible language may be the greatest scientific accomplishment of all time.

The end result is a 3.1 billion-letter instruction manual, which reveals a massive quantity of information and unlocks many mysteries of the human body.

This scientific advancement has opened up many additional research opportunities, which will undoubtedly prove to be both beneficial and intriguing.

Just considering the massive volume of the code gives one a feeling of awe and that mankind is about to have **a glimpse into the mind of God**.

Logical Conclusion

Never before has it been so obvious, that **only** the **hand of the Almighty** could have created such complex human beings.

Therefore, it is only natural and rational to accept the account of the creation in Genesis, rather than to assume that our complex universe came into existence by random chance.

E. Fear of the Lord is the Basis of all Knowledge, Wisdom and Understanding

Due to the eternal consequences, Spiritual Knowledge of the Godhead should be considered of immense importance.

(1) The fear of God is a significant subject, which is found throughout the Old Testament.

In the following verse, we discover that the fear of God is the beginning of knowledge, wisdom and understanding.

PROVERBS 9:10
The fear of the LORD is the beginning of wisdom, and knowledge of the Holy One is understanding.

Additional References: JOB 22:21, JOB 23:13-16, JEREMIAH 5:22, JEREMIAH 9:23-24, PSALMS 2:11; 19:9; 33:8; 34:11; 86:11; 111:10, PROVERBS 1:7

(2) Summation of King Solomon as he neared the end of his life.

ECCLESIASTES 12:13
Let us hear the conclusion of the whole

matter: **Fear God, and keep his commandments: for this is the whole duty of man.**

F. The Godhead, a Divine Entity

The Godhead (also known as the Trinity, an expressive term, which is not used in the Bible) is defined as a religious concept which declares that there is only one, true and living God existing in the Divine form of three interrelated Persons: God, the Father, God, the Son, and God, the Holy Spirit.

As the scriptures do not reveal any degrees of Deity, it is assumed that each has the same essence and all three are equal in their Attributes.

The Godhead acts when all three are acting or when one or two is the driving force, on behalf of all.

Furthermore, submission of one member of the Godhead to another does not result in the disruption of the Godhead or the removal of the submitting member from the Godhead.

1 JOHN 5:7
For there are three that bear record in heaven, *the Father, the Word, [Jesus Christ] and the Holy Ghost: and these three are one.*

This complex topic will be presented in greater detail in a planned follow-up advanced manual.

Important note: In order to avoid confusion in this volume, we will use the term "God" to denote the Godhead only.

Terms for the three separate interrelated elements will be **(1)** God, the Father, **(2)** God, the Son, the Son of God, the Son of Man, Jesus, Christ or a combination thereof, and the Lamb of God, **(3)** the Holy Spirit or the Holy Ghost.

G. Earthly Structures Similar to the Divine Composition

Many individuals find it difficult to understand how the God of the Bible is able to function in three separate and different ways at the same time as the God, the Father God, the Son and the Holy Spirit.

The best way is to simply accept what the Bible has to say on this topic, however, humans have an ingrained desire to understand the way things work.

This concept can be more difficult to comprehend, if an individual attempts to relate it to a similar earthly occurrence in nature that can be easily seen with human eyes.

To the knowledge of the author, an exact occurrence does not exist in nature.

However, prior to the widely known scientific explanation of the various forms of water, it may have been difficult for people, at that time, **to understand that rain, snow, ice; steam and fog are <u>all forms</u> of water.**

This is not a perfect example and many may never comprehend fully how the Father, the Son and Holy Spirit are <u>interrelated parts of one Godhead.</u>

The following verses confirm that there is only one God.

References: GENESIS 1:1, GENESIS 1:26, JOHN 1:1-3, ISAIAH 45:15, 21, JOHN 1:10-14, 1 CORINTHIANS 8:6

H. Understanding the Nature of the God of Heaven

(1) Research indicates that misconceptions regarding the physical nature of God exist widely in our modern society.

Many visualize God as a kindly old gentleman akin to Santa Claus, the Statue entitled God the Father, created by Artus Quellin II in 1682, the famous painting The Creation of Man by Michelangelo, a fresco in the Sistine Chapel or other physical images.

In order to know God, we must understand that He is **an invisible Spirit,** which is in constant attendance not only in all parts of the earth and the heavens, but throughout the **entire universe** and quite possibly far beyond.

Key Point to carefully consider

It is significant to note that it is possible that our immense universe is only a **small speck in the Realm of God.**

1 CORINTHIANS 2:9
But as it is written (ISAIAH 64:4), Eye hath not seen, nor ear heard, neither have entered into the heart of man, the things which God hath prepared for them that love him.

(2) Mankind has been provided a revelation of God through His Son, Jesus Christ, the Holy inspired Scriptures, our physical world and the night sky.

Jesus provided the greatest source of information and nature of God in the assumed physical form.

JOHN 14:9
Jesus saith unto him, Have I been so long time with you, and yet hast thou not known me, Philip? *He that hath seen me hath seen the Father;* and how sayest thou then, Show us the Father?

Although the revelation provided by Jesus was extensive, we cannot be certain that the written record is complete, since the **Scriptures do not contain a record of all the achievements, events and Words of Jesus.**

JOHN 21:25
And there are also many other things which Jesus did, the which, if they should be written every one, I suppose that even the world itself could not contain the books that should be written. Amen

Additional reference: JOHN 20:30-31

Key Point to remember

We must accept that it is beyond the finite capability of the human mind to achieve a complete understanding of our infinite Creator, as many aspects *remain the secret things of God.*

DEUTERONOMY 29:29
The secret things belong unto the LORD our God: but those things which are revealed belong unto us and to our children forever, that we may do all the words of this law

We have been provided with all the information required to develop a basic understanding and to create a relationship with our Creator by carefully following the Directives provided in His Word of Truth.

Awareness of our God will increase, after one has submitted completely to His Will by following His Pattern or Plan of salvation, regularly attending His Church and remaining faithful by following the Narrow Way or the *Path of Obedience*.

References: JOHN 7:17, JOHN 9:31.

I. The Interrelationship and Interaction of the Godhead

The precise nature of these interrelationships is not clearly revealed, but biblical scholars generally agree that the on-going mission of the Godhead from the beginning was and is the redemption of mankind.

God, the Father is believed to be the divine designer and architect of the overall plan.

The role of God, the Son, in addition to assisting in the design of the overall plan, emerges as that part of the Godhead, which actively interacts with mankind and executed the Will of God, the Father.

The exact role of the Holy Spirit, which operates in the background, is the least understood.

Each element or person of the Godhead serves and defers to each other in perfect harmony.

(1) God, the Father witnesses, glorifies and directs mankind to listen to the Son.

MATTHEW 17:5
While he yet spake, behold, a bright cloud overshadowed them: and behold a voice out of the cloud, which said, *This is my beloved*

Son, in whom I am well pleased; hear ye him.

Additional references: JOHN 8:16-18, JOHN 8:54

(2) Jesus clearly indicated that He taught only the Will of God, the Father

JOHN 12:49-50
For I have not spoken of myself; but the Father which sent me, he gave me a commandment, what I should say, and what I should speak. And I know that his commandment is life everlasting: whatsoever I speak therefore, even as the Father said unto me, so I speak.

(3) God, the Father and the Son honor the Holy Spirit.

JOHN 14:26
But the Comforter, which is the Holy Ghost, whom the Father will send in my name, *he shall teach you all things,* and bring all things to your remembrance, whatsoever I have said unto you.

Additional reference: JOHN 14:16

(4) Jesus Christ, also known as the Word and the Son of God had a leading role in the Creation.

JOHN 1:1-3
In the beginning was the Word, [Jesus Christ] and the Word was with God, and the Word was God. The same was in the beginning with God. *All things were made by him; and without him was not any thing made that was made.*

Additional references: EPHESIANS 3:9, COLOSSIANS 1:16, REVELATION 4:11, REVELATION 10:6

(5) The universe and earth were created by His spoken word.

GENESIS 1:1-3
In the beginning God created the heaven and the earth. And the earth was without form, and void; and darkness was on the face of the deep. And the Spirit of God was hovering over the face of the waters. *And God said,* **'Let there be light';** **and there was light.**

PSALMS 33:6, 9
By the word of the LORD were the heavens made; and all the host of them by the breath of his mouth. **For he spoke, and it was done; he commanded, and it stood fast.**

Additional reference: JOHN 1:1-3

(6) The Word of God later came to earth, in the form of a humble man, as the Savior of the world, in the person of Jesus Christ.

JOHN 1:14
And the Word was made flesh, and dwelt among us, (and we beheld his glory, the glory as of the only begotten of the Father,) full of grace and truth.

(7) The Words of Jesus indicate that He visited the earth several times during Old Testament times.

The following New Testament passages indicate that Jesus had visited the earth several times before His virgin birth.

His Words provide the most conclusive and unmistakable evidence that the component of the Godhead, who walked and talked with Adam, Eve and numerous other human beings in the Old Testament, **was not God, the Father as many believe,** but was the same Divine Being, who was born of a virgin several thousand years later.

This contention is based upon the following:

(a) Recorded statements of Jesus, in which He teaches that no man has ever seen God, the Father.

JOHN 1:18
No man hath seen God [the Father] at any time; the only begotten Son, which is in the bosom of the Father, he hath declared him.

Additional reference: JOHN 6:46

(b) Warning issued to Jewish leaders by Jesus.

JOHN 8:24
I said therefore unto you, that ye shall die in your sins: for if ye believe not that **I AM** he, ye shall die in your sins.

(c) Jesus confirmed His Old Testament name (I AM recorded in EXODUS 3:13-14)

MATTHEW 22:32
I AM the God of Abraham, and the God of Isaac, and the God of Jacob *God is not the God of the dead, but of the living*.

JOHN 8:58
Jesus said unto them, Verily, verily, I say unto you, *Before Abraham was,* **I AM.**

ISAIAH 44:6
Thus saith the LORD the King of Israel, and his redeemer the LORD of hosts; **I AM** the first, and **I AM** the last; and beside me there is no God.

(8) Examples of interaction between Jesus and mankind, recorded in the Old Testament.

(a) Adam was placed in the Garden and provided with a mate.

Read the full account: GENESIS 2:15-25

(b) Adam and Eve committed the first sins

The first Adam was only given **one Commandment,** but he demonstrated the weakness of human by transgressing and violating the trust of His Creator.

Reference: GENESIS 3:8-24

(c) Cain

Reference: GENESIS 4:9-11

(d) Enoch

References: GENESIS 5:24, HEBREWS 11:5

(e) Noah

Reference: GENESIS 6:9.

(f) Abram

Reference: GENESIS 17:3

(g) Jacob

Reference: GENESIS 35:13-15.

(h) Lord Jesus from within a burning bush first spoke directly with Moses and then on other occasions.

Reference: EXODUS 3:13-14

New Testament reference: In the first ten verses of 1 CORINTHIANS 10, the Great Apostle Paul refers to and confirms the role of Christ in Old Testament.

(9) Role of the Holy Spirit

As indicated in the introductory statement, the exact role of the Holy Spirit, which operates in the background, is the least understood.

There are multiple views of exactly how the Holy Spirit interacts with mankind in these last days, which resulted from a lack of specific guidance in the Scriptures.

Comparing and contrasting the various views of His interaction, is very interesting, but adds nothing to the quest of finding and following the Narrow Way to heaven.

Therefore, the author has determined to defer an in-depth discussion to the planned follow-up advanced volume, which will fully address this issue.

Frequent questions regarding the Holy Spirit are "Why is the Holy Spirit referred to as the Holy Ghost, in the King James Version?" or Are the Holy Spirit and the Holy Ghost the same entity?

The meaning of the word "ghost" has changed, since the translation of the King James Version, some 400 years ago. At the time of the translation, the word in Old English meant "guest".

Therefore, the translators referred to Him, as the Holy Guest. The terms Holy Spirit and the Holy Ghost, refer to the same entity.

J. Attributes of the Godhead

The following is a sampling of the numerous Attributes of the Godhead.

(1) God is a Spirit (Immortal, Invisible)

In JOHN 4:24 Jesus affirmed that God is spirit. Therefore, God has no physical body or measurable structure.

Paul confirmed that God is invisible.

1 TIMOTHY 1:17
Now unto the King eternal, immortal, invisible, the only wise God, be honor and glory forever and ever. Amen.

While Jesus Christ did assume a visible human form during His sojourn to earth, His natural essence is invisible.

(2) God is everywhere (Infinitude)

The spirit of God is not only present all over the earth, but throughout the entire universe the sum total of His reality that God created for mankind and beyond.

God has no boundaries is without measure or is infinite.

1 KINGS 8:27
But will God indeed dwell on the earth? behold, the heaven and heaven of heavens cannot contain thee; how much less this house that I have built?

Additional reference: MATTHEW 28:20

(3) God is All Powerful (Omnipotence, Almighty)

The power of God is without limits therefore all things are possible. Christ promised in MARK 9:23 that with **God all things are possible for believers.**

MARK 14:36
And he said, Abba, Father, all things are possible unto thee; take away this cup from me: nevertheless not what I will, but what thou wilt.

Additional references: JOB 5:17, MARK 10:27, REVELATION 1:8

(4) God is All Knowing

The wisdom, knowledge and understanding of God is infinite or complete and without limits. He knows the thoughts, motives and intentions of every man and woman.

It is simply not possible to conceal anything from God.

Knowledge and understanding of God will naturally increase with regular church service attendance and personal study.

ROMANS 11:33
O the depth of the riches both of the **wisdom and knowledge** of God! how unsearchable are his judgments, and his ways past finding out!

PSALMS 147:5
Great is our Lord, and of great power: his **understanding is infinite.**

Additional references: ECCLESIASTES 12:13-14, PSALMS 139:2-4, PSALMS 139:11-12, 1 KINGS 8:39, JOB 37:16

James directs the faithful followers of Christ, who feel they lack wisdom, to simply ask in prayer and it will be provided.

JAMES 1:5
If any of you lack wisdom, let him ask of God, that giveth to all men liberally, and upbraideth not; and it shall be given him

(5) God Is Eternal

Eternity is a human term, which means endless time. God has always been, is now and will be forever. Since God is all knowing, He has complete knowledge of the past, present and future.

1 TIMOTHY 1:17
Now unto the King eternal, immortal, invisible, the only wise God, be honor and glory forever and ever. Amen.

God created the concept of time at the creation of heaven and earth for the benefit of mankind. The method of timekeeping, if any, employed by God is beyond our understanding.

2 PETER 3:8
But, beloved, be not ignorant of this one thing, **that one day is with the Lord as a thousand years, and a thousand years as one day.**

(6) God is the Supreme Deity (Potentate, King of kings and Lord of lords)

1 TIMOTHY 6:14-15
That thou keep this commandment without spot, unrebukable, until the appearing of our Lord Jesus Christ: Which in his times he shall show, who is the blessed and only **Potentate, the King of kings, and Lord of lord**

Additional references: REVELATION 15:3, REVELATION 17:14, REVELATION 19:16, PSALMS 47:7, PSALMS 95:3, JEREMIAH 10:10

(7) God is Holy

The Holiness of God refers to His perfect moral purity, which exalts Him above all things. Being Holy, He requires holiness in all His children. Holiness is a gift of God that is received as a result of faith and obedience to our Lord Jesus.

LUKE 4:34
Saying, Let us alone; what have we to do with thee, thou Jesus of Nazareth? art thou come to destroy us? I know thee who thou art; the **Holy One of God.**

EPHESIANS 4:24
And that ye put on the new man, which after God is created in righteousness and true holiness.

(8) God Is Righteous

Righteousness as applied to God either refers to His pronouncement of moral laws of human conduct, such as the Ten Commandments, or assurance that obedient Christians are in a state of righteousness or being right with God, through the cleansing effect of the blood of Christ, which resulted from His sacrificial death.

ROMANS 1:16-17
For I am not ashamed of the gospel of Christ: for it is the power of God unto salvation to every one that believeth; to the Jew first, and also to the Greek. For therein is the **righteousness of God** revealed from faith to faith: as it is written, The just shall live by faith.

Additional reference: ROMANS 3:24-26

(9) God is the Ancient of Days

DANIEL 7:22
Until the *Ancient of days* came, and judgment was given to the saints of the most High; and the time came that the saints possessed the kingdom.

(10) God is Everlasting (Creator, Wonderful, Counselor, Mighty God, and Prince of Peace)

ISAIAH 9:6
For unto us a child is born, unto us a son is given: and the government shall be upon his shoulder: and his name shall be called *Wonderful, Counselor, The mighty God, The everlasting Father, The Prince of Peace.*

(11) God is Great and Dreadful

DANIEL 9:4
And I prayed unto the LORD my God, and made my confession, and said, *O Lord, the great and dreadful God,* keeping the covenant and mercy to them that love him, and to them that keep his commandment

Additional reference: NEHEMIAH 1:5

(12) God is Unchanging (Immutability)

God is perfect and does not change. **Therefore that which we learn from His Word can be believed with absolute certainty**.

HEBREWS 13:8
Jesus Christ the same yesterday, and today, and forever

(13) God is Self-sufficiency (Has life within Himself, all other life is His gift to mankind)

JOHN 5:26
For as the Father hath life in himself; so hath he given to the Son to have life in himself;

(14) God Is Truth

2 THESSALONIANS 2:13
But we are bound to give thanks always to God for you, brethren beloved of the Lord, because God hath from the beginning chosen you to salvation through

sanctification of the Spirit and <u>belief of the truth</u>:

Additional references: TITUS 1:2, DEUTERONOMY 32:4, 1 KINGS 17:24, 1 TIMOTHY 3:15

(15) God is Merciful, Gracious, Longsuffering, Good and True

It is impossible for God to lie. His faithfulness is our assurance that every promise will come to pass.

This is important to all Christians, since our hope is based upon His promise that our sins will be forgiven and we will live forever in His presence.

HEBREWS 6:18
That by two immutable things, in which it was **impossible for God to lie,** we might have a strong consolation, who have fled for refuge to lay hold upon the hope set before us:

EXODUS 34:6
And the LORD passed by before him, and proclaimed, The LORD, The LORD God, **merciful and gracious, longsuffering, and abundant in goodness and truth**

Additional references: 1 CORINTHIANS 10:13, HEBREWS 2:17, HEBREWS 4:16, 1 PETER 4:19, 2 JOHN 1:3

(16) God is our Fortress, Refuge and Rock

PSALMS 91:2
I will say of the LORD, He is my **refuge** and my **fortress:** my God; in him will I trust.

PSALMS 42:9
I will say unto God my **rock**, Why hast thou forgotten me? why go I mourning because of the oppression of the enemy?

(17) God provides His true followers with Wisdom, Righteousness, Sanctification and redemption

1 CORINTHIANS 1:30
But of him are ye in Christ Jesus, who of God is made unto us **wisdom**, and **righteousness**, and **sanctification,** and **redemption**

(18) God is our Shepherd

JOHN 10:14
<u>I am the good shepherd,</u> and know my sheep, and am known of mine.

Additional references: PSALMS 23:1, JOHN 10:16, HEBREWS 13:20

(19) God is our Savior

JUDE 1:25
To the only wise God <u>our Savior,</u> be glory and majesty, dominion and power, both now and ever. Amen.

Additional references: 2 SAMUEL 22:47, JOHN 4:42

(20) God is our Righteous Judge

JOHN 5:22
For the Father judgeth no man, **but hath committed all judgment unto the Son**:

JOHN 12:48
He that rejecteth me, and receiveth not my words, hath one that judgeth him: the word that I have spoken, **the same shall judge him in the last day.**

Additional references: DEUTERONOMY 32:4, ECCLESIASTES 3:17, PSALMS 9:8, ACTS 17:29-31, 2 TIMOTHY 4:8

(21) God is the Resurrection and the Life

JOHN 11:25
Jesus said unto her, <u>I am the resurrection, and the life</u>: he that believeth in me, though he were dead, yet shall he live:

(22) Wrath, Love, Grace and Mercy are Attributes of the Godhead, which warrant special consideration

K. Examples of the ferocious Wrath of God and His awesome Power

(1) Adam and Eve

Adam was created by God, thus became the first human son of God, who was destined to become the father of all mankind.

He was given a beautiful garden to live in, the task of tending and the joy of its fruits and delights.

From one of Adam's ribs God fashioned a female named Eve, who became his wife and soul mate, with all the associated pleasures.

God gave them total authority over earth and all living things that move on the earth.

Reference: GENESIS 1:28

Together they were given the gifts of the love of God, free-will freedom and righteousness.

(a) The first couple was only encumbered by one solitary commandment.

Upon the counsel of a snake, the Mother of all mankind, made a near fatal error of disobeying and violating the trust of her Creator, **enticed by a longing for increased self-importance and a yearning for a forbidden delight**.

Eve then persuaded her husband, to join her rebellion against the Lord.

Reference: GENESIS 3:5-6

Adam demonstrated the weakness of human beings by violating the trust of His Creator, which allowed sin and death to enter the world.

This was passed on to all men and women, thus paradise and the earthly lives of bliss that Adam and Eve had enjoyed were forever lost.

(b) The consequences for their transgressions were:

(1) Eve was **penalized** for her sin.

God had intended that her relationship with Adam would produce offspring who would live in the paradise He had created.

Alas, Eve had not only rebelled against God, but shared her transgression with her husband and when confronted blamed her failure to obey on the serpent.

It is ironic that *the penalty of intense pain was closely related to the purpose for which she was created. The lesson is that sin often brings on suffering.*

In addition, Eve lost her status as an equal by being placed in *permanent subjection* to her husband.

GENESIS 3:16
Unto the woman he said, *I will greatly multiply thy sorrow and thy conception;* in sorrow thou shalt bring forth children; and thy desire shall be to thy husband**,** *and he shall rule over thee.*

EPHESIANS 5:22-23
Wives, submit yourselves unto your own husbands, as unto the Lord. *For the husband is the head of the wife,* even as Christ is the head of the church: and he is the savior of the body.

1 TIMOTHY 2:14
And Adam was not deceived, *but the woman being deceived was in the transgression.*

(2) Adam, who lived for 930 years, *paid the price of hard labor* for his transgression

References: GENESIS 5:5, GENESIS 3:17-19

(3) Loss of innocence and being in the state of righteousness or being right with God

Reference: GENESIS 3:7

(4) Separation from God

Reference: GENESIS 3:23-24

(5) Adam and Eve exchanged their marvelous life of ease and happiness, for a brutal existence, in a cruel world.

Reference: GENESIS 3:17-19

Today, most people are trading a few years of fleeting worldly pleasures for their place in Heaven.

The first couple undoubtedly immediately realized they had made a dreadful error in judgment, **just as the vast majority will,** when they find themselves in the domain of Satan and his angels, but then it will be too late.

Reference: 2 THESSALONIANS 1:9

(6) The serpent and all his kind was made to suffer until the end of time for his lies

Reference: GENESIS 3:14

(7) Created a continuing enmity or antagonism between the seed of the woman [Christ] and the seed of the snake [Satan and his evil disciples]

References: GENESIS 3:15, GALATIANS 3:16, JOHN 8:44

(8) The effect of their disobedience on all mankind was offset and overcome by Christ, the "last Adam", by providing His redeemed followers with justification and eternal life.

The New Testament emphasizes the oneness of Adam and Eve and the far reaching result of their sin. Their disobedience affected all members of the human race, which have and will continue to pay a price, until the end of earthly time.

Fortunately for the faithful, the death of Christ provided humanity with *an eternal solution (justification) and reward (eternal life)*.

1 CORINTHIANS 15:22
For as in Adam all die, even so in Christ shall all be made alive.

Additional Reference: ROMANS 5:12-21

(3) The Great Flood

In GENESIS 7:11 God marked the day, in terms of the life span of Noah, on which the flood began. Underground springs were released and the windows of Heaven opened.

The torrents of rain continued for forty days and nights until the level of the water was approximately 22 feet above the highest mountain peaks.

The flood destroyed all land-based life; however it would appear that the flood had little or no effect on sea life.

References: GENESIS 7:4, GENESIS 7:11-12, GENESIS 7:20-24

(a) As it was, only eight souls out of an estimated population of 200,000,000 were saved.

If not for the righteousness and obedience of Noah and his family, *the great flood could have been the end of mankind's existence* on the face of the earth, due to the sinful ways of the vast majority, which resulted in the intense anger of God.

The ark was the vessel used to save Noah, his family and other living things as commanded. **Hence, the future of the human race was preserved.**

Reference: 1 PETER 3:20

In MATTHEW 7:13-14 Jesus warned that *few would find the Narrow Way.*

With the benefit of the Teachings of Jesus and His Disciples, a much greater percentage of the believers, who are honestly seeking to follow the Narrow Way, will be saved from the terrors of Hell.

As a token of the covenant entered into between God, Noah and perpetual generations, God placed His rainbow in the clouds.

GENESIS 9:13
I do set my bow in the cloud, and it shall be for *a token of a covenant between me and the earth.*

The Rainbow represents the **Promise of God** not to destroy the earth with water again.

The **Rainbow** also serves as a **solemn reminder** of the **awe-inspiring Power and fierce Wrath of Lord God Almighty**.

Read the full story: GENESIS 6:5-9:17

(4) The Tower of Babel

GENESIS 11:9
Therefore is the name of it called Babel;

because the *LORD did there confound the language of all the earth:* and from thence did the LORD scatter them abroad upon the face of all the earth.

The complete story is told in GENESIS 11:1-9

Another remarkable example is the narrative of the Destruction of Sodom and Gomorrah, as well as, the Story of Lot's wife recorded in GENESIS 19:15-29

(5) Disobedience of the Jewish Nation

The complete story of the recurring theme of sin, disobedience and forgiveness makes up a significant portion of the Old Testament.

The following are some notable examples.

(a) The Jewish nation was sentenced to wander 40 years in the wilderness

This is one of the most famous stories of the Old Testament, however the details of the reason why an entire nation was sentenced to forty years in the wilderness much less well known.

Basically, the Lord commanded Moses to send 12 men, one from each tribe to search out the Promised Land and bring back samples of its fruits.

Upon the return of the spies, 10 lacked faith and provided negative reports, while the faithful Joshua and Caleb were in favor of an immediate invasion.

When Moses and Aaron, expressed faith and indicated an intention to proceed, the people rebelled and refused to enter Canaan.

NUMBERS 14:33
And your children shall wander in the wilderness forty years, and bear your whoredoms, *until your carcasses be wasted in the wilderness*

(b) Joshua and Caleb were the only individuals that had experienced bondage in Egypt who survived to enter the Promised Land.

God was angered and with the exception of Joshua and Caleb, all adults were condemned to wander in the wilderness for the balance of their natural lives.

Reference: NUMBERS 13:32-33

(c) The Sons of Aaron served as Priests and died in flaming fire as a direct result of adding to the Worship service.

The deadly results of adding to Worship is found in LEVITICUS 10:1-2 "And Nadab and Abihu, the sons of Aaron, took either of them his censer, and put fire therein, and put incense thereon, and offered strange fire before the LORD, which he commanded them not. **And there went out fire from the LORD, and devoured them, and they died before the LORD."**

(d) Three members of the Jewish nation were swallowed alive

Korah, Dathan, and Abiram charged Moses and Aaron with overstepping their priestly authority. Being swallowed alive in an astonishing earthquake was the punishment suffered by these individuals

Reference: NUMBERS 16:32-33

The Israelites became irate at this occurrence and God may have destroyed them all, if Moses had not intervened on their behalf.

(e) Many abandoned God by practicing idol worship

A full explanation of the unfortunate events leading to the exile of the Jewish people fills numerous pages in Old Testament and therefore is beyond the scope of this guide.

(6) The following is a brief summary

Sin sometimes has unexpected all encompassing results, particularly when it involves a large number of individuals.

The magnitude of the alteration to their way of life, which resulted from their collective sins, simply could not have been accurately predicted.

The ancient Hebrew language of the Patriarchs had served His people for centuries.

They had the ability to read the Law and teach it to the children, as God had commanded.

The Hebrew people had grown into a strong wealthy independent nation and enjoyed countless Blessings from their Heavenly Father.

Then came a time when large numbers of His chosen people had abandoned their God by worshipping idols, failing to keep the Sabbath as Commanded and disregarding the words of His Prophets, as well as the written Word.

(a) Jewish Nation was driven into Bondage

As a result, the Lord drove His people into exile, by delivering them into the hands of the heathen Assyrians and Babylonians.

Reference: 2 CHRONICLES 36:21

Just as sin had created a major negative change in the lives of Adam and Eve, the Hebrew people transgressed the Law in mass and thus traded their marvelous lifestyle for the brutal reality of bondage

The northern tribes of Israel never returned, and only a tiny remnant of the tribe of Judah, which **included the forefathers of Jesus,** returned to the land.

During the threescore and ten (70) years of banishment, many changes occurred among the members of the tribe of Judah.

(b) They became much closer to their God and more obedient to His Law.

However, they had lost their status as a separate people and the previous glory of the Hebrew nation.

In addition, many had married foreign women and produced children, who unfortunately were not educated in the language of their ancestors.

Many remained in the lands to which they had been exiled and generally lost their ability to read or write the Hebrew language.

Reference: NEHEMIAH 13:23-24.

L. The Wrath of God

In Old Testament times, our Lord demonstrated beyond a shadow of a doubt His inflexibility in regards to His demand for complete obedience to His Divine Will, **without exception.**

It is critical that the user clearly understand that the same standards fully apply today!

His Word is still His absolute final Edict or Decree!

The Old and New Testaments were written and maintained over the centuries so that mankind would have a valid source of reliable information regarding the comprehensive Will or the requirements of their Creator.

(1) Our God is a God of fierce Anger and Wrath

Over the past seventy years almost universal change of attitude has occurred in the general beliefs regarding the Wrath of God.

Unfortunately, an erroneous view of this significant Divine characteristic of God has resulted in downgrading the seriousness of failing to obey the Commandments of our Lord and Savior, in the mind of man.

False teachers have created an artificial feeling of security and belief; by teaching that our Creator is a God of Grace and Mercy, who loves His children, which is **true.**

However, the wide spread belief that He would never punish those individuals who attempted to live a life of goodness for all eternity is **false.**

Many preach that Hell is reserved for the absolutely worst members of Humanity, which is also **not true.**

Hell will be filled by a countless number of good people who simply failed to meet the

Divine requirements for entry into the Kingdom of Heaven

Most of those good people could have been saved from this fate, which is much worse than death, if they would have simply submitted to the Will of their Creator.

A common roadblock is the simplicity of His requirements.

Many feel these Commands are far too elementary to be of any real importance.

This assumption is incorrect!

One must remember that the Patterns, Commandments, Instructions and Examples included in the New Testament were designed for those living in the first century, **many of which were poor and uneducated.**

Yes, His requirements are, elementary, simple, direct, so they are easily understood.

(2) However, our Lord demands precise and total obedience to His complete Will.

Therefore, if one wishes to spend eternity in Glory - he or she must simply obey each and every Divine Directive, regardless of personal preferences.

Alfred Lord Tennyson, summed it up in his famous 1854 narrative poem, "The Charge of the Light Brigade", by stating "**Ours is not to reason why, ours is but to do or die**"

(3) The following are examples of the numerous passages warning of the Wrath of God.

HEBREWS 12:28-29
Wherefore we receiving a kingdom which cannot be moved, let us have grace, whereby we may serve God acceptably with reverence and godly fear: *For our God is a consuming fire.*

2 THESSALONIANS 1:8-9
In flaming fire taking vengeance on them that know not God, and that obey not the gospel of our Lord Jesus Christ: Who shall be punished with everlasting destruction from the presence of the Lord, and from the glory of his power;

Additional references: DEUTERONOMY 4:24, DEUTERONOMY 9:3-4, ZECHARIAH 7:12, JEREMIAH 10:10, LUKE 12:4-5, ROMANS 2:5-8, ROMANS 11:22, 2 PETER 3:7-10

(4) Examples of sins, which resulted in stern warnings of the fierce Wrath of God:

(a) Apostasy or drifting away and idol worship or idolatry

Reference: 2 CHRONICLES 34:24-25

(b) Fellowship with ungodly individuals

Reference: 2 CHRONICLES 19:2

That righteous individuals could endanger their spiritual integrity by interactions with the wicked should come as no surprise. In the following verse the Great Apostle Paul confirmed the potential of immorality.

1 CORINTHIANS 15:33
Be not deceived: *evil communications corrupt good manners.*

Important Point to carefully consider

During the early and mid-twentieth century, hellfire and brimstone was a frequent topic of Sunday morning sermons.

Today, sermons related to the Wrath of God are rarely, if ever delivered.

This lack of information has caused serious harm to the younger generation, since the *fear of the Lord is the key to understanding and obeying the Will of God.*

M. The Love of God

(1) A very significant attribute of God's nature is <u>Love</u>.

A large percentage of the population has a general appreciation of this Divine Attribute of God.

His great Love for mankind was clearly demonstrated by the earthly Virgin Birth of His only begotten Son.

JOHN 3:16
For God so loved the world, that he gave his only begotten Son, that whosoever believeth in him should not perish, but have everlasting life.

The first coming of Christ was prophesied in numerous passages in the Old Testament, which was completed approximately 400 years before His birth.

Bible scholars claim to have isolated over 300 prophecies of the Messiah who would be put to death, thus providing salvation for mankind. Christ fulfilled each prophecy completely.

Approximately 25 prophecies were completed on the day He died on the cross, including His final words.

PSALMS 31:5
Into thine hand I commit my spirit: thou hast redeemed me, O LORD God of truth.

LUKE 23:46
And when Jesus had cried with a loud voice, he said, Father, *into thy hands I commend my spirit:* and having said thus, he gave up the ghost.

(a) His Resurrection, 3 days later, not only provided solid proof of the Divinity of God, the Son, but also confirmed the immense <u>Love of God</u>, the Father for all of humanity, by proving that He has the absolute Power and willingness to defeat death and raise human beings from the dead.

(b) There are many Scriptures that express the Love of God. In fact, one of the major topics of both the Old and New Testaments is the Love of God for the Jewish Nation, His people and for all of mankind.

Jesus laid down His life so that we might have a relationship with God by simply believing, following His Pattern or Plan of Salvation and continued obedience to His Directives for the balance of our earthly lives.

JOHN 15:13
Greater love hath no man than this, that a man lay down his life for his friends.

ROMANS 5:8
But God commendeth his love toward us, in that, while we were yet sinners, Christ died for us.

1 JOHN 4:10
Herein is love, not that we loved God, but that he loved us, and sent his Son to be the *propitiation for our sins.*

(c) While we live on earth the Love of God is unconditional. He offers freely to every man and woman the opportunity to become a child of God, regardless of how much he or she has sinned.

(d) Once an individual passes from this world or the Second Coming of Christ occurs, this golden opportunity will immediately expire and then all that will be left is the Day of Judgment and the Wrath of God.

(2) Under the Old Law retribution, on occasion, was immediate.

For example; the sons of Aaron violated a Pattern of God by offering strange fire

Two priests, the sons of Aaron failed to act in accordance with God's Pattern by adding strange fire to the Tabernacle service, thus violating His Law.

God responded instantaneously with an all-consuming fire from Heaven and they died before Him.

Reference: LEVITICUS 10:1-3

In section U of this chapter, additional examples of the disobedience to the Patterns of God are provided.

(3) The death of Christ marked the end of the Old Law or Covenant.

COLOSSIANS 2:14
Blotting out the handwriting of ordinances that was against us, which was contrary to us, and took it out of the way, *nailing it to his cross*

Thus removing this type of instantaneous terror, however, the Words of our Lord must be heeded and strictly obeyed in order to escape His Wrath on the Day of Judgment.

(4) His death also marked the beginning of the New Covenant

Changes came about in the manner God handles His relationship with mankind.

Mankind was directed to strictly follow that form of teaching or "The Faith" which was originally delivered or taught orally.

Reference: JUDE 1:3.

This is a direct reference to the Teachings of the New Covenant or New Testament, *which reflects a greater emphasis on love and how it overcomes fear.*

Important Point to Remember

The "Faith" is a distinctive unchanging body of "Truth" which will set you free from fear and an ever-increasing burden of sin, so you may be acceptable in the sight of God.

JOHN 8:32
And ye shall know the truth, and the truth shall make you free.

(5) Love is the centerpiece of the New Covenant

In JOHN 15:12-13, Jesus speaking to His Disciples declared, "This is my commandment, That ye love one another, as I have loved you. **Greater love hath no man than this, that a man lay down his life for his friends.**"

(a) And that is exactly what He did, not only for His friends in the first century, but for all of mankind until He comes again.

MATTHEW 26:28
For this is my blood of the new testament, **which is shed for many for the remission of sins.**

(b) In order to provide the user with an overall appreciation of the much greater emphasis on love and how it overcomes fear, the author has taken the liberty of updating the language of two applicable passages in 1 JOHN 4.

It is recommended that the reader **compare** these updated passages with his or her personal Bible.

1 JOHN 4:7-12 KJV **updated**
Beloved, Let us love one another, for love comes from God. Everyone who loves has been born of God and knows God. Whosoever does not love does not know God, because God is love. This is how God showed his love among us: He sent his one and only Son into the world that we might live through him. This is love: not that we loved God, but that he loved us and sent his Son as an atoning sacrifice for our sins. Since God so loved us, we also ought to love one another. No one has ever seen God; but if we love one another, God lives in us and his love is made complete in us.

1 JOHN 4:18 KJV **updated**
There is no fear in love. Perfect love drives out fear, because fear has punishment. The one who fears is not made perfect in love.

(c) Passages from New Testament that confirm the importance of Love in the New Covenant

2 TIMOTHY 1:7
For *God has not given us a spirit of fear, but of power and of love and of a sound mind. God demonstrates his Love for us: While we were still sinners, Christ died for us*

EPHESIANS 2:4
But God, who is rich in mercy, for *his great love wherewith he loved us,*

JAMES 1:12
Blessed is the man that endureth temptation: for when he is tried, he shall receive the crown of life, *which the Lord hath promised to them that love him.*

Additional references: ROMANS 8:39, EPHESIANS 1:4, (famous chapter devoted to love) 1 CORINTHIANS 13:1-13

(6) In response to a clear understanding of the enormous scale of His Love, we are encouraged to develop

a sincere insightful faith and a willingness to yield cheerfully to His Commandments, such as;

(a) Love the Lord thy God with all thy heart, and with all thy soul, mind and strength: this is the first commandment. (MARK 12:30)

(b) Thou shall love thy neighbor as thyself. There is none other commandment greater than these. (MARK 12:31)

(c) If you love me, keep my commandments. (JOHN 14:15)

(d) You shall love one another. (GALATIANS 5:14)

(7) More Good News for His faithful followers! God has promised to renew the strength of His faithful followers.

ISAIAH 40:31
But they that wait upon the LORD shall **renew their strength**; they shall mount up with wings as eagles; they shall run, and not be weary; and they shall walk, and not faint.

N. The Grace of God

The Grace of God is closely related to the Love of God, and it is very important to gain a clear understanding of this attribute.

Grace is a kindness or favor bestowed upon a person, regardless of the worthiness of that individual or what he or she actually deserves.

(1) Salvation is only possible by the immense Love, Grace and Mercy of God

EPHESIANS 2:5-9
But God, who is **rich in mercy**, for his **great love** wherewith he loved us, Even when we were dead in sins, hath quickened us [made us alive] together with Christ, by (grace ye are saved); And hath raised us up together, and made us sit together in heavenly places in Christ Jesus: That in the ages to come he might show the exceeding riches of his grace in **his kindness** toward us through Christ Jesus. For by grace are ye saved through faith; and that not of yourselves: it is the gift of God: Not of works, lest any man should boast.

(a) From this verse, we learn that the Grace of God is made up of three elements, <u>mercy, love</u> and <u>kindness</u>

(2) Paul teaches we are saved by grace through faith; however Jesus and James and others clearly indicated the importance of works, therefore both <u>faith and works</u> are required.

MATTHEW 16:27
For the Son of man shall come in the glory of his Father with his angels; **and then he shall reward every man according to his works.**

JAMES 2:24
Ye see then how that by **works** a man is justified, **and not by faith only**

Additional references: ACTS 15:11, TITUS 3:5, 2 PETER 3:9

(3) The Mercy of God

HEBREWS 4:16
Let us therefore **come boldly** unto the throne of grace, *that we may obtain mercy, and find grace to help in time of need.*

1 PETER 1:3
Blessed be the God and Father of our Lord Jesus Christ, *which according to his abundant mercy* hath begotten us again unto a lively hope by the resurrection of Jesus Christ from the dead

(a) God is Merciful, therefore He expects His children to be merciful

LUKE 6:36
Be ye therefore merciful, as your Father also is merciful.

MATTHEW 5:7
Blessed are the merciful: for they shall obtain mercy.

(4) The Kindness of God

EPHESIANS 2:7
That in the ages to come he might show the exceeding riches of *his grace in his kindness toward us through Christ Jesus.*

TITUS 3:4
But after that the *kindness and love* of God our Savior toward man appeared

O. Patterns of God

A general comprehension of the basic Patterns of God, which are detailed in later chapters, is an important element in developing an overall understanding of the Will of God.

(1) One must use the highest level of care to worship precisely in accord with the Patterns provided in the Word of God. Scriptural Worship and other Patterns of the Faith are not the creation of man, but were ordained by God.

(2) Christians are encouraged to lift their thoughts above the ideas and concepts of mankind towards the requirements, thoughts and ways of God.

Reference: ISAIAH 55:8-9.

Some ask themselves, when in difficult situations the question "What would Jesus do?" as an aid to lifting their thoughts.

P. Our God is a God of Patterns

(1) One of the most fascinating elements of both the Old and New Testaments is the <u>extensive use</u> of Patterns by God.

(2) Unfortunately, the vast majority of the specific Patterns provided in the New Testament have been almost universally DISREGARDED OR REPLACED by the teachings, convictions, opinions or commandments of men.

A brief review and comparison of the beliefs of the major religions in Appendix 5 (Comparative analysis of selected religious organizations) reveals substantial differences in basic doctrine, which confirms the validity of this declaration

(3) Jesus issued a clear warning against this type of behavior

MATTHEW 15:9
But in vain they do worship me, teaching [for] doctrines the commandments [traditions, teachings or convictions] of men.

PROVERBS 14:12
There is a way which seemeth **right** unto a man; But the end thereof are the ways of death. [Eternal Punishment]

Additional reference: JEREMIAH 10:23,

(4) The vast majority of believers are totally <u>unaware</u> of His Patterns

Research indicates that the majority of individuals claiming to be followers of Christ are completely unaware of the existence of the all-important Patterns of God.

A brief study of Old Testament history will provide graphic examples of how God, the Father made use of a specific plan or Pattern in His Creation and provided Noah specific Instructions or a Pattern for the construction of the Ark.

Noah, his family and every generation that followed him, *enjoyed the reward for his strict obedience* to the blueprints provided by his Creator.

The purpose of the next sections following is to provide examples of **how God has utilized Patterns,** throughout the ages and supplied blueprints for believers to follow.

(5) We must be conformed to His Will, not our own!

MATTHEW 7:21
Not every one that saith unto me, Lord, Lord, shall enter into the kingdom of heaven; *but he that doeth the will of my Father,* which is in heaven.

LUKE 6:46
And why call ye me, Lord, Lord, and *do not the things which I say*

A summary of examples of the startling results of human violations of His Patterns is provided in Section U.

Such violations of His Holy Patterns are not punished today as they were in Old Testament times, but make no mistake;

each of us will be held to account for any such transgression on the Day of Judgment.

Q. Examples of the Blueprints or Patterns of God

(1) A review of the Creation reveals a definite design.

The following creation sequence of God (GENESIS 1:1-31) reveals a distinctive, logical design, in providing the elements necessary for the survival of plant life, mankind and all other living creatures.

Day	Creation
1	light/darkness
2	atmosphere/sky
3	separated waters/dry land/vegetation
4	sun/moon/stars
5	fish/birds
6	man/animals
7	rested – not because He was tired, but to provide an example for mankind

The atmosphere was fashioned on the second day, thus providing the environment required by flora to exist. The following day He separated the waters, thus producing dry land and a favorable environment for vegetation to flourish. On the fourth day, sunlight the final component required by all plants, was added. Thus provisions were provided for all creatures and mankind, which were created on the two days following.

There exist, at least, two schools of thought regarding the actual time periods referred to as days. Many believe "day" represents a standard 24-hour period, while others believe thousands, if not millions of years elapsed between each "day".

The author would encourage the reader to consider logically the expected negative effect on vegetation, if sunshine had not existed for any period of years after creation.

On the other hand consider, the Teaching of Jesus in MARK 14:36 "Father, all things are possible unto thee" and words of the Apostle in 2 PETER 3:8 "that one day is with the Lord as a thousand years, and a thousand years as one day".

Accordingly, the duration of day number six is open to discussion, but the true answer will remain one of the secret things of God.

Regardless of the opinion held, it will not have any effect on your final place of residence for eternity.

(2) The blueprint provided to Noah was perfect.

The specifications or blueprint provided by God in the following passage describes a rectangular object resembling a barge rather the barn-like structure depicted in Sunday school training materials.

(a) God provided Noah with a Pattern for the construction of the Ark in just three verses.

Reference: GENESIS 6:14-16

(b) The following verse indicates the approval of the work of Noah by the Lord.

GENESIS 6:22
Thus did Noah; according to all that God commanded him, so did he.

(c) The obedience of Noah was verified by his faith.

Reference: HEBREWS 11:7

(d) The exact size of Noah's Ark is open to discussion.

History records two different measurements known as a "cubit". The Hebrew cubit measured 17.5 inches and the Egyptian cubit equals 20.65 inches. An argument in favor of the Egyptian cubit is that Moses, the writer of Genesis, was educated in Egypt.

Depending on the actual cubit measurement used, the dimension of length of 300 cubits in feet range from 437.5 feet (Hebrew) to 516.25 (Egyptian). The width or beam of 50 cubits in feet equals 72.9 feet using the Hebrew measure to 86 feet using the Egyptian method. The height measured either 43.75 or 51.6 feet.

Regardless of the actual measurement system used, the overall size of the ark was huge, with an estimated volume of 1.4 million cubic feet and a gross tonnage of 14,000 tons, with capacity of carrying over 120,000 animals the size of a sheep. It is interesting to note that an estimated 18000 species of land animals exist today, with an average size of less than a sheep.

(e) The Dimensions provided by God were ideal.

Extensive testing of a model ark using the 50 x 5 x 3 ratio in a large specialized container was constructed with the capacity to simulate the severest of ocean conditions. This test was performed at the highly respected Scripps Institute of Oceanography at La Jolla, California, proving it was impossible to capsize the rectangular shaped ark. This simply proved that the design endowed by God was perfect for the harsh and perilous conditions that Noah and his family faced during the great flood.

R. Patterns provided to Moses and the nation of Israel

As God promised, He led the children of Israel out of the slavery of Egypt to the base of Mount Horeb or the mountain of God.

This is the same mountain on which Moses heard God, the Son speak through the burning bush.

References: EXODUS 3:1-6, EXODUS 3:12

Note: The exact location of Mount Horeb cannot be confirmed with absolute certainty; however, tradition has long held that it is Gebel Musa (7363 feet) in the southern portion of the Sinai Peninsula.

(1) God provided the Jewish Nation a Pattern of Laws or the Ten Commandments

(a) Some confusion exists regarding whether the Ten Commandments from the Old Testament are in force today or not.

Upon the death of Jesus, the Old Covenant (Testament) passed away and was replaced by the New Covenant (Testament)

COLOSSIANS 2:14
Blotting out the handwriting of ordinances [Old Law] that was against us, which was contrary to us, and took it *out of the way, nailing it to his cross.*

Technically the Commandments of Old Testament passed away upon the death of Christ.

However, during His time on earth, Jesus affirmed or brought forward into the New Testament, nine of the original Ten Commandments, which become an important part of the foundation of the Faith in the New Testament.

Only one of the original commandments was changed. The Holy day was changed from the seventh or Sabbath day (EXODUS 20:8) to Sunday; the **first** day of the week (ACTS 20:7).

The following comparison between the: original Ten Commandants (EXODUS 3-17) and appropriate passages from the New Testament provide the support for this declaration:

I. You shall have no other Gods before Me

MATTHEW 4:10
Then saith Jesus unto him, Get thee hence, Satan: for it is written, *Thou shalt worship the Lord thy God, and him only shalt thou serve.*

II. You shall not make for yourself any idol

MATTHEW 6:24
No man can serve two masters: for either he will hate the one, and love the other; or else he will hold to the one, and despise the other. *Ye cannot serve God and mammon* [wealth and other idols].

III. You shall not take the Name of the Lord in vain

Reference: MATTHEW 5:33-37

IV. Remember the Sabbath Day and keep it Holy

References: MARK 2:23-27, MARK 3:1-6

The following verse confirms the change of the day of the week to be devoted to the worship of God.

ACTS 20:7

And upon the first day of the week, when the disciples came together to break bread, Paul preached unto them, ready to depart on the morrow; and continued his speech until midnight.

V. Honor your father and mother

MATTHEW 15:4
For God commanded, saying, *Honor thy father and mother*: and, He that curseth father or mother, let him die the death.

MATTHEW 19:19
Honor thy father and thy mother: and, Thou shalt love thy neighbor as thyself.

VI. You shall not kill

MATTHEW 5:21
Ye have heard that it was said by them of old time, *Thou shalt not kill;* and whosoever shall kill shall be in danger of the judgment:

VII. You shall not commit adultery

MATTHEW 5:27-28
Ye have heard that it was said by them of old time, *Thou shalt not commit adultery:* But I say unto you, That whosoever looketh on a woman *to lust after her* [fantasizing having sexual relations with her] hath committed adultery with her already in his heart.

VIII. You shall not steal

MATTHEW 19:18
He saith unto him, Which? Jesus said, Thou shalt do no murder, Thou shalt not commit adultery, *Thou shalt not steal,* Thou shalt not bear false witness,

IX. You shall not give false witness

MARK 10:19
Thou knowest the commandments, Do not commit adultery, Do not kill, Do not steal, *Do not bear false witness,* Defraud not, Honor thy father and mother.

X. You shall not covet

LUKE 12:15
And he said unto them, Take heed, and *beware of covetousness:* for a man's life *consisteth not in the abundance of the things which he possesseth.*

(2) The Patterns for the Tabernacle were provided in much greater detail.

As God provided Moses this Divine Pattern for the Tabernacle and it's furnishings, He also cautioned Moses to carefully follow His instructions **"According to all that I show thee, after the pattern of the tabernacle, and the pattern of all the instruments thereof, even so shall ye make it."** (EXODUS 25:9)

And He repeated this warning: "And look that thou **make them after their pattern,** which was shown thee in the mount" (EXODUS 25:40).

While the Lord provided Noah with a Pattern for the Ark, in the space of just three verses, the patterns for the Tabernacle and the related elements required four chapters. These very *detailed and fascinating Patterns* of God are recounted in Exodus chapter 25 - Exodus chapter 28.

First, the Lord directed Moses to ask the children of Israel to participate in creating the Tabernacle by donating certain items required for completing the project, which the Lord detailed in verses 3 through 7.

(3) Ark of the Covenant or His Testament

The most important sacred object of the Nation of Israel, as well as, the only article of furniture in the Holy of Holies or the innermost room of the Tabernacle was the Ark of the Covenant or His Testament.

It is beyond the scope of this manual to specify the elements of the entire project, but in order to provide an example of the level of detail in the Pattern provided, a detailed description of the Ark, which is also known as the Ark of the Covenant of the LORD, (NUMBERS 14:44), the Ark of the

LORD (JOSHUA 6:11), the Ark of God (1 SAMUEL 3:3) the Ark of the Testimony (EXODUS 25:22), the Ark of His Testament or Covenant (REVELATION 11:19) is outlined as follows:

Additional information: Appendix 12

The Ark was a sanctified transportable container with a top cover, known as a Mercy Seat with a pair of Cherubim, winged angelic creatures, facing each other attached to ends of the Mercy Seat.

The lower portion of the Ark was made of shittim (aka acacia) wood completely overlaid with pure gold inside and out. Around the top was a crown (rim) of pure gold, possibly to hold the Mercy Seat in place while the Ark was being transported.

The measurements were length 2.5 cubits, breadth 1.5 cubits and height 1.5 cubits.

Just as the actual dimensions of the Ark built by Noah are open to debate, due to the differences between Hebrew and Egyptian cubits, the measurements of Ark of the Covenant are also in question.

An argument in favor of the Egyptian cubit is that Moses, the writer of Exodus, was educated in Egypt. On the other hand, since Moses was supervising Jewish craftsman, it would be logical to assume the use of the Hebrew measurement system.

Reference: EXODUS 25:10-11

On each corner was a cast gold ring. Two staves of shittim wood, overlain with gold, placed thru the rings, which were not to be removed, were used to carry the Ark. (EXODUS 25:12-15)

The Mercy Seat was made of pure gold. The measurements were length 2.5 cubits and breadth 1.5 cubits.

Attached to the ends of the Mercy Seat was a pair of Cherubim with wings stretched to a height that would cover the Mercy Seat, made of beaten gold. (EXODUS 25:17-20)

(a) The following verses clearly indicate that God was pleased with the work.

References: EXODUS 39:42, EXODUS 36:1

(b) It is interesting to note that the Tabernacle or the Tent of God, which was constructed in the wilderness, served the Israelites, for several hundred years, as the house of the Living God, until Solomon completed the Temple in Jerusalem.

S. Pattern of the Temple

The discussion of the building of the Temple begins in the seventh chapter of Second Samuel.

(1) King David would have preferred to build the Temple for the Lord, but his offer was declined in favor of his son Solomon, because David had been a warrior and had blood on his hands.

Reference: 1 CHRONICLES 28:1-3

Key passage: 1 CHRONICLES 28:3 "But God said unto me, *Thou shalt not build a house for my name, because thou hast been a man of war, and hast shed blood.*"

(2) King David revealed that God had chosen Solomon to sit upon the Throne of the Kingdom of the LORD over Israel and to build His Temple.

Reference: 1 CHRONICLES 28:4-9

Key passage: 1 CHRONICLES 28:5 "And of all my sons, (for the LORD hath given me many sons,) *he hath chosen Solomon my son to sit upon the throne of the kingdom of the LORD over Israel*".

(3) King David provided Solomon with encouragement and the details of the Pattern of the Temple.

Reference: 1 CHRONICLES 28:10-21

Key passage: 1 CHRONICLES 28:19 "All this, said David, the LORD made me understand in writing by his hand upon me, *even all the works of this pattern.*"

Detailed instructions regarding the Temple continue into the final chapter of First Chronicles, which also records the death of King David.

The first few chapters of Second Chronicles reveal the construction process of the Temple, which required approximately seven years to complete.

Additional details of the Pattern of the Temple, which King David provided to his son Solomon, are recorded in 1 KINGS 6:1-38.

(4) Upon the completion of the temple the people rejoiced when the approval of their efforts to conform to His Pattern was clearly indicated by the Presence and Glory of God.

Reference: 2 CHRONICLES 5:13-14

Key Passage: "So that the priests could not stand to minister by reason of the cloud: *for the glory of the LORD had filled the house of God.*"

T. God requires strict obedience to His Patterns and Commandments.

The detailed Patterns and His warnings are a clear indication of the lofty level of obedience required by Lord God Almighty, not only from the nation of Israel, but from all His subjects for all time.

For those living in the modern age, God has provided a series of Patterns in the New Testament, which are fully discussed in this manual. **These Patterns must be followed carefully, in order to gain His approval and salvation from the eternal fires of hell.**

(1) Numerous passages expose the tendency of mankind to alter the Instructions or Divine Patterns of God to suit their own needs and ideas.

For example, Moses a faithful man of God *was not allowed to lead the people into the Promised Land,* a goal, which he had pursued for many years, *because he failed to specifically and precisely follow the Instructions of His Creator.*

(a) Moses was commanded in EXODUS 17:5-6 to take his rod and STRIKE the rock, in order to obtain water.

(b) On another occasion, Moses was instructed to take the rod along with his brother Aaron and to SPEAK to the rock before the assembled people.

(c) Rather than SPEAKING to the rock, as commanded, Moses STRUCK the rock with his rod. When the water did not begin to flow immediately, he STRUCK the rock a second time, thus, DISOBEYING the direct Command of His Lord.

Reference: NUMBERS 20:7-11.

(d) The RESULT of this Act of Disobedience is recorded in NUMBERS 20:12

In the minds of many, this act of **disobedience by Moses may be regarded as minor or trivial.** However, it has stood as a significant example of His firm, absolute and ageless requirement **for total compliant and strict obedience** to His Patterns and Commandments for thousands of years.

U. Examples of Disobedience to the Patterns of God

In Old Testament times, disobedience occasionally resulted in immediate, sometimes fatal consequences.

(1) The Golden Calf

While Moses was on Mount Sinai receiving the Commandments of God, Aaron was charged with the responsibility of leading the nation of Israel. The people apparently grew restless, due to a delay in the return of Moses. A group, possibly large, confronted Aaron with a demand that Aaron create a god to worship. Aaron offered little or no resistance, but rather directed a collection of gold earrings from which he fashioned a calf of gold, thus committing a grave sin.

EXODUS 32:1-10
And when the people saw that Moses delayed to come down out of the mount, the people gathered themselves together unto Aaron, and said unto him, Up, make us gods, which shall go before us; *for as for this Moses, the man that brought us up out of the land of Egypt, we know not what is*

become of him. And Aaron said unto them, Break off the golden earrings, which are in the ears of your wives, of your sons, and of your daughters, *and bring them unto me.* And all the people broke off the golden earrings, which were in their ears, and brought them unto Aaron. And he received them at their hand, and fashioned it with a graving tool, after he had *made it a molten calf:* and they said, *These be thy gods, O Israel, which brought thee up out of the land of Egypt.* And when Aaron saw it he built an altar before it; and Aaron made proclamation, and said, Tomorrow is a feast to the LORD. And they rose up early on the morrow, and offered burnt offerings, and brought peace offerings; *and the people sat down to eat and to drink, and rose up to play.* And the LORD said unto Moses, Go, get thee down; for thy people, *which thou broughtest out of the land of Egypt, have corrupted themselves:* They have turned aside quickly out of the way which I commanded them: they have made them a molten calf, and have worshiped it, and have sacrificed thereunto, and said, These be thy gods, O Israel, which have brought thee up out of the land of Egypt. And the LORD said unto Moses, I have seen this people, and, behold, it is a stiff necked people: *Now therefore let me alone, that my wrath may wax hot against them, and that I may consume them*: and I will make of thee a great nation.

(a) If not for the fervent intervention by Moses, God may have destroyed Aaron and the entire Nation of Israel for creating and worshiping the golden calf.

Additional references: EXODUS 32:10-14, DEUTERONOMY 9:20

The following examples demonstrate how God reacted to people who violated His Directives, even if they had the best of intentions.

(2) King Saul failed to "utterly destroy" the nation of the Amalek, as Commanded

King Saul deviated from the Commandment of the Lord to "utterly destroy" the nation of the Amalek and follow a course of action he felt (Saul) would be best. Saul spared the Amalek King and saved the finest animals for the purpose of sacrifice. Saul reasoned that sacrifices to God are good. The response of the Lord is recorded in 1 SAMUEL 15:22-23

Key passage: 1 SAMUEL 15:23 "Because thou hast rejected the word of the LORD, **he hath also rejected thee from being king.**"

(3) King David disregarded the Pattern for transporting the Ark of His Testament

(a) David and his followers attempted to transport the Ark of God to Jerusalem using a cart.

David disregarded a specific Instruction of God, which was that only members of the tribe of Levi were authorized to carry or touch the Ark.

Reference: DEUTERONOMY 10:8

(b) The end result of the disobedience was the death of Uzza before the Ark.

Reference: 1 CHRONICLES 13:7-10

Key passage: 1 CHRONICLES 13:9-10

(c) King David was angry with God and became fearful.

Reference: 2 SAMUEL 6:8-10

(4) King Uzziah violated the Pattern of God by entering the Temple to offer incense.

(a) King Uzziah entered the Temple to offer incense, with full and complete understanding that such was an exclusive service of the priests.

(b) For this crass transgression, the LORD rewarded him with the dreaded disease of leprosy.

Reference: 2 CHRONICLES 26:16-20

(5) Manasseh, king of Judah violated the Pattern of God by bringing abominations into the Temple

(a) Manasseh, king of Judah, brought abominations into the Temple of the Lord, which brought the Wrath of God on him and <u>destruction</u> upon his nation.

Reference: 2 CHRONICLES 33:1-11

V. Final Comments

(1) The general view or concept of our God today is much too narrow, diminutive and minuscule!

The following overview has been included to provide the user with an opportunity to gain a greater appreciation of the, holiness, grandeur and majesty of God.

(2) Names and Titles of God revealed in Scriptures, provide insights into His Glorious Grandeur [a]

Elohim or Elohay is first used as a designation for God in GENESIS 1:1, "In the beginning God [Elohim] created the heaven and the earth." From the Hebrew root word *meaning "strength" or "power",* which has the **unusual attribute of being plural in form,** is found over 2000 times in the Old Testament. *From the very beginning this plural form for the name of God was used to describe the One and Only True Living God.*

(a) The following examples denote how Elohim was combined with other Hebrew words in the Old Testament to portray various characteristics of God.

Holy God - Elohim Kedoshim

References: LEVITICUS 19:2, LEVITICUS 11:45

God of Gods - Elohay Elohim

References: DEUTERONOMY 10:17, JOSHUA 22:22

God of the Beginning - Elohay Kedem

Reference: DEUTERONOMY 33:27

God of Forgiveness - Elohay Selichot

Reference: NEHEMIAH 9:17

God of My Salvation - Elohay Yishi

Reference: PSALMS 25:5

God of Judgment - Elohay Mishpat

Reference: ISAIAH 30:18

Living God - Elohim Chaiyim

Reference: JEREMIAH 10:10

(b) The following are examples of the simple form of Elohim or El, which is another designation for God, which was combined with other terms to provide an illuminating enunciation.

The Highest God - El Elyon

Reference: GENESIS 14:18

The Everlasting God - El Olam

Reference: GENESIS 21:33

The Faithful God - El HaNe'eman

Reference: DEUTERONOMY 7:9

The Great God - El HaGadol

Reference: DEUTERONOMY 10:17

The God of Knowledge - El De'ot

Reference: 1 SAMUEL 2:3

The God of Israel - El Yisrael

Reference: PSALMS 68:35

The God Of Heaven - El HaShamayim

Reference: PSALMS 136:26

God is with us - Immanu El

Reference: ISAIAH 7:14

(c) A third name for God, which was used about 70 times is Elah. When combined with other words, additional characteristics of God are revealed as follows:

God of Heaven and Earth - Elah Sh'maya V'Arah

Reference: EZRA 5:11

Elah Yerush'lem - God of Jerusalem

Reference: EZRA 7:19

(d) YHVH is by far the preferred Hebrew word for Lord. YHVH was used

approximately 7,000 times in the Old Testament, which is much greater than other designations for God. YHVH was derived from the Hebrew verb meaning "to be", which is the unique name revealed to Moses at the burning bush.

Reference: EXODUS 3:14-15

The LORD who revealed Himself as YHVH or I AM to Moses in the Old Testament is revealed as Yeshua (Jesus) in the New Testament. Since Jesus as God the Son shares the same attributes as YHVH and clearly claimed to be YHVH.

JOHN 8:58
Jesus said unto them, Verily, verily, I say unto you, **Before Abraham was, I am.**

(e) Paul confirmed the Truth of this declaration of Jesus

Reference: ROMANS 10:9

(f) The use of YHVH, by Old Testament writers, is reflected in the following verses.

LORD God - YHVH Elohim

Reference: GENESIS 2:4

The LORD our Maker - YHVH O'saynu

Reference: PSALMS 95:6

The LORD our Righteousness - YHVH Tzidkaynu

Reference: JEREMIAH 33:16

Centuries ago, *the Jewish nation discontinued the use of this name out of fear of violating the commandment to strictly avoid taking the name of the LORD in vain. (EXODUS 20:7)* Today, while some pronounce YHVH Jehovah or Yaweh, Biblical scholars are generally uncertain as the original articulation.

Reference:

[a] **The Names of God in the Old Testament,** Blue Letter Bible, **www.blueletterbible.org,** April 1 2002.

Disregard of the Commandments and Patterns of the Most High unfortunately <u>will thwart</u> most believers' goal of entering the Gates of the Glorious Kingdom of Heaven.... Heaven Awaits!

Chapter II
Guide to the Divine Format of the Bible

Chapter Contents

A. Introduction

B. Overview of the Divine Mosaic

C. Simple technique of determining the Divine Will of God

D. Keystones of the Faith

E. Cornerstones of the Faith

F. Generally accepted Biblical facts regarding Lord Jesus and His Church.

G. Examples of general elements of the Divine Mosaic

H. Closing Comments

A. Introduction

As previously acknowledged, in the opinion of the author, most individuals have *a yearning for* and to varying degrees, are *eager and open to gaining a greater comprehension* of the Divine Will of God.

The purpose of this chapter is to begin the process of *eliminating the confusion and uncertainty,* which has existed among the majority of human beings for centuries.

(1) Scriptures were provided in a Divine Format!

(a) As stated in the General Prologue, it is the firm belief of the author, that a leading reason, the vast majority have difficulty in understanding Bible or the Message of Christ is due to the **failure of most to recognize** that the Word of God was from the very beginning, provided to mankind in a **Divine Format.**

(b) The author has labeled and refers to this celestial system or Divine Format as the **Divine Mosaic,** due to its similarity to a very large and highly detailed mosaic, montage or tapestry.

The term **Divine Mosaic** was coined for the purpose of increasing clarity and enabling greater understanding.

Most, if not all, knowledgeable and faithful followers would agree that the **Divine format of presentation is difficult to comprehend.**

(c) On the other hand, the vast majority would also agree that **the elements** of the Message of Christ are **quite simple and easy to understand.**

(d) His requirements are simple, but make no mistake, your Lord demands that His faithful followers make their very best efforts to comply precisely and faithfully to each and every Pattern, Commandment, Instruction or Example provided, without addition, subtraction or creative enhancement.

(e) Jesus and His Disciples originally taught the specifics of his Divine Will, which was identified, in the first century, as the **Gospel or Message of Christ**, the **Truth** or the **Faith,** in order to develop belief, faith; trust in Jesus Christ and to explain His Divine Directives or the specific **Divine Will of God, the Father.**

Reference: JOHN 12:49-50

(f) In the opinion of the writer, the <u>entire</u> New Testament should be considered the Gospel of Christ. However, *confusion and uncertainty exists regarding the precise meaning of the term Gospel of Christ,* which is detailed in Chapter III.

(g) Therefore, the author will make use of: the *Message of Christ* or the specific *Divine Will of God,* in order to reduce confusion.

In essence, an essential purpose of this manual is to illuminate the elements of the Message of Christ, which is also known in the pages of the New Testament Bible as the Truth or the Faith. The definition of each of these terms is; the complete, explicit details of the all important specifics of the Divine Will of God.

(2) Expanded definition of the Message of Christ

While many definitions of the Message or Gospel of Christ exist, most do not provide the level of detail required to provide a clear understanding.

(a) While researching references, the author located an expanded method of presentation attributed to Walter Scott, a Presbyterian Preacher during the Restoration Movement.

(b) Scott wrote, "The Gospel consists of facts to be believed, commands to be obeyed and promises to be anticipated."

(c) While this explanation would serve well in most instances, the author determined the need to develop an expanded innovative definition which presented this vital subject matter in greater detail.

This endeavor resulted in the creation of the following approach, which is used as the definition in Chapter III.

The Elements of the Message of Christ includes;
(1) Patterns to be observed
(2) Truths to be believed
(3) Commands to be obeyed
(4) Instructions or Examples to be followed
(5) Warnings to be heeded and
(6) Assurances to be anticipated.

(d) The author believes this approach to the definition of the Message of Christ is an enhanced method of presentation, but clearly understands that it **does not include the abstract elements of His Divine Message.**

Abstract concepts, such as beauty, cannot be defined, only described.

(e) After considering the alternatives, the author determined to resolve this dilemma, by providing the user with a **fundamental foundation**, of Biblical knowledge, in this chapter, including the following, all of which have been *assigned a label created by the writer*:

(1) A group of key Commandments of the Master and significant Commandments of His Disciples, which the author has labeled as **Keystones of the Faith.**

(2) **Cornerstones of the Faith,** such as forgiveness, mercy, fellowship, good works and kindness are abstract concepts, to varying degrees, which cannot be reduced to a simple model or pattern.

(3) A sampling of **generally accepted Biblical facts** regarding Lord Jesus and His Church.

(4) Examples of the **general elements** of the Divine Mosaic.

(f) An understanding of these basic Biblical principles along with the additional knowledge provided in Chapter III will provide the user with a *general comprehension of His Divine Message.*

(g) An important objective of the author is to assist the user in developing his or her ability to search out the *Divine Will of God and identify false or erroneous religious teachings.*

After the user has gained a solid understanding of the information provided in this manual, he or she will be empowered to come to their own **independent logical conclusions** and **make informed decisions** regarding spiritual issues.

B. Overview of the Divine Mosaic

(1) The writer refers to the Divine Format or Heavenly System of Revelation as the Divine Mosaic, due to its similarity to a very large and highly detailed mosaic, montage or tapestry, which can only be accurately observed, using a wide panoramic view

(2) Each word, verse, chapter and book is an essential element of the Divine Format and is exactly in order of presentation ordained by God. This type of format requires rigorous effort to search out and understand.

(3) The use of this handbook, removes most of the effort involved, by the careful arrangement of the information, in the form of a series of explanations, outlines or lists; which is a format preferred by the mind of man and easily assimilated.

(4) All information is presented in a clear, simple to understand format, based exclusively on the inspired Holy Bible, which is our only source of trustworthy information.

(5) The author has intentionally limited the amount of commentary by **allowing the Bible, His Holy and eternal Word to speak for itself.**

(6) Every declaration is supported with one or more passages from the Word of God.

In addition, the author has also provided a limited quantity of general background information in order to increase the depth and enhancement of the understanding of the user.

(7) This Divine method of presentation did not happen by random chance. The revelation of His Will using Divine Format was a part of the planning of God, possibly developed long before the beginning of the world.

(8) By the use of this Divine method, God clearly indicates that He requires each individual to make a sincere effort and to labor diligently in order to obtain a clear understanding of His Word, **which is confirmed by the extensive use of the parable in the earthly teachings of Jesus.**

(9) A parable is usually defined as **an earthly story with a Heavenly meaning.**

The primary purpose of the parable was to conceal the Truth from the casually curious, because hardness had developed in the hearts of many members of the Jewish faith, who simply refused to believe His Words.

At the same time, the Disciples' attitude allowed them to be blessed with the ability to learn the mysteries of the Kingdom of Heaven.

Reference: MATTHEW 13:10-17

On occasion not even His Disciples could understand his meaning and therefore had no choice, but to request the Master to explain His Parables.

References: MARK 4:33-34, MATTHEW 13:34-43

(10) Parables were used by Jesus to explain **Heavenly secrets or the unknown, by comparing Heavenly secrets to known earthly facts, thus, shedding light on the unknown.**

C. Simple technique of determining the Divine Will of God

(1) Introduction

(a) The following is a real world illustration of the simple technique used by the author to **research and determine the Divine Will of God or test the validity of religious teachings, principles or briefs.**

(b) When attempting to determine the Will of God in regarding a specific issue or religious teaching, one *must consider all interrelated verses, before making a final determination.*

(c) The author highly recommends the use of the advanced key word search function found within the **free** software offered by **Eveningdew.com Bible System** or similar, to perform key word searches to locate all applicable passages. An alternative is the use of a comprehensive concordance.

(2) For example, millions believe that only faith is required to be saved.

(a) This belief is commonly known as "faith only." (Additional information is provided in Appendix 4).

(3) The key question to be resolved is: Does this belief match the teachings found within Divine Mosaic?

(a) This belief is based upon the words of Apostle Paul in EPHESIANS 2:8-9 "For by grace are ye saved through faith, and that not of yourselves: it is the gift of God: Not of works, lest any man should boast."

(b) This verse clearly states that faith is required, but **does not** plainly indicate that faith is **all** that is essential.

(c) EPHESIANS 2:8-9 **does teach** that we cannot qualify for entrance into Heaven by our "works" and that **we are not to be too proud or boastful** of our accomplishments.

(d) The statement "Not of works, lest any man should boast" refers to the teaching of Lord Jesus in LUKE 17:10 *that our works are nothing more that our assigned duty.*

(e) A word search of "**faith**" using the eveningdew.com software produced many references, which included the following, which *confirm faith is definitely required.*

Romans 1:17
For therein is the righteousness of God revealed from faith to faith: as it is written. *The just shall live by faith.*

HEBREWS 11:6
But without faith it is impossible to please him: for he that cometh to God must believe that he is, and that he is a rewarder of them that diligently seek him.

(f) *The next step was to search the New Testament for verses with the exact phrase* "**faith only**".

(1) This search yielded only one passage.

JAMES 2:24
Ye see then how that by *works a man is justified*, and **not by faith only.**

(g) Next, the word "works" in the New Testament was searched, which produced over 100 matches. After a careful review, the list was narrowed down to following applicable verses.

MATTHEW 16:27
For the Son of man shall come in the glory of his Father with his angels; and then he shall reward every man *according to his works.*

JAMES 2:17
Even so faith, *if it hath not works, is dead,* being alone.

JAMES 2:18
Yea, a man may say, Thou hast faith, and I have works: shew me thy faith without thy works, and I will shew thee my faith by my works.

Additional reference: REVELATION 20:12-13

(h) The Apostle Paul teaches we are saved by grace through faith; however Jesus, James and **Paul in 1 TIMOTHY 6:18-19** point out the **importance of works; therefore both faith and works are required.**

Conclusion: The concept of faith only **does not match** the teachings found within Divine Mosaic and **can only be considered a false teaching, which must be strictly avoided.**

It is important to appreciate that vast majority have the ability to employ this simple system to accurately resolve the most scriptural or religious issues and questions, by simply following the procedure outlined above and **allowing the Bible to speak for itself.**

D. Keystones of the Faith

(1) The author has selected a series of the basic elements of Divine Mosaic and labeled them as Keystones of the Faith.

The elements mentioned are not necessarily more important than others not cited but have either been referred to by **the Master as first** or in the opinion of the writer, have *far-reaching authority.*

(2) Examples of Keystone Teachings of Lord Jesus

(a) Seek first the Kingdom of God

MATTHEW 6:33
But seek ye **first** the kingdom of God, and his righteousness; and all these things shall be added unto you.

In order to be acceptable and be saved from the terrors of Hell, Jesus has made it clear that our Creator must be made **first** in our lives. *This is the reason why the discussion of our God is presented in Chapter I.*

(b) Love your God, with all your Heart, Soul and Mind

MATTHEW 22:37-38
Jesus said unto him, Thou shalt love the Lord thy God with all thy heart, and with all thy soul, and with all thy mind. This is the **first** and **greatest** commandment.

Additional references: LUKE 10:27, MARK 12:30, DEUTERONOMY 6:5
DEUTERONOMY 10:12;11:13;13:3; 30:6, JOSHUA 22:5,

(c) Love all members of humanity or your neighbors as yourself

MATTHEW 22:39
And the **second** is like unto it, Thou shalt love thy neighbor as thyself.

Additional references: MARK 12:31, MARK 12:33, JOHN 13:34

(d) The Worship of God is to be in Spirit and in Truth

JOHN 4:24
God [is] a Spirit: and they that worship him must worship [him] **in spirit and in truth**

(1) The term **"in Spirit"** is an **abstract concept**, like beauty it cannot be defined, only described.

(2) The term **"in Truth"** is interchangeable with and comparable to the term the **"Will of God"**.

(e) Search the Scriptures

References: JOHN 5:39

(f) Do unto others, as they would have them do unto them.

References: MATTHEW 7:12, LUKE 6:31

(g) Biblical Injunction against adding to or taking away from His Word

Reference: REVELATION 22:18-19

(h) Jesus will be our Righteous Judge on the Day of Judgment

References: ACTS 17:31, ROMANS 14:12, JOHN 5:22, JOHN 12:48, 1 CORINTHIANS 14:37, 2 TIMOTHY 4:8, ECCLESIASTES 3:17

(3) Examples of Keystone Teachings of His Apostles

(a) Commandments of Apostles are binding

Reference: 1 Corinthians 14:37

(b) Save yourself first and then all those who will hear you

Reference: 1 TIMOTHY 4:16

(c) Study the Word and consider the entire Counsel of God

Reference: 2 TIMOTHY 2:15, ACTS 20:27

(d) A child of God who continues in sin has fallen away and can be lost.

References: GALATIANS 5:4, 1 CORINTHIANS 10:12, HEBREWS 3:12-19, 2 PETER 2:20-22

(e) A believer who falls away and repents may return to His Church.

References: ACTS 8:22, JAMES 5:16.

(f) Walk by Faith, not by sight.

Reference: 2 CORINTHIANS 5:7

(g) Be prepared to provide others with the Biblical basis of your beliefs or convictions.

Reference: 1 PETER 3:15

E. Cornerstones of the Faith

Fellowship, good works, forgiveness, kindness and mercy are **abstract concepts,** to varying degrees, which cannot be reduced to a simple model or pattern.

(a) Christian Fellowship

ACTS 2:42
And they continued steadfastly in the apostles' doctrine and **fellowship,** and in breaking of bread, and in prayers

1 CORINTHIANS 1:9
God is faithful, by whom ye were called unto the **fellowship** of his Son Jesus Christ our Lord.

2 CORINTHIANS 8:4
Praying us with much entreaty that we would receive the gift, and take upon us the **fellowship** of the ministering to the saints.

Additional references: 1 JOHN 1:31, JOHN 1:7

(b) Good Works

2 CORINTHIANS 9:8
And God is able to make all grace abound toward you; that ye, always having all sufficiency in all things, may abound to every **good work**:

EPHESIANS 2:10
For we are his workmanship, created in Christ Jesus unto **good works**, which God hath before ordained that we should walk in them.

JAMES 3:17
But the wisdom that is from above is first pure, then peaceable, gentle, and easy to be entreated, **full of mercy and good fruits,** without partiality, and without hypocrisy.

Additional references: EPHESIANS 6:8, COLOSSIANS 1:10, 1 TIMOTHY 2:10, 1 THESSALONIANS 5:15, 2 THESSALONIANS 2:17, 1 TIMOTHY 1:5, 1 TIMOTHY 6:18, 2 TIMOTHY 2:21, 2 TIMOTHY 3:17, TITUS 2:14, TITUS 3:1, TITUS 3:8, TITUS 3:14, HEBREWS 10:24, HEBREWS 13:16, HEBREWS 13:21, , 1 PETER 2:12, 3 JOHN 1:11

(c) Forgiveness

MATTHEW 6:14-15
For if ye **forgive** men their trespasses, your heavenly Father will also **forgive** you: But if ye **forgive not** men their trespasses, neither will your Father **forgive** your trespasses.

LUKE 17:3
Take heed to yourselves: If thy brother trespass against thee, rebuke him; and if he repent, **forgive** him.

LUKE 23:34
Then said Jesus, Father, **forgive them**; for they know not what they do. And they parted his raiment, and cast lots.

Additional references: MATTHEW 6:12, , LUKE 6:37, MARK 11:25-26

(d) Mercy

LUKE 6:36
Be ye therefore **merciful,** as your Father also is **merciful.**

MATTHEW 5:7
Blessed are the **merciful**: for they shall obtain **mercy.**

(e) Kindness

2 CORINTHIANS 6:6
By pureness, by knowledge, by longsuffering, **by kindness,** by the Holy Ghost, by love unfeigned,

COLOSSIANS 3:12
Put on therefore, as the elect of God, holy and beloved, bowels of mercies, **kindness,** humbleness of mind, meekness, longsuffering;

2 PETER 1:7
And to godliness brotherly **kindness**; and to brotherly kindness charity.

Additional references: EPHESIANS 2:7, TITUS 3:4

F. Generally accepted Biblical facts regarding Lord Jesus and His Church

(1) Jesus has all power [authority] in Heaven and on Earth. Believers submit respectfully to the supreme power and authority of Christ. (COLOSSIANS 3:1, MATTHEW 28:18)

(2) Believers acknowledge that Jesus Christ founded His Church. (MATTHEW 16:18)

(3) Believers acknowledge that Christ is the Head of His Church, which is His Body. (EPHESIANS 1:22-23)

(4) Our Lord is the Savior of the Body, which is His Church. (EPHESIANS 5:23)

(5) Jesus pleaded for religious unity in one Faith. (JOHN 17:20-21)

(6) Jesus Christ shed his blood for His Church. (ACTS 20:28)

(7) Only the Lord can add saved people to His Church. (ACTS 2:47)

(8) Jesus Christ loves His Church. (EPHESIANS 5:25)

(9) His followers proudly wear the name of Christ. (ACTS 4:12, ACTS 11:26, 1 PETER 4:16)

(10) His followers are to be faithful to Christ (REVELATIONS 2:10)

(11) Lord Jesus requires complete obedience to His Words in the New Testament. (MATTHEW 23:23, MARK 13:31, JOHN 14:23, JOHN 15:7)

G. Examples of general elements of the Divine Mosaic

The following are basic elements that stand-alone and simply must be accepted. Each component is part of the **Divine Mosaic,** which provides the knowledge, understanding and overall plans for living a Christian life acceptable to God.

(1) Members of His Church are guided by the same Message as was originally delivered to the first century Christians, which is accepted unconditionally, as the complete Inspired Word of God. (2 TIMOTHY 3:15-17, 1 PETER 1:22-25)

(2) Paul pleaded for religious unity in one Faith and confirmed that only one Church is the true Church of our Lord. (EPHESIANS 4:4-6, 1 TIMOTHY 3:15, COLOSSIANS 1:18, EPHESIANS 1:22)

(3) His Church has no earthly organization as its headquarters are in Heaven. (ACTS 2:47, COLOSSIANS 3:1)

(4) His faithful followers recognize the distinctions between the Old and New Testaments. (COLOSSIANS 2:14, JEREMIAH 31:31-34, HEBREWS 8:7-13, HEBREWS 8:6, HEBREWS 9:15-24, JOHN 1:17, 1 PETER 1:10-12, 2 TIMOTHY 3:16, ROMANS 15:4)

It is important to study the examples provided in the Old Testament, which was written for our benefit and is a part of God's Word. The Old Covenant passed away, including, animal sacrifices, polygamy, incense, Sabbath Day etc. It was replaced with the New Covenant or Testament at the moment of Christ's Death. The Blood of Christ paid the price on the Cross, on behalf of all mankind for the forgiveness of all repented sins.

(5) Worship, according to the teachings or commandments of men is prohibited. (MATTHEW 15:9)

(6) Words spoken by Jesus were not spoken on His own Authority, but He spoke only what God instructed Him to speak. (JOHN 12:49-50)

(7) There is only one Pattern (Plan) of Salvation. (EPHESIANS 4:4-6)

(8) His Church was not built by the Apostle Paul or by any other human or group. (MATTHEW 16:16-18, 1 CORINTHIANS 1:13-15)

E. Closing Comments

The author has struggled to provide an example that *contrasts thought patterns using the wide panoramic view compared with the normal thought pattern of man*, to no avail.

Therefore, will make use of the following illustration, which compares the normal thought pattern of mankind with the recorded details of the Divine thought process

If a mature human male reviews his life, he will usually consider each component, beginning with earliest memories of childhood proceeding through each segment up to the present day.

Most find that in some instances, memory fails, *but overall is able to produce a general panoramic view,* which one is able to review one segment at a time, with a few gaps.

HEBREWS 4:12
For the word of God [Jesus Christ] is quick, and powerful, and sharper than any two-edged sword, **piercing even to the dividing asunder of soul and spirit,** and of the joints and marrow, and **is a discerner of the thoughts and intents of the heart.**

Additional references: ROMANS 11:33, 1 CORINTHIANS 4:5, PSALMS 147:5, PSALMS 139:2-4, PSALMS 139:11-12, 1 KINGS 8:39, JOB 37:16

On the other hand, based upon Hebrews 4:12 (above) among the innumerable **Attributes of Christ is the ability to instantaneously examine a panoramic view,** of every kindness and righteous thought, word and deed, as well as, every sin, or evil thought, word and deed, completely down to the last infinitesimal detail, without exception, the total and net results of the life of that mature human male, as well as all other human beings who ever walked the face of the earth.

Thus, Lord Jesus has the ability to render an instantaneous Judgment, since nothing can be hidden from His view.

ECCLESIASTES 12:14
For God shall bring every work into judgment, **with every secret thing, whether it be good, or whether it be evil.**

It is important to remind the reader that His faithful followers, who are properly prepared, need **not** be concerned with this Divine Review, simply because their sins have been washed away and their souls will have been cleansed or purified by the Blood of Christ, thus, will be whiter than the purest snow. Therefore, His faithful followers will be directed to rest among His sheep or to the right side of His Throne.

Oh Happy Day!

The author has endeavored in the development of this guide to faithfully follow the advice of the Great Apostle Peter, who in 1 PETER 3:15 wrote "But sanctify in your hearts Christ as Lord: **being ready always to give answer to every man that asketh you a reason concerning the hope that is in you, yet with meekness [humbleness] and fear.**"

This passage of scripture teaches that we must be ready to provide others with the Biblical basis of our beliefs or convictions.

Therefore, each statement or contention expressed by the author is supported by one or more references or passages and is based solely upon the Word of God.

The author currently holds the opinion that a complete understanding and mastery of the entire Bible would require an entire lifetime of devoted study and *is possibly beyond the grasp of the average human being.*

Nevertheless, it is clear that in order to be acceptable in the eyes of the Lord, one must endeavor to increase his or her level of understanding by personal study, listening carefully to sermons and making use of commentaries or guides, such as the one you are currently reading.

However, each of us must also **carefully compare the words of men** against the Word of God to determine their validity

Fortunately, Christ does not require a complete mastery of the entire Bible, but rather that we develop **a complete understanding of Divine Will of God.**

Important Point to carefully consider

Decisions made during our earthly existence will determine our ultimate destiny forever...Heaven Awaits!

Chapter III

The Message of Christ

Chapter Contents

A. Introduction

B. Overview of the Message of Christ

C. Elements of the Message of Christ

D. Lord Jesus did NOT promise

A. Introduction

After the fall of Adam and Eve, the redemption of mankind was a continuously evolving subject in the Old Testament.

(1) Tidings of Great Joy were announced upon the earthly birth of Jesus

LUKE 2:10-14
And the **angel said** unto them, Fear not: for, behold, I bring you good **tidings of great joy,** which shall be to all people. For unto you is born this day in the city of David a Savior, which is Christ the Lord. And this shall be a sign unto you; Ye shall find the babe wrapped in swaddling clothes, lying in a manger. And suddenly there was with the angel a multitude of the heavenly host praising God, and saying, Glory to God in the highest, and on earth peace, good will toward men.

(2) Many have questioned what the Angel was referring to in His proclamation "tidings of great joy".

(a) At the core of the Message is the Promise that God, the Father has provided Remission of Sins and Redemption through His Son Christ Jesus.

(b) The Good Tidings also included the Divine Plan for deliverance, liberation and freedom from the state of sin in which every human had lived in since the fall of Adam and Eve.

(c) In addition the good tidings included an Assurance of a joyful life for all eternity.

(3) In Order to gain these Spiritual benefits of the Gospel one must obey or conform to His Pattern of Salvation and then remain faithful by obeying the other elements of His Message or Gospel.

(4) Stern warnings were issued to all those who refuse to obey or fail to gain a clear understanding of the Message or Gospel of Christ.

References: 2 THESSALONIANS 1:8, 1 PETER 4:17, ROMANS 1:31

(5) Gospel Message preached by Jesus, His Apostles and Disciples is the absolute final and authoritative Will of God, the Father.

Reference: JOHN 12:49-50

(6) The terms tidings of great joy, and good tidings were the original meaning of the word Gospel.

Gospel is from the Greek word *euangelion* and Old English word *godspell*. Modern translations of the New Testament now generally define the Gospel as the Good News.

(7) Although the Bible clearly teaches the concept of obedience to the Gospel, for some undetermined reason, such as confusion, misunderstanding or the trickery of Satan, substantial uncertainty exists today regarding the exact definition or meaning of this term.

(a) Possible causes of Uncertainty

(1) The use of synonymous terms; in New Testament, such as good tidings of great joy (LUKE 2:10) glad tidings of good things (ROMANS 10:15) and the modern term "Good News" for the word Gospel

(2) To add to the confusion, the term Gospel is also referred to by several other expressions in the New Testament, such as:

(a) *Message*

Reference: 1 JOHN 1:5

(b) *Gospel of Christ*

Reference: ROMANS 15:19

(c) *Glorious Gospel of Christ*

Reference: 2 CORINTHIANS 4:4

(d) *Gospel of Jesus Christ*

Reference: MARK 1:1

(f) *Gospel of God*

Reference: 1 THESSALONIANS 2:9

(g) *Gospel of the Grace of God*

Reference: ACTS 20:24

(h) *Gospel of Peace*

References: EPHESIANS 6:15, ROMANS 10:15

(i) *Gospel of your Salvation*

Reference: EPHESIANS 1:13

(j) *The Gospel of the Kingdom*

Reference: MATTHEW 4:23

(3) The Gospel is also synonymous with "common salvation" and "the faith which was **once*** [***once** in this verse means **once and for all**] delivered unto the saints" (JUDE 1:3), as well as, "that form of doctrine which was delivered you" (ROMANS 6:17)

(4) These various terms for word Gospel, had a very specific meaning in the time of Jesus. However, the same term applies to many things today, *which have little or nothing in common* with His Divine Message, such as:

(a) The term "Gospel Music" encompasses not only the Spiritual songs and Hymns, based upon passages or Bible themes, suitable for praising God in congregational services of His Church, but also worldly instrumental music with few Christian references, which, in many instances are completely foreign to the Words of the Master.

(b) In many churches, ministers purport to preach the gospel by teaching self-improvement, financial management and other topics, which are not remotely related to the Message of Christ

(c) In the first century the term Gospel was never used to denote any book of the New Testament, as the first four books of the New Testament are now commonly called.

(8) Today, even between knowledgeable, well-versed faithful followers there is no universally accepted definition of the Gospel

(a) One group takes the position that the Gospel refers only to His Pattern or Plan of Salvation or the narrow view.

(b) The other group contends that the term the Gospel or the Message of Christ refers to the entire specific Divine Will of God, which includes the <u>sum total</u> of Patterns, Teachings, Commandments, Instructions or Examples provided by Christ and His Disciples in the New Testament.

(c) The author agrees with and makes use of this wider, all-inclusive view or definition and therefore will generally make use of the term the Message of Christ to avoid further confusion.

B. Overview of the Message of Christ

The Gospels (Matthew, Mark, Luke and John) are devoted to a detailed account of the Life of Jesus including His Birth, Mission, Death, Resurrection and Ascension to the right hand of God, from four points of view.

Woven within these four inspired Books are also His Patterns, Teachings, Commandments, Instructions or Examples, which are clarified and supplemented, by His inspired Disciples in the remaining books of the New Testament.

(1) The Message of Christ is a Belief System with Reverence for God, who is acknowledged as the Creator or Master Designer and Supreme Sovereign of the universe and all creation.

(a) The end result of carefully obeying the Message of Christ is a faith or trust-grace based relationship between each faithful servant and his Creator.

C. Elements of the Message of Christ

(1) The Elements of the Message of Christ includes;

(a) Patterns to be observed
(b) Truths to be believed
(c) Commands to be obeyed
(d) Instructions or Examples to be followed
(e) Warnings to be heeded
(f) Assurances to be anticipated

(2) Examples of Patterns to be observed

The Message of Christ in part, is an organized system of Divine Patterns.

(a) His Divine Pattern or Plan of Salvation
Detailed information: Chapter VI

(b) Divine Pattern of Prayer
Full information: Chapter VI

(c) Divine Pattern of Worship
Comprehensive information: Chapter V,

(d) Divine Pattern of the Organizational Structure of His Church
In depth information: Chapter V

(e) Divine Pattern of the Work of the Congregation
Complete information: Chapter V

Important Point to Remember

In order to successfully follow the Narrow Way and be saved from the flames of Hell, one must regularly attend a Church which actively Worships God "in Spirit", as well as being structured and functions absolutely "in Truth" or strictly in accord with the *specific Divine Will of God*, in the prescribed manner provided in the Scriptures.

Only the Eldership is empowered to set the structure and function of Worship service, however each member has the absolute right to make his or her personal determination.

If for any reason a member concludes that one or more elements of the Worship service are not scriptural they may point out the error(s) to a member of the Eldership and request the necessary correction(s).

If a satisfactory solution cannot be accomplished, it is recommended that the member(s) *simply move their membership to a congregation, which strictly conforms to His Patterns*.

(3) Examples of Truths to be believed

(a) God exists

HEBREWS 11:6
But without faith it is impossible to please him: for **he that cometh to God must believe that he is,** and that he is a rewarder of them that diligently seek him.

(b) God is a Spirit

JOHN 4:24
God is a Spirit: and they that worship him must worship him in spirit and in truth.

(c) Jesus Christ is All Powerful

MATTHEW 28:18
And Jesus came and spake unto them, saying, **All power is given unto me in heaven and in earth**.

(d) Jesus is the Resurrection and the Life

JOHN 11:25
Jesus said unto her, **I am the resurrection, and the life:** he that believeth in me, though he were dead, yet shall he live:

(e) Jesus is our Savior

JOHN 4:42
And said unto the woman, Now we believe, not because of thy saying: for we have heard him ourselves, and know that this is indeed the **Christ, the Savior of the world.**

(f) God is Love

JOHN 3:16
For God so loved the world, that he gave his only begotten Son, that whosoever believeth in him should not perish, but have everlasting life.

(g) Jesus is the only Way to God, the Father

JOHN 14:6
Jesus saith unto him, **I am the way,** the truth, and the life: no man cometh unto the Father, but by me.

(4) Examples of Commands to be obeyed

(a) Love your God, with all your Heart, Soul, and Mind and thy neighbor

LUKE 10:27-28
Thou shalt love the Lord thy God with all thy heart, and with all thy soul, and with all thy strength, and with all thy mind; and thy neighbour as thyself.

(b) Seek first the Kingdom of God

MATTHEW 6:33
But seek ye first the kingdom of God, and his righteousness; and all these things shall be added unto you.

(c) Worship God in Spirit and in Truth

JOHN 4:24
God [is] a Spirit: and they that worship him **must worship [him] in spirit and in truth.**

(d) Search and study the Scriptures

JOHN 5:39
Search the Scriptures; for in them ye think ye have eternal life: and they are they which *testify of me.*

2 TIMOTHY 2:15
Study to shew thyself approved unto God, a workman that needeth not to be ashamed, **Rightly [correctly] dividing the word of truth.**

(e) Save yourself first and then all those who will hear you

1 TIMOTHY 4:16
Take heed unto thyself, and unto the doctrine; continue in them: for in doing this **thou shalt both save thyself, and them that hear thee.**

(f) Consider the entire Counsel of God

ACTS 20:27
For I have not shunned to declare unto you **all the counsel of God.**

(g) Commandments were further clarified, amplified and added to by His Apostles in the remaining books.

1 CORINTHIANS 14:37
If any man think himself to be a prophet, or spiritual, let him acknowledge that the things that I write unto you are the **Commandments of the Lord.**

(h) Old Testament Commandments, which were ratified by Christ

MARK 10:19
Thou knowest the commandments, Do not commit adultery, Do not kill, Do not steal, Do not bear false witness, Defraud not, Honour thy father and mother.

ROMANS 13:9
For this, Thou shalt not commit adultery, Thou shalt not kill, Thou shalt not steal, Thou shalt not bear false witness, Thou shalt not covet; and if [there be] any other commandment, it is briefly comprehended in this saying, namely, Thou shalt love thy neighbour as thyself.

(5) Examples of Instructions or Examples to be followed

(a) His faithful followers are to assemble for Worship on the first day of each and every week

ACTS 20:7
And upon the first day of the week, when the disciples came together to break bread, Paul preached unto them, ready to depart on the morrow; and continued his speech until midnight.

(b) His faithful followers are to observe the Lord's Supper on the first day of each and every week

MATTHEW 26:26-28
And as they were eating, Jesus took bread, and blessed it, and broke it, and gave it to the disciples, and said, **Take, eat; this is my body.** And he took the cup, and gave thanks, and gave it to them, saying, **Drink ye all of it; For this is my blood of the New Testament, which is shed for many for the remission of sins.**

ACTS 20:7
And upon the first day of the week, when the disciples came together to break bread, Paul preached unto them, ready to depart on the morrow; and continued his speech until midnight.

Additional reference: 1 CORINTHIANS 11:23-26

(c) His faithful followers are to cheerfully give of their means on Sunday, the first day of each and every week.

1 CORINTHIANS 16:2
Upon the first day of the week let every one of you lay by him in store, as God hath prospered him, that there be no gatherings when I come

2 CORINTHIANS 9 6-7
But this [I say], He which soweth sparingly shall reap also sparingly; and he which soweth bountifully shall reap also bountifully. **Every man according as he purposeth in his heart, [so let him give]; not grudgingly, or of necessity: for God loveth a cheerful giver.**

(6) Examples of Warnings to be heeded

In MATTHEW 16:26 Jesus pointed out the importance of gaining a complete understanding of His Message and the eternal value of each individual Soul, by asking two simple questions.

For what is a man profited, if he shall gain the whole world, and lose his own soul?

What shall a man give in exchange for his soul?

Of course, nothing a human could possibly offer would equal to the value of his Soul. Therefore it is clear that it is our most valuable possession and as such we must take every precaution to protect it.

(a) Stern warnings were issued to all those who refuse to obey

2 THESSALONIANS 1:8
In flaming fire taking vengeance on them that know not God, and that obey not the gospel of our Lord Jesus Christ:

1 PETER 4:17
For the time is come that judgment must begin at the house of God: and if it first begin at us, *what shall the end be of them that obey not the gospel of God?*

(b) Severe warnings to those who fail to gain a clear understanding of the Message of Christ.

ROMANS 1:31
Without understanding, covenant breakers, without natural affection, implacable, unmerciful:

(c) We must have Biblical Authority or support for every belief and practice

EPHESIANS 5:10-11
Proving what is acceptable unto the Lord. And have no fellowship with the unfruitful works of darkness, but rather reprove them

(d) Strict Biblical Injunction against adding or taking away from His Word

His Holy Will is to be esteemed and definitely not to be altered, by any man under penalty of the second death.

REVELATION 22:18-19
For I testify unto every man that heareth the words of the prophecy of this book, **If any man shall add unto these things, God shall add unto him the plagues that are written in this book: And if any man shall take away from the words of the book of this prophecy, God shall take away his part out of the book of life,** and out of the holy city, and [from] the things which are written in this book.

(e) Warnings of false teachers and teaching

MATTHEW 24:11
And many false prophets shall rise, and shall deceive many.

MATTHEW 24:24
For there shall arise false Christs, and false prophets, and shall shew great signs and wonders; insomuch that, if it were possible, *they shall deceive the very elect*

In MATTHEW 7:16, Jesus further explains **"Ye shall know them by their fruits."**

In this context "Fruits" includes the beliefs, physical worship and practices of the religion, which must be compared directly with the Bible and no other source of information

ACTS 20:29-30
For I know this, **that after my departing shall grievous wolves enter in among you, not sparing the flock. Also of your own selves shall men arise, speaking perverse things, to draw away disciples after them.**

2 CORINTHIANS 11:13-15
For such are false apostles, deceitful workers, transforming themselves into the apostles of Christ. And no marvel; for Satan himself is transformed into an angel of light. Therefore it is no great thing if his ministers **also be transformed as the ministers of righteousness;** whose end shall be according to their work

(7) Examples of Assurances to be anticipated

Assurance is much more than just a simple promise. It is a splendid state of being assured; which provides freedom from fear, distrust and ambiguity. The believer who has compiled with His Pattern of Salvation is assured that supreme penalty has been paid by Christ, for all their sins. If they overcome the evil one and remain faithful their final destiny is the Glorious Kingdom of Heaven!

(a) Lord Jesus Assures His faithful servants a Glorious Heavenly home

MATTHEW 16:27
For the Son of man shall come in the glory of his Father with his angels; *and then he shall reward every man according to his works*.

MATTHEW 25:34
Then shall the King say unto them on his right hand, *Come, ye blessed of my Father, inherit the kingdom prepared for you from the foundation of the world*:

Additional references: MATTHEW 5:11-12, MATTHEW 13:43, MATTHEW 25:21, JOHN 4:36, JOHN 14:3, REVELATION 2:7, REVELATION 2:10-11, REVELATION 2:26-28, REVELATION 3:5, REVELATION 3:20-21, REVELATION 22:14

(b) Lord Jesus Assures us He will confess all who Confess Him before men

MATTHEW 10:32
Whosoever therefore shall confess me before men, *him will I confess also before my Father which is in heaven.*

LUKE 12:8
Also I say unto you, Whosoever shall confess me before men, *him shall the Son of man also confess before the angels of God:*

(c) Lord Jesus Assures us an abundant, life on earth

JOHN 10:10
The thief cometh not, but for to steal, and to kill, and to destroy: I am come that **they might have life, and that they might have [it] more abundantly.**

JOHN 16:23-24
And in that day ye shall ask me nothing. Verily, verily, I say unto you, *Whatsoever ye shall ask the Father in my name, he will give [it] you*. Hitherto have ye asked nothing in my name: ask, **and ye shall receive, that your joy may be full.**

Additional references: MATTHEW 6:6, MATTHEW 6:33, MATTHEW 21:22, MARK 9:23, MARK 10:28-30, MARK 11:24, LUKE 6:38, JOHN 15:7, JOHN 15:10-11

(d) Lord Jesus Assures us that He will always be with us

MATTHEW 18:20
For where two or three are gathered together in my name, *there am I in the midst of them.*

MATTHEW 28:20
Teaching them to observe all things whatsoever I have commanded you: and, lo, *I am with you alway, [even] unto the end of the world.* Amen.

(e) Lord Jesus Assures us that He will come again

MATTHEW 24:30-31
And then shall appear the sign of the Son of man in heaven: and then shall all the tribes of the earth mourn, and they shall see the *Son of man coming in the clouds of heaven with power and great glory. And he shall send his angels with a great sound of a trumpet, and they shall gather together his elect from the four winds, from one end of heaven to the other.*

LUKE 21:27-28
And then shall they see the Son of man coming in a cloud with power and great glory. *And when these things begin to come to pass, then look up, and lift up your heads; for your redemption draweth nigh.*

MATTHEW 24:27
For as the lightning cometh out of the east, and shineth even unto the west; so shall also the coming of the Son of man be.

MATTHEW 25:31
When the Son of man shall come in his glory, and all the holy angels with him, then shall he sit upon the throne of his glory:

(f) Another Assurance that Lord Jesus has made is that there will definitely be a Judgment Day, <u>which we all must attend.</u>

Every human being, over the age of accountability, who has ever walked the earth, will be in attendance. Each shall be judged as how they did or did not obey the Commandments and conformed to His other requirements. There is no choice as this is an unconditional Assurance.

JOHN 5:26-29
For as the Father hath life in himself; so hath he given to the Son to have life in himself; *And hath given him authority to execute judgment also, because he is the Son of man.* Marvel not at this: for the hour is coming, in the which all that are in the graves shall hear his voice, *And shall come forth; they that have done good, unto the resurrection of life; and they that have done evil, unto the resurrection of damnation.*

Important Point to Remember

His judgment is absolutely final, without any further appeal, as this is the Highest Tribunal of all.

D. Lord Jesus did NOT promise

(1) Lord Jesus did NOT promise to save any individual who is not a faithful member of His Church, which He purchased with His own blood.

ACTS 20:28
Take heed therefore unto yourselves, and to all the flock, over the which the Holy Ghost hath made you overseers, *to feed the church of God, which he hath purchased with his own blood*.

EPHESIANS 1:22
And hath put all [things] under his feet, and gave him [to be] *the head over all [things] to the church,*

EPHESIANS 5:23
For the husband is the head of the wife, even as *Christ is the head of the church: and he is the saviour of the body.*

(2) Lord Jesus did NOT promise to give us another hour to live.

The prudent individual lives each hour as if it was their last and is thankful each time they awake.

JAMES 4:14
Whereas ye know not what [shall be] on the morrow. For what [is] your life? It is even a vapour, that appeareth for a little time, and then vanisheth away.

(3) Lord Jesus did NOT promise us another chance after death.

Every person who has ever been conceived or lived on the face of the earth will live eternally. Under God's plan the spark of life in all people is their Soul. Each life begins with the Soul being contained in an earthly body. At some point the earthly body expires, but the Soul, which is the essence of the person, lives on forever.

The first part of the existence of the Soul could be called the trial period. This is the time lived on earth beginning at the age of accountability and ending with the death of the earthly body. If the body of the individual dies before the attainment of accountability, then the Soul of that individual moves directly to Paradise.

In LUKE 16:19-31, Jesus indicates that at the end of the trial period or the moment of our death a Divine Determination of our eternal destiny will be completed. There is no second chance to serve our Lord and Master.

If the proper preparations have not been made during this life with complete obedience to our Lord Jesus, we shall find ourselves **without Hope in the Lake of Fire.**

(4) Lord Jesus did NOT promise us a life free of hardships and sacrifices.

Our Lord and Master never promised a life free of evil, troubles, problems, trials and tribulations.

2 TIMOTHY 3:12
Yea, and all that will live godly in Christ Jesus *shall suffer persecution.*

(5) Lord Jesus did NOT promise to accept man's excuses.

Our Lord **did not accept the pleas Adam and Eve gave for their disobedience** and it is unlikely that He will accept the excuses of modern man for failure to conform their lives to His specific Will.

Key Passage: GENESIS 3:16-19
"Unto the woman he said, *I will greatly multiply thy sorrow and thy conception;* in sorrow thou shalt bring forth children; and thy desire [shall be] to thy husband, and he shall rule over thee.And unto Adam he said, Because thou hast hearkened unto the voice of thy wife, and hast eaten of the tree, of which I commanded thee, saying, Thou shalt not eat of it: cursed [is] the ground for thy sake; in sorrow shalt thou eat [of] it all the days of thy life; Thorns also and thistles shall it bring forth to thee; and thou shalt eat the herb of the field; In the sweat of thy face shalt thou eat bread, till thou return unto the ground; for out of it wast thou taken: for dust thou [art], and *unto dust shalt thou return."*

The effect of carefully obeying the Message of Christ is a faith or trust-grace based indestructible relationship between each faithful servant and Lord God, Almighty... Heaven Awaits!

Chapter IV
The Authority of Christ

Chapter Contents

A. The Divine Authority of Christ

B. True and false authority.

A. The Divine Authority of Christ

(1) Christ has been given All Power in Heaven and Earth.

(a) Therefore, He has All Authority and is All Powerful.

(b) Jesus Christ is today, has always been and will always be our absolute Lord and Master.

MATTHEW 28:18
And Jesus came and spake unto them, saying, *All power [excousia] is given unto me in heaven and in earth.*

The Greek word **"exousia",** which translates **authority or power** is a noun that comes from the Greek verb **"exesti"** meaning **"it is right, lawful or rightfully held."**

(2) Lord Jesus purchased His Church with His shed blood

ACTS 20:28
Take heed therefore unto yourselves, and to all the flock, over the which the Holy Ghost hath made you overseers, to feed the church of God, *which he hath purchased with his own blood.*

(3) Christ is the Head of His Church, which is His Body

COLOSSIANS 1:18
And he is the head of the body, the church: who is the beginning, the firstborn from the dead; that in all things he might have the preeminence.

EPHESIANS 1:22-23
And hath put all things under his feet, and *gave him to be the head over all things to the church, Which is his body,* the fullness of him that filleth all in all.

EPHESIANS 5:23
For the husband is the head of the wife, even as *Christ is the head of the church: and he is the savior of the body.*

(4) Jesus is the Author of Eternal Salvation to all who obey him

HEBREWS 5:9
And being made perfect, *he became the author of eternal salvation unto all them that obey him.*

(5) Our Lord requires complete obedience to His Words in the New Testament

MATTHEW 23:23
Woe unto you, scribes and Pharisees, hypocrites! for ye pay tithe of mint and anise and cummin, and *have omitted the weightier matters of the law, judgment, mercy, and faith: these ought ye to have done, and not to leave the other undone.*

MARK 13:31
Heaven and earth shall pass away: **but my words shall not pass away.**

JOHN 14:23
Jesus answered and said unto him, *If a man love me, he will keep my words: and my Father will love him, and we will come unto him, and make our abode with him.*

JOHN 15:7
If ye abide in me, and my words abide in you, ye shall ask what ye will, and it shall be done unto you.

Important Point to Remember

In essence, the lesson that Jesus is teaching is that we are *to conform strictly to the Directives as provided, as well as, following His example of Holiness.*

One without the other is empty, hollow and completely without value.

(6) Jesus will be our Righteous Judge on the Day of Judgment

ACTS 17:31
Because he hath appointed a day, in the which *he will judge the world in righteousness by that man whom he hath*

ordained; whereof he hath given assurance unto all men, in that he hath raised him from the dead.

ROMANS 14:12
So then every one of us shall give account of himself to God.

JOHN 5:22
For the Father judgeth no man, but hath committed all judgment unto the Son:

JOHN 12:48
He that rejecteth me, and receiveth not my words, hath one that judgeth him: the word that I have spoken, the same shall judge him in the last day.

2 TIMOTHY 4:8
Henceforth *there is laid up for me a crown of righteousness, which the Lord, the righteous judge, shall give me at that day: and not to me only, but unto all them also that love his appearing.*

ECCLESIASTES 3:17
I said in mine heart, **God shall judge the righteous and the wicked:** for there is a time there for every purpose and for every work.

(7) His true followers cherish Jesus Christ as Lord and have the highest respect for His Authority and Power, which is one of the distinguishing traits of His Church

(a) The following passage clearly indicates that God has not and will not provide mankind with any revelations other than those, which were included in His Holy Word.

REVELATION 22:18-19
For I testify unto every man that heareth the words of the prophecy of this book, *If any man shall add unto these things, God shall add unto him the plagues that are written in this book: And if any man shall take away from the words of the book of this prophecy, God shall take away his part out of the book of life,* and out of the holy city, and [from] the things which are written in this book.

(b) In addition adding to, or subtracting from, the simple instructions of Jesus is failing to respect His Authority and will result in eternal punishment.

Therefore, His Church has no conferences, synods, councils, earthly headquarters or denominational governmental associations are maintained or considered, as Christ condemned such.

MATTHEW 15:9
But **in vain** they do worship me, teaching for doctrines the commandments of men.

(c) Unauthorized traditions added to Worship of God are unacceptable

The term "**traditions**" is from the Greek word "**paradosis**", Jesus and the Apostles Paul and Peter **denounced** *the use of religious traditions, rules or regulations that originated in the minds of men and then were handed down.*

MATTHEW 15:3
But he answered and said unto them, *Why do ye also transgress the commandment of God by your tradition?*

MARK 7:9
And he said unto them, Full well *ye reject the commandment of God, that ye may keep your own tradition.*

MARK 7:13
Making the word of God of none effect through your tradition, which ye have delivered: and many such like things do ye.

COLOSSIANS 2:8
Beware lest any man spoil you through philosophy and vain deceit, after the tradition of men, after the rudiments of the world, and not after Christ.

1 PETER 1:18
Forasmuch as ye know that ye were not redeemed with corruptible things, as silver and gold, *from your vain conversation received by tradition from your fathers;*

(d) Apostle Paul commanded that Christians hold fast to only the traditions they had been taught

2 THESSALONIANS 2:15
Therefore, brethren, *stand fast, and hold*

the traditions which ye have been taught, whether by word, or our epistle.

(8) Apostle Paul taught that each faithful follower must be certain that they have Biblical Authority or support for every belief and practice

1 THESSALONIANS 5:21
Prove all things; hold fast that which is good.

EPHESIANS 5:10-11
Proving what is acceptable unto the Lord. And have no fellowship with the unfruitful works of darkness, but rather reprove them.

(9) Apostle John warned each faithful follower that it is sinful to condone unauthorized or condemned beliefs or practices

2 JOHN 1:9-11
Whosoever transgresseth, and abideth not in the doctrine of Christ, hath not God. He that abideth in the doctrine of Christ, he hath both the Father and the Son. *If there come any unto you, and bring not this doctrine, receive him not into your house, neither bid him Godspeed: For he that biddeth him Godspeed is partaker of his evil deeds.*

B. True and False Authority

True Authority

(1) True Authority comes from Heaven, which is defined as the authority or power to command which, is right and lawful or the power which is rightfully held by Jesus Christ

References: MATTHEW 21:23-27, MATTHEW 28:18, 2 JOHN 1:9

(2) True Authority is revealed in the Word of God

References: ROMANS 6:17, TITUS 2:10, 1 TIMOTHY 6:1, 2 TIMOTHY 3:16

(3) Individuals conducting themselves in accord with the Commandments of Christ have direct Authority from Heaven for their Worship.

Reference: COLOSSIANS 3:17

(4) Individuals who obey the full Message of Christ have respected the Authority of Christ and will be saved!

Reference: HEBREWS 5:9

False Authority

(1) False authority or power to command is unlawfully assumed by demons or men by adding or subtracting from the Commands or Examples of Jesus and His Apostles.

1 TIMOTHY 4:1-3
Now the *Spirit speaketh expressly, that in the latter times some shall depart from the faith, giving heed to seducing spirits, and doctrines of devils;* Speaking lies in hypocrisy; *having their conscience seared with a hot iron; Forbidding to marry, and commanding to abstain from meats,* which God hath created to be received with thanksgiving of them which believe and know the truth.

2 CORINTHIANS 11:13-15
For such are **false apostles, deceitful workers, transforming themselves into the apostles of Christ.** And no marvel; for **Satan himself is transformed into an angel of light.** Therefore it is no great thing if his ministers also be **transformed as the ministers of righteousness**; whose end shall be according to their works.

Additional reference ROMANS 16:17

(2) Individuals conducting themselves in accord with the commandments of men or demons do not have authority from Heaven and therefore their worship is in vain

References: MATTHEW 15:8-9, MATTHEW 15:11-14, MARK 7:6-8

(3) Individuals not functioning or worshiping in accord with the specific Divine Will of God do so without His

Authority, which will only **result in eternal retribution in Hell**

Reference: REVELATION 22:18-19

Important Points to Remember

(1) The Holy Spirit, revealed the Word of God, to the Writers of the New Testament.

1 CORINTHIANS 2:6-12
Howbeit we speak wisdom among them that are perfect: yet not the wisdom of this world, nor of the princes of this world, that come to naught: But we speak the wisdom of God in a mystery, even the hidden wisdom, which God ordained before the world unto our glory: Which none of the princes of this world knew: for had they known it, they would not have crucified the Lord of glory. But as it is written, Eye hath not seen, nor ear heard, neither have entered into the heart of man, the things which God hath prepared for them that love him. But God hath revealed them unto us by his Spirit: for the Spirit searcheth all things, yea, the deep things of God. For what man knoweth the things of a man, save the spirit of man which is in him? even so the things of God knoweth no man, *but the Spirit of God. Now we have received*, not the spirit of the world, but the *Spirit which is of God; that we might know the things that are freely given to us of God.*

EPHESIANS 3:3-5
How that by revelation he made known unto me the mystery; (as I wrote afore in few words, Whereby, when ye read, ye may understand my knowledge in the mystery of Christ) Which in other ages was not made known unto the sons of men, as it is now *revealed unto his holy apostles and prophets by the Spirit*;

(2) The Holy Spirit revealed all Truth to the Writers of the New Testament.

References: JOHN 16:13, 2 PETER 1:20-21

JOHN 16:13
Howbeit when he, *the Spirit of truth, is come, he will guide you into all truth: for he shall not speak of himself; but whatsoever he shall hear, that shall he speak: and he will show you things to come.*

2 PETER 1:21 For the prophecy came not in old time by the will of man: *but holy men of God spake as they were moved by the Holy Ghost.*

Important Point to clearly understand

Since all Truth was revealed to these Writers, therefore, nothing further could be revealed after their death.

Hence, we can know with certainty that anything written or spoken by any man, which is not present in the Holy Scriptures, is a false teaching.

MATTHEW 7:15
Beware of false prophets, which come to you in sheep's clothing, but inwardly they are ravening wolves.

GALATIANS 1:8 But though we, or *an angel from heaven, preach any other gospel unto you than that which we have preached unto you, let him be accursed.*

Logical Conclusion

Therefore, Christians must base their personal convictions solely upon the inspired Word of God, as it is our ONLY source of Divine Authority.

Trust and Obey.... Heaven Awaits!

Chapter V

The Church that Jesus Built

Chapter Contents

A. Introduction

B. Importance of understanding the Message of Christ

C. Divine Authority is Mandatory

D. Divine Patterns of the Faith

E. Jesus Christ established His Church

F. His Divine Pattern of Scriptural Worship

G. His Divine Pattern of Organizational Structure

H. His Divine Pattern of the Work of the Congregation

I. Christianity is much more than a succession of Patterns

J. Role of female members of His Church

K. Christians must be properly attired

L. Eternal future of His Church

A. Introduction

(1) Identifying His Church

(a) Anyone willing to make the effort is able to identify His Church by the process of elimination or by simply comparing beliefs, practices and structure of each religious group against the Words of the New Testament.

The reader may find Appendixes 2, 3, 4, 5, and 6, one or more of the *Suggested Outside References* listed near the end of this guide or internet key-word searches useful in making this all important determination.

(b) His Church is the largest and most conservative of the five groups that came into being as a result of Restoration Movement that occurred during the Second Great Awakening in the early years of the nineteen century in the eastern and southern regions of the United States.

The basic objective of the Restoration pioneers was to eliminate all unsupported non-Biblical components in Worship Services and restore the purity of the Church by a complete return to the primitive or original Church of the first century.

Members of His Church in the United States generally mark the beginning of the Restoration in the United States as August 7, 1801 or the opening day of the famous revival held at Cane Creek, Kentucky, which was attended by tens of thousands seeking to understand the specific Divine Will of God. For over one hundred years, the various factions of the Restoration worked to attain unity and finally agree upon common doctrine, based solely upon the Word of God.

Unfortunately, these efforts failed and in 1906 the separate factions of the Restoration split and formed independent churches.

Additional information is provided in Section E of this Chapter.

B. Importance of understanding the Message of Christ

(1) Jesus requires that we understand the Message of Christ or the specific Divine Will of God, and promises that through obedience, we will be made free from fear and an ever-increasing burden of sin.

JOHN 8:31-32
Then said Jesus to those Jews which believed on him, **If ye continue in my word, then are ye my disciples indeed; And ye shall know the truth, and the truth shall make you free.**

(2) God wishes that each and every member of His creation would be saved from the fires of Hell, but has given to mankind the absolute freedom of choice.

(a) The Great Apostle Peter confirms this declaration in 2 PETER 3:9; "The Lord is not slack concerning his promise, as some men count slackness; but is longsuffering to us-ward, not willing that any should perish, but that all should come to repentance."

(b) Our Creator has expressed His strong desire that everyone in the world would be faithful; "Who will have all men to be saved, and to come unto the knowledge of the truth." (1 TIMOTHY 2:4)

(c) What is the meaning of the words knowledge and truth referred to in this passage?

In this context, the word **knowledge means comprehension or understanding** and the **Truth** is interchangeable with and comparable to **the specific Divine Will of God.**

The source of the **Truth is the Scriptures,** which is defined in JOHN 17:17; "Sanctify them by your truth, **your word is truth**."

Therefore, the phrase **"your word is truth"** is a direct reference to the specific **Divine Will of God.**

(d) The Great Apostle Paul provides additional support and certainty by stating, in 2 TIMOTHY 3:16-17; that the Scriptures are sufficient for all our needs. This verse assures the followers of Christ that the Scriptures contain all the information required to be saved.

C. Divine Authority is Mandatory

(1) We must have Biblical Authority or support for every belief and practice.

(a) Our personal beliefs must be based upon clearly defined convictions of standards.

(1) These convictions or standards must be based solely upon the Word of God, *as it is our only source of Divine Authority.*

(2) This set of convictions or standards must embrace His total counsel, while including only the Patterns, Commandments, Instructions and Examples provided by Jesus, and His Disciples.

EPHESIANS 5:10-11
Proving what is acceptable unto the Lord. And have no fellowship with the unfruitful works of darkness, but rather reprove them.

Additional references: 1 THESSALONIANS 5:21, 2 TIMOTHY 1:13

(b) The Apostle Paul commanded that Christians hold fast to only the traditions they had been taught

Key Passage: 2 THESSALONIANS 2:15

(2) We must understand the everlasting consequences of unauthorized beliefs or practices.

Key Passage: MATTHEW 7:21-23

(3) We must understand that it is sinful to condone unauthorized or condemned beliefs or practices.

Key Passage: 2 JOHN 1:9-11

D. Divine Patterns of the Faith

(1) The Greek word "tupos" means a model for imitation, a pattern, form or exact replication. Each time a pattern [tupos] is duplicated certain characteristics and distinctiveness will always be present and identifiable.

Consider why the modern fast food franchises are successful. The developers of these franchises created successful and profitable methods of operations and then expanded by selling exact duplications to individuals seeking to purchase a successful business, making great gains in the process.

In doing so, these developers use the same methods that were employed in the Old Testament and the first century.

(2) The Patterns of the Faith are distinctive.

The following examples confirm that the concept of those Patterns is an integrated element of God's Plan.

(a) The Greek word "pistis" translates as religious truth, or the truthfulness of God, especially reliance upon Christ for salvation, abstractly, the system of religious (Gospel) truth itself: assurance, belief, faith or fidelity.

(b) The Apostle Paul, in EPHESIANS 4:4-6 clearly states there is only ONE faith.

EPHESIANS 4:4-6
There is one body, [His Church] and one Spirit, even as ye are called **in one hope of your calling**; One Lord, **one faith,** [pistis] **one baptism**, One God and Father of all, who is above all, and through all, and in you all.

(c) Jude used the same Greek word [pistis] to denote the <u>Faith</u>.

JUDE 1:3
Beloved, when I gave all diligence to write unto you of the common salvation, it was needful for me to write unto you, and exhort you *that ye should earnestly contend for the faith [pistis]* which was once delivered unto the saints.

(3) The Faith consists of a distinctive unchanging Body of Truth.

(a) Jesus and His Disciples originally taught the Message of Christ in order to develop belief, faith, trust in Jesus Christ and to explain His Divine Directives.

(b) Almost immediately after the very beginning of His Church, this precious Body of Truth, His Message was being altered or misrepresented.

(c) Unfortunately, even today generally the full Message of Christ either is not being taught or is seriously distorted by the vast majority of teachers.

Note: An overview of the Patterns and related elements of the Message of Christ has been provided in Appendix 6: Summary of selected Elements of the Divine Mosaic.

E. Jesus Christ established His Church

(1) Introduction

(a) The Greek word for His Church is "ekklesia", which means "the called out assembly" and people called from one realm (this world) to another (His Spiritual Kingdom or His Church.)

(b) This term was first applied to Christianity by Jesus in Matthew 16:18 and refers to either the worldwide or universal assembly. It is headquartered in Heaven and composed of saved believers who are in fellowship with Lord Jesus and one another.

(c) This assembly is known as the Body of Christ or His Church, which includes all local congregations of His Church throughout the world.

(2) Jesus Christ purchased His Church with His shed blood

Reference: ACTS 20:28

(3) Jesus Christ has all Power (Authority) over His Church.

(a) Jesus Christ is today, has always been and will always be our absolute Lord and Master.

(b) Members of His Church submit respectfully to the supreme power and authority of Christ.

(c) The acknowledgement of the Authority of Christ is one of the distinguishing traits of His Church.

Reference: MATTHEW 28:18

(4) Jesus Christ is the Head of His Church, which is His Body.

Reference: EPHESIANS 1:22-23

(5) Jesus is the Author of Eternal Salvation.

Reference: HEBREWS 5:9

(6) Lord Jesus requires complete obedience to His Words in the New Testament.

References: MATTHEW 23:23, MARK 13:31, JOHN 14:23, JOHN 15:7

(a) In essence, the lesson that Jesus is teaching is that we are <u>to conform strictly</u> to all Directives provided and to follow His example of Holiness.

One without the other is empty, hollow and completely without value

(7) Jesus will be our Righteous Judge on the Day of Judgment

References: ACTS 17:31, ROMANS 14:12, JOHN 5:22, JOHN 12:48, 2 TIMOTHY 4:8, ECCLESIASTES 3:17

(8) Place and Date of the beginning of His Church

A few months prior to being crucified Christ proclaimed, as recorded in MATTHEW 16:18, "upon this rock **I will build my Church;** and the gates of hell shall not prevail against it."

Isaiah stated in Chapter 2:2-3, that when the law and the word of the Lord went forth from **Jerusalem**, the house of the Lord, would establish and all nations would flow into it

In ZECHARIAH 1:16, the Lord made it clear, speaking through His prophet, that His house or church would be built in Jerusalem "Therefore thus saith the LORD; *I am returned to Jerusalem with mercies: my house shall be built in it,*"

In MARK 9:1, Jesus enlightened His Apostles regarding the coming of His Kingdom or Church, "Verily I say unto you, That there be some of them that stand here, which shall not taste of death, till they have seen the kingdom of God [His Church] come with power." (Power was provided later to the Apostles by the Holy Spirit - ACTS 2:1.)

According to the record of the gathering of Jesus and His Apostles after his Resurrection in LUKE 24:44-47, Jesus said "These [are] the words which I spake unto you, while I was yet with you, that all things must be fulfilled, which were written in the Law of Moses, and [in] the prophets, and [in] the psalms, concerning me." Then opened He their understanding, that they might understand the scriptures, And said unto them, "Thus it is written, and thus it behoved Christ to suffer, and to rise from the dead the third day: And that repentance and remission of sins should be preached in his name among all nations, beginning at Jerusalem."

We learn in ACTS 1:2-9 that this meeting occurred 40 days after the Resurrection of Jesus Christ, that he revealed details regarding the Kingdom of God. Jesus instructed them "Not to depart from Jerusalem, but wait for the promise of the Father". In verse 8, He said, "But you shall receive power, after the Holy Spirit is come upon you, and you shall be witnesses unto me both in Jerusalem and Judah and in Samaria and unto the uttermost parts of the earth".

Verse 9 tells us "when he had spoken these things, while they beheld, he was taken up; and a cloud received him out of their sight." In verse 12, we are told "Then returned they unto Jerusalem from the mount called Olivet, which is from Jerusalem a Sabbath day's journey." This account is also recorded in LUKE 24:48-53.

(a) It is clear that His Church or Kingdom began in Jerusalem.

Beginning in the first verse of ACTS Chapter 2, we are told that ten days later on the Sunday which marked Day of Pentecost, 50 days after the Resurrection of Christ, the Apostles were together and suddenly a sound from Heaven, like a rushing mighty wind and they were all filled with the Holy Ghost and began to speak in other languages.

Reference: ACTS 2:5-6

On that glorious day of Pentecost, when His Church began in Jerusalem, the renowned Apostle Peter delivered one of the most monumental and significant sermons of all time, on the Life, Death, the Burial, and the Resurrection of Jesus Christ, which also marked the beginning of the preaching of the Message of Christ or His Gospel, which proclaimed Salvation through obedience and the remission of sins.

References: ACTS 2:14, LUKE 24:47

A large percentage of the audience was the same horde of barbaric unfaithful Jews, who less than two months before had subjected their Lord and Savior, the King of all earthly kings, to one of the most brutal and vindictive forms of death, ever conceived by the evil mind of man.

Many of these individuals had shown no interest in His Message and were overtly hostile towards Christ.

When Peter had finished preaching, it must have been a time of critical sorrow among those who believed. They knew in their hearts and had no other alternative, but to admit that they had demanded that, the Messiah, whom they had awaited for centuries, be murdered in a bloodbath. They were carrying the immense guilt of slaughtering the only man who ever lived a totally sinless life.

At the moment of realization, a great fear must have come upon the Jews. Luke relates in verse 37 that when the assembly understood their situation, "they were pricked in their heart", and they begged Peter and the other Apostles for a way out by asking, "Men [and] brethren, what shall we do?"

Peter answered in verse 38, "Repent, and be baptized every one of you in the name of Jesus Christ for the remission of sins, and ye shall receive the gift of the Holy Ghost."

Repentance is an alteration of one's heart and mind, brought about by Godly sorrow (2 CORINTHIANS 7:9-10), the results of which is a change of lifestyle, in which sin is avoided and obedience to His Message becomes a personal concern.

The second part of Peter's instruction was to repent and be baptized (ACTS 2:38) for the forgiveness of all their sins. Their belief, confession and repentance were of no value, until they were willing to submit to His Will by an act of faith and be saved.

ACTS 2:38
Then Peter said unto them, **Repent,** and **be baptized** every one of you **in the name of Jesus Christ for the remission of sins**, and ye shall receive the gift of the Holy Ghost.

We learn in verse 41 that "Then they that gladly received his word were baptized: and the same day there were added [unto them] about three thousand souls." In verse 47, we discover that the Church continued to grow, "Praising God and having favor with all the people, **and the Lord added to the Church daily such as should be saved**".

The Scriptures clearly indicate that the words of Peter prompted three thousand Souls to follow the simple Commandments of the Lord. Thus, founding the **first congregation of His Church in Jerusalem,** which began with a membership of over 3000 souls, which was guided by the Holy Spirit, as well as, from the Thrones of God the Father and Lord Jesus in Heaven, in **approximately 30 AD,** (Bible scholars differ on the actual year, estimates range from AD 29 to AD 33), on the Day of Pentecost.

This occurred ten days after the Ascension of our Lord and Savior to His Glorious Throne of Light, at the right hand of God, in Heaven.

That Day of Pentecost also marked the beginning of the Christian Age

This is confirmed by the fact that this is the first time in the New Testament that the Church was spoken of as being in existence

REVELATION 11:2 and 12:5 plainly state that His Church would suffer severe hardship, but would **survive** and be in **continuous existence**, without exception, **forever!**

This is **confirmed** by the words of the Great Apostle Paul in EPHESIANS 3:21 ASV "unto him `be' the glory in the church and in Christ Jesus unto all generations **for ever and ever.** Amen" and the passages listed below.

Additional references: GENESIS 17:19, DANIEL 2:44, DANIEL 7:13-14, MATTHEW 16:18, HEBREWS 12:28

Many Biblical scholars agree that the prophecy of John foretold in REVELATION 12:6 of the persecution of His Church (figuratively as a woman who fled into the wilderness where God had prepared a place of refuge). It is also generally accepted that the time period "thousand two hundred and threescore days" equals 1260 years.

His Church and Catholicism (REVELATION 16:13, REVELATION 19:20, REVELATION 20:10) were in conflict, but did not completely part ways until 533 AD.

It was during this year when **Justinian I renamed himself John II,** and **declared** himself to be the **Lord of the Church**, in **place of Jesus Christ**.

After 533 AD His Church went into hiding (as prophesied in Revelation 12:6) as Catholicism became extremely aggressive, in the evil attempt to eradicate all traces of His Spiritual Kingdom or Church, as the leadership of that church gained, with the assistance of Satan, virtually control and vast influence over the Emperors of the Byzantine Empire.

Historical Note: The Justinian Dynast was a family who ruled over the Byzantine Empire from 518 to 602. This dynast originated with Justin I, who ruled from 518 to 527. Petrus Sabbatius, the adopted son of Justin, rose to the rank of emperor, and ruled as **Justinian I** from 527 to 565.

As a result of the declaration of Justinian and the intense oppression and persecution (2 TIMOTHY 3:12) of the Catholic hierarchy, **the members of His Church** were forced into **hiding** for the 1260 prophetic years.

Americans as a result of the successful Revolution gained religious freedom in 1776. As a result of the promise of religious freedom, a large number of British citizens, who were members of His Church, which had existed and been oppressed by the Church of England for centuries, fled to America.

Then in 1793 or **exactly** 1260 years from the date of the declaration of Justinian, James O'Kelley, in an successful effort to return to the Teaching of the Bible, withdrew from the Methodist Episcopal Church and called upon others to join his movement, to which several thousand responded.

His Church experienced rapid expansion in America, a new land that God provided for his believers, as a result of the massive "Back to the Bible" restoration movement that united members of many faiths in one common goal, which was to worship, conduct services and to live daily lives precisely in the manner, as commanded in His Holy Scriptures.

Members of His Church in the United States generally mark the beginning of the Restoration or *more properly the date of the formal introduction of His Church in the United States* as August 7, 1801 or the opening day of the famous revival held at Cane Creek, Kentucky, which was attended by tens of thousands seeking to understand the specific Divine Will of God.

(b) Importance of determining when and where His Church began

To allow believers to **differentiate** His Church from religious organizations of modern human origin, by gaining an understanding of <u>when and where</u> His One True Church began

There is only **one** Church of our Lord and Savior, Jesus Christ. (Ephesians 4:4-6)

(c) Only the Lord may add members to His Church

Individuals who have conformed themselves to His Divine requirement are added to His Church by the Lord. No man or woman has ever been added to His Church through a vote of the congregation or any other method created by man. This is confirmed in ACTS 2:47

(d) His Church has no earthly organization as the headquarters of His Church is in Heaven.

(1) The membership rolls of His Church or the Book or Life is maintained in Heaven.

References: PHILIPPIANS 4:3, REVELATION 20:15, REVELATION 3:5, ACTS 2:47, COLOSSIANS 3:1

(9) Jesus Christ pleaded for religious unity in one Faith and prayed that His Church would not be divided.

References: JOHN 17:11, JOHN 17:20-21

(a) The Apostle Paul appealed for religious unity in one Faith.

Reference: 1 CORINTHIANS 1:10

The Church of our Lord is best known for its distinctive plea for religious unity based exclusively upon the Words of Jesus and His Disciples

(b) The Apostle Paul predicted Denominationalism.

Reference: ACTS 20: 29-30

Logical Conclusion

His Church is nondenominational. Jesus and His Apostles clearly indicated that divisions or Denominationalism is NOT acceptable to the Lord; therefore, millions are in danger of the Judgment.

(10) The modern name of His Church is Scriptural

Numerous descriptive expressions for His Church or the Faith appear upon the pages of the New Testament. However, **no formal name for His Church** or the Faith was provided in the first century, as it is unnecessary, **since there was only one**.

Many of the moons of other planets have names, but our moon has remained unnamed. Why? **Because there is only one!**

God provided a Pattern to follow. The use of any name, which is mentioned in the Word of God, would be Scriptural. However, the acceptability of other church names, which are not in accord with the Scriptures or that glorify a human name, is questionable.

(a) The modern name of His Church glorifies His Holy Name.

His Church has about 40 different designations in the Bible, which usually relate to or glorify Christ or God, but no official name. Christ has clearly indicated that Christians are to glorify Him and His Name.

While only one Church existed in the first century, at the time of the restoration, in the early nineteenth century, hundreds, if not thousands of churches were in existence. The restorers obeyed His Commandments, followed the Biblical pattern and reestablished His Church with a Scriptural modern name in tribute to the magnificence of our Lord and Savior.

References: JOHN 13:32, JOHN 16:14, JOHN 17:1, JOHN 17:5

(b) Members of His Church wear the name of Christ.

Isaiah prophesied that the Lord would give the children of God a new everlasting name. For this reason the members of His Church wear the name of **Christians only**, in Honor of Christ and to His Glory. His true disciples do not make use of worldly labels such as Catholics, Mormons, Lutherans, Baptists or the thousands of other names individuals call themselves to identify their religious affiliation, as these are not mentioned in the Word of God.

References: ISAIAH 56:5, ACTS 11:26 ISAIAH 62:2, 1 PETER 4:16

(11) Jesus Christ Loves and will save the faithful Disciples of His Church from the horrors of Hell.

EPHESIANS 5:23
For the husband is the head of the wife, even as **Christ** is the head of the church: and he is the **savior** of the body.

Additional references: ACTS 4:12, EPHESIANS 1:22-23, EPHESIANS 5:25

F. His Divine Pattern of Scriptural Worship

(1) Spiritual Elements of Worship

The Authority for each act of Worship is based solely on inspired Scriptures of the New Testament. The Leadership and members of congregations of His Church actively seek to be guided in all they do by the Word of God. The Great Apostle Paul assures us that *the Scriptures are <u>sufficient</u> for all our needs*.

Key Passage: 2 TIMOTHY 3:15-17

(a) God revealed to the world through his Son, in the first century, precisely how Christians are to Worship Him each Lord's Day

Reference: JOHN 12:49-50

(b) The purpose of Worship is the Glorification and Worship of God

References: 1 PETER 4:11, PSALMS 100:1-5, 1 PETER 2:9, 1 PETER 4:11

(c) The Worship of God is to be truly in Spirit and in Truth

JOHN 4:24
God [is] a Spirit: and they that worship him must worship [him] in spirit and in truth.

Important Definition to fully understand

The term "in Spirit" is an abstract concept, like beauty it cannot be defined, only described. People usually know when they move into a spiritual state, which only occurs when an individual is in the proper frame of mind. The spiritual plane is higher than the realm of reality, in which we normally function. We will usually rapidly reach this higher plane, when reaching out to God, in sincere and humble prayer.

It is a mental activity, which requires the proper attitude and willingness to focus our minds on spiritual concerns, while consciously attempting to eliminate all unnecessary worldly issues from the active part of our mind during worship services or at times of prayer.

God requires that we Worship with all our Heart, Mind and Soul, which was created in His image. (GENESIS 1:26) We all have the ability, but it requires effort and a willingness to conform to His Commandments in order to offer the Spiritual form of Worship that is sincere, humble, holy, and pure, which corresponds with the Spiritual Disposition of God.

The term "in Truth" is interchangeable with and comparable to the term the "Will of God".

The Truth or the Will of God simply means to carefully follow the Patterns, Commandments, Examples and Instructions which are recorded in the Word of God.

(d) Now that we understand the Biblical meaning of Truth, the next step is to conform, organize and harmonize the Worship of God, just as He directs in His Word, without any unauthorized additions, subtractions or creative enhancements which violate the clear, intense and unmistakable Command of Christ in REVELATION 22:18-19

Important Point to Remember

In order to successfully follow the Narrow Way, one must regularly attend a Church which actively Worships God **"in Spirit"**, as well as being structured and functions absolutely **"in Truth"** or strictly in accord with the specific Will of God, in the prescribed manner provided in the Scriptures.

(2) Physical Elements of Worship

(a) His Church Meets on the first day of each and every week

ACTS 20:7
And upon the first day of the week, when the disciples came together to break bread, Paul preached unto them, ready to depart on the morrow; and continued his speech until midnight.

(b) Several Prayers are offered to God during each Worship Service.

Prayer is a central component of all worship services with several prayers lead by Christian male members.

1 TIMOTHY 2:8
I will therefore that men pray every where, lifting up holy hands, *without wrath and doubting*.

Additional references: ACTS 2:42, ACTS 12:5, ACTS 12:12, JAMES 5:16 1 TIMOTHY 2:1

(c) Vocal or a cappella* singing and making melody in their hearts, without instrumental accompaniment, is an important component of Worship.

*The word a cappella literally means "as in the chapel" or "in the manner of the church"

EPHESIANS 5:19
Speaking to yourselves in psalms and hymns and spiritual songs, **singing and making melody in your heart to the Lord;**

Additional references: COLOSSIANS 3:16, HEBREWS 2:12, 1 CORINTHIANS 14:15

(1) In the Old Testament, God Commanded and was Worshipped with harps and other instruments.

Reference: 2 CHRONICLES 29:25

(2) However, the New Testament contains no such directive related to the use of any type of musical instrument and several other Patterns for specific actions were commanded under the Old Law (Testament) such as, animal sacrifices in the worship of God.

Since we live and worship under the New Covenant (Testament), all members of His Church sing without the aid of instrumental music.

Since the use of musical instruments is not mentioned or commanded in the Holy Scriptures it can only be considered an unauthorized and illegitimate addition to the Worship service.

Hence, any such use would be a violation of the unyielding Biblical Injunction, against "adding to" in REVELATION 22:18-19 and would likely result in each individual, who affirms its use, *to be eternally lost*.

(d) Teaching and Preaching of the Word to one another each time we gather for Worship.

(1) The Bible is to be the exclusive basis of all Teachings in classes and from the pulpit.

MATTHEW 24:14
And this gospel of the kingdom shall be *preached in all the world for a witness unto all nations; and then shall the end come.*

Additional references: ROMANS 10:15, 1 CORINTHIANS 9:14, 2 TIMOTHY 4:2

(e) The Lord's Supper is observed on Sunday, the first day of each and every week

MATTHEW 26:26-28
And as they were eating, Jesus took bread, and blessed it, and broke it, and gave it to the disciples, and said, **Take, eat; this is my body**. And he took the cup, and gave thanks, and gave it to them, saying, Drink ye all of it; **For this is my blood of the New Testament, which is shed for many for the remission of sins**

ACTS 20:7
And upon the first day of the week, when the disciples came together to break bread, Paul preached unto them, ready to depart on the morrow; and continued his speech until midnight.

1 CORINTHIANS 11:23-26
For I have received of the Lord that which also I delivered unto you, That the Lord **Jesus the same night in which he was betrayed took bread:** And when he had given thanks, he broke it, and said, Take, eat: this is my body, which is broken for you: **this do in remembrance of me.** After the same manner also **he took the cup,** when he had supped, saying, This cup is the new testament in my blood: **this do ye, as oft as ye drink it, in remembrance of me.** For as often as ye eat this bread, and drink this cup, **ye do show [proclaim] the Lord's death till he come[s].**

We are **commanded to remember** and **to review in our minds His Death** and **His Life** (Including but not limited to His Birth, Accomplishments, Directives, events leading up to His Death, Resurrection etc.) of **our Lord and Savior each week before and during the Lord's Supper**

We are **not** commanded to celebrate the Birth or Resurrection of our Lord. Therefore any cerebration or activities related to the earthly holidays (Easter or Christmas) within or as a part of the Worship services can only be considered as **an unauthorized and illegitimate addition** to the Worship service.

Hence, any such cerebration or activities would be a violation of the unyielding Biblical Injunction, against "adding to" in REVELATION 22:18-19 and would likely result in each individual, who affirms its use, to be eternally lost

On the other hand, private or personal celebrations are **not prohibited** in the pages of the New Testament. Therefore, personal or public celebrations of His Birth or Resurrection, which are **not** included as a part of the Worship services of His Church, **would be acceptable**

(f) Members cheerfully give of their means on Sunday, the first day of each and every week.

Each week, members are given the opportunity to support the work of the Church by returning to the Lord a portion of the amount they have been prospered.

1 CORINTHIANS 16:2
Upon the first day of the week let every one of you lay by him in store, as God hath prospered him, that there be no gatherings when I come

Additional reference: 2 CORINTHIANS 9:6-8

(3) Throughout the Worship services, four principles govern all Elements:

(a) Glorification and Worship of God.

References: PSALMS 100:1-5, 1 PETER 2:9, 1 PETER 4:11

(b) Worship of the Father in Spirit and in Truth

JOHN 4:24
God [is] a Spirit: and they that worship him must *worship [him] in spirit and in truth.*

Additional reference: 1 CORINTHIANS 14:15

(c) All things are done for Edification (Instruction)

Reference: 1 CORINTHIANS 14:25-26

(d) All things are to be done decently and in order

1 CORINTHIANS 14:40
Let all things be done decently and in order.

G. His Divine Pattern of Organizational Structure

Following the example of first century Congregations of His Church, congregations of His Church, today make use of the congregational type of church government, as follows:

(1) Jesus Christ is the Head of His Church, which is His Body.

EPHESIANS 1:22-23
And hath put all things under his feet, and gave him to be the **head** over all things to the church, **Which is his body,** the fullness of him that filleth all in all.

Additional references: 1 TIMOTHY 6:14-15, COLOSSIANS 1:18, JAMES 4:12

A widespread misconception exists regarding the Scriptural government of the Church. Since the people of the United States and several other countries live in a democracy, many believe that the congregation *should vote upon any issue that affects the majority.*

This perception is <u>erroneous</u>, due to the fact that His Church is <u>not</u> a democracy, but a <u>monarchy</u> and Jesus Christ is the everlasting King.

(2) Each mature Congregation or local Church had Elders (Bishops), who

oversaw and tended to the flock (members)

Governing each Congregation of the early Church was a group of two or more ordained Elders, who oversaw and tended to the spiritual needs of its members. The Elders ordained at that location independently governed each Congregation or local Church.

Thus each Congregation or local Church had complete autonomy and were bound to other local churches or congregations, only through Jesus as the Head of His Church and their shared Faith.

Biblical scholars assume this type of church government was employed to circumvent widespread apostasy.

1 TIMOTHY 5:17
Let the elders that rule well be counted worthy of double honor, especially they who labor in the word and doctrine.

Additional references: ACTS 14:23
1 PETER 5:2

(3) Today, Elders of each congregation, who are subject only to the King, oversee their congregation and must meet the qualifications defined in 1 TIMOTHY 3:1-7

Today, following the Pattern set by the congregations of the first century Church, wherever Christians join together to extend fellowship to each other in Worship, we find a congregation or local church and if mature, with ordained Elders overseeing and tending to the flock with complete autonomy, bound to other local churches or congregations, only through Jesus as the Head of His Church and a shared Faith.

In addition, churches in these last days conform to all other aspects of the first century Church government, which includes;

(4) Today, each local Church has two or more Deacons, subject to the Elders, who actively serve the Church and must meet the qualifications defined in 1 TIMOTHY 3:8-13

(5) That each local Church has Evangelists, Ministers, Preachers or Teachers who teach or proclaim the Gospel

Reference: EPHESIANS 4:11-12

(6) That each local Church has Members, who love the Lord and each other

References: 1 JOHN 5:1-2, PHILIPPIANS 2:1-3

(7) Members of His Church collectively esteem Jesus Christ as Lord and have the highest regard for His absolute Power and Authority.

Reference: MATTHEW 28:18

H. His Divine Pattern of the work of the Congregation

(1) Evangelism

References: MATTHEW 28:19-20, MARK 16:15-16, ROMANS 1:16

(2) Benevolence

References: 1 TIMOTHY 6:18-19, 2 CORINTHIANS 1:3-5

(3) Edification (Instruction) and Spiritual Growth

References: HEBREWS, 10:24-25 EPHESIANS 4:11-16, ACTS 9:31, GALATIANS 6:1

I. Christianity is much more than a succession of Patterns

The **Divine Mosaic** is rigid and very specific in regards to many aspects of the Faith, such as the elements of Worship, and the organizational structure of His congregations.

It is vital to understand that Christianity is not merely a succession of Patterns to be followed, but from a very wide perspective is a non-legalistic individual

faith-love-grace-mercy arrangement of immense grandeur.

(1) Cornerstones of the Faith such as; Fellowship, Good Works, Forgiveness, Kindness and Mercy, are abstract terms and simply cannot be reduced to a simple model or pattern.

(a) Fellowship

ACTS 2:42
And they continued steadfastly in the apostles' doctrine and *fellowship*, and in breaking of bread, and in prayers

1 CORINTHIANS 1:9
God is faithful, by whom ye were called unto the *fellowship* of his Son Jesus Christ our Lord.

2 CORINTHIANS 8:4
Praying us with much entreaty that we would receive the gift, and take upon us the *fellowship* of the ministering to the saints.

1 JOHN 1:3
That which we have seen and heard declare we unto you, that ye also may have *fellowship* with us: and truly our *fellowship* is with the Father, and with his Son Jesus Christ.

1 JOHN 1:7
But if we walk in the light, as he is in the light, we have *fellowship* one with another, and the blood of Jesus Christ his Son cleanseth us from all sin

(b) Good Works

2 CORINTHIANS 9:8
And God is able to make all grace abound toward you; that ye, always having all sufficiency in all things, may abound to every *good work*:

EPHESIANS 2:10
For we are his workmanship, created in Christ Jesus unto *good works,* which God hath before ordained that we should walk in them.

JAMES 3:17
But the wisdom that is from above is first pure, then peaceable, gentle, and easy to be entreated, *full of mercy and good fruits*, without partiality, and without hypocrisy.

COLOSSIANS 1:10
That ye might walk worthy of the Lord unto all pleasing, *being fruitful in every good work*, and increasing in the knowledge of God;

Additional references: EPHESIANS 6:8, 1 TIMOTHY 2:10, 1 THESSALONIANS 5:15, 2 THESSALONIANS 2:17, 1 TIMOTHY 1:5, 1 TIMOTHY 6:18, 2 TIMOTHY 2:21, 2 TIMOTHY 3:17, TITUS 2:14, TITUS 3:1, TITUS 3:8, TITUS 3:14, HEBREWS 10:24, HEBREWS 13:16, HEBREWS 13:21, , 1 PETER 2:12, 3 JOHN 1:11

(c) Forgiveness

MATTHEW 6:14-15
For if ye *forgive* men their trespasses, your heavenly Father will also *forgive* you: But if ye *forgive not* men their trespasses, neither will your Father *forgive* your trespasses.

LUKE 17:3
Take heed to yourselves: If thy brother trespass against thee, rebuke him; and if he repent, *forgive* him.

LUKE 23:34
Then said Jesus, Father, *forgive them*; for they know not what they do. And they parted his raiment, and cast lots.

Additional references: MATTHEW 6:12, LUKE 6:37, MARK 11:25-26

(d) Mercy

LUKE 6:36
Be ye therefore *merciful*, as your Father also is *merciful*.

MATTHEW 5:7
Blessed are the *merciful:* for they shall obtain *mercy*.

(e) Kindness

COLOSSIANS 3:12
Put on therefore, as the elect of God, holy and beloved, bowels of mercies, *kindness,* humbleness of mind, meekness, longsuffering;

2 PETER 1:7
And to godliness brotherly *kindness*; and to brotherly kindness charity.

Additional references: 2 CORINTHIANS 6:6, EPHESIANS 2:7, TITUS 3:4

J. Role of female members of His Church

(1) Female members face certain Divine Limitations.

(a) Women are commanded not to teach or to exercise authority over adult males.

(b) Women are to remain silent in all Worship Services, during which the Lord's Supper is observed.

Key Passage: 1 TIMOTHY 211-14:

Additional references: 1 TIMOTHY 2:11-14, 1 CORINTHIANS 14:34, 1 CORINTHIANS 11:3, EPHESIANS 5:22-24

(2) Female members of His Church are commanded to teach.

Reference: TITUS 2:3-5

(a) Women taught other women and children in New Testament times

Reference: 2 TIMOTHY 1:5,

(b) Female members are generally better than men as instructors of women.

Women are usually superior to male members due to several reasons. Feminine members, unlike males, clearly understand the feeling of other females. These members can directly approach the subject of sexual sin in a manner rarely matched by their male counterparts. In a period of great stress a feminine teacher will become a much-needed friend and can easily telephone just to chat or drop in for a social visit.

(3) Many opportunities exist for women to advance the cause of Christ within their congregations.

In addition to being encouraged to develop their God given talents as soul winners, much of what the congregations of His Church actually accomplish is realized through the efforts of women. Hospitality is almost always dependent on wives. Benevolence is often the direct result of the ability of female members to determine real world needs and many times, the delivery of food or clothing.

(4) Only one's imagination limits the work that women may accomplish in the Church, within the bounds set forth by God in His Holy Word.

(a) Works of the church in which female members may be freely involved include, but are definitely not limited to:

Preparation of the communion
Assisting women at baptism
Maintain and washing of baptismal towels & garments
Visiting the sick, shut-ins, weak members, newcomers, nursing homes
Manage classified advertising program
Take part in a personal telephone evangelism program
Manage, grade, handle mailing, follow-up of Bible correspondence courses
Print and mail welcome letter to visitors
Prepare bulletins
Clean the church building
Baby-sit for others, while they perform work on behalf of the congregation
Arrange and maintain bulletin boards
Maintain the church library
Plant and maintain flowers
And many other tasks

K. Christians must be properly attired

(1) Society has radically reduced its concept of proper dress, however we will be judged by Biblical standards

(2) Inappropriate wearing apparel or the lack of proper coverings may cause impure thoughts, which can lead to sin.

(3) One of the darkest periods in King David's life began by his viewing of Bathsheba while she bathed.

Reference 2 SAMUEL 11:2-5

(4) Our Lord expects both men and women to clothe themselves properly, which will usually avoid unintentional impure thoughts by another individual. When we cause another to stumble, we are guilty of sin ourselves.

(a) In the Old Testament the Lord made his intentions quite clear. After Adam and Eve sinned they attempted to cover their nakedness with aprons of fig leafs

Reference: GENESIS 3:7

(b) God found these garments to be unacceptable and provided them with coats made from animal hides.

GENESIS 3:21
Unto Adam also and to his wife did the LORD God make coats of skins, and clothed them.

Hebrew scholars have determined, based the full meaning of the terms used in this passage that the *coats provided covered their bodies from shoulder to knee.*

(c) God's intentions are further confirmed by his commands in Exodus and Isaiah.

References: EXODUS 28:42, ISAIAH 47:2-3

(5) The New Testament contains numerous warnings regarding lust and the lust of the eye. The wearing of improper apparel may lead others to commit mental adultery

Key reference: 1 JOHN 2:16

Additional references: MATTHEW 5:27-28, ROMANS 6:12, GALATIANS 5:16, JAMES 1:14-15, 1 PETER 2:11, 1 PETER 4:2-3

Important Point to Remember

Simply stated, improper wearing apparel may cause others to sin. It is sinful to dress in such a manner that is intended to excite the lustful eye of the opposite sex.

Such conduct and manner of dress is called <u>Lasciviousness</u>.

GALATIANS 5:19
Now the works of the flesh are manifest, which are these; adultery, fornication, uncleanness, **lasciviousness**

(6) Christian women are directed to adorn themselves in modest apparel.

Reference: 1 TIMOTHY 2:9

L. Eternal future of His Church

(1) Jesus is Coming Again

At such time will He gather together all the faithful members of His Church, which is also known as the Kingdom of God.

Reference: 1 THESSALONIANS 4:16-17

(2) Jesus will then deliver the Kingdom or His Church to God the Father

1 CORINTHIANS 15:24
Then cometh the end, *when he shall have delivered up the kingdom [His Church] to God*, even the Father; when he shall have put down all rule and all authority and power

In order to be saved, we must use our very best efforts to clearly understand, obey and faithfully practice all elements of the Faith until the end of our life without distortion or the addition of creative enhancements ...

Heaven Awaits!

Chapter VI

Preparing for your place in Heaven

Chapter Contents

A. Becoming a Disciple of Christ

B. Counting the Cost of becoming a Christian

C. His Divine Pattern or Plan of Salvation

D. Remaining Faithful

E. Examples of how Christians exhibit faithfulness

F. Cleansing Power of the Blood of Christ

G. Pattern of Prayer, our access to God

H. Developing an appropriate Attitude

I. Common concern and misperception

J. Jesus urged vigilance and opposition to false prophets and teachings

K. Warnings of false teachers and teaching issued by His Apostles

L. Expect to be criticized for basing your beliefs upon the Words of Jesus

A. Becoming a Disciple of Christ

Once His Church is identified, it is suggested that the reader request the assistance of the minister or leaders of a local congregation, in order to give this important decision proper consideration and to complete His Pattern or Plan of Salvation.

B. Counting the Cost of becoming a Christian

Salvation, which is free to all, was purchased with the blood of Christ, upon which an earthly value cannot be placed. Jesus taught that just one soul has a greater value than the entire wealth of the world.

MATTHEW 16:26
For what is a man profited, if he shall gain the whole world, and lose his own soul? Or what shall a man give in exchange for his soul?

Other elements that could be considered a part of the cost are, the time involved, the monetary requirements and the elimination of many of the pleasures of this world, in order to become a living sacrifice.

ROMANS 12:1-2
I beseech you therefore, brethren, by the mercies of God, that ye present your bodies a living sacrifice, holy, acceptable unto God, which is your reasonable service. And be not conformed to this world: but be ye transformed by the renewing of your mind, that ye may prove what is that good, and acceptable, and perfect, will of God.

Christ indicated one should carefully consider the cost of following Him with the following question in mind: LUKE 14:28 "For which of you, intending to build a tower, sitteth not down first, and counteth the cost, whether he have sufficient to finish it?"

On the other hand, Jesus offers a Crown of Life to His faithful followers.

REVELATION 2:10
Fear none of those things which thou shalt suffer: behold, the devil shall cast some of you into prison, that ye may be tried; and ye shall have tribulation ten days; **be thou faithful unto death, and I will give thee a crown of life.**

Only one question remains:

Which will you choose?

C. His Divine Pattern or Plan of Salvation

While on earth, Jesus Christ and His Disciples commanded seven things; we must do, in order to become a child of God.

(1) The new convert must acknowledge, in his or her heart that in the light of God's word, he or she is a sinner.

JAMES 1:13-15
Let no man say when he is tempted, I am tempted of God: for God cannot be tempted with evil, neither tempteth he any man: But every man is tempted, when he is drawn away of his own lust, and enticed. Then when lust hath conceived, it bringeth forth sin: and sin, when it is finished, bringeth forth death.

In this passage, James clearly teaches that temptation and sin are personal, which makes sin a responsibility we must assume.

Even after we have become a child of God, we must constantly guard against allowing our personal desires, which are not in accord with His revealed Will, from separating ourselves from God.

In addition, the passage indicates that sin brings forth the harsh consequence of the second death, which includes eternal separation from God and endless punishment in darkness, as well as, the perpetual fires of hell.

ROMANS 3:23
For all have sinned, and come short of

ROMANS 6:23
For the wages of sin is death; but the gift of God is eternal life through Jesus Christ our Lord.

LUKE 18:13
And the publican, standing afar off, would not lift up so much as his eyes unto heaven, but smote upon his breast, saying, *God be merciful to me a sinner*.

(2) The new convert must hear or study the Word of God.

ROMANS 10:17
So then faith *cometh by hearing, and hearing by the word of God.*

JOHN 5:24
Verily, verily, I say unto you, *He that heareth my word, and believeth on him that sent me,* hath everlasting life, and shall not come into condemnation; but is passed from death unto life.

(3) The new convert must have faith or trust and be obedient.

(a) The first step is to develop an absolute belief in the existence of God.

An excellent foundation for this belief is the size and design of the universe, which is the same basis offered by the Great Apostle Paul in ROMANS 1:20 *"For the invisible things of him from the creation of the world are clearly seen, being understood by the things that are made, even his eternal power and Godhead"*.

Today, two theories are presented for the origin of the universe, evolution and creationism. It is clear from the previous verse that creationism is the position held by the Apostle Paul, which is the same position held by Moses (GENESIS 1:1, EXODUS 20:11), David (PSALMS 19:1) and Isaiah (ISAIAH 45:18).

By logically considering the universe, our world, nature and the workings of the human body, one can recognize that a most powerful and Divine God not only exists, but the glory of God;

ROMANS 5:12
Wherefore, as by one man [Adam] sin entered into the world, and death by sin; and so death passed upon all men, *for that all have sinned*: that He alone is responsible for all living things.

HEBREWS 11:6
But without faith it is impossible to please him: for he that cometh to God must believe that he is, and that he is a rewarder of them that diligently seek him.

(b) The sincere belief that God created all things, both seen and unseen, as well as, all life is a <u>fundamental</u> requirement of becoming a Christian

Without this rational acceptance, it is simply <u>not</u> possible to please Him.

In addition, we must believe that God rewards those who seek to understand Him. It is natural to have questions and that, in part, is the purpose of the Bible. The

Apostle Paul assures us that "All Scripture is given by inspiration of God, and is profitable for doctrine, for reproof, for correction, for instruction in righteousness:" (2 TIMOTHY 3:16) and James confirms the value of scripture "receive with meekness the engrafted word, which is able to save your souls." (JAMES 1:21)

(c) His inspired Word is our only source of revelation regarding our God and the way of life He requires, in order to be pleasing in his sight.

ROMANS 16:26
But now is made manifest, and by the Scriptures of the prophets, according to the commandment of the everlasting God, made known to all nations for the obedience of faith:

Additional references: 2 CORINTHIANS 10:5, GALATIANS 3:26

(4) The new convert must sincerely believe that Jesus is the Son of God

MARK 16:15-16
And he said unto them, Go ye into all the world, and preach the gospel to every creature. *He that believeth and is baptized shall be saved;* but he that believeth not shall be damned.

JOHN 3:16
For God so loved the world, that he gave his only begotten Son, *that whosoever believeth in him should not perish, but have everlasting life.*

Additional references: JOHN 3:36, JOHN 8:24, JOHN 17:21, ACTS 8:37, ACTS 16:31, 1 JOHN 5:13

(5) The new convert must truly repent of your sins and turn away from sin.

LUKE 13:3
I tell you, Nay: but, *except ye repent, ye shall all likewise perish.*

ACTS 3:19
Repent ye therefore, and be converted, that your sins may be blotted out, when the times of refreshing shall come from the presence of the Lord;

Additional References: ACTS 17:30, ACTS 20:21, ROMANS 2:4, 2 CORINTHIANS 7:10, 2 PETER 3:9

(6) The new convert must confess Jesus as his or her Lord and the Son of God.

MATTHEW 10:32-33
Whosoever therefore shall confess me before men, him will I confess also before my Father which is in heaven. But whosoever shall deny me before men, him will I also deny before my Father which is in heaven.

LUKE 12:8
Also I say unto you, Whosoever shall confess me before men, him shall the Son of man also confess before the angels of God:

ROMANS 10:9-10
That if thou shalt confess with thy mouth the Lord Jesus, and shalt believe in thine heart that God hath raised him from the dead, thou shalt be saved. For with the heart man believeth unto righteousness; and *with the mouth confession is made unto salvation.*

Additional Reference: 1 JOHN 4:15

(7) The new convert must be baptized into Christ, by total immersion, for the remission of sins in the name of the Father, the Son and the Holy Ghost [Spirit]

MATTHEW 28:19
Go ye therefore, and teach all nations, *baptizing them in the name of the Father, and of the Son, and of the Holy Ghost*:

ACTS 2:38
Then Peter said unto them, *Repent, and be baptized every one of you in the name of Jesus Christ for the remission of sins,* and ye shall receive the gift of the Holy Ghost

MARK 16:16
He that believeth and is baptized shall be saved; but he that believeth not shall be damned.

Additional References: JOHN 3:3-5, ACTS 10:47, ACTS 22:16, ROMANS 6:3,

GALATIANS 3:27, TITUS 3:5, HEBREWS 10:22

(a) Baptism is a burial by immersion.

MATTHEW 3:16-17
And Jesus, *when he was baptized, went up straightway out of the water:* and, lo, the heavens were opened unto him, and he saw the Spirit of God descending like a dove, and lighting upon him: And lo a voice from heaven, saying, This is my beloved Son, in whom I am well pleased.

ACTS 8:38-39
And he commanded the chariot to stand still: and they went down both into the water, both Philip and the eunuch; and he baptized him. *And when they were come up out of the water,* the Spirit of the Lord caught away Philip, that the eunuch saw him no more: and he went on his way rejoicing.

(b) Baptism is a resurrection.

COLOSSIANS 2:12
Buried with him in baptism, wherein also ye are risen with him through the faith of the operation of God, who hath raised him from the dead

ROMANS 6:3-6
Know ye not, that so many of us as were baptized into Jesus Christ were baptized into his death? *Therefore we are buried with him by baptism into death: that like as Christ was raised up from the dead by the glory of the Father, even so we also should walk in newness of life.* For if we have been planted together in the likeness of his death, we shall be also in the likeness of his resurrection: Knowing this, that our old man is crucified with him, that the body of sin might be destroyed, that henceforth we should not serve sin.

(c) When an individual is baptized, he or she goes into the water a sinner, is buried in the water and raised sinless through the blood of Christ.

REVELATION 1:5
And from Jesus Christ, who is the faithful witness, and the first begotten of the dead, and the prince of the kings of the earth. Unto him that loved us, *and washed us from our sins in his own blood,*

At that very moment:

(d) You have been saved from your sins.

1 PETER 3:21
The like figure whereunto *even baptism doth also now save us* (not the putting away of the filth of the flesh, but the answer of a good conscience toward God,) by the resurrection of Jesus Christ:

(e) You have put on Christ and become a child of God.

GALATIANS 3:26-27
For ye are all the children of God by faith in Christ Jesus. *For as many of you as have been baptized into Christ have put on Christ.*

(f) You have been born again

JOHN 3:3
Jesus answered and said unto him, Verily, verily, I say unto thee, *Except a man be born again, he cannot see the kingdom of God.*

1 PETER 1:23
Being born again, not of corruptible seed, but of incorruptible, by the word of God, which liveth and abideth forever.

(g) You have gained Justification

1CORINTHIANS 6:11
And such were some of you: *but ye are washed, but ye are sanctified, but ye are justified in the name of the Lord Jesus, and by the Spirit of our God.*

(h) You have gained entrance into the Kingdom or His Church

JOHN 3:5
Jesus answered, Verily, verily, I say unto thee, Except a man be born of water and of the Spirit, *he cannot enter into the kingdom of God.*

1 CORINTHIANS 12:13 *For by one Spirit are we all baptized into one body,* whether we be Jews or Gentiles, whether we be

bond or free; and have been all made to drink into one Spirit.

(i) One will be added to His Church, after following His Pattern of Salvation or has been saved, at which time; your name is added to the membership rolls, in Heaven, by our Lord God Almighty.

ACTS 2:47
Praising God, and having favor with all the people. *And the Lord added to the church daily such as should be saved.*

(j) After an individual has been baptized, he or she is commanded to Remain Faithful!

One must walk in newness of life (having put away the previous life filled with sin) and continue in faithful obedience.

ROMANS 6:3-4
Know ye not, that so many of us as were baptized into Jesus Christ were baptized into his death? Therefore we are buried with him by baptism into death: that like as Christ was raised up from the dead by the glory of the Father, *even so we also should walk in newness of life.*

Conclusions

There are seven requirements to be saved

The number seven is a divine number, which denotes entirety or completeness

These seven things do not constitute simple "church ordinances".

When we obey these seven things we do not merely comply with "church doctrines"

These are seven things commanded by our Lord and Savior, Jesus Christ, and His Disciples

In submitting to these things we obey our King.

Jesus is the One who died to set us free and we obey Him in order to accept the freedom that is found only in Him!

If we fail to submit to these commands, we reject the authority of the One who died for us...the only One who can set us free!

Such rejection will only result in eternal damnation!

2 THESSALONIANS 1:8
In flaming fire taking vengeance on them that know not God, and that obey not the gospel of our Lord Jesus Christ

Now, make your commitment to your Lord and Savior PERSONAL!

(Your name) will be mine" says the Lord God Almighty, "in the day when I gather my treasured possessions." (MALACHI 3:17 – Updated)

D. Remaining Faithful

Now the Challenge, which is not difficult, is to Remain Faithful and to follow the Narrow Path that leads to eternal Life, until death.

(1) What does it mean to Remain Faithful?

(a) After an individual has been saved, it becomes his or her personal mission to continue to be saved by remaining faithful. The steps we took leading us to salvation are of no value, if we <u>do not</u> keep the Faith.

The Greek word for faithful is "pistos", which means faithful, reliable, trustworthy and dependable.

(b) Remaining faithful is carefully and strictly following the specific Commandments, Instructions, Warnings, Examples and Patterns set forth by Jesus and his Disciples.

There are many facets or elements of remaining faithful to God. God, your Creator, is well aware of the sinful nature of man, as well as, the perfection He requires.

(c) God has provided everything we need in his Word to gain everlasting life and to be happy while on Earth.

Fortunately, the path leading to perfection is stated within the pages of the Bible.

(d) It is a process that naturally develops as you begin to spend ever-increasing time in prayer, study and associating with other Christians in the work of the Lord.

This begins, like a journey of ten thousand miles, with a single step. All the new Christian has to do is to begin and the various components will fall into place.

God will help you and to the surprise of many, the progression is filled with joy and self-satisfaction.

In order to simplify this important topic we will first examine this Commandment by dividing it into two parts or elements.

(2) Individual Element

(a) Every Christian is commanded to be faithful unto death.

Reference: REVELATION 2:10

(b) Each Christian is obligated to be faithful to our Lord and Savior and to stand up for the cause of Christ, as required.

TITUS 2:12-13
Teaching us that, *denying ungodliness and worldly lusts, we should live soberly, righteously, and godly, in this present world; Looking for that blessed hope, and the glorious appearing of the great God and our Savior Jesus Christ;*

(c) Each Christian must accept the Bible as the inspired Word of God, which contains His complete Message to mankind.

Reference: 2 TIMOTHY 3:16-17

(d) Each Christian must demonstrate his or her faithfulness in their way of life.

Examples of which are provided in the section following Congregational Element

(3) Congregational Element

(a) A congregation is a group of Christians with shared beliefs, who have banded together in an area or community to serve and worship God in Spirit and in Truth.

(b) Each Christian must faithfully attend and make a personal commitment to a local congregation of His Church, which is a part of the Church that Christ purchased with His own blood.

(c) Each Christian has responsibility to attend a congregation of His Church, which is structured and strictly conforms to the Patterns provided by Christ and His Disciples.

MATTHEW 28:20
Teaching them to observe all things whatsoever I have commanded you: and, lo, I am with you always, even unto the end of the world. Amen.

E. Examples of how Christians exhibit faithfulness

(1) Our most important Mission is sharing the "Good News" of Christ with others

MATTHEW 28:19
Go ye therefore, and teach all nations, baptizing them in the name of the Father, and of the Son, and of the Holy Ghost:

ROMANS 1:16
For I am not ashamed of the gospel of Christ: for it is the *power of God unto salvation to every one that believeth*; to the Jew first, and also to the Greek.

Important Point to Review

(2) Worshipping God in spirit and in truth

JOHN 4:23-24
But the hour cometh, and now is, when the true worshippers shall worship the Father **in spirit and in truth**: for the Father seeketh such to worship him.

(a) What is the meaning of "in Spirit and in Truth"?

"In Spirit" is a matter of proper attitude and appropriately focusing our minds on spiritual concerns, while consciously attempting to eliminate worldly issues from the active part of our mind, during worship services or at times of prayer.

"In Truth" is interchangeable with and comparable to the term the "Will of God". Christians are directed to conform, organize and harmonize their worship of God in precise accordance with the examples, Commandments and instructions of Jesus and His Apostles, *without unauthorized additions or enhancements.*

(b) In order to be saved, one must regularly attend a Church that is structured and functions absolutely in accordance with the "Will of God" or "in Truth".

(3) Obeying the Commandments

JOHN 14:23
Jesus answered and said unto him, *If a man love me, he will keep my words:* and my Father will love him, and we will come unto him, and make our abode with him.

(4) Seeking to actively serve the Lord

JAMES 2:24
Ye see then how that *by works a man is justified, and not by faith only.*

JAMES 1:25
But whoso looketh into the perfect law of liberty, and continueth therein, he being not a forgetful hearer, *but a doer of the work, this man shall be blessed in his deed*

JAMES 1:27
Pure religion and undefiled before God and the Father is this, *To visit the fatherless and widows in their affliction,* and to keep himself unspotted from the world.

COLOSSIANS 1:10
That ye might walk worthy of the Lord unto all pleasing, *being fruitful in every good work, and increasing in the knowledge of God*;

Additional reference: 1 CORINTHIANS 15:58

(5) Caring for our Brethren in Christ and others in need

(a) Christians must be willing to assist our Brethren in their spiritual growth or who are discouraged or have been overcome by sin or fallen away.

GALATIANS 6:1-2
Brethren, if a man be overtaken in a fault, ye which are spiritual, restore such a one in the spirit of meekness; considering thyself, lest thou also be tempted. Bear ye one another's burdens, and so fulfill the law of Christ.

Additional reference: EPHESIANS 4:11-15

(b) Christians must be considerate, accommodating and have a willingness to share worldly wealth, with those who are less fortunate, feeble, ailing or in distress.

GALATIANS 2:10
Only they would that we should remember the poor; the same which I also was forward to do.

Additional reference: JAMES 1:27

(6) Avoiding Temptation and Sin

1 THESSALONIANS 5:22
Abstain from all appearance of evil.

MATTHEW 26:41
Watch and pray, that ye enter not into temptation: **the spirit indeed is willing, but the flesh is weak.**

Additional references: JOHN 3:6, JAMES 1:12

(7) Living a Simple Life

Materialism is an updated word for covetousness, which is condemned in both the Old and New testaments. In His Sermon on the Mount (MATTHEW 6:19-34), Jesus spoke more on this topic than any other, centered around "**For where your treasure is, there will you heart be also**".

1 TIMOTHY 6:10
For the **love of money is the root of all evil:** which while some coveted after, they have erred from the faith, and pierced themselves through with many sorrows.

Additional references: ROMANS 13:8, HEBREWS 13:5

(8) Studying your Bible Regularly

Use the Bible as your ultimate and absolute guide. The printed Bible is truly a gift to all mankind. God has provided us with all the information we need to be pleasing in His sight.

Therefore, it is important to study, understand and apply its richness to our lives on a daily basis.

1 PETER 2:2
As newborn babes, desire the sincere milk of the word, that ye may grow thereby:

JAMES 1:21
Wherefore lay apart all filthiness and superfluity of naughtiness, and *receive with meekness the engrafted word, which is able to save your souls.*

Additional references: JOHN 5:39, ACTS 17:11, 2 TIMOTHY 2:15, 2 PETER 3:18

(9) Regularly going to your Heavenly Father in Prayer

PHILIPPIANS 4:6-7
Be careful for nothing; but in every thing by prayer and supplication with thanksgiving let your requests be made known unto God. And **the peace of God, which passeth all understanding,** shall keep your hearts and minds through Christ Jesus.

COLOSSIANS 4:2
Continue in prayer, and watch in the same with thanksgiving;

HEBREWS 4:16
Let us therefore come boldly unto the throne of grace, that we may obtain mercy, and find grace to help in time of need.

Additional references: EPHESIANS 6:18, 1 PETER 3:12

(10) Controlling your tongue, emotions and thoughts

MATTHEW 12:36-37
But I say unto you, That every idle word that men shall speak, they shall give account thereof in the day of judgment. **For by thy words thou shalt be justified, and by thy words thou shalt be condemned.**

JAMES 1:26
If any man among you seem to be religious, and bridleth not his tongue, but deceiveth his own heart, this man's religion is vain.

JAMES 5:12
But above all things, my brethren, swear not, neither by heaven, neither by the earth, neither by any other oath: but let your yea be yea; and your nay, nay; lest ye fall into condemnation.

Additional references: EPHESIANS 4:24-27, EPHESIANS 5:4, 2 CORINTHIANS 10:5

(11) Avoid False Doctrine

(a) The Doctrine of the Church, built by the hands of Jesus Christ, is pure and simple.

(b) The only way to know exactly what God desires is to put your trust in His Words rather than the convictions of man.

(c) Christ and His Apostles have warned us to avoid false teachers and their false doctrine.

Unfortunately, from the very beginning of Christianity, there have been individuals who were unwilling to abide within the Message of Christ.

Beware of and avoid such individuals, regardless of their earthly position.

TIMOTHY 4:3-4
For the time will come when they will not endure sound doctrine; but after their own lusts shall they heap to themselves teachers, having itching ears; *And they shall turn away their ears from the truth, and shall be turned unto fables.*

(12) Characteristics of a faithful follower

(a) Is absolutely certain of the unlimited power and supremacy of our Creator (HEBREWS 11:1)

(b) Is convinced of the legitimacy and authenticity of the Assurances of our God (HEBREWS 11:1)

(c) Completely accepts the account of the creation and believes that the design of our immeasurable universe was created by our supreme Deity (HEBREWS 11:3)

(d) Believes in and takes appropriate action based upon the Assurances of our Lord (HEBREWS 11:8-22)

(e) Holds Jesus in immense esteem and appreciation far above all else (HEBREWS 11:26)

(f) Is absolutely assured that with the support of God, has the ability to overcome incredible odds (HEBREWS 11:29-38)

F. The Cleansing Power of the Blood of Christ

(1) The Blood of Christ is a reoccurring theme in the New Testament, an important element of the Divine Mosaic

An understanding of this topic is necessary to fully understand the reasons why it was necessary for our Lord to leave His glorious Heavenly throne to sojourn on the earth as a humble homeless man and suffer a cruel death on the Cross, which is detailed in the chapter following.

(2) After one has been baptized and God has washed away every sin he or she has ever committed and has raised them to walk in newness of life.

ACTS 22:16
And now why tarriest thou? arise, and be baptized, and wash away thy sins, calling on the name of the Lord

ROMANS 6:3-4
Know ye not, that so many of us as were baptized into Jesus Christ were baptized into his death? Therefore we are buried with him by baptism into death: that like as Christ was raised up from the dead by the glory of the Father, even so we also should walk in newness of life.

(3) Two common questions are:

(a) What are we to do if we commit other sins?

(b) How do we gain forgiveness for these sins?

Our God understands the problem and provided a solution in the first century by inspiring the Great Apostle John to write "But if we walk in the light as he is in the light, we have fellowship one with another, and the blood of Jesus Christ His Son cleanses us from all sin." (1 JOHN 1:7)

(4) Please note that this verse includes two conditions;

(a) We must "walk in the light", which means we must be in obedience to the Word of God

(b) We must be in "fellowship" or we must be regularly attending services of His Church and going to our Heavenly Father in prayer, as well as studying His Holy Scriptures.

"If we confess our sins, He is faithful and just to forgive us our sins and to cleanse [katharizo] us from all unrighteousness." God will forgive, if we truly repent and respectfully ask Him to forgive us. (1 JOHN 1:9)

(5) The original Greek word "katharizo" that is translated "cleanse" in this verse actually means continual cleansing.

Important Point to Remember

It is quite comforting to know that we are being continually cleansed, by the precious Blood of Christ and **therefore have no fear of death,** since we are assured that on that glorious day of Judgment, we will be among the few to enter the pearly gates of Heaven, which is why **we should always be exceedingly thankful** for the willing sacrifice made by Jesus on the cruel Cross of Calvary.

G. Pattern of Prayer, our access to God

1 THESSALONIANS 5:17
Pray without ceasing. In everything give thanks: for this is the will of God in Christ Jesus concerning you.

(1) Christ provided each of us with a perfect pattern for prayer in MATTHEW 6:7-13, which is <u>not intended</u> to be recited, but to be used, as a Divine example to follow.

MATTHEW 6:7-13
But when ye pray, use not vain repetitions, as the heathen do: for they think that they shall be heard for their much speaking. Be not ye therefore like unto them: for your Father knoweth what things ye have need of, before ye ask him. **After this manner therefore pray ye:**

Our Father which art in Heaven, hallowed be Thy Name.

We are instructed, by example, to have great reverence for His Holy Name

Thy kingdom come. Thy will be done in earth, as it is in heaven.

We are directed to have an open and compliant attitude toward His Will.

Give us this day our daily bread.

We must understand and acknowledge that our "daily bread" is completely dependent on Him.

And forgive us our debts, as we forgive our debtors.

We must have a complete awareness of our weakness and sinfulness. We should ask for His constant forgiveness of our sins through the Cleansing Power of the Blood of Christ

It is vital to understand that forgiveness will not be granted, unless we are willing to forgive those who have "sinned" against us.

And lead us not into temptation, but deliver us from evil: For thine is the kingdom, and the power, and the glory, forever. Amen.

God will lead us, if we look to Him and walk with Him in our every step. God will not lead us into temptation, but if we will allow, He will deliver us from evil.

It should be noted that this Prayer begins with Honor and ends with Praise and Worship.

The Lord's Prayer, as this passage is commonly known, is a Divine Pattern of acceptable Prayer.

This Prayer is addressed to God, the Father, His Holy Name is Honored, followed with pleas regarding Heavenly and Earthly issues and is closed with Praise and Worship of God.

It is quite brief, consisting of only sixty words.

This Prayer covers both physical and spiritual human needs.

The structure of the Prayer is so simple and specific that even a youngster can understand the meaning and content.

For additional Prayers of Jesus and selected Prayers of the Faithful, please refer to Appendix 8 and 9

H. Development of an appropriate Attitude

The obligation for an appropriate attitude towards our God, ourselves and our fellow Christians cannot be overemphasized.

Talent cannot overcome or make up for a set of improper attitudes.

However, with the right attitudes, not only will our efforts to serve the Lord be enhanced, but we allow ourselves to live up to our full potential.

(1) Attitudes toward God

(a) We must grow in Love for God, the Father as Jesus Commanded

Reference: MATTHEW 22:34-40

(b) We must develop faith and trust.

Without faith, which is a strong conviction and complete trust in the Words of His Son, it is simply impossible to please God, the Father

HEBREWS 11:1
Now faith is the substance of things hoped for, the evidence of things not seen.

HEBREWS 11:6
But without faith it is impossible to please him: for he that cometh to God must believe that he is, and that he is a rewarder of them that diligently seek him.

(c) We must develop an attitude of Gratitude and Thankfulness.

Such an attitude will usually alleviate the possibility of bitterness or animosity that has the potential of damaging the spirit of any congregation of His followers.

EPHESIANS 5:20
Giving thanks always for all things unto God and the Father **in the name of our Lord Jesus Christ;**

Please note the righteous indignation of God towards those who were not thankful, that is reflected in the following verse

ROMANS 1:21
Because that, when they knew God, they glorified him not as God, neither were thankful; but became vain in their imaginations, and their foolish heart was darkened.

(2) Attitudes toward Ourselves

It is suggested that our attitudes be considered on a daily basis, in order to avoid the possibility of our hearts and minds becoming distracted.

(a) We must be willing to humble ourselves and maintain an appropriate level of humility.

ROMANS 12:3
For I say, through the grace given unto me, to every man that is among you, *not to think of himself more highly than he ought to think; but to think soberly,* according as God hath dealt to every man the measure of faith.

ROMANS 12:16
Be of the same mind one toward another. *Mind not high things, but condescend to men of low estate. Be not wise in your own conceits.*

Additional reference: JOHN 13:6-17

(b) We must be willing to assume a proper spirit of submissiveness

EPHESIANS 5:21
Submitting yourselves one to another in the fear of God

HEBREWS 13:7
Remember them which have the rule over you, who have spoken unto you the word of God: whose faith follow, considering the end of their conversation.

(c) We must be willing to study, learn and benefit from constructive advice or criticism

JAMES 5:16
<u>Confess</u> your faults one to another, and pray one for another, that ye may be healed. **The effectual fervent prayer of a righteous man availeth much.**

Additional reference: PROVERBS 15:31-32

(3) Attitudes towards Our Brothers and Sisters in Christ

(a) Jesus taught that we have an obligation to love our Brothers and Sisters.

JOHN 13:34-35
A new commandment I give unto you, That ye love one another; as I have loved you, that ye also <u>love one another</u>. By this shall all men know that ye are my disciples, if ye have love one to another.

Additional reference: 1 PETER 1:22-23

(b) Christian Love allows brethren to easily work effectively together, as God intended

1 CORINTHIANS 12:21
And the eye cannot say unto the hand, I have no need of thee: nor again the head to the feet, I have no need of you.

(c) Sincere appreciation for the efforts of others will greatly reduce or eliminate destructive condemnation, gossip and divisiveness.

1 THESSALONIANS 5:12-13
And we beseech you, brethren, to know them which labor among you, and are over you in the Lord, and admonish you; And *to esteem them very highly in love for their work's sake. <u>And be at peace among yourselves.</u>*

Question to seriously consider

Are we humble enough to serve our brothers and sisters, in Christ?

(4) We must earnestly assume the responsibility of a mediator or peacemaker

ROMANS 14:19
Let us therefore *follow after the things which make for peace, and things wherewith one may edify another.*

MATTHEW 5:9
Blessed are the peacemakers: for they shall be called the children of God.

Additional reference: EPHESIANS 4:1-3, JAMES 3:17-18

The true children of God are those who are willing to attempt to resolve conflicts, then work and display their righteousness in an environment of harmony.

(5) We genuinely endeavor to increase our hospitality; warmth, friendliness and openness.

HEBREWS 13:2
Be not forgetful to entertain strangers: **for thereby some have entertained angels unawares**.

Additional references: ACTS 11:27-30, ROMANS 12:13

One of the reasons the Church spread so rapidly, in the first century, was the cordial generosity and heartfelt friendship extended by early Christians.

(6) We must develop a sincere attitude of Gentleness, Meekness, Forgiveness, Forbearance, Patience and Longsuffering

GALATIANS 6:1
Brethren, if a man be overtaken in a fault, ye which are spiritual, restore such a one in the spirit of meekness; considering thyself, lest thou also be tempted.

EPHESIANS 4:2
With all lowliness and meekness, with longsuffering, forbearing one another in love;

Additional reference: EPHESIANS 4:32

Attitudes are critical to Christian growth, and as such this section demonstrates this topic is more involved than is usually assumed at first glance.

It is important to recognize that in most congregations, members are usually at different levels of spiritual development. Therefore improvements should be an ongoing effort of the membership.

Proper attitudes are of great assistance in overcoming the obstacles or complications, which Satan constructs, in his efforts to derail or devastate local congregations of His Church.

Ideal attitudes would make for near perfect working conditions among the members of a local congregation, which is a worthwhile goal for each member to work toward.

Attitude improvement could be compared to the woodsman sharpening his axe. If we would like the efforts of the congregation to proceed smoothly, we ought to continuously hone our attitudes, which hopefully will make us useful to our Lord and Master, preparing us for every good work.

2 TIMOTHY 2:21
If a man therefore purge himself from these, he shall be a vessel unto honor, sanctified, and meet for the master's use, *and prepared unto every good work.*

Question to seriously consider

Are you developing or are you willing to develop the types of attitudes, which are necessary to properly prepare yourself for the work of the Lord?

I. Common concern and misperception

(1) A common concern is how to move from a very weak to high level of Spirituality, which appears to be enjoyed by Elders, Ministers, and other experienced Christians.

Many also **assume** that those members of the human race mentioned in the Bible, who had the privilege of walking and talking with God, were some sort of a "super" believer.

(a) Unfortunately, these usually unspoken doubts have caused countless believers to suffer under the misconception that they could never achieve such high standards as those who appear to be so strong in their walk with God.

Such impressions result from misperceptions created by the devil to deceive, discourage and dampen the spirit of the believer.

Since the writer silently experienced the results of this misperception for an extended period before discovering the Truth, he requests that each reader consider the following:

(2) Moses, a man who spoke with the Lord, as a man converses with his friend

EXODUS 33:11
And the LORD spoke unto Moses face to face, as a man speaketh unto his friend. And he turned again into the camp: but his servant Joshua, the son of Nun, a young man, departed not out of the tabernacle.

A highly respected leader of the Jewish nation, who was credited with penning the first five books of the Old Testament, unfortunately, also demonstrated human failing and weaknesses.

(a) Murderer – took the life of an Egyptian taskmaster

EXODUS 2:11-12
And it came to pass in those days, when Moses was grown, that he went out unto his brethren, and looked on their burdens: and he spied an Egyptian smiting a Hebrew, one of his brethren. And he looked this way and that way, and when he saw that there was no man, *he slew the Egyptian, and hid him in the sand.*

Read the balance of the story: EXODUS 2:13-22, ACTS 7:24-29

(b) Doubted, complained and questioned His God

EXODUS 3:11
And Moses said unto God, *Who am I, that I should go unto Pharaoh, and that I should bring forth the children of Israel out of Egypt?*

EXODUS 5:22-23
And Moses returned unto the LORD, and said, Lord, wherefore hast thou so evil entreated this people? why is it that thou hast sent me? For since I came to Pharaoh to speak in thy name, he hath done evil to this people; neither hast thou delivered thy people at all.

(3) David, the glorious King of Israel who defeated Goliath and was called the Chosen of God (PSALMS 78:70) also lived on the dark side as:

(a) An adulterer

2 SAMUEL 11:2-5
And it came to pass in an eveningtide, that David arose from off his bed, and walked upon the roof of the king's house: and from the roof he saw a *woman washing herself; and the woman was very beautiful to look upon.* And David sent and inquired after the woman. And one said, *Is not this Bath-sheba, the daughter of Eliam, the wife of Uriah the Hittite?* And David sent messengers, and took her; and **she came in unto him, and he lay with her;** for she was purified from her uncleanness: and she returned unto her house. And the woman conceived, and sent and told David, and said, **I am with child**

(b) A murderer

2 SAMUEL 11:14-15
And it came to pass in the morning, that *David wrote a letter to Joab,* and sent it by the hand of Uriah. And he wrote in the letter, saying, *Set ye Uriah in the forefront of the hottest battle,* **and retire ye from him, that he may be smitten, and die**

Read the full story: 2 Samuel 11:26-12:10

(4) The Great Apostle Peter

(a) Was audacious, impulsive and rash

MATTHEW 16:21-23
From that time forth began Jesus to show unto his disciples, how that he must go unto Jerusalem, and suffer many things of the elders and chief priests and scribes, and *be killed, and be raised again the third day. Then Peter took him, and began to rebuke him,* saying, Be it far from thee, Lord: this shall not be unto thee. But he turned, and said unto Peter, *Get thee behind me, Satan: thou art an offense unto me: for thou savorest not the things that be of God, but those that be of men.*

(b) Struggled with his faith

MATTHEW 14:28-31
And Peter answered him and said, Lord, if it be thou, bid me come unto thee on the water. And he said, Come. *And when Peter was come down out of the ship, he walked on the water, to go to Jesus. But when he saw the wind boisterous, he was afraid; and beginning to sink, he cried, saying, Lord, save me.* And immediately Jesus stretched forth his hand, and caught him, and said unto him, **O thou of little faith, wherefore didst thou doubt?**

(c) Acted without thinking

MATTHEW 26:50-51
And Jesus said unto him, Friend, wherefore art thou come? Then came they, and laid hands on Jesus, and took him. And, behold, one of them which were with Jesus stretched out his hand, and *drew his sword, and struck a servant of the high priest's, and smote [cut] off his ear.*

(d) Lied and thus, denied his Lord and Savior

Reference: MATTHEW 26:69-75

(5) The Great Apostle Paul

(a) Was prideful

Reference: ACTS 22:3.

(b) Persecutor and Killer of Christians

ACTS 22:4-5
And I persecuted this way unto the death, binding and delivering into prisons both men and women. As also the high priest doth bear me witness, and all the estate of the elders: from whom also I received letters unto the brethren, and went to Damascus, *to bring them which were there bound unto Jerusalem, for to be punished.*

Additional references: ACTS 7:58-59, ACTS 8:1-3, ACTS 9:1-2

(c) Claimed to be the chief sinner

1 TIMOTHY 1:15-16
This is a faithful saying, and worthy of all acceptation, *that Christ Jesus came into the world to save sinners; of whom I am chief.* Howbeit for this cause I obtained mercy, that in me first Jesus Christ might show forth all longsuffering, *for a pattern to them which should hereafter believe on him to life everlasting.*

Additional reference: EPHESIANS 3:7-9

(d) Struggled continuously with sin

Reference: ROMANS 7:14-25.

(6) One might ask, considering their shortcomings, what made these men great servants of God?

(a) The answer is: Willingness to confess, repent of their sins and ask for forgiveness.

2 SAMUEL 12:13
And David said unto Nathan, I have sinned against the LORD. And Nathan said unto David, **The LORD also hath put away thy sin; thou shalt not die.**

(7) The more an individual grows in Christ, the greater their personal realization of their weaknesses and shortcomings.

MATTHEW 26:41
Watch and pray, that ye enter not into temptation: **the spirit indeed is willing, but the flesh is weak.**

(8) If you ever feel that you will never be the kind of Christian that God wants...be assured that you are in good company.

You are no different from the vast majority of other Christians.

When we sin, God is able to forgive. Jesus continually intercedes on our behalf with our heavenly father.

(9) All that is expected is that we humble ourselves in sincere prayer, confess, repent and ask for forgiveness.

1 JOHN 1:8-10
If we say that we have no sin, we deceive ourselves, and the truth is not in us. *If we confess our sins, he is faithful and just to forgive us our sins, and to cleanse us from all unrighteousness.* If we say that we have not sinned, we make him a liar, and his word is not in us.

1 JOHN 2:1-2
My little children, these things write I unto you, that ye sin not. And if any man sin, we have an advocate with the Father, Jesus Christ the righteous: *And he is the propitiation for our sins: and not for ours only, but also for the sins of the whole world.*

J. Jesus urged vigilance and opposition to false prophets and teachings

(1) His intense concern is clearly reflected in the following verses.

In MATTHEW 7:15, Jesus stated the following in regards to false prophets (teachers, ministers, evangelists etc.) "Beware of false prophets, which come to you in sheep's clothing, but inwardly they are ravening wolves."

MATTHEW 24:11
And many false prophets shall rise, and shall deceive many.

MATTHEW 24:24
For there shall arise false Christs, and false prophets, and shall shew great signs and wonders; insomuch that, if it were possible, *they shall deceive the very elect*

In MATTHEW 7:16, Jesus further explains *"Ye shall know them by their fruits."* In this context "Fruits" includes the beliefs, physical worship and practices of the religion, which must be compared directly with the Bible and no other source of information.

The writer understands that many churches claim to be the original church; however, the vast majority employ doctrines not supported by the Holy Scriptures and/or make use of uninspired documents written by men.

Satan has inspired men, during the time since the birth of Christ, to become teachers of false doctrines and practices as a snare for the believers who are unwilling to learn or have failed to sincerely seek the Truth.

The Bible, the inspired Word of God, makes it crystal clear that this type of worship is simply **unacceptable.**

Unfortunately, many people blindly accept any religious teaching without any thought as to whether it is based upon Biblical Truth or is a twisted doctrine of man.

Following this path may result in a faithful, deeply religious individual being unacceptable to God in the end.

Regrettably millions have died believing their souls were in Christ while actually being in great danger, simply because they failed to seek the Truth.

As Jesus plainly stated in MARK 7:9 "And he said unto them, *Full well ye reject the commandment of God, that ye may keep your own tradition."*

MATTHEW 15:9
But in vain they do worship me, teaching for doctrines the commandments [traditions, teachings or convictions] of men.

K. Warnings of false teachers and teaching issued by His Apostles

ACTS 20:29-30
For I know this, *that after my departing shall grievous wolves enter in among you, not sparing the flock. Also of your own selves shall men arise, speaking perverse things, to draw away disciples after them.*

2 PETER 3:17
Ye therefore, beloved, seeing ye know these things before, beware lest ye also, being led away with the error of the wicked, fall from your own steadfastness.

COLOSSIANS 2:8
Beware lest any man spoil you through philosophy and vain deceit, after the tradition of men, after the rudiments of the world, and not after Christ.

Additional references: 2 CORINTHIANS 11:13-15, GALATIANS 1:8-10, 2 PETER 3:17, 1 JOHN 4:5-6, 2 THESSALONIANS 2:3

(1) The following verse clearly affirms that to support false teachers or teachings is sinful.

2 JOHN 1:9-11
Whosoever transgresseth, and abideth not in the doctrine of Christ, hath not God. He that abideth in the doctrine of Christ, he hath both the Father and the Son. *If there come any unto you, and bring not this doctrine, receive him not into your house, neither bid him Godspeed: For he that biddeth him Godspeed is partaker of his evil deeds.*

L. Expect to be criticized for basing your beliefs upon the Words of Jesus

(1) Many members of the denominations take the position that an individual who endeavor to live in accord with the teachings of Jesus or that form of teaching that Paul referred to in ROMANS 6:17-18 are legalists.

ROMANS 6:17-18
But God be thanked, that ye were the servants of sin, **but ye have obeyed from the heart that form of doctrine which was delivered you.** Being then made free from sin, ye became the servants of righteousness

The Webster's dictionary defines a legalist as "an advocate or adherent of moral legalism or one who views things from a legal standpoint, and one who places primary emphasis on legal principle."

"Legalist" is a codeword for equating believers who strive to strictly obey the Word of God contained in the New Testament with first century scribes and Pharisees, who Jesus condemned in MATTHEW 23:23, for paying very close attention to minor details of the Old Law, while overlooking much more important and significant religious matters.

(2) Christians who carefully follow the specific Divine Will of God are His faithful followers, not legalist!

As an individual grows in Christ, his or her personal understanding and consciousness of their weaknesses and shortcomings will be increased and enhanced.... Heaven Awaits!

Chapter VII

The Way of the Cross

Chapter Contents

A. Why did our Savior come to earth?

B. Three days that altered the course of world history

C. The universal problem of sin

D. Why was it necessary for Christ to die on the cross?

E. Satan, the evil prince of this world

F. What happens after death?

G. The Second Coming of Christ

H. The Day of Judgment

I. Knowledge of the absolute certainty of the Day of Judgment

J. The final Verdict

K. The Glory of Heaven

L. Who will be given Divine permission to enter the magnificent Realm of God?

M. Final Comments

A. Why did our Savior come to earth?

(1) God, the Father sent Him

Jesus understood clearly, prior to His first coming to earth, that he would suffer the excruciating agony of crucifixion in order to provide the perfect sacrifice of the sins of mankind and provide each of us the Hope of Eternal Salvation.

MATTHEW 20:28
Even as the Son of man came not to be ministered unto, but to minister, and *to give his life a ransom for many.*

JOHN 3:16-18
For God so loved the world, *that he gave his only begotten Son, that whosoever believeth in him should not perish, but have everlasting life.* For God sent not his Son into the world to condemn the world; *but that the world through him might be saved. He that believeth on him is not condemned:* but he that believeth not is condemned already, because he hath not believed in the name of the only begotten Son of God.

1 JOHN 4:10
Herein is love, not that we loved God, but that he loved us, and **sent his Son to be the propitiation [atonement] for our sins**.

JOHN 6:38,
For I came down from heaven, not to do mine own will, *but the will of him that sent me.*

Additional reference JOHN 20:21

(2) Jesus provided us with additional reasons why he came to earth

MATTHEW 5:17
Think not that I am come to destroy the law, or the prophets: *I am not come to destroy, but to fulfil.*

LUKE 19:10
For the Son of man is come *to seek and to save that which was lost.*

MATTHEW 9:13
But go ye and learn what that meaneth, I will have mercy, and not sacrifice: **for I am not come to call the righteous, but sinners to repentance**

Additional references: MATTHEW 10:34-35, MARK 2:17, JOHN 10:10, JOHN 12:46, ACTS 3:26, ROMANS 8:3-4, GALATIANS 4:4-5, 1 TIMOTHY 1:15, 1 JOHN 4:10, JOHN 18:37

(3) His Disciples provided confirmation of His Divine purpose.

ROMANS 8:3-4
For what the law could not do, in that it was weak through the flesh, God sending his own Son in the likeness of sinful flesh, and for sin, *condemned sin in the flesh: That the righteousness of the law might be fulfilled in us, who walk not after the flesh, but after the Spirit.*

1 TIMOTHY 1:15
This is a faithful saying, and worthy of all acceptation, *that Christ Jesus came into the world to save sinners;* of whom I am chief.

B. Three days that altered the course of world history

(1) Crucifixion of Jesus Christ

His crucifixion was predicted by Christ in MATTHEW 20:19 and prophesied in detail in the Old Testament.

PSALM 22:16 predicted His death on the cross and in verse 18 foretold of His garments being divided by the casting of lots.

Crucifixion was a punishment usually reserved for the hardened criminals. It was illegal to impose It upon a Roman citizen, and rarely employed on members of the Jewish faith.

(a) It was selected as the penalty for our Lord Jesus, because the Jewish horde present at His questioning by Pilate demanded it.

JOHN 19:6
When the chief priests therefore and officers saw him, they cried out, saying, **Crucify him, crucify him.** Pilate saith unto them, *Take ye him, and crucify him: for I find no fault in him.*

Additional references: MARK 15:13, MARK 15:14, LUKE 23:21

(2) The Miracle of His Resurrection resulted in the Launching of His Church

ACTS 2:1
And when the day of Pentecost was fully come [the morning sun had risen], they [His twelve apostles] were all with one accord in one place.

(3) A Miracle occurred; when His Apostles were filled by the Holy Ghost [Spirit] and were empowered to communicate in many languages.

ACTS 2:2-4
And suddenly there came a sound from heaven as of a rushing mighty wind, and it filled all the house where they were sitting. And there appeared unto them cloven tongues like as of fire, and it sat upon each of them. *And they were all filled with the Holy Ghost, and began to speak with other tongues,* as the Spirit gave them utterance.

(a) On that day His Church began, with a membership of approximately 3000 souls, in Jerusalem, on a Sunday, which is marked as the Day of Pentecost, AD 30.

C. The Universal Problem of Sin

In addition to the very Good News found within the pages of the Bible, is some really bad news. Usually, if given a choice, people will choose to hear the bad news first.

(1) Humanity is faced with one major problem, which is beyond human ability to completely solve. That problem is sin or the transgression of the Will of God.

The Apostle Paul stated in ROMANS 3:23 *"all have sinned, and fallen short of the glory of God."*

(2) In other words, we sin each time we do something that God does not want us to do or every time we fail to do something God requires.

ISAIAH 59:1-2
Behold, the Lord's hand is not shortened, that it cannot save; neither his ear heavy, that it cannot hear: But your iniquities [sins or transgressions] have separated between you and your God, and your sins have hid his face from you, that he will not hear.

(3) So the bad news is; we have sinned and are separated from God.

Therefore, we are lost, since the wages of sin is death.

There are two types of death; physical and spiritual. The Greek word for death in this context is "thanatos", which means separation.

Physical death is separation of the body and the soul. Spiritual death is separation between our soul and God. Hence, due to our sins we are separated from God, thus are **Spiritually Dead.**

EZEKIEL 18:4
Behold, all souls are mine; as the soul of the father, so also the soul of the son is mine: *the soul that sinneth, it shall die.*

The Great Apostle Paul referred to Spiritual Death in ROMANS 6:23, *"For the wages of sin is death*; but the gift of God is eternal life through Jesus Christ our Lord."

(4) It is basically not possible for us to maintain a relationship with God by our own efforts, which places each of us in the ominous situation of being condemned and required to carry an ever-increasing burden of sin until we yield to our Creator.

(a) The Great Apostle Paul summarized Good News as; the reconciliation of mankind with God through the Gospel of our Lord and Savior, which has the Power to Save every individual who truly believes.

2 CORINTHIANS 5:19
To wit, that *God was in Christ, reconciling the world unto himself*, not imputing their trespasses unto them; and hath committed unto us the word of reconciliation.

ROMANS 1:16
For I am not ashamed of the gospel of Christ: **for it is the power of God unto salvation to every one that believeth**; to the Jew first, and also to the Greek.

(5) Many individuals believe that doing good works will make up for their sins.

(a) Unfortunately, this is simply not possible, as we are taught that Our Master owes us nothing for faithful service, as all good works are considered only a part of our obligation to our Creator.

LUKE 17:10
So likewise ye, when ye shall have done all those things, which are, commanded you, say, We are unprofitable servants: **we have done that which was our duty to do**.

(b) Isaiah declared that even the most righteous were lacking and characterized the very best of His followers, as filthy rags.

ISAIAH 64:6
But we are all as an unclean thing, *and all our righteousness are as filthy rags;* and we all do fade as a leaf; and our iniquities, like the wind, have taken us away.

D. Why was it necessary for Christ to die on the cross?

The following is a partial listing of the reasons He was required by His dedication and love of mankind to suffer this barbaric form of torture, which was usually reserved for the very worst of criminals.

(1) God, the Father required the shedding of blood or the sacrifice of a sinless man, without blemish or spot

EPHESIANS 5:2
And walk in love, as Christ also hath loved us, and *hath given himself for us an offering and a sacrifice to God* for a sweet smelling savor.

(a) Christ alone was without sin and therefore was spotless or perfect.

1 JOHN 3:5
And ye know that he was manifested to take away our sins; and *in him is no sin.*

1 PETER 1:19-20
But with the precious blood of Christ, **as of a lamb without blemish and without spot**: Who verily was foreordained before the foundation of the world, but was manifest in these last times for you,

Additional reference: 2 CORINTHIANS 5:21

(2) Required for the redemption or salvation of mankind

EPHESIANS 1:7
In whom we have *redemption through his blood, the forgiveness of sins,* according to the riches of his grace;

(3) Provided the cleansing Power of the Blood of Christ

(a) The cleansing Power of the Blood of Christ is a reoccurring theme in the New Testament and is a vital aspect of the Divine Mosaic.

MATTHEW 26:28
For this is my blood of the new testament, **which is shed for many for the remission of sins.**

HEBREWS 9:28
So Christ was once offered to bear the sins of many; and unto them that look for him shall he appear the second time without sin unto salvation.

REVELATION 1:5
And from Jesus Christ, who is the faithful witness, and the first begotten of the dead, and the prince of the kings of the earth. Unto him that loved us, and *washed us from our sins in his own blood,*

(b) When an individual is properly baptized, God washes away every sin he or she has ever committed and raises them to walk in newness of life.

ACTS 22:16
And now why tarriest thou? arise, and *be baptized, and wash away thy sins,* calling on the name of the Lord.

ROMANS 6:4
Therefore we are buried with him by baptism into death: that like as Christ was raised up from the dead by the glory of the Father, *even so we also should walk in newness of life.*

(c) Beginning almost immediately after baptism, each Christian must face the ongoing problem of sin.

JOHN 1:29
The next day John seeth Jesus coming unto him, and saith, *Behold the Lamb of God, which taketh away the sin of the world.*

Important Point to Review

1 JOHN 1:7
But if we **walk in the light** as he is in the light, we have **fellowship** one with another, and **the blood of Jesus Christ His Son cleanses us from all sin.**

Please note that 1 JOHN 1:7 includes two important Divine conditions;

- ❖ We must "**walk in the light**", which means we must be in obedience to the Word of God,
- ❖ We must be in **"fellowship"** or we must be regularly attending services of His Church and going to our Heavenly Father in prayer, as well as studying His Holy Scriptures.

God promises to pardon us, if we truly repent and respectfully ask Him to forgive us.

1 JOHN 1:9
If we confess our sins, He is faithful and just to forgive us our sins and to cleanse [katharizo] us from all unrighteousness.

The original Greek word "katharizo" that is translated "cleanse" in this verse actually means **continual cleansing.**

It is reassuring to know that we are being continually cleansed and therefore **have no fear of physical death**, since we are assured that on that glorious day of Judgment, we will be among the few to enter the Pearly Gates of Heaven, which is why **we should always be especially thankful** for the willing sacrifice made by the Son of God on the Cross of Calvary.

(4) Predicted by Isaiah

ISAIAH 53:12
Therefore will I divide him a portion with the great, and he shall divide the spoil with the strong; because he hath poured out his soul unto death: *and he was numbered with the transgressors; and he bore the sin of many, and made intercession for the transgressors.*

(5) Predicted by Christ

MATTHEW 20:18-19
Behold, we go up to Jerusalem: and the Son of man shall be betrayed unto the chief priests and unto the scribes, and they shall condemn him to death, And shall deliver

him to the Gentiles to mock, and to scourge, and to crucify him: and the third day he shall rise again.

(6) Symbolizes the destruction of sin

GALATIANS 2:20
I am crucified with Christ: nevertheless I live; yet not I, but Christ liveth in me: and the life which I now live in the flesh I live by the faith of the Son of God, who loved me, and gave himself for me.

(7) To assist mankind in overcoming the universal problem of sin.

Reference: JOHN 1:29

E. Satan, the evil prince of this world

The Bible does not provide details regarding the origin of Satan, but does provide a few clues.

In the opinion of the author we can safely assume, due to the absolute holiness of the Godhead, that this evil entity is the source of all wickedness.

We can also assume that he was originally created to be an obedient servant of Almighty God.

(1) The Fall of Satan and his followers

Apparently, at some point possibly before the creation of mankind, Satan led a group of angels of Heaven in rebellion against God.

REVELATION 12:7-9
And there was war in heaven: Michael and his angels fought against the dragon; and the dragon fought and his angels, And prevailed not; neither was their place found any more in heaven. *And the great dragon was cast out, that old serpent, called the Devil, and Satan, which deceiveth the whole world: he was cast out into the earth, and his angels were cast out with him.*

(2) The forces of Satan were defeated and cast out of Heaven onto the earth.

REVELATION 12:12
Therefore rejoice, ye heavens, and ye that dwell in them. Woe to the inhabiters of the earth and of the sea! for the devil is come down unto you, *having great wrath, because he knoweth that he hath but a short time.*

(3) Satan was allowed by God to roam freely, but many of his followers, were cast down into hell in chains of darkness to await their final Judgment.

1 PETER 5:8
Be sober, be vigilant; because your adversary the devil, as a roaring lion, walketh about, *seeking whom he may devour:*

2 PETER 2:4
For if God spared not the angels that sinned, but cast them down to hell, and delivered them into chains of darkness, to be reserved unto judgment;

JUDE 1:6
And the angels which kept not their first estate, but left their own habitation, he hath reserved in *everlasting chains under darkness unto the judgment of the great day.*

(4) The old serpent, which may have been Satan in the form of a snake, deceived Eve and upon the sin of Adam, the evil one became the god of this world

By yielding to the will of the evil, Adam and Eve brought sin upon themselves and into the world.

Their sin immediately resulted in spiritual death or a complete separation from their God.

In effect, Adam and Eve handed the evil one his crown of power and dominion and at that very moment, **Satan became the god of this world.**

2 CORINTHIANS 4:4
In whom **the god of this world** hath blinded the minds of them which believe not, lest the light of the glorious gospel of Christ, who is the image of God, should shine unto them.

(5) This is confirmed by the offer made by the devil to Christ in the wilderness.

LUKE 4:5-8
And the devil, taking him up into a high mountain, showed unto him all the kingdoms of the world in a moment of time. And the devil said unto him, All this power will I give thee, and the glory of them: for that is delivered unto me; and to whomsoever I will I give it. If thou therefore wilt worship me, all shall be thine. And Jesus answered and said unto him, Get thee behind me, Satan: for it is written, **Thou shalt worship the Lord thy God, and him only shalt thou serve**

(6) Satan is known by numerous names in the Bible, including the devil

MATTHEW 25:41
Then shall he say also unto them on the left hand, Depart from me, ye cursed, into everlasting fire, prepared for the *devil and his angels:*

Other names of Satan include Beelzebub (MATTHEW 12:24), wicked one, (MATTHEW 13:19) old serpent (REVELATION 12:9) and Belial, which means worthlessness (2 CORINTHIANS 6:15)

Jesus called him, among several other names, the prince of this world (JOHN 12:31, JOHN 14:30, JOHN 16:11)

(7) Jesus expressed His absolute contempt, disdain and disapproval of the evil one in the following verse.

JOHN 8:44
Ye are of your father the devil, and the lusts of your father ye will do. *He was a murderer from the beginning, and abode not in the truth*, because there is no truth in him. When he speaketh a lie, he speaketh of his own: *for he is a liar, and the father of it.*

(8) Examples of schemes used by Satan since the days of the apostles in the first century

(a) Deception

EPHESIANS 4:14
That we henceforth be no more children, *tossed to and fro, and carried about with every wind of doctrine,* by the sleight of men, and cunning craftiness, *whereby they lie in wait to deceive;*

EPHESIANS 5:6
Let no man deceive you with vain words: for because of these things cometh the wrath of God upon the children of disobedience.

2 THESSALONIANS 2:3
Let no man deceive you by any means: for that day shall not come, except there come a falling away first, and **that man of sin be revealed, the son of perdition;**

(b) Temptation

MATTHEW 4:3
And when the tempter came to him, he said, If thou be the Son of God, command that these stones be made bread.

MATTHEW 26:41
Watch and pray, *that ye enter not into temptation: the spirit indeed is willing, but the flesh is weak.*

LUKE 8:13
They on the rock are they, which, when they hear, receive the word with joy; and these have no root, which for a while believe, *and in time of temptation fall away.*

1 TIMOTHY 6:9
But they that will be rich fall into temptation and a snare, and **into many foolish and hurtful lusts, which drown men in destruction and perdition.**

JAMES 1:12
Blessed is the man that endureth temptation: for when he is tried, **he shall receive the crown of life, which the Lord hath promised to them that love him.**

Additional references: HEBREWS 3:8, REVELATION 3:10

(c) Confusion and spiritual blindness

2 CORINTHIANS 4:3-4
But if our gospel be hid, it is hid to them that are lost: In whom the **god of this world**

hath blinded the minds of them which believe not, lest the light of the glorious gospel of Christ, who is the image of God, should shine unto them.

(9) Examples of the modern schemes of Satan

(a) Atheism

Followers of Atheism deny the existence of a Divine being in any form. Therefore, they are free to live as they please within the limits of civil law. This scheme of Satan usually causes deep pessimism, due to the high value on material possessions and worldly pleasures, which usually leads to a question, such as, **"Is that all there is?"**

(b) Legalism

This is a form of personal religion in which the follower believes that he or she can be justified only by doing certain works or living up to certain, generally undefined standards. This type of belief usually creates doubt and an incessant sense of personal guilt. *The followers generally feel they are not doing enough and are continuously concerned about falling short of the mark.* Legalism usually results in trepidation, with no assurance of salvation.

(c) Liberalism

Followers believe everything is relative. Truth is an abstract concept and its determination must be based upon the circumstances at the time. Some believe that Christianity is continuously evolving as the progress of mankind advances. No certainty exists regarding the meaning of the Scriptures, which permits infinite changes.

(10) Additional tactics employed by Satan and his evil angels

(a) Distraction

The diversion of the mind of man from His Word to the carnal attractions of this world

(b) Delay

The endeavor to influence mankind to put off addressing spiritual concerns, until it is too late

(c) Defeat

The attempt to create a feeling of failure to such extent that the individual loses his or her willingness to even attempt to obey

(d) Doubt

An evil effort to create doubt regarding their Creator, His Word and their personal ability to become His faithful follower

(e) Discourage

Encourages mankind to focus on the negative aspect of this life and not on the positive aspects of working toward and attaining Glorious Immorality

(11) Satan is powerful, but not all-powerful

Only God is all-powerful. However, Satan has been allowed to tempt, entice and deceive all of mankind.

Human beings by nature are weak, which allows Satan and his evil angels to allure and lead many astray.

Christians must be constantly on guard and offer resistance to sin and iniquity, which usually result in rapid departure of his evil forces.

JAMES 4:7
Submit yourselves therefore to God. **Resist the devil, and he will flee from you.**

(12) Christians are equipped to struggle with and overcome the devil

REVELATION 12:11
And they overcame him [devil] by the blood of the Lamb [Christ], and by the word of their testimony; and they loved not their lives unto the death.

HEBREWS 7:25
Wherefore he is able also to save them to the uttermost that come unto God by him, seeing *he [Lord Jesus] ever liveth to make intercession for them.*

EPHESIANS 6:13-18
Wherefore take unto you the *whole armor of God, that ye may be able to withstand in the evil day,* and having done all, to stand. Stand therefore, having your loins girt about with truth, and having on the breastplate of righteousness; And your feet shod with the preparation of the gospel of peace; Above all, taking the shield of faith, wherewith ye shall be able to quench all the fiery darts of the wicked. And take the helmet of salvation, and the sword of the Spirit, which is the word of God: Praying always with all prayer and supplication in the Spirit, and watching thereunto with all perseverance and supplication for all saints;

GALATIANS 5:16
This I say then, *Walk in the Spirit,* and ye shall not fulfill the lust of the flesh.

1 CORINTHIANS 10:13
There hath no temptation taken you but such as is common to man: but God is faithful, *who will* not suffer you to be tempted above that ye are able; but will with the temptation also make a way to escape, that ye may be able to bear it.

(13) Final destiny of the devil and his evil angels

(a) The following verses are a clear indication and harsh warning of the hopelessness and wretchedness of the future everlasting punishment prepared for the devil, the beast, the false prophet and the overwhelming majority of the human race!

REVELATION 20:10
And the devil that deceived them was cast into the lake of fire and brimstone, where the beast and the false prophet [are], and shall be tormented day and night for ever and ever

MATTHEW 8:12
But the children of the kingdom [of the devil] shall be cast out into outer darkness: there shall be weeping and gnashing of teeth.

MATTHEW 25:41
Then shall he say also unto them on the left hand, Depart from me, ye cursed, into everlasting fire, prepared for the devil and his angels:

Additional Information is provided in the Prologue within the fictional account of "**The very first day of Eternity**"

F. What Happens after Death?

(1) Two Schools of thought, based upon the limited information provided

(a) Unconscious in the grave

JOHN 5:29-29
Marvel not at this: for the hour is coming, in the which all that are in the graves shall hear his voice, And shall come forth; they that have done good, unto the resurrection of life; and they that have done evil, unto the resurrection of damnation.

(b) In Hades

Hades is from the Greek word "haides" which means unseen or the place or state of departed souls, grave or hell.

The following verse indicates that Jesus spent those 3 days in Hades. If not, where did he go? The tomb was empty.

ACTS 2:31
He seeing this before spake of the resurrection of Christ, that his soul was not left in hell [Hades], neither his flesh did see corruption

(2) The Promise of Jesus to the thief on the cross

Another factor to consider is His promise to the thief on the cross, recorded in LUKE 23:43 "And Jesus said unto him, Verily I say unto thee, Today shalt <u>thou be with me in paradise.</u>"

(3) The account in LUKE 16 indicates that Hades is divided into two divisions:

(a) An area of great comfort, which is called Paradise by many Biblical scholars

(b) A place devoted to punishment

LUKE 16:19-31
There was a certain rich man, which was clothed in purple and fine linen, and fared sumptuously every day: And there was a certain beggar named Lazarus, which was laid at his gate, full of sores, And desiring to be fed with the crumbs which fell from the rich man's table: moreover the dogs came and licked his sores.

And it came to pass, that the beggar died, and was carried by the angels into Abraham's bosom: [paradise] the rich man also died, and was buried; And in **hell** he lifted up his eyes, **being in torments,** and seeth Abraham afar off, and Lazarus in his bosom. And he cried and said, *Father Abraham, have mercy on me, and send Lazarus, that he may dip the tip of his finger in water, and cool my tongue; for I am tormented in this flame.*

But Abraham said, Son, remember that thou in thy lifetime receivedst thy good things, and likewise Lazarus evil things: *but now he is comforted, and thou art tormented. And beside all this, between us and you there is a great gulf fixed: so that they which would pass from hence to you cannot; neither can they pass to us, that would come from thence.*

Then he said, *I pray thee therefore, father, that thou wouldest send him to my father's house: For I have five brethren; that he may testify unto them, lest they also come into this place of torment.*

Abraham saith unto him, *They have Moses and the prophets; let them hear them.* And he said, Nay, father Abraham: *but if one went unto them from the dead, they will repent.* And he said unto him, If they hear not Moses and the prophets, neither will they be persuaded, though one rose from the dead.

Important Question to carefully consider:

Is this passage a parable or a glimpse into the reality of Eternity?

G. The Second Coming of Christ

(1) The destiny of Faithful followers alive at the time of His Second Coming

1 THESSALONIANS 4:16-17
For the Lord himself shall descend from heaven with a shout, with the voice of the archangel, and with the trump of God: *and the dead in Christ shall rise first: Then we which are alive and remain shall be caught up together with them in the clouds to meet the Lord in the air: and so shall we ever be with the Lord.*

(2) Certainty of the Second Coming of Christ

MATTHEW 16:27
For the Son of man shall come in the glory of his Father with his angels; and then he shall reward every man according to his work.

JOHN 14:3
And if I go and prepare a place for you, I will come again, and receive you unto myself; that where I am, there ye may be also.

REVELATION 22:12
And, behold, *I come quickly; and my reward is with me, to give every man according as his work shall be.*

Additional references: ACTS 1:10-11, HEBREWS 9:28

(3) For His true followers - a time of Immense Elation and Joy

2 THESSALONIANS 1:10
When he shall come to be glorified in his saints, and to be admired in all them that believe (because our testimony among you was believed) in that day

2 TIMOTHY 4:7-8
I have fought a good fight, I have finished my course, I have kept the faith: Henceforth there is laid up for me a crown of

righteousness, which the Lord, the righteous judge, shall give me at that day: and not to me only, but unto all them also that love his appearing.

LUKE 21:27-28
And then shall they see the Son of man coming in a cloud with power and great glory. And when these things begin to come to pass, then look up, and lift up your heads; for your redemption draweth nigh.

(4) In light of the foregoing, please consider how the non-believers or those who did not carefully follow His Commandments will react to the arrival of their Lord and Master.

(a) Will it be with immense elation and joy or with great shock, terror, panic and fear?

MARK 13:24-26
But in those days, after that tribulation, the sun shall be darkened, and the moon shall not give her light, And the stars of heaven shall fall, and the powers that are in heaven shall be shaken. *And then shall they see the Son of man coming in the clouds with great power and glory.*

1 CORINTHIANS 4:5
Therefore judge nothing before the time, until the Lord come, *who both will bring to light the hidden things of darkness,* and will make manifest the counsels of the hearts: and then shall every man have praise of God.

2 THESSALONIANS 1:7-10
And to you who are troubled rest with us, when the Lord Jesus shall be revealed from heaven with his mighty angels, In flaming fire taking vengeance on them that know not God, and that obey not the gospel of our Lord Jesus Christ: Who shall be punished with everlasting destruction from the presence of the Lord, and from the glory of his power; When he shall come to be glorified in his saints, and to be admired in all them that believe (because our testimony among you was believed) in that day.

(5) The Time of His return is not known, except by God, the Father.

MATTHEW 25:13
Watch therefore, **for ye know neither the day nor the hour wherein the Son of man cometh**

MARK 13:32
But of that day and that hour knoweth no man, no, not the angels which are in heaven, **neither the Son,** but the Father.

Additional references: MARK 13:32, PETER 3:10-13, REVELATION 3:3

(6) Resurrection of every human being that was ever conceived or walked the face of the earth

JOHN 5:28-29
Marvel not at this: for the hour is coming, in the which all that are in the graves shall hear his voice, *And shall come forth; they that have done good, unto the resurrection of life; and they that have done evil, unto the resurrection of damnation.*

1 CORINTHIANS 15:23-28
But every man in his own order: Christ the firstfruits; afterward they that are Christ's at his coming. *Then cometh the end, when he shall have delivered up the kingdom to God, even the Father; when he shall have put down all rule and all authority and power. For he must reign, till he hath put all enemies under his feet.* <u>The last enemy that shall be **destroyed is death**.</u> For he hath put all things under his feet. But when he saith all things are put under him, it is manifest that he is excepted, which did put all things under him. And when all things shall be subdued unto him, then shall the Son also himself be subject unto him that put all things under him that God may be all in all.

(7) The body of every individual shall be changed from corruptible to an incorruptible state that will endure time without end.

1 CORINTHIANS 15:50-57
Now this I say, brethren, that *flesh and blood cannot inherit the kingdom of God; neither doth corruption inherit incorruption.* Behold, I show you a mystery; We shall not

all sleep, but we shall all be changed, In a moment, in the twinkling of an eye, at the last trump: for the trumpet shall sound, and the dead shall be raised incorruptible, and we shall be changed. For this corruptible must put on incorruption, and this mortal must put on immortality. *So when this corruptible shall have put on incorruption, and this mortal shall have put on immortality,* then shall be brought to pass the saying that is written, *Death is swallowed up in victory. O death, where is thy sting? O grave, where is thy victory?* The sting of death is sin; and the strength of sin is the law. But thanks be to God, *which giveth us the victory through our Lord Jesus Christ. Therefore, my beloved brethren,* be ye steadfast, unmovable, always abounding in the work of the Lord, forasmuch as ye know that your labor is not in vain in the Lord.

PHILIPPIANS 3:21
Who shall change our vile body, that it may be fashioned like unto his glorious body, according to the working whereby he is able even to subdue all things unto himself.

1 JOHN 3:2
Beloved, now are we the sons of God, and it doth not yet appear what we shall be: but we know that, when he shall appear, we shall be like him; for we shall see him as he is.

H. The Day of Judgment

(1) Someday we will all die and there will definitely be a Judgment Day.

ECCLESIASTES 12:13-14
Let us hear the conclusion of the whole matter: Fear God, and keep his commandments: for this [is] the whole [duty] of man. **For God shall bring every work into judgment, with every secret thing, whether [it be] good, or whether [it be] evil.**

HEBREWS 9:27
And as it is appointed unto men once to die, *but after this the judgment*

(2) A day has been appointed for the Judgment, which is unknown to all, except God, the Father.

MARK 13:32
But of that day and that hour knoweth no man, no, not the angels which are in heaven, neither the Son, but the Father.

LUKE 21:34-36
And take heed to yourselves, lest at any time your hearts be overcharged with surfeiting, and drunkenness, and cares of this life, and so that day come upon you unawares. For as a snare shall it come on all them that dwell on the face of the whole earth. *Watch ye therefore, and pray always, that ye may be accounted worthy to escape all these things that shall come to pass, and to stand before the Son of man.*

ACTS 17:31
Because he hath appointed a day, in the which he will judge the world in righteousness by that man whom he hath ordained; whereof he hath given assurance unto all men, in that he hath raised him from the dead.

(3) The Judgment shall take place after the Second Coming of Christ

MATTHEW 25:31
When the Son of man shall come in his glory, and all the holy angels with him, *then shall he sit upon the throne of his glory:*

(4) Jesus Christ will be the Righteous Judge of all mankind on Judgment Day.

HEBREWS 4:12
For the word of God [Jesus Christ] is quick, and powerful, and sharper than any two-edged sword, piercing even to the dividing asunder of soul and spirit, and of the joints and marrow, and **is a discerner of the thoughts and intents of the heart.**

JOHN 5:22
For the Father judgeth no man, but hath committed all judgment unto the Son:

JOHN 5:27
And hath given him authority to execute

judgment also, because he is the Son of man.

ACTS 10:42
And he commanded us to preach unto the people, *and to testify that it is he which was ordained of God to be the Judge of quick and dead.*

ROMANS 14:10
But why dost thou judge thy brother? or why dost thou set at naught thy brother? *for we shall all stand before the judgment seat of Christ.*

2 CORINTHIANS 5:10
For we must all appear before the judgment seat of Christ; that every one may receive the things done in his body, according to that he hath done, whether it be good or bad.

2 TIMOTHY 4:1
I charge thee therefore before God, and the Lord Jesus Christ, *who shall judge the quick and the dead at his appearing and his kingdom*;

(5) Standards of Judgment

(a) Members of the Jewish Faith, who lived and died under the Old Covenant, shall be judged by the Law of Moses

(b) Heathens shall be judged by the contents of their conscience

ROMANS 2:12-15
For as many as have sinned without law shall also perish without law: and as many as have sinned in the law shall be judged by the law;(For not the hearers of the law are just before God**, but the doers of the law shall be justified**. For when the Gentiles, which have not the law, do by nature the things contained in the law, these, having not the law, are a law unto themselves: Which show the work of the law written in their hearts, **their conscience also bearing witness**, and their thoughts the mean while accusing or else excusing one another;)

(c) The Gospel or Words of Jesus in the New Testament will judge every individual, above the age of accountability, who lives or had lived since the death of Christ on Judgment Day.

JOHN 12:48
He that rejecteth me, and receiveth not my words, hath one that judgeth him: **the word that I have spoken, the same shall judge him in the last day.**

ROMANS 2:16
In the day when God shall judge the secrets of men by Jesus Christ according to my gospel

(d) Upon the approach of each individual to His Holy Seat of Judgment, Christ will immediately view a complete, to the last infinitesimally small detail, without exception, the total and net results of the life of each individual.

Unfortunately, the Divine panoramic view of the vast majority *will be filled with the hideous darkness of sin with, to a greater or lesser degree, glimpses of the light of righteousness.*

On the other hand, the panoramic of His true Disciples, will be free of the darkness of sin and *will be filled with the glorious light of righteousness produced during their time on earth*

Jesus will carefully consider and judge every aspect, including every kindness and righteous thought, word and deed, as well as, every sin of your life, *except sins, which have been confessed, repented of and forgiven and cleansed by the Blood of Christ*.

(6) Examples of aspects of the life of an individual, which His Word states will be judged:

(a) Individual actions or works

REVELATION 20:12
And I saw the dead, small and great, *stand before God; and the books were opened: and another book was opened, which is the book of life:* and the dead were *judged out of those things which were written in the books, according to their <u>works</u>.*

REVELATION 20:13
And the sea gave up the dead which were in it; and death and hell delivered up the dead which were in them: **and they were judged every man according to their works.**

ECCLESIASTES 11:9
Rejoice, O young man, in thy youth; and let thy heart cheer thee in the days of thy youth, and walk in the ways of thine heart, and in the sight of thine eyes: **but know thou, that for all these things God will bring thee into judgment.**

(b) The words of each individual

MATTHEW 12:36-37
But I say unto you, That *every idle word that men shall speak, they shall give account thereof in the day of judgment. For by thy words thou shalt be justified, and by thy words thou shalt be condemned.*

JUDE 1:15
To execute judgment upon all, and to convince all that are ungodly among them of all their ungodly deeds which they have ungodly committed, *and of all their hard speeches which ungodly sinners have spoken against him.*

(c) Their secrets

1 CORINTHIANS 4:5
Therefore judge nothing before the time, *until the Lord come, who both will bring to light the hidden things of darkness,* and will make manifest the counsels of the hearts: and then shall every man have praise of God.

ECCLESIASTES 12:14
For God shall bring every work into judgment, *with every secret thing,* whether it be good, or whether it be evil.

(d) The evil thoughts of each individual

MATTHEW 5:28
But I say unto you, **That whosoever looketh on a woman to lust after her hath committed adultery with her already in his heart.**

MATTHEW 15:18-19
But those things which proceed out of the mouth come forth from the heart; and they defile the man. *For out of the heart proceed evil thoughts, murders, adulteries, fornications, thefts, false witness, blasphemies:*

I. Knowledge of the absolute certainty of the Day of Judgment

Provides a powerful motivation and inspiration for:

(1) Faith and Obedience

HEBREWS 11:1
Now faith is the substance of things hoped for, the evidence of things not seen.

HEBREWS 11:6
But without faith it is impossible to please him: for he that cometh to God must believe that he is, and that he is a rewarder of them that diligently seek him.

Additional references: ROMANS 1:5, ROMANS 6:16, ROMANS 16:26, 2 CORINTHIANS 7:15, 2 CORINTHIANS 10:5, GALATIANS 3:26

(2) Confession of Sins

JAMES 5:16
Confess your faults one to another, and pray one for another, that ye may be healed. The effectual fervent prayer of a righteous man availeth much.

1 JOHN 1:9
If we confess our sins, he is faithful and just to forgive us our sins, and to cleanse us from all unrighteousness.

(3) Repentance of Sins

ACTS 17:30-31
And the times of this ignorance God winked at; but now commandeth all men every where to repent: Because he hath appointed a day, in the which he will judge the world in righteousness by that man whom he hath ordained; whereof he hath given assurance unto all men, in that he hath raised him from the dead.

LUKE 13:3
I tell you, Nay: but, except ye repent, ye shall all likewise perish.

Additional references: ROMANS 2:4, 2 CORINTHIANS 7:10, 2 PETER 3:9

(4) Holiness

2 PETER 3:11-14
Seeing then that all these things shall be dissolved, *what manner of persons ought ye to be in all holy conversation and godliness,* Looking for and hasting unto the coming of the day of God, wherein the heavens being on fire shall be dissolved, and the elements shall melt with fervent heat? Nevertheless we, according to his promise, look for new heavens and a new earth, wherein dwelleth righteousness. Wherefore, beloved, seeing that ye look for such things, be diligent that ye may be found of him in peace, without spot, and blameless.

(5) Prayer and watchfulness

MARK 13:33
Take ye heed, *watch and pray:* for ye know not when the time is.

(6) Obeying the Commandments

TITUS 2:12-13
Teaching us that, denying ungodliness and worldly lusts, *we should live soberly, righteously, and godly,* in this present world; Looking for that blessed hope, and the glorious appearing of the great God and our Savior Jesus Christ;

JOHN 14:23
Jesus answered and said unto him, If a man love me, *he will keep my words:* and my Father will love him, and we will come unto him, and make our abode with him.

(7) Actively seeking to serve the Lord

JAMES 2:24
Ye see then how that by works a man is justified, and **not by faith only.**

Additional references: JAMES 1:25, JAMES 1:27 COLOSSIANS 1:10, 1 CORINTHIANS 15:58

(8) Caring for our Brethren and others in need

GALATIANS 6:1-2
Brethren, if a man be overtaken in a fault, ye which are spiritual, restore such a one in the spirit of meekness; considering thyself, lest thou also be tempted. Bear ye one another's burdens, *and so fulfill the law of Christ.*

GALATIANS 2:10
Only they would that we should remember the poor; the same which I also was forward to do.

(9) Sharing the "Good News" with others

ROMANS 1:16
For I am not ashamed of the gospel of Christ: **for it is the power of God unto salvation** to every one that believeth; to the Jew first, and also to the Greek.

MATTHEW 28:19
Go ye therefore, and teach all nations, baptizing them in the name of the Father, and of the Son, and of the Holy Ghost:

(10) Actively avoiding sin and temptation

MATTHEW 26:41
Watch and pray, that ye enter not into temptation: **the spirit indeed is willing, but the flesh is weak.**

JAMES 1:12
Blessed is the man that endureth temptation: for when he is tried, **he shall receive the crown of life,** which the Lord hath promised to them that love him.

Additional references: JOHN 3:6, 1 THESSALONIANS 5:22, REVELATION 3:5

(11) Living simply

1 TIMOTHY 6:10
For the love of money is the root of all evil: which while some coveted after, *they have erred from the faith, and pierced themselves through with many sorrows.*

HEBREWS 13:5
Let your conversation be without

covetousness; and be content with such things as ye have: for he hath said, I will never leave thee, nor forsake thee

Additional references: MATTHEW 19:23-24, ROMANS 13:8

(12) Regularly studying the Bible

2 TIMOTHY 2:15
Study to shew thyself approved unto God, a workman that needeth not to be ashamed, *rightly [correctly] dividing the word of truth.*

Additional references: 2 PETER 3:18, JAMES 1:21, ACTS 17:11

J. The final verdict

(1) And before Christ shall be gathered all nations: and He shall separate them one from another. His sheep will be moved to the right side and the goats to the left.

MATTHEW 25:31-33
When the Son of man shall come in his glory, and all the holy angels with him, then shall he sit upon the throne of his glory: **And before him shall be gathered all nations:** and he shall separate them one from another, as a shepherd divideth [his] sheep from the goats: **And he shall set the sheep on his right hand, but the goats on the left.**

(2) Christ will reward His sheep (faithful followers), at the Judgment.

MATTHEW 25:34
Then shall the King say unto them on his right hand, **Come, ye blessed of my Father, inherit the kingdom prepared for you from the foundation of the world:**

REVELATION 3:5
He that overcometh, the same shall be clothed in white raiment; and I will not blot out his name out of the book of life, but I will confess his name before my Father, and before his angels.

Additional reference: 2 TIMOTHY 4:8, REVELATION 11:18

(3) Our righteous judge will then sentence the goats to everlasting punishment

MATTHEW 25:46
And these shall go away into everlasting punishment: but the righteous into life eternal.

REVELATION 20:15
And **whosoever was not found written in the book of life was cast into the lake of fire.**

Additional reference: 1 CORINTHIANS 4:5

(4) Who will be sentenced to eternal retribution in the fires and darkness of Hell?

The short answer is everyone who has come of age, has normal mental capabilities and **is not a faithful member of His Church.**

A faithful follower is defined as an individual who is an active member of His Church and has used his or her best efforts carefully followed all the Patterns, Commandments, Examples and Instructions of Jesus and His Disciples.

This conclusion is based on a careful study of the New Testament; however no human will judge mankind. Therefore **it is possible that certain exceptions** may be made by our Righteous Judge, **but please do not count on it.**

(5) Examples of common reasons why the majority will be punished in the darkness and fires of hell forever

(a) If any individual fails to hear or understand the Gospel of Christ, he or she will be doomed to the horror of everlasting punishment

ROMANS 1:18; 31
For the wrath of God is revealed from heaven against all ungodliness and unrighteousness of men, who hold the truth in unrighteousness; **Without understanding**, covenant breakers, without natural affection, implacable, unmerciful:

Additional references: ROMANS 10:17, EPHESIANS 4:18

(b) If a person does not believe, that individual will be eternally lost to the fires of hell.

JOHN 3:16
For God so loved the world, that he gave his only begotten Son, that whosoever believeth in him should not perish, but have everlasting life.

JOHN 6:47
Verily, verily, I say unto you, He that believeth on me hath everlasting life.

Additional references: MARK 16:16, JOHN 11:25

(c) If an individual does not repent, he or she will be lost in the flames of hell forever.

LUKE 13:3
I tell you, Nay: but, *except ye repent, ye shall all likewise perish.*

Additional references: ACTS 17:30-31, 2 PETER 3:9

(d) If a person does not confess their faith in Christ, Jesus will not confess that individual before His Father in Heaven and will be everlastingly punished.

MATTHEW 10:32-33
Whosoever therefore shall confess me before men, him will I confess also before my Father which is in heaven. *But whosoever shall deny me before men, him will I also deny before my Father which is in heaven.*

ROMANS 10:10
For with the heart man believeth unto righteousness; and *with the mouth confession is made unto salvation.*

Additional references: LUKE 12:8-9, ROMANS 10:9,1 JOHN 4:15, REVELATION 3:5, 2 JOHN 1:7, JOHN 12:42,

(e) If any person is not baptized by immersion for the forgiveness of sins, that individual will be lost to the service of the devil for evermore in total darkness and unending agony.

MARK 16:16
He that believeth and is baptized shall be saved; but he that believeth not shall be damned.

MATTHEW 28:19
Go ye therefore, and teach all nations, *baptizing them in the name of the Father, and of the Son, and of the Holy Ghost:*

ACTS 2:38
Then Peter said unto them, Repent, and be baptized every one of you in the name of Jesus Christ *for the remission of sins,* and ye shall receive the gift of the Holy Ghost

Additional references: LUKE 7:30, JOHN 3:3-5, ROMANS 6:3

(6) Two important aspects of living a victorious Christian life is avoiding sin and temptation, as well as, remaining faithful.

In order to be successful, each activity and conversation must be carefully considered to determine if, any sin was committed.

For example, REVELATION 21:8 **clearly indicates that "all liars" will have a part in the lake of fire.**

REVELATION 21:8
But the fearful and unbelieving, and abominable, and murderers, and whoremongers, and sorcerers, and idolaters, and **all liars,** shall have their part in the lake which burneth with fire and brimstone: which is the second death

Lying has almost become our national pastime.

Studies have shown that the average individual lies several times each day.

A lie may be labeled as: a white lie, a fib, falsehood, propaganda, tall story, and others. In the view of our Lord, a lie of any kind, for any reason is a sin.

Please don't expect to correct this common flaw overnight, but now that you are aware of it, simply begin the process of considering your words carefully, before speaking.

The evil one is constantly trying to find ways to cause Christians to fail in their quest for Heaven, and therefore we must be vigilant.

In addition to all liars, Christ listed the fearful [cowards, timid souls too fearful to act] unbelieving [which includes infidels, atheists, and individuals unwilling to take the time to understand or those who rejected His Gospel], sexual sinners [abominable unnatural sex acts, whoremongers], murderers, sorcerers [doers of evil magic, spells and incantations] and idolaters or worshippers of idols or heathen gods.

The Great Apostle Paul in ROMANS 1:18-31 lists several additional including false teachers, dishonor of parents and individuals who fail to understand the Teachings of Christ.

Among the most common reasons for being punished will be unforgiven sin, which is totally unnecessary.

The demands of Christ are reasonable, and He clearly expressed His great Love and concern for us coming down from Heaven, walking as a humble man and enduring an excruciating death on the Cross, in order to provide Remission or Forgiveness of our Sins.

The Divine Instructions for His faithful followers are simply to pray, confess your sin(s), truly repent and ask for forgiveness.

Regardless, the vast majority will be relegated to hell for one or more unforgiven sins, including once active members of His Church, who simply drifted away due to a lack of faith or interest.

K. The Glory of Heaven

God in His wisdom has chosen not to provide comprehensive information as what we can look forward to in Heaven, but has provided Blessed Assurance. In 1 Corinthians 2:9, the Great Apostle Paul relates the following promise. No eye has seen, no ear heard nor is it possible for the mind to conceive what God has prepared for those who love him.

Likewise we have been provided with few details regarding the physical attribute of Heaven, but from the limited information mankind has been supplied, we have been blessed with an unmistakable impression of a Paradise, so beautiful and glorious that it absolutely defies description.

JOHN 14:2-3
In my Father's house are many mansions: if it were not so, I would have told you. I go to prepare a place for you. And if I go and prepare a place for you, I will come again, and receive you unto myself; that where I am, there ye may be also.

REVELATION 21:18
And the building of the wall of it was of jasper: and the city was pure gold, like unto clear glass. And the foundations of the wall of the city were garnished with all manner of precious stones. The first foundation was jasper; the second, sapphire; the third, a chalcedony; the fourth, an emerald;

Additional references: REVELATION 21:3-4, REVELATION 21:11, REVELATION 22:1-2, REVELATION 22:5

L. Who will be given Divine permission to enter the magnificent Realm of God?

An immense number of people have already qualified for a Heavenly home, including but not limited to the righteous from Patriarchal and Mosaic Dispensations from the other side of the Cross, children who died before the age of accountability, which includes over **fifty-five million** babies, which have been aborted in the United States and a total worldwide of over **one billion, two hundred and fifty million** unborn children, who have been annihilated since 1980!

Others include, primitive people who had no opportunity to hear the Word, but lived in a manner pleasing to the Lord, the mentally handicapped or retarded, who did not have the mental capacity to understand His teaching and all those who successfully fulfilled His requirements to be saved since His death on the Cross, including being an active, faithful member of His Church.

It is important to note that thousands of individuals who regularly attended His Church will be lost as a result of failing to follow carefully one or more of His Commandments or other reasons.

For example, one may have failed to worship in Spirit, refused to spread His Word or maintained a secret life.

M. Final Comments

Many people do not even want to think about the concept of forever or everlasting. This concept is difficult for many to comprehend. Some like to think of forever as a circle or never ending. Others look at the night sky and try to imagine where it begins and ends. It is the opinion of many that the universe is like eternity or unending.

Make no mistake; you will not accidentally or unintentionally wind up in Heaven.

Jesus promised to prepare an eternal home in Glory (JOHN 14:2-3) for all serious minded people who are willing to study, comprehend and conform to His Will and then make a persistent, unwavering and **intentional** effort to carefully follow His simple Directives in order to prepare themselves for their everlasting place of joyfulness in the Glorious Kingdom of Heaven. (REVELATION 2:7)

In MATTHEW 6:33, our Lord Commands us "But seek first the kingdom of God, and His righteousness."

Jesus warned in REVELATION 20:15 results of **not** being listed in the Book of Life. "And whosoever was not found written in the book of life was cast into the lake of fire."

It is imperative that each of our names be found in the Book of Life.

Is your name in that book?

Please take a few minutes of quiet time and consider intensely the concepts of eternity and continuous ceaseless retribution. Then make a choice, before it is too late.

Once you pass away from this life you have lost the golden opportunity to have the hope of heaven.

If you fail to accept God's grace and love, by becoming His faithful servant, you have selected hell and to spend eternity as an angel of Satan, in everlasting fire, **by default.**

Faithful followers have the blessed reassurance of knowing they are being continually cleansed of all sin and therefore have no fear of physical death, since they are certain that on the glorious Day of Judgment, they will be among the few to be given permission to enter the Pearly Gates of the Glorious Kingdom of God.... Heaven Awaits!

Chapter VIII

Introduction to the Life of Christ

Chapter Contents

A. Pre-existence of Lord Jesus

B. Prophecies and predictions of the Messiah

C. Setting the Stage for His Divine Birth

A. Pre-existence of Lord Jesus

Jesus Christ did not begin His existence upon His birth in Bethlehem, or when He was conceived within the Virgin Mary.

In the first three verses of chapter 1 (Key Passage: JOHN 1:1-3) in the inspired book of John, the Father reveals that His Son, *Jesus [the Word] is part of the eternal Deity or Godhead, which has no beginning or end and that Jesus Christ or the Word was responsible for all creation.* The segment "The same was in the beginning with God" *refers to the beginning of our universe* (GENESIS 1:1).

In the key Passage, JOHN 1:13-14, we learn that Christ was born of God and confirms the fact that the eternal spiritual **invisible** state of the Word [Jesus] was transformed to the fleshly form.

Additional references: EXODUS 3:14, COLOSSIANS 1:15-16, 1 CORINTHIANS 8:6, HEBREWS 1:1-2, JOHN 1:15, JOHN 8:58 JOHN 16:26-27, JOHN 16:28, JOHN 17:5

B. Prophecies and predictions of the Messiah

The First Coming of the Messiah, our Lord and Savior Jesus Christ, was prophesied and predicted in amazing detail over hundreds of years by numerous men of God. The apparent purpose was to provide the Jewish Nation with a method of confirming that the Messiah, whom they had awaited for centuries, had actually arrived so they could accept Him.

In light of the fulfilled prophecies, miracles, healing and His vastly superior knowledge, one of the **great mysteries of life** is why the majority of believers did not quickly accept Him. (#17 below)

The following is a cross section of the prophecies and predictions regarding the Messiah in the Old Testament, which are confirmed in the Gospels.

(1) The Messiah would be born of a virgin

References: ISAIAH 7:14, MATTHEW 1:21-23

(2) That the seed of the woman would bruise the head of the serpent

References: GENESIS 3:14-15, ROMANS 16:20

(3) The Messiah would be born in Bethlehem

References: MICAH 5:2, MATTHEW 2:1, LUKE 2:4-7

(4) The Messiah would be of the Seed of Abraham

References: GENESIS 12:1-3, GENESIS 22:18, MATTHEW 1:1, GALATIANS 3:16

(5) The Messiah would be of the tribe of Judah

References: GENESIS 49:10, LUKE 3:33, HEBREWS 7:14

(6) The Messiah would be of the house of David

References: 2 SAMUEL 7:12-16, MATTHEW 1:1

(7) Herod would conspire to murder the children

References: JEREMIAH 31:15, MATTHEW 2:16-18

(8) The infant Jesus would be taken to Egypt

References: HOSEA 11:1, MATTHEW 2:14-15

(9) The Messiah would be anointed by the Holy Spirit

References: ISAIAH 11:1-2, MATTHEW 3:16-17

(10) The Messiah would be preceded by a messenger - (John the Baptist)

References: ISAIAH 40:3-5, MALACHI 3:1, MATTHEW 3:1-3, MATTHEW 3:11-12, MARK 1:2-5, MARK 1:7-8, LUKE 3:16-17

(11) The Messiah engaged in a Ministry of Miracles

References: ISAIAH 35:5-6, MATTHEW 9:35

(12) The Messiah would preach the "Good News"

References: ISAIAH 61:1; LUKE 4:14-21

(13) The Messiah would teach in parables

References: PSALMS 78:1-4, MATTHEW 13:34-35

(14) The Messiah would minister in Galilee

References: ISAIAH 9:1, MATTHEW 4:12-16

(15) The Messiah would cleanse the Temple

References: MALACHI 3:1, ISAIAH 56:7, MATTHEW 21:12-13.

(16) The Messiah would enter Jerusalem as a King on a donkey

References: ZECHARIAH 9:9, MATTHEW 21:4-9

(17) The Messiah would be rejected by His people, the Jews

References: PSALMS 118:22, 1 PETER 2:7, ISAIAH 53:3, JOHN 1:10-11

(18) The Messiah would be betrayed by a friend

References: PSALMS 41:9, LUKE 22:3-4, JOHN 13:18

(19) The Messiah would be betrayed for thirty pieces of silver

References: ZECHARIAH 11:12, MATTHEW 26:14-15

(20) The Messiah would be silence before His accusers

References: ISAIAH 53:7, MATTHEW 27:13-14

(21) The Messiah would be mocked

References: PSALMS 22:7-8, MATTHEW 27:31

(22) The Messiah would be severely beaten

References: ISAIAH 52:14, MATTHEW 27:26

(23) The Messiah would be spit upon

References: ISAIAH 50:6, MATTHEW 27:30

(24) The hands and feet of the Messiah would be pierced

References: PSALMS 22:16, MATTHEW 27:31, JOHN 20:24-28

(25) The Messiah would be crucified with thieves

References: ISAIAH 53:12, MATTHEW 27:38.

(26) The Messiah would pray for His persecutors

References: ISAIAH 53:12, LUKE 23:34

(27) The Messiah would be given gall and vinegar to drink

References: PSALMS 69:21, MATTHEW 27:34, LUKE 23:36

(28) The soldier would divide the clothing of the Messiah and cast lots

References: PSALMS 22:18, JOHN 19:23-24.

(29) The side of Messiah would be pierced

References: ZECHARIAH 12:10, JOHN 19:34

(30) No Bones in the body of the Messiah would be broken

References: PSALMS 34:20, JOHN 19:32-36

(31) The Messiah would be buried in the tomb of a rich man

References: ISAIAH 53:9, MATTHEW 27:57-60

(32) The Messiah would arise from the dead!

References: PSALMS 16:10, MARK 16:6, ACTS 2:31

(33) The Messiah would ascend into Heaven

References: PSALMS 68:18, ACTS 1:9.

(34) The Messiah would sit down at the right hand of God

References: PSALMS 110:1, HEBREWS 1:3

C. Setting the Stage for His Divine Birth

(1) Divine communications with earthly parents of Jesus Christ and John, the Baptist

(a) The birth of John the Baptist was foretold to Zacharias [Father of John, the Baptist], by the Angel Gabriel

Locality: **Jerusalem (Temple)**

Date: **7 B.C.**

Reference: LUKE 1:5-23

(b) The Angel Gabriel promises the birth of Jesus to the Virgin Mary

Locality: **Nazareth**

Date: **6 B.C.**

Reference: LUKE 1:24-38

(c) Annunciation of the Birth of Jesus to Joseph, by Angel in a dream

Locality: **Nazareth**

Messianic Prophecy fulfilled: ISAIAH 7:14

Date: **5 B.C.**

Reference: MATTHEW 1:18-25

(2) The Divine answer to the question: "When does life begin?"

(a) Mary visits Elisabeth

Locality: **Hill Country Judah, which is located approximately 100 miles, by footpath south of Nazareth**

Date: **6 B.C.**

LUKE 1:39-44
And Mary arose in those days, and went into the hill country with haste, into a city of Judah; And entered into the house of Zacharias, and saluted Elisabeth. And it came to pass, that, when Elisabeth heard the salutation of Mary, **the babe leaped in her womb;** and Elisabeth was filled with the Holy Ghost: And she spake out with a loud voice, and said, **Blessed art thou among women, and blessed is the fruit of thy womb.** And whence is this to me, that the mother of my Lord should come to me? For, lo, as soon as the voice of thy salutation sounded in mine ears, **the babe leaped in my womb for joy.**

(b) Song of Mary

Locality: **Hill Country Judah**

Date: **6 B.C.**

LUKE 1:46-55
And Mary said, My soul doth magnify the Lord, And my spirit hath rejoiced in God my Savior. For he hath regarded the low estate of his handmaiden: for, behold, from henceforth all generations shall call me blessed. For he that is mighty hath done to me great things; and holy is his name. **And his mercy is on them that fear him from generation to generation.** He hath showed strength with his arm; he hath scattered the proud in the imagination of their hearts. He hath put down the mighty from their seats, and exalted them of low degree. He hath filled the hungry with good things; and the rich he hath sent empty away. He hath

helped his servant Israel, in remembrance of his mercy; As he spake to our fathers, to Abraham, and to his seed forever.

(c) After about three months, Mary returned to her Home in Nazareth

Reference: LUKE 1:56.

(d) Birth, youth and future purpose of John the Baptist

Locality: **Hill Country Judah**

Date: **6 B.C.**

LUKE 1:57-80
Now Elisabeth's full time came that she should be delivered; and she brought forth a son. And her neighbors and her cousins heard how the Lord had showed great mercy upon her; and they rejoiced with her. And it came to pass, that on the eighth day they came to circumcise the child; and they called him Zacharias, after the name of his father. And his mother answered and said, **Not so; but he shall be called John. And they said unto her, There is none of thy kindred that is called by this name. And they made signs to his father, how he would have him called. And he asked for a writing table, and wrote, saying, His name is John.** And they marveled all. And his mouth was opened immediately, and his tongue loosed, and he spake, and praised God. And fear came on all that dwelt round about them: and all these sayings were noised abroad throughout all the hill country of Judea. And all they that heard them laid them up in their hearts, saying, What manner of child shall this be! And the hand of the Lord was with him. And his father Zacharias was filled with the Holy Ghost, and prophesied, saying, **Blessed be the Lord God of Israel; for he hath visited and redeemed his people, And hath raised up a horn of salvation for us in the house of his servant David; As he spake by the mouth of his holy prophets, which have been since the world began:** That we should be saved from our enemies, and from the hand of all that hate us; **To perform the mercy promised to our fathers, and to remember his holy covenant; The oath which he sware to our father Abraham, That** he would grant unto us, that we being delivered out of the hand of our enemies might serve him without fear, In holiness and righteousness before him, all the days of our life. And thou, child, shalt be called the prophet of the Highest: **for thou shalt go before the face of the Lord to prepare his ways; To give knowledge of salvation unto his people by the remission of their sins,** Through the tender mercy of our God; whereby the dayspring from on high hath visited us, To give light to them that sit in darkness and in the shadow of death, to guide our feet into the way of peace. **And the child grew, and waxed strong in spirit, and was in the deserts till the day of his showing unto Israel.**

(e) The Imperial Decree of Caesar Augustus

Caesar Augustus, issued a decree that the world, be taxed. Each subject was required to register in the town or city of his birth. Joseph and Mary great with child, traveled on foot from Nazareth to Bethlehem. This census was preliminary to the taxing process in the provinces. At that time in history, the Roman Empire encompassed the vast majority of the civilized world.

LUKE 2:1-6
And it came to pass in those days, **that there went out a decree from Caesar Augustus, that all the world should be taxed.** (And this taxing was first made when Cyrenius was governor of Syria.) And all went to be taxed, every one into his own city. And *Joseph also went up from Galilee, out of the city of Nazareth, into Judea, unto the city of David,* **which is called Bethlehem;** because (he was of the house and lineage of David:) **To be taxed with Mary his espoused wife, being great with child.** And so it was, that, while they were there, **the days were accomplished that <u>she should be delivered</u>.**

Jesus Saves.... Heaven Awaits!

Chapter IX

The Life of Christ

Chapter Contents

A. Introduction

B. Life of Christ prior to His Ministry

C. Role of John the Baptist

D. Jesus prepares for His Ministry

E. Launches His Ministry in Galilee, Judea and Samaria

F. Great Galilean Ministry

G. Further training of the Twelve

H. Later Judean Ministry

I. Perean Ministry

J. Culmination of His Miracles and Teachings

K. The Final Days of Jesus in Jerusalem

L. His Last Day with His Apostles

M. The Final Day of His earthly Life

N. His Resurrection

O. His Appearances

P. His Ascension to His Father

Q. Many actions and sayings of Jesus not recorded

R. From His Ascension to Pentecost

S. Divine Involvement and Appearances since His Ascension

T. Yesterday, today, until He comes again and forever Lord Jesus or the Word of God is God and High Priest

A. Introduction

This chapter contains an easy-to-use comprehensive overview (not a common harmony, synopsis or parallel) primarily based upon the four Gospels with related references, as required, to highlight the most important of all chronicles, the life of our Lord and Savior in a manner that does not bury His Story in a sea of Bible verses.

The approach is different from the usual because many of His Teachings, Miracles, Parables and Warnings, along with brief notes have been incorporated in order to provide the user an opportunity to quickly develop an understanding of this all important topic. Events referenced in more than one Gospel, are grouped together.

This overview categorizes recorded events from the Life of Christ in an approximate chronological order. The New Testament does not provide a timeline, but does provide many clues and hints which allowed the author to develop a probable arrangement.

The author has also included a probable timeline of events, in order to provide the reader with an additional frame of reference.

There exists numerous, well supported theories which date the Death Burial and Resurrection of Christ from AD 29 to AD 33.

The author selected the timeline, which appears to be most widely accepted, which dates His Ascension in AD 30.

(1) Introduction - The Gospel of Luke

LUKE 1:1-4
Forasmuch as many have taken in hand to set forth in order a declaration of those things which are most surely believed among us, Even as they delivered them unto us, *which from the beginning were eyewitnesses, and ministers of the word;* It seemed good to me also, *having had perfect understanding of all things from the very first,* to write unto thee in order, most excellent Theophilus, That thou mightest know the certainty of those things, wherein thou hast been instructed.

(2) Genealogical Ancestors of the Son of Man

The reason these genealogies are different is that Matthew provided the ancestry of

Joseph, while Luke recorded the lineage of Mary.

Jesus was miraculously conceived in the Virgin Mary by the Holy Spirit. Since Joseph was Mary's husband, he was assumed to be the father of Jesus. The genealogy of Luke addressed this issue by stating Jesus was "as was supposed the son of Joseph" (LUKE 3:23).

MATTHEW 13:55
Is not this the carpenter's son? is not his mother called Mary? and his brethren, James, and Joses, and Simon, and Judas?

Since Jesus was born into the family of Joseph, He was a legal heir. Through Joseph, Jesus obtained a rightful claim to the throne of David. Jesus was the first born and legal descendant of Joseph, but was not a physical descendant.

(a) Matthew used the Septuagint, the Greek translation of the Hebrew Old Testament, to assemble 42 names, each representing a generation in MATTHEW 1:1-17. Then he separated them in three groups of 14 generations each, as follows:

(1) Abraham to David, 14 names
(2) Solomon to the Captivity, 14 names
(3) Jeconiah to Jesus, 14 names

This genealogy was traced through Joseph. It is interesting to note that Mary, the mother of Jesus is listed in verse 16.

(b) In LUKE 3:23-38, Luke listed 77 names, almost twice as many names as Matthew and also used the number seven as a basis for organizing Christ's pedigree in terms of 77 names.

Luke's genealogy included four groups, as follows:

(1) Jesus to Zerubbabel, 21 names
(2) Shealtiel to Nathan, 21 names
(3) David to Isaac, 14 names
(4) Abraham to Adam, 21 names.

Please note that Luke provided Adam with the title of **"son of God"**, which, of course, is correct, in verse 38

(3) The travels of the Master

A prime objective of the author is to allow the reader to grasp and appreciate the extraordinary length and breadth of the exertion and effort expensed, as well as the distances traveled on foot, which amounted to several thousand miles, by our Lord Jesus, His earthly parents and Disciples during His brief life of approximately 33 years and ministry of about three years.

For example, His parents traveled over 1000 miles, apparently on foot, just before and after His birth.

The following listing of distances between geographical sites, presents only a fraction of the sites, villages, towns and cities actually visited by Jesus and His Disciples.

For example the seventy Disciples were sent to sites previously visited. (LUKE 10:1-16) This would have amounted to a minimum of 35 sites, but could have easily numbered in the hundreds, if each pair had been assigned a number of locations within a specific area.

(4) Approximate distances between geographical sites mentioned in the first four books of the New Testament: [b]

(a) From Jerusalem to:

Bethany, site of His Ascension - **2 miles**
Bethlehem, birthplace of Jesus - **6 miles**
Bethphage, located near Bethany - **1 mile**
Caesarea Philippi, site of the Great Confession of the Apostle Peter and near the site of the Transfiguration - **105 miles**
Capernaum, adopted base of operations or hometown of Jesus, after His rejection at Nazareth - **85 miles**
Emmaus, site of an appearance of Jesus to His Disciples after His Resurrection - **16 miles**
Jericho, site of the miracle of restoring the sight of the blind Bartimaeus - **15 miles**
Jordan River, site of the baptism of Jesus, near Salim - **50 miles**
Sychar, Samaria, Site of Jacob's Well where Jesus taught a wayward woman the true nature of worship - **35 miles**

Sea of Galilee, site where Jesus and Peter walked on water - **70 miles**

(b) From Capernaum to:

Bethsaida, hometown of Philip, Andrew and Peter - **6 miles**

Caesarea Philippi, site of the Great Confession of the Apostle Peter and near the site of the Transfiguration - **27 miles**

Cana, site of the first miracle, water changed into wine - **16 miles**

Dalmanutha, site visited just after the feeding of the 4000, Pharisees requested a sign from Heaven, Jesus left in disgust - **6 miles**

Gennesaret, site near where Jesus and Peter walked on water - **3 miles**

Nain, site where Jesus raised the son of a widow, from the dead - **22 miles**

Nazareth, hometown of Jesus, was rejected and relocated to Capernaum - **20 miles**

Tyre, site where Jesus cast out a devil from the daughter of a Syrophenician woman - **35 miles**

Sidon, site north of Tyre - **50 miles**

Sychar, same as above - **55 miles**

B. Life of Christ prior to His Ministry

(1) Jesus was born of a Virgin

Locality: **Bethlehem,** which is approximately six miles south of Jerusalem, on the road to Hebron.

Messianic Prophecies fulfilled: MICAH 5:2 born in Bethlehem, ISAIAH 7:14 born of a Virgin

Probable Date: **September 5 BC (Details below)**

Reference: LUKE 2:4-7

Key Passage LUKE 2:7 And she brought forth her firstborn son, and wrapped him in swaddling clothes, and laid him in a manger; because there was no room for them in the inn.

Biblical Support for date of His birth

(2) While much of the world celebrates the birth of our Lord Jesus on December 25, a careful study of the Scriptures and logic would point toward a more temperate time of the year:

(a) The Romans, just like taxing authorities of today, relied upon voluntary compliance. Compliance levels would naturally be much lower if the census were scheduled for the dead of winter, when the temperatures dip below freezing, the wind howls and the roads are in poor condition, making travel in the hilly regions of the Holy Land quite difficult.

Compliance would be much greater, if the Roman officials governing the Jewish Nation planned the collection of data during a religious celebration with obligatory attendance of the faithful.

If this were the case, the reason why there was no room at the inn becomes quite clear.

(b) We know based upon LUKE 2:8 that shepherds were tending their sheep, which was their total livelihood, at night at the time Christ was born.

It is highly unlikely that shepherds would have exposed their flocks to the normally inclement weather at night in December, due to the risks of loss involved and natural lack of forage.

A study of the history of the Roman Empire reveals that the 25th of December was the date of a pagan festival, which was held in honor of the Roman sun god when the sun was in its winter solstice.

By late in the third century the Church had become divided and a major fraction introduced the celebration of the "Christ Mass" so its members could take part in the merriment.

An observant study of the Scriptures indicates that the actual date was in the fall of the year.

(c) Service of priests in the Temple was organized and divided into 24 "courses" during the time of King David.

(d) An important clue is provided in LUKE 1:5. The father of John the Baptist,

Zacharias was priest of the course of Abia or Abijah.

(e) Zacharias learned during his course of service (mid-June), that his then barren wife, Elisabeth would have a child (LUKE 1:8-13).

Upon the completion of his service traveled home and she conceived (LUKE 1:23-24), leading to the birth of John in the following March.

(f) In verses 31 and 36 of the first chapter of Luke, we learn the Virgin Mary had been selected by God to be the mother of Jesus and that her cousin Elisabeth was in her sixth month of pregnancy (mid-December).

(g) Mary traveled to visit her cousin and was "with child" when she arrived. (LUKE1:39-44)

(h) Mary stayed for three months, until Elisabeth delivered her son in mid-March (LUKE 1:56-57).

(i) Therefore, the most likely time of the birth of our Lord was in September or during the time of the festival of Tabernacles, the third and final major festival of the year, when all the males of Israel gathered in Jerusalem for services in the Temple.

(j) We are not commanded to celebrate the birth of our Lord annually, nor are such celebrations prohibited in the pages of the New Testament.

(k) Therefore personal or public celebrations of His Birth, which are not included as a part of the Worship services (weekly services during which the Lord's Supper is served) of His Church, would be acceptable.

(l) However the inclusion of any cerebration or activities related to Christmas as a part of the Worship services can only be considered as an unauthorized addition to the Worship service.

Hence, any such cerebration or activities would be a violation of the unyielding Biblical Injunction, against "adding to" in REVELATION 22:18-19 and would likely result in each individual, who affirms its use, to be eternally lost

(m) Today, just like Christians did in the first century; His faithful followers celebrate the Lord's Supper by remembering and reviewing in our minds, His Sacrifice, Life and Resurrection from the dead, on the first day of each and every week, as Christ commanded. (MATTHEW 26:26-28, ACTS 20:7, 1 CORINTHIANS 11:23-26)

(n) Without His Resurrection - His Birth would have been meaningless

(o) Christ is the only example of a Virgin Birth in all of history. His virgin Birth and Resurrection were both Miracles, which demonstrates the immense, limitless Supremacy and Power of our Almighty God.

Additional information: Appendix 12

(3) Angel proclaimed the birth of Jesus and Tidings of Great Joy to shepherds

Locality: **Near Bethlehem**

Reference: LUKE 2:8-14

Key Passage: LUKE 2:10 "And the angel said unto them, Fear not: for, behold, I bring you **good tidings of great joy,** which shall be to all people".

Key Passage: LUKE 2:13-14 "And suddenly there was with the angel a multitude of the heavenly host praising God, and saying, Glory to God in the highest, and on earth peace, good will toward men"

Many have pondered the specific meaning of the term **"good tiding of great joy"**.

The tidings of great joy included full remission of sin and redemption, as well as, everlasting life for all, who would **accept His Blessings under the Divine terms offered.**

The Christ was born specifically to spread His Message, to shed His Blood **and give His Life as a ransom for the sins of all mankind.**

(4) Shepherds visit Jesus and then praised God

Locality: **Bethlehem**

Reference: LUKE 2:15-20

(5) Naming and circumcision of Jesus

Locality: **Bethlehem**

Time frame: **Eight days after His birth**

LUKE 2:21
And when eight days were accomplished for the circumcising of the child, his name was called JESUS, which was so named of the angel before he was conceived in the womb.

(6) Presentation and purification in the Temple

Locality: **Jerusalem**

Time frame: **Forty days after His birth**

Messianic Prophecy fulfilled: LEVITICUS 12:8

Reference: LUKE 2:22-38

(7) Wise men from the East visit, bearing gifts of gold, frankincense and myrrh

Locality: **Jerusalem and Bethlehem**

Probable Date: **4 BC**

Reference: MATTHEW 2:1-12

Key Passage: MATTHEW 2:1-2 Now when Jesus was born in Bethlehem of Judea in the days of Herod the king, behold, **there came wise men from the east** to Jerusalem, Saying, **Where is he that is born King of the Jews?** for we have seen his star in the east, and are come to worship him.

Key Passage: MATTHEW 2:11-12 **And when they were come into the house,** they saw the young child with Mary his mother, and fell down, and worshiped him: and when they had opened their treasures, they presented unto him gifts; gold, and frankincense, and myrrh. *And being warned of God in a dream that they should not return to Herod, they departed into their own country another way*

It is possible that the providence of God encouraged the wise men to present gifts to the parents of the newborn King, which in turn, were used to finance the unexpected extended sojourn in Egypt.

(8) Flight to Egypt

Locality: **Bethlehem to Egypt, a trip of approximately 400 miles, on foot**

Messianic Prophecy fulfilled: HOSEA 1:1.

Reference: MATTHEW 2:13-15

In a vain attempt to murder Jesus, Herod determined to put to the sword, all the small children in the area of Bethlehem. An Angel warned Joseph in a dream, which resulted in Joseph and Mary fleeing immediately to Egypt.

(9) Massacre of the children

Locality: **Bethlehem**

Messianic Prophecy fulfilled: JEREMIAH 31:15

Reference: MATTHEW 2:16-18.

(10) Return to Nazareth

Locality: **Egypt to Nazareth, a trip of approximately 485 miles, on foot**

Significant event:

King Herod died on March 13, 4 BC

Reference: MATTHEW 2:19-23

(11) Childhood of Jesus

Locality: **Nazareth**

Probable Dates: **5 BC to AD 8**

Reference: LUKE 2:40

(12) Jesus converses and deliberates with religious leaders in the Temple

Locality: **Jerusalem**

Probable Date: **April, AD 8**

About the age of 12, Jesus was left behind in Jerusalem. His parents searched for three days before locating Jesus in the Temple. When questioned, Jesus simply stated that He must be about His Father's business.

Reference: LUKE 2:41-51

(13) Youth to manhood of Jesus

Locality: **Nazareth**

Probable Dates: **AD 8 to AD 26**

Reference: LUKE 2:52

After Caesar Augustus passed away, Tiberius began his reign on August 19, AD 14. Augustus and Tiberius had jointly reigned for over two years prior to the death of Augustus.

This fact has caused a question regarding the date of the beginning of the ministry of John, the Baptist, which Luke stated was in the fifteenth year of the reign of Tiberius (LUKE 3:1).

C. Role of John the Baptist

(1) Youth of John the Baptist

Locality: **Judea**

Reference: LUKE 1:80

(2) John the Baptist prepares the way for the Messiah

Locality: **Desert near Jordon River**

Messianic Prophecies fulfilled: ISAIAH 40:3-5, MALACHI 3:1

Probable Date: **Summer, AD 26**

Reference: MATTHEW 3:1-6

Additional references: MARK 1:1-8, LUKE 3:1-6,

(3) Example of the boldness of his ministry and testimony of John the Baptist

Locality: **Bethabara, a place east of Jordan River**

Reference: JOHN 1:19-28

Key Passage JOHN 1:23 "He said, I [am] the voice of **one crying in the wilderness,** Make straight the way of the Lord, as said the prophet Esaias". (Refers to: ISAIAH 40:3)

Additional references: MATTHEW 3:7-12, LUKE 3:7-18

(4) John reluctantly Baptizes Christ

Locality: **Bethabara**

Messianic Prophecy fulfilled: ISAIAH 11:2 Christ anointed by the Holy Spirit

Probable Date: **Winter, AD 26**

Reference: MATTHEW 3:13-17

Additional references: MARK 1:9-11, LUKE 3:21-22

John may have been reluctant because from his point of view, repentance or baptism was unnecessary, due to the sinless nature of the Son of God and his apparent feeling of being unworthy. Jesus understood his position, but also was keenly aware of the long standing Divine Plan, which called His Obedient Submission to the Will of His Father, Who immediately and clearly expressed His approval.

When Jesus came up out of the water, He was Praying and Heaven opened (LUKE 3:21) and the all engulfing voice of God, the Father declared, **"You are My beloved Son; in You I am well pleased",** this indicated that He fulfills His destiny described centuries earlier by the prophet Isaiah (ISAIAH 11:2). **The descent of the dove was a sign that Jesus was the One anointed by the Spirit of God as the Servant-Messiah of His chosen people.**

(5) John the Baptist declares Jesus to be the Messiah

Reference: JOHN 1:29-34

Key Passage: JOHN 1:29 "The next day John seeth Jesus coming unto him, and saith, Behold the Lamb of God, which taketh away the sin of the world."

(6) John, the Baptist continues his ministry and acknowledgment of Jesus, as the Son of God

Locality: **Aenon**

Reference: JOHN 3:23-36

Key Passage: JOHN 3:35-36 "The Father loveth the Son, and hath given all things into his hand. **He that believeth on the Son hath** everlasting life: and he that believeth not the Son shall not see life; but the wrath of God abideth on him."

(7) John, the Baptist arrested by Herod, the Tetrarch

Locality: **Arrested in Anenon, taken to and imprisoned in Machaerus, which is located east of the Dead Sea.**

Probable Date of his death: **March, AD 28**

Reference: MATTHEW 14:1-9

Key Passage MATTHEW 14:8 "And she, being before instructed of her mother, said, Give me here John Baptist's head in a charger."

Additional references: MARK 6:14-29, LUKE 3:19-20, LUKE 9:7

(8) John, the Baptist, Beheaded

References: MATTHEW 14:10-11, LUKE 9:8-9

(9) Disciples bury the body of John the Baptist

References: MATTHEW 14:12, MARK 6:29

D. Jesus prepares for His Ministry

(1) Temptation and Triumph of Jesus in the Wilderness

Localities: **(a) In the wilderness, (b) in Jerusalem, (c) on a high mountain**

Comments: In the Gospels of Matthew, Mark, and Luke, His Baptism is followed immediately by the Temptation in the wilderness.

The purpose of this testing may have been to confirm His understanding and acceptance of the path which had been preordained for His earthly life.

It is interesting to note, that during these trials He refused to use His Awesome Power to attain personal needs, to astonish others, or to rule the earth by political and military force.

MATTHEW 4:1-10
Then was Jesus led up of the spirit **into the wilderness** to be tempted of the devil. And when he had fasted forty days and forty nights, he was afterward hungry. And when the **tempter came to him,** he said, **If thou be the Son of God, command that these stones be made bread.**

But he answered and said, It is written, **Man shall not live by bread alone, but by every word that proceedeth out of the mouth of God.** (Recorded several centuries earlier by Moses in DEUTERONOMY 8:3)

Then the devil taketh him up into the holy city, and setteth him on a pinnacle of the temple, And saith unto him, **If thou be the Son of God, cast thyself down: for it is written, He shall give his angels charge concerning thee:** and in their hands they shall bear thee up, lest at any time thou dash thy foot against a stone. Jesus said unto him, It is written again, **Thou shalt not tempt the Lord thy God.** (Originally written by Moses in DEUTERONOMY 6:16)

Again, the devil taketh him up into an **exceeding high mountain,** and showeth him all the kingdoms of the world, and the glory of them; And saith unto him, All these things will I give thee, if thou wilt fall down and worship me. Then saith Jesus unto him, Get thee hence, Satan: for it is written, **Thou shalt worship the Lord thy God, and him only shalt thou serve.**

Additional references: MARK 1:12-13, LUKE 4:1-13

E. Launches His Ministry in Galilee, Judea and Samaria

(1) Jesus considered potential Apostles

Locality: **Bethabara**

Probable Date: **Winter, AD 26**

Reference: JOHN 1:35-51

(2) Miracle, first - Jesus turned water into wine

Locality: **Cana, was located about 5 miles northeast of Nazareth in Galilee**

Messianic Prophecy fulfilled: ISAIAH 35:5-6
Jesus would perform miracles

Probable Date: **Winter, AD 27**

Reference: JOHN 2:1-11

(3) Sojourn of Jesus, His family and disciples in Capernaum

Locality: **Capernaum, located approximately 16 miles from Cana, on the northwest shore of the Lake of Galilee, near the main road from Damascus to Egypt**

Reference: JOHN 2:12

(4) Journey to Jerusalem for Passover

Locality: **The distance from Capernaum to Jerusalem was approximately 85 miles or a four to five day journey on foot.**

Probable Date: **April, AD 27**

Reference: JOHN 2:13

(5) The First Temple Clearing and Cleansing

Locality: **Jerusalem**

Key Passages: **(a)** JOHN 2:16 "And said unto them that sold doves, Take these things hence; make not my Father's house an house of merchandise." **(b)** JOHN 2:19 "Jesus answered and said unto them, Destroy this temple, and in three days I will raise it up."

Reference: JOHN 2:13-19

The Words of Jesus in JOHN 2:19 provided the basis for the claim of the two false witnesses at His trial who stated that Jesus said, "I am able to destroy the temple of God and to build it in three days" (MATTHEW 26:61), which was a reference to His earthly human body and not the Temple built by King Solomon.

(6) Teaching (Commandment) of Jesus: Do not make my Father's house into a house of merchandise.

Messianic Prophecy fulfilled: PSALMS 69:9

This commandment indicates clearly that the collective local membership, which is His Church or the physical church building, is not to be used for worldly activities, such as selling products, fund raising or bingo games. The purpose of all gatherings is exclusively for fellowship, study of His Word and above all the Worship of God, the Father.

(7) Teaching of Jesus - Nicodemus visits Jesus under cover of darkness

Locality: **Jerusalem**

Key Passage - Message: JOHN 3:3 - "**Each believer must be born of water [baptized] and the Spirit, in order to enter the Kingdom**"

Read the whole story: JOHN 3:1-21

(8) His disciples baptize many in Judea

References: JOHN 3:22-24, JOHN 4:1-2

(9) Jesus learns of the capture of John, the Baptist, departs Judea

Locality: **Depart Judea travels to Galilee via Samaria,** a journey of several days

References: MATTHEW 4:12 MARK 1:14, JOHN 4:3

(10) Teaching of Jesus - Samaritan woman at the well

Locality: **Well of Jacob, located near Sychar, Samaria**

Key Passages - Messages: **(a)** JOHN 4:10 **Introduction of the Water of Life** **(b)** JOHN 4:23-24 "**God is a Spirit: and they that worship him must worship him in Spirit and in Truth**"

Reference: JOHN 4:4-24

(11) Jesus declared that He is the Messiah

Locality: **Well of Jacob, located near Sychar, Samaria**

Key Passage: JOHN 4:25-26 "The woman saith unto him, I know that Messiah cometh, which is called Christ: when he is come, he will tell us all things. Jesus saith unto her, **I that speak unto thee am he.**"

(12) Teaching of Jesus - He speaks of the Spiritual Harvest to His Disciples

Locality: **Well of Jacob, located near Sychar, Samaria**

Key Passages - Message: JOHN 4:32-38 –
(a) "My meat is to do the will of him that sent me, and to finish his work."

(b) The pressing need for spreading or sowing the seeds the Truth, which another often reaps and the eternal reward that await each of them.

Reference: JOHN 4:27-38

(13) Numerous Samaritans believed the Word of Jesus

Reference: JOHN 4:39-42

F. Great Galilean Ministry

(1) Jesus enters Galilee with the Power of the Spirit.

Messianic Prophecies fulfilled: ISAIAH 9:1-2: **Jesus would minister in Galilee** and ISAIAH 61:1 **Jesus would preach the Good News**

Probable Date: **Winter, AD 28**

Key Passage: LUKE 4:14-15 "And Jesus returned in the **power of the Spirit into Galilee**: and there went out a fame of him through all the region round about. And he taught in their synagogues, being glorified of all"

Additional references: MATTHEW 4:12-17, MARK 1:14-15, JOHN 4:43-45

(2) Miracle - Jesus heals the son of an official, who demonstrates faith

Locality: **Cana**

Reference: JOHN 4:46-54

(3) First rejection of Christ in Nazareth, His hometown

In this celebrated discourse Jesus quoted Isaiah 61:1 to portray his ministry, which is recorded in Luke 4:18

Key passage: LUKE 4:24 **"And he [Jesus] said, Verily I say unto you, No prophet is accepted in his own country"**

Messianic Prophecy fulfilled: ISAIAH 53:3

Reference: LUKE 4:16-27

(4) Miracle - Members of synagogue are filled with wrath, attempt to kill Jesus, who is mysteriously able to easily evade.

Locality: **Nazareth**

Key passage: LUKE 4:28-30 "And all they in the synagogue, when they heard these things, were filled with wrath, And rose up, and thrust him out of the city, and led him unto the brow of the hill whereon their city was built, **that they might cast him down headlong. But he passing through the midst of them went his way,**"

(5) Similar unexplained mysterious occurrences:

References: JOHN 8:59, JOHN 10:39, JOHN 20:19, MATTHEW 27:52-53

(6) Teaching of Jesus - He travels to Capernaum, His new home base and begins to preach: Repent! The Kingdom of Heaven is at hand.

Key passages: **(a)** MATTHEW 4:17 From that time Jesus began to preach, and to say, "**Repent: for the kingdom of heaven is at hand.**" **(b)** MARK 1:15 "And saying, **The time is fulfilled, and the kingdom of God is at hand: repent ye, and believe the gospel.**"

References: MATTHEW 4:13-17, LUKE 4:31-32

(7) Fishermen become fishers of men

Jesus Called Simon (Peter), his brother Andrew, James, son of Zebedee and his brother John

Locality: **Shore Lake of Galilee**

Key passage: MATTHEW 4:19 "And he saith unto them, Follow me, and **I will make you fishers of men.**"

References: MATTHEW 4:18-22, MARK 1:16-20,

(8) Miracle - Jesus provides a miraculous catch of fish

Locality: **Shore Sea of Galilee, which means harp shaped in Hebrew. Was also known as Lake Gennesaret (LUKE 5:1) and Lake Tiberias because the palace of Herod was located on its shore** (JOHN 6:1)

Key passage: LUKE 5:9-10 "For he was astonished, and all that were with him, at the draught of the fishes which they had taken: And so was also James, and John, the sons of Zebedee, which were partners with Simon. And Jesus said unto Simon, Fear not; from henceforth thou shalt catch men"

Reference: LUKE 5:1-11

(9) Jesus teaches with Great Authority

Locality: **Capernaum**

Key passage: MARK 1:21-23 "And they went into Capernaum; and straightway on the sabbath day he entered into the synagogue, and taught. **And they were astonished at his doctrine: for he taught them as one that had authority,** and not as the scribes. And there was in their synagogue a man with an unclean spirit; and he cried out"

(10) Miracle - Jesus expels that unclean spirit

Locality: **Capernaum**

Key passages: MARK 1:24 "Saying, Let us alone; what have we to do with thee, thou Jesus of Nazareth? art thou come to destroy us? I know thee who thou art, the Holy One of God."

References: MARK 1:24-28, LUKE 4:33-37

(11) Miracle - Mother-in-Law of Peter is healed - She suffered from a fever. Jesus touched her hand and the fever left her. She then arose and ministered unto them.

Locality: **Capernaum**

References: MATTHEW 8:14-15, MARK 1:29-31, LUKE 4:38-39

(12) Miracles - many healed at sunset - Many were possessed by devils, which He cast out by His Word and healed all that were sick.

Locality: **Capernaum**

References: MATTHEW 8:16-17, MARK 1:32-34, LUKE 4:40-41

(13) Jesus toured Galilee with four Disciples preaching in many synagogues

References: MATTHEW 4:23-25, MARK 1:38-39, LUKE 4:43-44

(14) Miracles - healing the sick, casting out devils, a great multitude followed Him

Key passage: MARK 1:39 **"And he preached in their synagogues throughout all Galilee, and cast out devils."**

References: MATTHEW 4:23-25, MARK 1:28-39, LUKE 4:43-44

(15) Miracles - Jesus cleanses a man of leprosy, great multitudes came to hear Him and were healed

References: man cleansed of leprosy: MATTHEW 8:1-4, MARK 1:40-45, LUKE 5:12-14

After Jesus had cleansed the leper, He asked the man **not** to say anything regarding his cleansing, however the man was apparently overcome with great joy and went about broadcasting his good fortune

Thus, Jesus was prevented from entering the city, so they came to him from every quarter to hear and be healed of their infirmities.

Reference, multitudes healed: LUKE 5:15

(16) Miracle - Jesus cures a paralyzed man, lowered through the roof of Peter's house

Locality: **Capernaum**

References: MATTHEW 9:1-8, MARK 2:1-12, LUKE 5:17-26,

Comments: Note the procedure used by Jesus, first He attended to spiritual needs of the individual by forgiving his sins in MATTHEW 9:2, then proceeded to cure him physically in MATTHEW 9:6.

It is also interesting to note the unbelief and beginning of enmity of certain scribes and Pharisees, who were watching and **their accusation of blasphemy is recorded in** MATTHEW 9:3, MARK 2:6-7 and LUKE 5:21.

(17) Matthew called to be a Disciple; Jesus shares a meal with sinners at the home of Matthew

Locality: **Capernaum**

References: MATTHEW 9:9-13, MARK 2:13-17, LUKE 5:27-32

(18) Some of the Disciples of John, the Baptist question why the Disciples of Christ did not fast

Locality: **Capernaum**

References: MATTHEW 9:14-17, MARK 2:18-22, LUKE 5:33-39,

His illustrations or answers are recorded in MATTHEW 9:15-17

(19) Jesus went to numerous towns, teaching in their synagogues the Gospel of the Kingdom and healing many people.

Locality: **Galilee**

Messianic Prophecy fulfilled: ISAIAH 9:1-2

Reference: MATTHEW 9:35

(20) Jesus traveled to Jerusalem for Passover

Locality: **Traveled approximately 85 miles from Capernaum on foot to Jerusalem**

Probable Date: **April, AD 28**

Reference: JOHN 5:1

(21) Miracle - A lame man healed by the Pool of Bethesda

Locality: **Jerusalem**

Reference: JOHN 5:2-15

(22) As a result the claim of Christ that He is the Son of God, a group of Jews conspire to kill Him

Locality: **Jerusalem**

Reference: JOHN 5:16-18

(23) Teachings of Jesus - provides strong support for His claim of being the Messiah.

Locality: **Jerusalem**

Reference: JOHN 5:19-47 - This passage contains several basic principles of His Gospel – **a must read.**

(24) Disciples pluck ears of corn on the Sabbath, criticism of Pharisees answered by Christ

References: MATTHEW 12:1-8, MARK 2:23-28, LUKE 6:1-5

(25) Miracle - Withered Hand is healed on the Sabbath, Pharisees plot against Jesus

References: MATTHEW 12:9-14, MARK 3:1-6

(26) Miracles - Jesus withdraws to the Sea of Galilee, a large throng follows, and many were healed

Locality: **Jesus traveled approximately 70 miles on foot, from Jerusalem to Sea of Galilee**

References: MATTHEW 12:15-21, MARK 3:7-8

(27) Jesus withdraws and prays all night, on a mountain

Locality: **Possibly the Hill of Hattin near Capernaum**

Reference: LUKE 6:12

(28) Jesus selects His Twelve Disciples

(a) *The Twelve selected included:*

(1) Simon, whom He surnamed Peter

(2) James, son of Zebedee, and his brother
(3) John, whom He surnamed Boanerges, which translates as "the sons of thunder"

(4) Andrew

(5) Philip

(6) Bartholomew

(7) Matthew

(8) Thomas

(9) James, son of Alphaeus

(10) Thaddeus

(11) Simon, the Canaanite

(12) Judas Iscariot

References: MATTHEW 10:2-4, MARK 3:13-19, LUKE 6:13-16

(29) Miracles - Jesus descends, heals the throng

Reference: LUKE 6:17-19

(30) Jesus ascends, sits down and prepares to address His Disciples

This was a widespread occurrence at this time in history for a teacher to sit in a prominent place where all could see and hear, then gather his disciples around and instruct, which is believed to be the setting of the Sermon on the Mount

Reference: MATTHEW 5:1

(31) Teachings of Jesus - The Sermon on the Mount

Locality: **Possibly the Hill of Hattin near Capernaum**

In this sermon, Jesus confirms that He was the long awaited Messiah, promised to Moses (DEUTERONOMY 18:17-18) as children of Israel prepared to enter the Promised Land.

He also began clarifying the Spiritual requirements for members of the soon to be established Kingdom of God. The Covenant that was in existence at the time or the Old Covenant required obedience to the Letter of the Law. Upon His death on the Cross, a New Covenant would replace the Old, followed by the establishment of the Kingdom, which occurred shortly after His Ascension to Heaven. The New Covenant requires obedience to both the Letter and Spirit of the Law, as had been prophesied in ISAIAH 42:21.

For example, Christians are not only to avoid committing adultery (Letter of Law), but also are to circumvent evil thoughts or lusting after the flesh (Spirit of Law), which is much more difficult, or to the act of murder, which was condemned for hundreds of years, Jesus added a prohibition against hatred.

References: MATTHEW 5:1-8:1, LUKE 6:20-49

(32) Teaching of Jesus - Beatitudes

References: MATTHEW 5:1-12, LUKE 6:17-26

It is interesting to note that Jesus not only provided the Pattern and Guide for Christian living, but also practiced that which He preached.

(33) Teaching of Jesus - Salt

Reference: MATTHEW 5:13

(34) Parable of Jesus - Lamp under a Basket

Reference: MATTHEW 5:14-16,

Message: **Let the Light of your Righteousness shine to the Glory of God**

(35) Teaching of Jesus - Law of Moses

Reference: MATTHEW 5:17-20

(36) Teaching of Jesus - Anger

Key passage: MATTHEW 5:21 **is an Affirmation of sixth Old Testament commandment** EXODUS 20:13

Reference: MATTHEW 5:21-24,

(37) Teaching of Jesus - Handling Adversaries

References: MATTHEW 5:25-26, LUKE 12:58-59

(38) Teaching of Jesus - Lust

Key passage: MATTHEW 5:27-28 **is an Affirmation of seventh Old Testament commandment** EXODUS 20:14

Reference: MATTHEW 5:27-30

(39) Teaching of Jesus - Divorce

Reference: MATTHEW 5:31-32

(40) Teaching of Jesus - Vows

Reference: MATTHEW 5:33-37 **is an Affirmation of third Old Testament commandment** EXODUS 20:7

Related passages: MATTHEW 6:9, MATTHEW 23:16-22

(41) Teaching of Jesus - Revenge

Reference: MATTHEW 5:38-42

(42) Teaching of Jesus - Loving your Enemies

References: MATTHEW 5:43-48, LUKE 6:27-36

(43) Teaching of Jesus - Giving to the Poor

Reference: MATTHEW 6:1-4

(44) Teaching of Jesus - Prayer

References: MATTHEW 6:5-15, LUKE 11:1-13

(45) Teaching of Jesus - Fasting

Reference: MATTHEW 6:16-18

(46) Teaching of Jesus - Money

Key passage: MATTHEW 6:24 **is an Affirmation of second Old Testament commandment** EXODUS 20:4-5

Reference: MATTHEW 6:19-24

(47) Teaching of Jesus - Worry

Key passage: MATTHEW 6:33 **is an Affirmation of first Old Testament commandment** EXODUS 20:3

Reference: MATTHEW 6:25-34

Related passage: MATTHEW 22:37-40

(48) Parable of Jesus - the Speck and Plank - regarding the criticism of others

Lesson: **Do not presume to judge others**

References: MATTHEW 7:1-6, LUKE 6:37-42

(49) Teaching of Jesus - Asking, Seeking and Knocking

Reference: MATTHEW 7:7-12

(50) Teaching of Jesus - Narrow Way to Heaven

References: MATTHEW 7:13-14, LUKE 13:24

(51) Warning of Jesus - warning of false prophets and teachings - you shall know them by their fruits!

References: MATTHEW 7:15-20, LUKE 6:43-45

(52) Parable of Jesus - Two Houses, compares building on a rock (firm foundation of His teachings) or shifting sands (following false teachings)

Message: Finding and following the narrow way requires strict obedience, to His Words

References: MATTHEW 7:21-29, LUKE 6:46-49

(53) Recap of Christ's Affirmation of the five original Old Testament Commandments within the text of the Sermon on the Mount and four others as follows:

(a) MATTHEW 6:33 - **Affirmation of first Old Testament commandment:** EXODUS 20:3

(b) MATTHEW 6:24 - **Affirmation of second Old Testament commandment:** EXODUS 20:4-5

(c) MATTHEW 5:33-37 - **Affirmation of third Old Testament commandment:** EXODUS 20:7

(d) MATTHEW 5:21 - **Affirmation of sixth Old Testament commandment:** EXODUS 20:13

(e) MATTHEW 5:27-28 - **Affirmation of seventh Old Testament commandment:** EXODUS 20:14

Jesus affirmed four other original Ten Old Testament Commandments in the following passages:

(f) MATTHEW 15:4 - **Affirmation of fifth Old Testament commandment:** EXODUS 20:12

(g) MATTHEW 19:18 - **Affirmation of eighth Old Testament commandment:** EXODUS 20:15

(h) MATTHEW 19:18 - **Affirmation of ninth Old Testament commandment:** EXODUS 20:16

(i) LUKE 12:15 - **Affirmation of tenth Old Testament commandment:** EXODUS 20:17

Note: The Fourth Old Testament commandment was NOT affirmed.

(j) Under the New Covenant the Day of the Lord was changed from Saturday to Sunday, the first day of the week. (ACTS 20:7)

(54) Miracle - Roman Centurion demonstrates great faith in Jesus to heal his servant

Locality: **Capernaum**

References: MATTHEW 8:5-13, LUKE 7:1-10

(55) Miracle - Son of a widow, was raised from the dead

Locality: **Nain, village southeast of Nazareth**

Reference: LUKE 7:11-17

(56) Followers of John, the Baptist question Jesus, uncertainties are eased

Locality: **Nain**

References: MATTHEW 11:1-6, LUKE 7:18-23

(57) Jesus commends John the Baptist

Locality: **Nain**

References: MATTHEW 11:7-15, LUKE 7:24-30

(58) Wickedness condemned

References: MATTHEW 11:16-19, LUKE 7:31-35

(59) Parable of Jesus - Children in the Marketplace

Occasion: **Self-righteous rejection of the baptism of John by the Pharisees**

Message: **Evils of a critical temperament**

References: MATTHEW 11:16-17, LUKE 7:32

(60) Jesus Rebukes and issues a strong warning to the Cities of Chorazin, Bethsaida and Capernaum

Reference: MATTHEW 11:20-24

(61) Teaching of Jesus - Jesus offers the invitation to find Rest (peace, serenity and tranquility) in Him

Reference: MATTHEW 11:25-30

(62) Jesus Dined with Simon a Pharisee, a sinful woman anoints His feet; Simon questioned why Jesus allows this immoral female to touch Him, which was answered in the form of the Parable of the Two Debtors.

Reference: LUKE 7:40-43

(63) Parable of Jesus - meaning of the Two Debtors

Key Passage: LUKE 7:48-50 **"And he said unto her, Thy sins are forgiven. And they that sat at meat with him began to say within themselves, Who is this that forgiveth sins also? And he said to the woman, Thy faith hath saved thee; go in peace".**

Message: **Our Lord is willing to forgive no matter the amount of debt (sins)**

Reference: LUKE 7:40-50

(64) Miracle - Jesus tours Galilee with the Twelve, heals followers

Locality: **Galilee**

In the congregate was **Mary called Magdalene**, *who had been healed of seven demons and infirmities,* as well as, other generous women who followed Jesus and ministered unto him of their substance.

Reference: LUKE 8:1-3

(65) Miracle - Jesus heals a demon-possessed man

Locality: **Capernaum**

Reference: MATTHEW 12:22-23

(66) Scribes and Pharisees accuse Jesus of using power of Satan to perform Miracles

Locality: **Capernaum**

References: MATTHEW 12:24, MARK 3:22

(67) Pharisees rebuked

References: MATTHEW 12:25-30, MARK 3:23-27

(68) Warning of Jesus - Blasphemy against the Holy Spirit is an Unpardonable Sin

References: MATTHEW 12:31-35, MARK 3:29

(69) Explanation of the Unpardonable Sin

When a demon-possessed man came to Jesus, he was healed. The multitudes were amazed. The religious leaders of the day (Scribes and Pharisees) claimed He was healing through Satan's power (MATTHEW 12:24). Jesus had cast out the demons by the power of the Holy Spirit; His enemies claimed He cast them out by the power of Satan. Such defamation of the Holy Spirit reveals a spiritual perversion, which situates an individual beyond any hope of repentance or forgiveness.

(70) Warning of Jesus - Mankind will be judged by their words

Locality: **Capernaum**

Reference: MATTHEW 12:36-37

(71) Jewish Leaders request that Jesus perform a miracle, Jesus declines - refers to the Sign of Jonah

Locality: **Capernaum**

Reference: MATTHEW 12:38-45

(72) Mother and brothers of Jesus seek an audience; Jesus, then defined His position regarding His true family

Key Passage: MATTHEW 12:50 **"For whosoever shall do the will of my Father which is in heaven, the same is my brother, and sister, and mother"**.

References: MATTHEW 12:46-50, MARK 3:31-35, LUKE 8:19-21

(73) Parable of Jesus - the Sower and Four Types of Soil

References: MATTHEW 13:1-9, MARK 4:1-9, LUKE 8:4-8

(a) Jesus explains reasons for the use of Parables

Key passage: MATTHEW 13:11 "He answered and said unto them, **Because it is given unto you to know the mysteries of the kingdom of heaven, but to them it is not given."**

References: MATTHEW 13:10-17, MARK 4:11-12, LUKE 8:10

(74) Jesus clarifies the meaning of The Parable, Sower and the Four Types of Soil

Message: Defines the Kingdom of Heaven and the Divine Power, the Word of God. The Sower of the good seed is the Son of Man or Jesus Christ (MATTHEW 13:37) The Seed is the Word or the Gospel of the Kingdom or Christ (MATTHEW 13:23)

The first soil (wayside) hears – does not understand (MATTHEW 13:19)

The second soil (stony places) hears – accepts with joy – has no roots – stumbles when persecution arises (MATTHEW 13:20-21)

The third soil (among the thorns) hears and accepts – is choked by cares of the world or deceitfulness of riches (MATTHEW 13:22)

The fourth soil (good ground) hears the word – understands – keeps the word and bears fruit with patience (MATTHEW 13:23)

Key Passage: MATTHEW 13:16-17 "But blessed are your eyes, for they see: and your ears, for they hear. For verily I say unto you, *That many prophets and righteous men have desired to see those things which ye see*, and have not seen them; and to hear those things which ye hear, and have not heard them."

References: MATTHEW 13:10-23; 13:36-37, MARK 4:10-25, LUKE 8:9-18

(75) Parable of Jesus - the Growing Seed

Message: The Kingdom grows as a result of the planting of Word of God, which is similar to sprouting and growth of field grains. At that time, the growth process was a mystery and today is beyond the comprehension of most individuals.

Reference: MARK 4:26-29

(76) Parable of Jesus - the Weeds (also known as Wheat and Tares or the Tares)

Message: Again the subject is the Kingdom of Heaven from a slightly different point of view.

He who sows the good seed is the Son of Man. The world is the field.

The good seed are those who receive the Word of God, submit to Him as their Lord and King, become sons or daughter of the Kingdom or His Disciples.

The enemy is the devil, who sows the tares or the sons of evil one.

The harvest will occur upon the Second Coming of Christ. Angels will accompany Christ and will act as the reapers, separating the tares from the faithful.

Reference: MATTHEW 13:24-30

(77) Parable of Jesus - the Mustard Seed

Message: Jesus used mustard seed, which was among the smallest seed used at the time, yet produces a mature plant ranging in height from 10 to 15 feet, as comparison to how the Kingdom of Heaven would begin with a small group and then enjoyed an incredible expansion, **growing from approximately 120 Disciples to over 3000 on first day of the existence of the Kingdom of Heaven or His Church.**

Rapid growth continued until the influence of His Church was felt in every corner of the world, in the first century and today.

References: MATTHEW 13:31-32, MARK 4:10-25, LUKE 13:18-21

(78) Parable of Jesus - the Leaven or Yeast

Message: Warning - avoid corrupting influences

Reference: MATTHEW 13:33

Additional Message: Jesus also warned of the leaven of the Pharisees and Sadducees in MATTHEW 16:5-12 and LUKE 12:1 in regards to their teachings and hypocrisy. The Apostle Paul warned that a little leaven leavens the whole lump, as he pointed out the requirement to withdraw from a rebellious, unrepentant member in 1 CORINTHIANS 5:1-13.

Alternative interpretation: Some scholars have suggested a meaning similar to the Parable of the Mustard Seed.

The leaven is Christ and His small band of Disciples and the meal or loaf is the world. The Word of God would eventually spread throughout the world.

(79) Jesus spoke to the multitude in Parables

Messianic Prophecy fulfilled: PSALMS 78:1-4

Reference: MATTHEW 13:34-35

(80) Jesus clarifies meaning of the Weeds Parable

Reference: MATTHEW 13:36-43

(81) Warning of Jesus - Heaven or Hell

Message: Warning of final destiny (Heaven or Hell) of all souls in the harvest, upon the Second Coming of Christ

Key Passage: MATTHEW 13:41-43 "The Son of man shall send forth his angels, and they shall gather out of his kingdom all things that offend, **and them which do iniquity; And shall cast them into a furnace of fire: there shall be wailing and gnashing of teeth.** Then shall the righteous shine forth as the sun in the kingdom of their Father Who hath ears to hear, let him hear".

Reference: MATTHEW 13:38-43

(82) Parable of Jesus - the Hidden Treasure

Message: A man finds a treasure hidden in a field. Proceeds to purchase field, the price of which requires that he sell everything he owns.

The man joyfully sells all in anticipation of the treasure, which will be rightfully his, when the purchase is completed.

Conclusion: The value of the reward or treasure of Kingdom of Heaven is much greater that the price of discipleship.

Those who understand the treasure will joyfully forgo the pleasures of the world, in order to obtain the reward (many benefits in this life and eternal joy in the world to come).

Reference: MATTHEW 13:44

Additional References: MARK 10:28-30, COLOSSIANS 2:2-3

(83) Parable of Jesus - the Pearl of Great Price

Message: A merchant seeks pearls, finds one of great price and sells everything he owns in order to acquire this rare pearl.

Conclusion: The message is the same as the Parable of the Hidden Treasure.

Reference: MATTHEW 13:44-46

(84) Parable of Jesus - the Fishing Net

Message: Importance of obedience to and proclaiming of the Gospel. Jesus clearly indicated there is simply no escape from the realm of God.

Reference: MATTHEW 13:47-50

(85) Warning of Jesus

Message: Just as the fish caught in the Parable of the Fishing Net are separated, so will the angels sever the wicked from the just at the end of time.

Reference: MATTHEW 13:49-50

(86) Parable of Jesus - the House Owner

Message: There are various approaches for teaching the Truth.

Reference: MATTHEW 13:52

(87) A great multitude gathers around Jesus, He directs His Disciples to cross to other side of the Sea of Galilee

References: MATTHEW 8:18, MARK 4:35, LUKE 8:22

(88) Miracle - Jesus sleeps, a storm arises; Disciples show a lack of faith, are rebuked, then Jesus quiets the stormy sea

Reference: MATTHEW 8:23-27

Memorable Passage: MARK 4:39 "And he arose, and rebuked the wind, and said unto the sea, **Peace, be still.** And the wind ceased, and there was a great calm."

Additional references: MARK 4:36-41, LUKE 8:23-25

(89) Miracle - Demons are transferred from two violent men to a herd of pigs, which run into and perish in the sea,

terrified local residents pleaded with Jesus to depart from the area

Locality: **possibly Gergesa, east side, Sea of Galilee**

References: MATTHEW 8:28-34, MARK 5:1-20, LUKE 8:26-39

(90) Jesus sails to Capernaum

References: MATTHEW 9:1, MARK 5:21, LUKE 8:40

(91) Jairus requests Jesus to heal his daughter

References: MATTHEW 9:18-19, MARK 5:22-24, LUKE 8:41-42

(92) Jairus learns of the death of his daughter

References: MARK 5:35-36, LUKE 8:49-50

(93) Miracle - Woman of great faith with an issue of blood was healed by touching the hem of His garment

Locality: **Capernaum,**

Key Passage: MATTHEW 9:22 "But Jesus turned him about, and when he saw her, he said, **Daughter, be of good comfort; thy faith hath made thee whole.** And the woman was made whole from that hour."

References: MATTHEW 9:20-22, MARK 5:25-34, LUKE 8:43-48

(94) Miracle - Jesus raised Jairus' daughter from the dead

Locality: **Capernaum**

Key Passage: MARK 5:36 "As soon as Jesus heard the word that was spoken, he saith unto the ruler of the synagogue, **Be not afraid, only believe.**"

References: MATTHEW 9:23-26, MARK 5:36-43, LUKE 8:51-56

(95) Miracle - Jesus heals Two Blind Men

Reference: MATTHEW 9:27-31

(96) Miracle - Jesus heals a mute, Possessed by a devil

The multitude marveled; once again the Pharisees had blasphemed the Holy Spirit, by charging that Jesus used power of the prince of darkness to cast out devils

MATTHEW 9:32-34
And when the devil was cast out, the dumb spake: and the multitudes marveled, saying, It was never so seen in Israel. **But the Pharisees said, He casteth out devils through the prince of the devils.**

(97) The final rejection of Jesus in Nazareth

Key passage: MARK 6:4 "But Jesus said unto them, **A prophet is not without honor,** but in his own country, and among his own kin, and in his own house."

References: MATTHEW 13:54-58, MARK 6:1-6

(98) Miracles - Healing of the sick in Nazareth

Reference: MARK 6:4-5

(99) Miracles - during third tour of Galilee, healed many among the people

Reference: MATTHEW 9:35

(100) Jesus expressed His compassion for mankind

Reference: MATTHEW 9:36-38

(101) Jesus bestows upon the Twelve, the power to cast out devils and heal the sick

Locality: **Capernaum**

References: MATTHEW 10:1-42, MARK 6:7-13, LUKE 9:1-6

(102) Jesus provides Disciples instructions for the Journey

References: MATTHEW 10:7-15, MARK 6:8-11, LUKE 9:3-5

(103) Jesus predicts persecution of His Disciples

Key passage: MATTHEW 10:32-33 "Whosoever therefore shall confess me before men, him will I confess also

before my Father which is in heaven. But whosoever shall deny me before men, him will I also deny before my Father which is in heaven."

Reference: MATTHEW 10:16-33

(104) Jesus delineates the high costs and rewards of discipleship or following Him

References: MATTHEW 8:19-22, MATTHEW 10:34-42, LUKE 9:57-62, LUKE 14:25-35

(105) The Twelve sent to spread the Good News, 2 by 2

References: MATTHEW 10:5-6; 11-1, MARK 6:7; 6:12-13, LUKE 9:2; 9:6

(106) Herod Antipas suffers from the immense fear that John, the Baptist had risen from the dead, as Jesus.

Reference: LUKE 9:7

(107) The Twelve return

References: MATTHEW 14:12-13, MARK 6:30-32, LUKE 9:10, JOHN 6:1

(108) Miracles - Jesus preaches and heals the masses

References: MATTHEW 14:14, MARK 6:33-34, LUKE 9:11, JOHN 6:2-3

G. Further training of the Twelve

(1) Miracle - Jesus feeds the 5,000

Locality: **Bethsaida**

Probable Date: **Spring, AD 29**

References: Matthew 14:15-21, Mark 6:35-44, Luke 9:12-17, John 6:4-13

(2) Jesus prays alone

References: MATTHEW 14:22-23, MARK 6:45-47, JOHN 6:14-15

(3) Miracle - Jesus walks on water

Peter exhibits his faith and great courage by attempting to emulate Christ, after a few moments of success, began to sink

References: MATTHEW 14:24-33, MARK 6:48-52, JOHN 6:16-21

(4) Miracles - Healings in Gennesaret

References: **MATTHEW 14:34-36, MARK 6:53-56**

(5) Teaching of Jesus - I am the Bread of Life

Locality: **Capernaum**

Key passage: JOHN 6:32-40 "Then Jesus said unto them, Verily, verily, I say unto you, Moses gave you not that bread from heaven; but my Father giveth you the true bread from heaven. For the bread of God is he which cometh down from heaven, and giveth life unto the world. Then said they unto him, Lord, evermore give us this bread.

And Jesus said unto them, **I am the bread of life:** he that cometh to me shall never hunger; and he that believeth on me shall never thirst. But I said unto you, That ye also have seen me, and believe not. All that the Father giveth me shall come to me; and him that cometh to me I will in no wise cast out. For I came down from heaven, not to do mine own will, but the will of him that sent me.

And this is the Father's will which hath sent me, that of all which he hath given me I should lose nothing, but should raise it up again at the last day. And this is the will of him that sent me, that every one which seeth the Son, **and believeth on him, may have everlasting life: and I will raise him up at the last day."**

Reference: JOHN 6:22-71

(6) The question of the Divinity of Jesus debated among the Jews

Reference: JOHN 6:41-59

(7) Many followers desert Jesus

Reference: JOHN 6:60-66

(8) One of the Twelve is a DEVIL!

Reference: JOHN 6:70-71

(9) Warning of Jesus - Believers who follow the commandments of men, Worship in Vain

References: ISAIAH 29:13, MATTHEW 15:7-9, MATTHEW 15:13-14, MARK 7:6-7

(10) Teaching of Jesus - Danger of Traditions - Failure to Honor Parents

References: MATTHEW 15:1-14, MARK 7:1-14

This passage (MATTHEW 15:1-14) begins with a challenge from the scribes and Pharisees regarding the apparent failure of His Disciples to wash their hands before meals, which was a transgression of the prevailing Jewish Tradition.

Jesus countered by pointing out the hypocrisy of creating traditions or the commandments of men, which invalidate the written law of God.

Jesus used the example of the fifth commandment for each to honor their father and mother. Under the Jewish tradition a man could declare that all his possessions had been **"given to God",** which relieved, in the opinion of the Jewish establishment, him of the responsibility of supporting his parents.

In addition to Jesus condemning the practice of attempting to invalidate the commandments of God,

He also clearly indicated that those **who follow the commandments, convictions or traditions of men simply worship in vain, and those who follow such will be sentenced to Hell for all eternity**.

The application today has not changed. In order to be saved from eternal damnation, God demands that each and every Commandment and Teaching of Christ and His Apostles, as well as, the Patterns provided be carefully followed, without exception or unauthorized additions or enhancements.

In addition, Christians must be a member of and regularly attend a Church, which is structured and functions absolutely in accordance with the Will of God.

(11) Teaching of Jesus - The inner Purity of Mankind is not Spiritually Defiled by that which is consumed, but that which <u>comes out of the mouth</u>

References: MATTHEW 15:11, MATTHEW 15:18-20, MARK 7:15

(12) Warning of Jesus - Plants not planted by God, the Father, shall be rooted up

Stern warnings against **(a) preaching of the false doctrines of men (b) blindly following such teachings without question**

Reference: MATTHEW 15:13-14

(13) Miracle - Faith of a woman, results in Jesus eliminating a demon from her daughter

Locality: **Tyre**

References: MATTHEW 15:21-28, MARK 7:24-30

(14) Multitude marvels at the healings of Jesus

Reference: MATTHEW 15:29-31

(15) Miracle - Jesus heals deaf man

Reference: MARK 7:31-37

(16) Miracle - Jesus feeds the 4,000

Locality: **Possibly Gennesart**

References: MATTHEW 15:32-39, MARK 8:1-10

(17) Pharisees seek a sign in the sky

References: MATTHEW 16:1-4, MARK 8:10-13

(18) Warning of Jesus - false teachings

References: MATTHEW 16:5-12, MARK 8:14-21

(19) Miracle - The Blind Man is cured in Bethesda

Reference: MARK 8:22-26

(20) The Great Confession - Peter Confesses That Jesus Is the Christ, is the Son of the living God

Key Passage: MATTHEW 16:15-18 "He saith unto them, But whom say ye that I am? And Simon Peter answered and said, **Thou art the Christ, the Son of the living God.** And Jesus answered and said unto him, Blessed art thou, Simon Bar-jona: for flesh and blood hath not revealed it unto thee, but my Father which is in heaven. And I say also unto thee, That thou art Peter, and **upon this rock I will build my church;** and the gates of hell shall not prevail against it."

Location: **Caesarea Philippi**

References: MATTHEW 16:13-20, MARK 8:27-30, LUKE 9:18-20

(21) Prediction of Jesus - predicts His death - first time

References: MATTHEW 16:2, MARK 8:31

(22) Jesus rebukes Peter

References: MATTHEW 16:22-23, MARK 8:32-33

(23) Teaching of Jesus - take up your cross and follow me

References: MATTHEW 16:24-27, MARK 8:34-38, LUKE 9:23-26

(24) Prediction of Jesus - Some of you will live to see the beginning of My Kingdom (Church)

Fulfillment: Act 2:14-42

References: MATTHEW 16:28, MARK 9:1, LUKE 9:27

(25) Miracle - The Transfiguration of Jesus

Locality: **Possibly Mount Hermon, near Caesarea Philippi**

Probable Date: **Summer, AD 29**

The Transfiguration and the appearance of Moses and Elijah were a mighty display of the unlimited Power and immense Glory of God.

It is difficult to imagine the appearance of Jesus when He was transfigured.

The Gospel writers speak of His face becoming bright like the sun, and of His clothes being dazzling white.

Jesus warns His apostles not to relate what they had seen until He had been risen from the dead.

In the following passage the great apostle cites the Transfiguration as historical proof of the Truth of the Gospel of Christ.

2 PETER 1:16-18
For we have not followed cunningly devised fables, when we made known unto you the power and coming of our Lord Jesus Christ, but were eyewitnesses of his majesty. For he received from God the Father honor and glory, when there came such a voice to him from the excellent glory, **This is my beloved Son, in whom I am well pleased.** And this voice which came from heaven we heard, when we were with him in the holy mount.

References: MATTHEW 17:1-13, MARK 9:2-13, LUKE 9:28-36

(26) Elijah was discussed while descending; Jesus discloses that Elijah had already returned in the person of John the Baptist.

This was a reference to: Malachi 4:5 "Behold, I will send you Elijah the prophet before the coming of the great and dreadful day of the LORD:"

References: MATTHEW 17:9-13, MARK 9:9-13

(27) Miracle - A demon is cast out of a boy

References: MATTHEW 17:14-18, MARK 9:14-27, LUKE 9:37-42

(28) The Disciples ask why they were unable to cast out the demon

Answer: Lack of faith, if your faith was the size of a mustard seed, [a very small seed] you could move mountains.

References: MATTHEW 17:19-21, MARK 9:28-29

(29) Predictions of Jesus - predicted treachery, His Death and Resurrection

Locality: **Galilee**

References: MATTHEW 17:22-23, MARK 9:30-32, LUKE 9:43-45

(30) Miracle - The Temple Tax - coin in mouth of a fish

Locality: **Capernaum**

Reference: MATTHEW 17:24-27

(31) Disciples contend as to which shall be the greatest in the Kingdom of the Messiah

Locality: **Capernaum**

References: MATTHEW 18:1-5, MARK 9:33-37, LUKE 9:46-48

(32) John forbids another to use the name of Jesus, is rebuked

References: MARK 9:38-41, LUKE 9:49-50

(33) Warnings of Jesus - Temptation

References: MATTHEW 18:7-9, MARK 9:43-50

(34) Parable of Jesus - the Lost Sheep

Message: God has great love for all mankind and there is great joy in Heaven when one sinner repents.

References: MATTHEW 18:11-14, LUKE 15:11-32

(35) Teaching of Jesus - Church Discipline

Reference: MATTHEW 18:15-17

(36) Instructions of Jesus - to His Apostles

Reference: MATTHEW 18:18-19

(37) Promise of Jesus

To be with us, whenever we gather in His name

Reference: MATTHEW 18:20

(38) Teaching of Jesus - Forgiveness

Reference: MATTHEW 18:21-22

(39) Parable of Jesus - the Unmerciful Servant

Locality: **Capernaum**

Message: Christians must be forgiving or merciful in order to be forgiven.

Forgiveness is one of the marks of a faithful follower and *an absolute requirement to be invited to enter the Gates of Heaven.*

Reference: MATTHEW 18:23-35

H. Later Judean Ministry

(1) Jesus travels to Jerusalem in secret

Probable Date: **Fall, AD 29**

Reference: JOHN 7:10

(2) Feast of Tabernacles

Locality: **Jerusalem**

Reference: JOHN 7:2

(3) Many Jews sought Jesus, but feared to speak openly due to the intimidation of the Jewish Leaders

Reference: JOHN 7:11-13

(4) Jesus teaches openly in the Temple during the feast

Reference: JOHN 7:14-15

(5) Many believe on Him

Reference: JOHN 7:31

(6) Pharisees conspire to seize Jesus, dispatch officers to arrest Him

Reference: JOHN 7:32-36

(7) Division among the people

Reference: JOHN 7:40-44

(8) Officers find no fault, decline to arrest Jesus, Pharisees question officers

Reference: JOHN 7:45-49

(9) Question of Nicodemus, who had previously visited Jesus under the cover of darkness

Reference: JOHN 7:50-51

(10) Observation of Nicodemus

Reference: JOHN 7:52

(11) Jesus retires to the Mount of Olives

Reference: JOHN 8:1

(12) Jesus begins to teach in the Temple early in the following morning

Reference: JOHN 8:2

(13) Scribes and Pharisees bring an adulterous woman, caught in the act, to Jesus

Locality: **Jerusalem**

Reference: JOHN 8:3-6

(14) Teaching of Jesus - Let him that is without sin cast the first stone

Key passage: JOHN 8:7 "So when they continued asking him, he lifted up himself, and said unto them, **"He that is without sin among you, let him first cast a stone at her"**

Reference: JOHN 8:7-11

(15) Teaching of Jesus - I am the Light of the World - sent by God, the Father

Reference: JOHN 8:12-30

(16) Teaching of Jesus - Spiritual Freedom

Key passage: JOHN 8:32 **"And ye shall know the truth, and the truth shall make you free"**.

Reference: JOHN 8:31-36

(17) Miracle - Jesus heals man born blind

Reference: JOHN 9:1-7

(18) Parable of Jesus - Christ is the Good Shepherd

Locality: **Jerusalem**

Message: **Jesus is the only Way to the Father**

Reference: JOHN 10:1-18

(19) Returns to Galilee; makes His final departure

Reference: LUKE 9:51

(20) Samaritan village rejects Jesus

Locality: **Samaria**

Reference: LUKE 9:52-53

I. Perean Ministry

(1) Seventy are sent out 2 by 2

Locality: **Perea,**

Probable Date: **November, AD 29**

Reference: LUKE 10:1-16

(2) The Seventy joyously return

Reference: LUKE 10:17-20

(3) Jesus Rejoices

Reference: LUKE 10:21-22

(4) Jesus privately blesses the Twelve

Reference: LUKE 10:23-24

(5) Lawyer tests Jesus

Reference: LUKE 10:25-29

(6) Parable of Jesus - the Good Samaritan

Locality: **Perea**

Message: **All men and women are our neighbors; all are directed to follow the golden rule**

Reference: LUKE 10:29-37

(7) Visit to Martha and Mary, Martha serves while Mary listens, Martha

requested Jesus to direct Mary to assist, Jesus declines

Locality: **Bethany**

Reference: LUKE 10:38-42

(8) Parable of Jesus - Friend at Midnight or Three Loaves

Message: Importance of proper prayer

Reference: LUKE 11:1-13

(9) Miracle - demon cast out of mute man

Reference: LUKE 11:14

(10) Immediately Jesus is accused of being in league with Beelzebub and is asked to provide a Sign from Heaven

Locality: **Perea**

Reference: LUKE 11:15-16

(11) Teaching of Jesus - demons

Reference: LUKE 11:17-26

(12) Woman blesses His mother - Jesus corrects her, saying blessed are those who hear and keep the Word of God

Reference: LUKE 11:27-28

(13) Sign of Jonah

Reference: LUKE 11:29-32

(14) Teaching of Jesus - the light of the body

Reference: LUKE 11:33-36

(15) Jesus dined with a Pharisee; fails to wash His hands

Locality: **Perea**

Reference: LUKE 11:37-38

(16) Jesus declares great woe (wretchedness) upon the Pharisees and lawyers

Reference: LUKE 11:39-52

(17) Pharisees, scribes and lawyers conspire against Jesus

Reference: LUKE 11:53-54

(18) Teaching of Jesus - teaches a great multitude regarding the deception or leaven of the Pharisees

Reference: LUKE 12:1-12

(19) Warning of Jesus - greed and covetousness

Reference: LUKE 12:13-15

(20) Parable of Jesus - Rich Fool

Message: Foolish reliance on worldly wealth

Reference: LUKE 12:16-21

(21) Teaching of Jesus - Trust in God for daily needs - layup treasure in Heaven

Reference: LUKE 12:22-34

(22) Parable of Jesus - Watchful Servant

Message: Watch for His Second Coming

Reference: LUKE 12:35-40

(23) Parable of Jesus - Wise Steward

Locality: **Perea**

Message: His Second Coming

Reference: LUKE 12:42-59

(24) Galileans slain by Pilate reported to Jesus

Reference: LUKE 13:1-5

(25) Parable of Jesus - the Barren Fig Tree

Message: Danger of disbelief among the Jewish people

Reference: LUKE 13:6-9

(26) Miracle - Woman with twisted back healed on the Sabbath in a synagogue

Locality: **Perea**

Reference: LUKE 13:10-13

(27) Synagogue ruler clashes with Jesus

Reference: LUKE 13:14-17

(28) Jesus Teaches as He journeys toward Jerusalem

Reference: LUKE 13:22

(29) The Pharisees warn Jesus regarding Herod

Reference: LUKE 13:31-33

(30) Jesus expressed concern and sorrow for Jerusalem

References: MATTHEW 23:37-39, LUKE 13:34-35

J. Culmination of His Miracles and Teachings

(1) The Feast of Dedication in the Temple

Locality: **Jerusalem**

Reference: JOHN 10:22-23

(2) Jesus declares that He is one with God, the Father

Reference: JOHN 10:30

(3) Jews confront Christ; they attempt to stone Him, He escapes

References: JOHN 10:31, JOHN 10:39

(4) Jesus retires beyond Jordan

Reference: JOHN 10:40-42

(5) On the Sabbath Jesus went to house of Chief Pharisee to eat bread

Locality: **Perea**

Reference: LUKE 14:1

(6) Miracle - Jesus heals a man suffering Dropsy

Reference: LUKE 14:2-6

(7) Parable of Jesus - the Wedding Guest

Message: Humility

Reference: LUKE 14:7-11

(8) Parable of Jesus - the Great Banquet

Message: Do not allow earthly concerns to take priority over spiritual matters

Reference: LUKE 14:15-24

(9) Jesus eats with publicans (tax collectors) and sinners

Locality: **Perea**

Reference: LUKE 15:1-2

(10) Parable of Jesus - Lost Coin

Message: Great love of our Father in Heaven for the lost, which is to be the pattern for all Christians.

Reference: LUKE 15:8-10

(11) Parable of Jesus - Prodigal Son

Message: Same as the Lost Coin

Reference: LUKE 15:11-32

(12) Parable of Jesus - Unjust Steward

Message: Use care and prudence in handling power, property or assets

Reference: LUKE 16:1-15

(13) Teaching of Jesus - Divorce and Adultery

Reference: LUKE 16:18

(14) Parable of Jesus - Rich Man and Lazarus

Locality: **Perea**

Message: (a) Importance of repentance (b) importance of understanding and following the Word of God (c) the realty of hell (d) the care for the faithful in death

Reference: LUKE 16:19-31

(15) Jesus instructs His Disciples in faith and service

Reference: LUKE 17:1-6

(16) Parable of Jesus - the Unprofitable Servant

Message: When all that is commanded is accomplished a servant has done no more than that which was expected. Any reward received is due to grace, not merit

Reference: LUKE 17:7-10

(17) Miracle - Raising Lazarus from the dead

Locality: **Bethany**

Reference: JOHN 11:1-44

(18) Many Jews who witnessed Miracle believed on Jesus

Reference: JOHN 11:45

(19) Unbelievers reported to the Pharisees

Reference: JOHN 11:46

(20) High ranking Jewish leaders conspire to slay Jesus

Locality: **Jerusalem**

Reference: JOHN 11:47-53

(21) Aware of their evil intentions, Jesus withdraws to Ephraim

Reference: JOHN 11:54

(22) Miracle - TEN Lepers are cleansed

Locality: **Samaria**

Reference: LUKE 17:11-14

(23) Only ONE returns to praise God and thank Jesus

Reference: LUKE 17:15-19

(24) Pharisees ask about the Kingdom

Locality: **Perea**

Key passage: LUKE 17:21 "Neither shall they say, Lo here! or, lo there! for, **behold, the kingdom of God is within you."**

Reference: LUKE 17:20-21

(25) Teaching of Jesus - the coming Kingdom

Reference: LUKE 17:22-37

(26) Parable of Jesus - the Persistent Widow

Message: Perseverance in Prayer, do not lose heart, pray without ceasing

Reference: LUKE 18:1-8

(27) Parable of Jesus - the Pharisee and the Publican

Locality: **Perea**

Message: Proper form and approach to prayer

Key passage: LUKE 18:13-14 "And the publican, standing afar off, would not lift up so much as his eyes unto heaven, but smote upon his breast, saying, **God be merciful to me a sinner.** I tell you, this man went down to his house justified rather than the other: *for every one that exalteth himself shall be abased; and he that humbleth himself shall be exalted."*

Reference: LUKE 18:9-14

(28) Jesus travels to coast of Judea

References: MATTHEW 19:1, MARK 10:1

(29) Multitudes Follow Jesus

Reference: MATTHEW 19:2

(30) Teaching of Jesus - Marriage

Key passage: MARK 10:7-9 "For this cause shall a man leave his father and mother, and cleave to his wife; And they twain shall be one flesh: so then they are no more twain, but one flesh. **What therefore God hath joined together, let not man put asunder**".

References: MATTHEW 19:3-9, MARK 10:2-9

(31) Christ blessed the little children

Locality: **Perea,**

References: MATTHEW 19:13-15, MARK 10:13-16, LUKE 18:15-17

(32) Young rich ruler

Key passage: MATTHEW 19:22-24 "But when the young man heard that saying, he went away sorrowful: for he had great possessions. Then said Jesus unto his disciples, Verily I say unto you, That a rich man shall hardly enter into the kingdom of heaven."

"And again I say unto you, *It is easier for a camel to go through the eye of a needle, than for a rich man to enter into the kingdom of God.*"

Note: The eye of a needle expression was probably a hyperbole or a dramatic overstatement for effect.

The lesson that the Master was teaching is, the tendency of mankind to hold their wealth very dear. This normal human trait adds an additional barrier that the rich man or woman must overcome in order to gain eternal life, which is the most valuable or the greatest prize of all

MATTHEW 6:24
No man can serve two masters: for either he will hate the one, and love the other; or else he will hold to the one, and despise the other. Ye cannot serve [both] God and mammon.

Therefore the message is:

(a) The rich must put God far ahead of their possessions and use his or her wealth to fulfill His purposes.

(b) Understand that only God can save.

(c) No man can achieve his Salvation solely by his personal efforts, as it is a Gift granted by the Grace of God. However, it is required that we conform to and follow the Commandments, Patterns, Instructions and Examples provided

References: MATTHEW 19:16-26, MARK 10:17-27, LUKE 18:18-27

(33) Disciples will be rewarded

References: MATTHEW 19:27-30, MARK 10:28-31, LUKE 18:28-30

(34) Parable of Christ - Laborers in the Vineyard

Message: Salvation is not related to amount of time spent in the service of the Lord.

Key passage: MATTHEW 20:16 "So the last shall be first, and the first last: **for many be called, but few chosen.**"

Reference: MATTHEW 20:1-16

(35) Jesus predicts His Crucifixion and Resurrection

Locality: **Traveling toward Jerusalem**

References: MATTHEW 20:17-19, MARK 10:32-34, LUKE 18:31-34

(36) Ambitions of James and John in the coming Kingdom

Locality: **Perea,**

Probable Date: **March, AD 30**

References: MATTHEW 20:20-28, MARK 10:35-45

(37) Miracle - Bartimeus & his companion regain their sight

Locality: **Jericho,**

Key Passage: LUKE 18:42-43 "And Jesus said unto him, *Receive thy sight: thy faith hath saved thee. And immediately he received his sight, and followed him, glorifying God:* and all the people, when they saw it, gave praise unto God."

References: MATTHEW 20:29-34, MARK 10:46-52, LUKE 18:35-43

(38) Conversion of Zaccheus

Locality: **Jericho**

Key Passage: LUKE 19:10 "For the Son of man is come **to seek and to save that which was lost.**"

Reference: LUKE 19:1-10

(39) Parable of Jesus - the Minas or Pounds

Locality: **Traveling toward Jerusalem**

Message: Faithful, productive service until the Lord returns

Reference: LUKE 19:11-28

(40) Hostility within the Sanhedrin

Locality: **Jerusalem**

Reference: JOHN 11:55-57

(41) Jesus arrives in Bethany

Reference: JOHN 12:1

(42) Dines with Martha, Mary & Lazarus, Mary anoints Jesus

Locality: **Bethany**

Probable Date: **Saturday, April 1, AD 30**

Key passage: JOHN 12:3 "Then took Mary a pound of ointment of spikenard, very costly, and anointed the feet of Jesus, and wiped his feet with her hair: and the house was filled with the odor [fragrance] of the ointment."

References: MATTHEW 26:6-13, MARK 14:3-9, JOHN 12:2-8,

(43) Large throng comes to see Jesus and Lazarus

Locality: **Bethany**

Reference: JOHN 12:9

(44) The Chief Priests conspire to exterminate Lazarus

Locality: **Jerusalem**

Reference: JOHN 12:10-11

(45) Two Disciples locate ass and a colt the foal of an ass

Messianic Prophecy fulfilled: DANIEL 9:25 **Jesus would present Himself as King**

References: MATTHEW 21:1-7, MARK 11:1-7, LUKE 19:29-35

K. The Final Days of Jesus in Jerusalem

(1) Triumphal Entry into Jerusalem, Followers express great Adulation and Joy

Locality: **Jerusalem**

Messianic Prophecy fulfilled: ZECHARIAH 9:9 **Jesus would enter Jerusalem as King on a donkey**

Probable Date: **Sunday, April 2, AD 30**

Key passage: MATTHEW 21:8-9 "And a very great multitude spread their garments in the way; others cut down branches from the trees, and strewed them in the way. And the multitudes that went before, **and that followed, cried, saying, Hosanna to the son of David: Blessed is he that cometh in the name of the Lord; Hosanna in the highest."**

References: MATTHEW 21:8-11, MARK 11:8-10, LUKE 19:36-38, JOHN 12:12-18

(2) Response of Pharisees

References: LUKE 19:39-40. JOHN 12:19

(3) Jesus wept for Jerusalem

Reference: LUKE 19:41-44

(4) In the evening, Jesus and the Twelve return to Bethany

Reference: MARK 11:11

(5) The following morning, Jesus Cursed a Fig Tree

Probable Date: **Monday, April 3, AD 30**

References: MATTHEW 21:18-19, MARK 11:12-14

(6) Second Temple Cleansing

Locality: **Jerusalem**

Messianic Prophecy fulfilled: MALACHI 3:1 **Jesus would cleanse the Temple**

Key passage: MATTHEW 21:13 "And said unto them, It is written, (ISAIAH 56:7) **My house shall be called the house of prayer;** but ye have made it a den of thieves".

References: MATTHEW 21:12-13, MARK 11:15-17, LUKE 19:45-46

(7) Miracles - Jesus healed many blind and lame

Locality: **Temple in Jerusalem**

Reference: MATTHEW 21:14

(8) The Jewish Leaders seek to eliminate Jesus

References: MATTHEW 21:15, MARK 11:18, LUKE 19:47

(9) Jesus retires to Bethany for the night

Reference: MATTHEW 21:17

(10) Miracle - Fig Tree Withers

Probable Date: **Tuesday, April 4, AD 30**

Key passage: MARK 11:23 "For verily I say unto you, That whosoever shall say unto this mountain, Be thou removed, and be thou cast into the sea; and **shall not doubt in his heart, but shall believe that those things which he saith shall come to pass; he shall have whatsoever he saith.**"

References: MATTHEW 21:20-22, MARK 11:20-26

(11) Authority of Jesus challenged

References: MATTHEW 21:23-27, MARK 11:27-33, LUKE 20:1-8

(12) Parable of Jesus - the Two Sons

Message: **Importance of actually doing the Will of God and not just simply discussing His Will.**

Reference: MATTHEW 21:28-32

(13) Parable of Jesus - the Wicked Tenants

Message: **God often bestows wonderful blessings. If blessings are improperly employed, may be removed or penalties may be imposed.**

References: MATTHEW 21:33-46, MARK 12:1-12, LUKE 20:9-18

(14) Parable of Jesus - the Wedding Feast

Message: Each of us has been blessed with an invitation to the wedding feast of His son, but we must be properly attired in order to attend by:**(1) putting on Christ (2) putting on a new man or woman by developing a Christian character and (3) perform righteous acts to the Glory of God**

Reference: MATTHEW 22:1-14

(15) Pharisees query Jesus about paying taxes to Caesar

Locality: **Jerusalem**

Key passage: MATTHEW 22:21 "They say unto him, Caesar's. Then saith he unto them, **Render therefore unto Caesar the things which are Caesar's; and unto God the things that are God's.**"

References: MATTHEW 22:15-22, MARK 12:13-17, LUKE 20:19-26

(16) Sadducees inquiry regarding the Resurrection

Key passage: MATTHEW 22:30 "For in the resurrection they neither marry, nor are given in marriage, but are as the angels of God in heaven."

References: MATTHEW 22:23-33, MARK 12:18-27, LUKE 20:27-38

(17) Pharisees question Jesus regarding the Greatest Commandment

Key passage: MATTHEW 22:37-40 "Jesus said unto him, **Thou shalt love the Lord thy God with all thy heart, and with all thy soul, and with all thy mind.** This is the first and great commandment. And the second is like unto it, **Thou shalt love thy neighbor as thyself.** On these two commandments hang all the law and the prophets."

References: MATTHEW 22:34-40, MARK 12:28-34

(18) Jesus asks Pharisees about ancestry

References: MATTHEW 22:41-46, MARK 12:35-37, LUKE 20:41-44

(19) Woes upon Scribes and Pharisees - Hypocrites

References: MATTHEW 23:1-39, MARK 12:38-40, LUKE 20:45-47

(20) Widow's mite

Key passage: MARK 12:44 "For all they did cast in of their abundance; **but she of her want did cast in all that she had,** even all her living." (Many gave of their funds, but this widow gave all)

References: MARK 12:41-44, LUKE 21:1-4

(21) Disciples admire the Temple, Jesus predicts Total Destruction

References: MATTHEW 24:1-2, MARK 13:1-2

(22) Disciples question Jesus

References: MATTHEW 24:3, MARK 13:3-4

(23) Jesus warns of future difficulties

References: MATTHEW 24:4-14, MARK 13:5-13, LUKE 21:8-19

(24) Jesus predicts fall of Jerusalem

Locality: **Jerusalem**

References: MATTHEW 24:15-28, MARK 13:14-23, LUKE 21:20-24

(25) Teaching of Jesus - His Second Coming

References: MATTHEW 24:27-31, MARK 13:24-27, LUKE 21:25-28

(26) Parable of Jesus - the Fig Tree

Message: Watch for the Second Coming of Christ

References: MATTHEW 24:32-33, MARK 13:28-29, LUKE 21:29-31

(27) Warning of Jesus - Be Watchful

Key passage: LUKE 21:33 **"Heaven and earth shall pass away: but my words shall not pass away."**

References: MATTHEW 24:34-51, MARK 13:30-37, LUKE 21:32-36

(28) Parable of Jesus - the Ten Virgins

Message: Diligently prepare for His Second Coming, heeding the call to grow in grace and knowledge. Understand that He is coming and live accordingly.

Reference: MATTHEW 25:1-13

(29) Parable of Jesus - the Talents

Message: Make productive use of the **abilities** and **opportunities** God has **granted** and **continuously press on to greater accomplishments.**

Reference: MATTHEW 25:14-30

(30) Warning of Jesus - regarding the Judgment

Key passage: MATTHEW 25:46 **"And these shall go away into everlasting punishment: but the righteous into life eternal."**

Reference: MATTHEW 25:31-46

(31) Jesus predicts the Day of His Crucifixion

Reference: MATTHEW 26:1-2

(32) Greeks request meeting with Jesus

Reference: JOHN 12:20-22

(33) Final Appeal to Unbelievers

Key passage: JOHN 12:48 48 "He that rejecteth me, and receiveth not my words, hath one that judgeth him: **the word that I have spoken, the same shall judge him in the last day."**

Reference: JOHN 12:23-50

(34) Plot to take the Life of Jesus, unfolds

Probable Date: **Wednesday, April 5, AD 30**

References: MATTHEW 26:3-5, MARK 14:1-2, LUKE 22:1-22

(35) Jesus retires to Bethany for the day and is anointed

References: MATTHEW 26:6-13, MARK 14:3-9

(36) Judas bargains to betray Jesus, for Thirty Pieces of Silver.

Messianic Prophecies fulfilled:
ZECHARIAH 11:12 Sold for 30 pieces of

silver, PSALM 22:7-8 Jesus betrayed by friend

References: MATTHEW 26:14-16, MARK 14:10-11, LUKE 22:3-6

L. His Last day with His Apostles

(1) Peter and John prepare for Passover

Locality: **Jerusalem**

Probable Date: **Thursday, April 6, AD 30**

References: MATTHEW 26:17-19, MARK 14:12-16, LUKE 22:7-13

(2) Fellowship in the Upper Room

Locality: **Jerusalem**

References: MATTHEW 26:20, MARK 14:17, LUKE 22:14

(3) Jesus washes the Disciples feet

Reference: JOHN 13:1-20

(4) Identity of traitor revealed

References: MATTHEW 26:21, MARK 14:18-21, JOHN 13:21-30

(5) Jesus institutes the Lord's Supper

Key Passage: MATTHEW 26:29-28 "And as they were eating, **Jesus took bread,** and blessed it, and broke it, and gave it to the disciples, and said, **Take, eat; this is my body. And he took the cup,** and gave thanks, and gave it to them, saying, Drink ye all of it; **For this is my blood of the new testament, which is shed for many for the remission of sins."**

References: MARK 14:22-25, LUKE 22:15-20, 1 CORINTHIANS 11:23-26

(6) A new Commandment

Reference: JOHN 13:34-35

(7) Contention as to who is the Greatest Disciple

Reference: LUKE 22:24-30

(8) Jesus warns Peter and tells of His Prayer for him

Reference: LUKE 22:31-32

(9) Jesus predicted the Denial of the Disciples

References: MATTHEW 26:31-32, MARK 14:27-28

(10) Jesus predicted Denials of Peter

References: MATTHEW 26:33-35, MARK 14:29-31, LUKE 22:33-34, JOHN 13:36-38

(11) Jesus advised his Disciples to prepare

Reference: LUKE 22:35-38

(12) Jesus comforted the Disciples

Reference: JOHN 14:1-4

(13) Response to Thomas

Key passage: JOHN 14:6 "Jesus saith unto him, **"I am the way, the truth, and the life: no man cometh unto the Father, but by me."**

Reference: JOHN 14:5-7

(14) Response to Philip

Key passage: JOHN 14:15 **"If ye love me, keep my commandments."**

Reference: JOHN 14:8-15

(15) Promise of Jesus - the Holy Spirit

Reference: JOHN 14:16-18

(16) Jesus responds to Judas (not Iscariot)

Reference: JOHN 14:22-31

(17) Farewell Discourse (Vine and Branches)

Messianic Prophecy fulfilled: PSALMS 69:4

Reference: JOHN 15:1-16

(18) Jesus prays for His Disciples

Reference: JOHN 17:1-26

(19) The assemblage sang a hymn

Reference: MATTHEW 26:30

(20) Garden of Gethsemane

Locality: **Mount of Olives**

References: MATTHEW 26:36, MARK 14:32-33, LUKE 22:39-40, JOHN 18:1

(21) Jesus, in agony, prayed in Gethsemane

References: MATTHEW 26:37-46, MARK 14:34-42, LUKE 22:41-46

(22) Rabble approached to arrest Jesus

References: MATTHEW 26:47, MARK 14:43, JOHN 18:2-3

(23) Judas betrayed Jesus with a kiss

References: MATTHEW 26:48-50, MARK 14:44-45, LUKE 22:47-48

(24) Jesus answered the horde

Reference: JOHN 18:4-9

(25) Peter wounded Malchus

References: MATTHEW 26:51-54, MARK 14:46-47, LUKE 22:49-50, JOHN 18:10-11

(26) Jesus healed Malchus

Reference: LUKE 22:51

M. The Final Day of His earthly Life

(1) Jesus is arrested - His Disciples flee

Probable Time & Date: **past midnight, Friday, April 7, AD 30**

Messianic Prophecy fulfilled: ZECHARIAH 13:7 (MARK 14:50)

References: MATTHEW 26:55-56, MARK 14:48-52, LUKE 22:52-53, JOHN 18:12

(2) Jesus taken to the palace of Annas, a High Priest

Locality: **Jerusalem**

Messianic Prophecy fulfilled: PSALMS 38:11

References: MATTHEW 26:57, MARK 14:53, LUKE 22:54, JOHN 18:13-14

(3) Peter followed at a distance

References: MATTHEW 26:58, MARK 14:54, LUKE 22:54, JOHN 18:15-16

(4) Peter's first Denial - damsel at the door of palace

References: MATTHEW 26:69-70, MARK 14:66-68, LUKE 22:55-57, JOHN 18:17-18

(5) Peter's second Denial - maid by the fire on porch

References: MATTHEW 26:71-72, MARK 14:69-70, LUKE 22:58, JOHN 18:25

(6) Peter's third Denial - relative of Malchus

References: MATTHEW 26:73-75, MARK 14:71-72, LUKE 22:59-62, JOHN 18:26-27

(7) Immediately the Cock Crowed, Peter remembered the Words of Jesus and wept bitterly

Reference: MATTHEW 26:74-75

(8) Annas questions Jesus, officer strikes Him

References: JOHN 18:12-14, JOHN 18:19-23

(9) Jesus taken to Caiaphas, in the Sanhedrin

Reference: JOHN 18:24

(10) Sanhedrin guards mock and beat Jesus

References: MATTHEW 26:67-68, MARK 14:65, LUKE 22:63-65

(11) False witnesses testify

Messianic Prophecy fulfilled: PSALMS 35:11; 20-21

References: MATTHEW 26:59-61, MARK 14:55-59

(12) Caiaphas, High Priest questions Jesus

Locality: **Jerusalem**

References: MATTHEW 26:62-66, MARK 14:60-64

(13) Council of religious leaders condemn Jesus to death

References: MATTHEW 27:1, MARK 15:1, LUKE 22:66-71

(14) Jesus was bound and delivered to Pontius Pilate

References: MATTHEW 27:2, LUKE 23:1

(15) The remorse and suicide of Judas Iscariot

Messianic Prophecy fulfilled: ZECHARIAH 11:13 - MATTHEW 27:5; 7-8 **30 pieces thrown in the temple, silver used by priests to purchase a potter's field**

Reference: MATTHEW 27:3-10

(16) Jesus first hearing before Pilate, offered no defense, remained silent

Locality: **Jerusalem**

Probable Time & Date: **6 A.M., Friday, April 7, AD 30**

Messianic Prophecy fulfilled: ISAIAH 53:7 Jesus remained silent before accusers

Key Passage: JOHN 18:36-37, "My kingdom is not of this world: Thou sayest that I am a king. To this end was I born, and for this cause came **I into the world, that I should bear witness unto the truth.**"

References: MATTHEW 27:11-14, MARK 15:2-5, LUKE 23:2-7, JOHN 18:29-38

(17) Pilate refers Jesus to Herod Antipas

Reference: LUKE 23:6-12

(18) Soldiers of Herod mock Jesus

Reference: LUKE 23:11

(19) It was the custom for the Governor to release one Jewish prisoner during the Passover feast

Reference: MATTHEW 27:15

(20) Pilate offers the assembled Jewish throng a choice of either Jesus or Barabbas, a brutal criminal

Reference: MATTHEW 27:16-17

(21) Jesus before Pilate a second time, releases Barabbas

Key Passage: MATTHEW 27:26 "Then released he Barabbas unto them: **and when he had scourged Jesus, he delivered him to be crucified."**

References: MATTHEW 27:20, MARK 15:6-15, LUKE 23:13-25, JOHN 18:39-40,

(22) Jesus severely beaten, which likely hastened His death

Messianic Prophecy fulfilled: ISAIAH 52:14

Reference: MATTHEW 27:26

(23) Soldiers dressed Jesus in a scarlet robe placed a Crown of Thorns on His head, spit upon and mocked Him.

Messianic Prophecy fulfilled: ISAIAH 50:6 Jesus was mocked and spit upon

References: MATTHEW 27:27-30, MARK 15:17-20, JOHN 19:1-3

(24) Pilate attempts to release Jesus

Reference: JOHN 19:4-7

(25) Pilate questioned and pleaded with Jesus again

Reference: JOHN 19:8-11

(26) The wife of Pilate warned him that Jesus was faultless and complained that Jesus had caused her great suffering in a dream

Reference: MATTHEW 27:19

(27) Pilate attempts to release Jesus a second time; the Jews expressed great resistance and demanded that He be crucified.

Messianic Prophecy fulfilled: ISAIAH 53:3 **Jesus was rejected by His own people**

References: MATTHEW 27:22-23, JOHN 19:12-15

(28) Pilate washes his hands of the whole affair

Reference: MATTHEW 27:22

(29) Pilate delivered Him to Roman soldiers to be crucified

Probable Time & Date: **8 A.M., Friday, April 7, AD 30**

Reference: JOHN 19:16

(30) His clothing was returned, soldiers lead the way to the place of the skull or Golgotha (Hebrew) aka Calvary (Greek), Jesus was forced to carry His Cross

References: MATTHEW 27:31, JOHN 19:17

(31) Probably due to the loss of blood, from the severe beating, Jesus was unable to continue, Simon of Cyrene compelled to bear the Cross.

References: MATTHEW 27:32, MARK 15:21, LUKE 23:26

(32) Jesus Warns the Weeping Women

Reference: LUKE 23:27-31

(33) Jesus is led to Calvary

Locality: **Near Jerusalem**

References: MATTHEW 27:33, MARK 15:22, LUKE 23:33

(34) Soldiers offered Jesus wine mingled with myrrh (vinegar and gall), He declined

Messianic Prophecy fulfilled: PSALMS 22:18, PSALMS 69:21

References: MATTHEW 27:34, MARK 15:23

(35) His crucifixion ordeal began at the third hour or 9 a.m., His hands and feet were pierced

Probable Time & Date: **9 A.M., Friday, April 7, 30 AD**

Messianic Prophecy fulfilled: PSALMS 22:16

Reference: MARK 15:25

(36) Soldiers cast lots for His garments

Messianic Prophecy fulfilled: PSALMS 22:18

References: MATTHEW 27:35-36, MARK 15:24, LUKE 23:34, JOHN 19:23-24

(37) Jesus crucified with two thieves, one right and left

Messianic Prophecy fulfilled: ISAIAH 53:12

References: MATTHEW 27:38, MARK 15:27, LUKE 23:32, JOHN 19:18

(38) Inscription on Cross of Jesus "JESUS OF NAZARETH THE KING OF THE JEWS" written in Hebrew, Greek and Latin

References: MARK 15:26, LUKE 23:38, JOHN 19:19-22

(39) His first words from the Cross: "Father, forgive them; for they know not what they do"

Messianic Prophecy fulfilled: ISAIAH 53:12

Reference: LUKE 23:34

(40) Citizens, priests, scribes and elders mock Jesus, wagged heads and stared

Messianic Prophecies fulfilled: PSALMS 22:7, PSALMS 109:25 **wagged heads** PSALMS 22:17 **stared**

References: MATTHEW 27:39-43, MARK 15:29-32, LUKE 23:35-37

(41) Jesus speaking to John and Mary from the Cross, "Woman, behold thy son! Behold thy mother!"

Reference: JOHN 19:25-27

(42) Thieves mocked Jesus

References: MATTHEW 27:44, MARK 15:32, LUKE 23:39

(43) One Thief rebuked the other

Reference: LUKE 23:40-42

(44) Jesus comforts the Thief "Today shalt thou be with me in paradise."

Probable Time & Date: **noon, Friday, April 7, AD 30**

Reference: LUKE 23:43

(45) Darkness covers the land for three hours

Probable Time & Date: **3 P.M., Friday, April 7, AD 30**

Messianic Prophecy fulfilled: AMOS 8:9

References: MATTHEW 27:45, MARK 15:33, LUKE 23:44

(46) The Temple Veil torn from top to bottom and the earth did quake

References: MATTHEW 27:51, MARK 15:38, LUKE 23:45

(47) Jesus cried in a loud voice "My God, my God, why hast thou forsaken me?"

Messianic Prophecy fulfilled: PSALMS 22:1

References: MATTHEW 27:46, MARK 15:34,

(48) Jesus called out from the cross "I thirst"

Messianic Prophecy fulfilled: PSALMS 22:15

Reference: JOHN 19:28

(49) Jesus is offered vinegar on a reed

References: MATTHEW 27:47-48, MARK 15:35-36, JOHN 19:29

(50) When Jesus had received the vinegar, He said, "Father, into thy hands I commend my spirit" and gave up the ghost (His Spirit).

Messianic Prophecy fulfilled: PSALMS 31:5
Jesus committed Himself to God, the Father

References: MATTHEW 27:50, MARK 15:37, LUKE 23:46, JOHN 19:30

(51) Soldier pierced His side with a spear

Messianic Prophecy fulfilled: ZECHARIAH 12:10

Reference: JOHN 19:34

(52) Jewish leaders requested Pilate to have His legs broken, so Jesus would die. The soldiers broke the legs of the thieves, but did not break His legs since He was already dead.

Messianic Prophecy fulfilled: PSALMS 22:15

Reference: JOHN 19:31-33

(53) A centurion who had been observing Jesus and the events surrounding His death becomes convinced that He is the Son of God

References: MATTHEW 27:54, MARK 15:39, LUKE 23:47

(54) The multitude departed grieving

Reference: LUKE 23:48

(55) Female followers observed from afar

Messianic Prophecy fulfilled: PSALMS 38:11

References: MATTHEW 27:55-56, MARK 15:40-41, LUKE 23:49

(56) Joseph of Arimathaea begged Pilate for His Body

References: MATTHEW 27:57-58, MARK 15:42-43, LUKE 23:50-52

(57) A centurion reported to Pilate - Jesus is dead

Reference: MARK 15:44-45

(58) Joseph of Arimathaea transported the body of Jesus to the tomb

Reference: JOHN 19:38

(59) Nicodemus and Joseph prepared the body of Jesus

Probable Time & Date: **6 P.M., Friday, April 7, AD 30**

Reference: JOHN 19:39-40

(60) The Body of Jesus is laid in a new garden tomb, originally prepared for Joseph of Arimathaea

Locality: **Gethsemane**

Messianic Prophecy fulfilled: ISAIAH 53:9

References: MATTHEW 27:59-60, MARK 15:46, LUKE 23:53, JOHN 19:41-42

(61) Mary Magdalene and Mary, mother of Joses watch the burial

References: MATTHEW 27:61, MARK 15:47

(62) Roman soldiers are posted to guard the tomb

Reference: MATTHEW 27:62-66

(63) Mary Magdalene and Mary the mother of Joses prepare spices

Reference: LUKE 23:56

(64) Angel rolls the stone away

Reference: MATTHEW 28:2-4

(65) Mary Magdalene and Mary the mother of Joses bring spices to the tomb

References: MATTHEW 28:1, MARK 16:1-4, LUKE 24:1-3, JOHN 20:1

(66) Passover celebrated

Probable Date: **Saturday April 8, AD 30**

N. His Resurrection

(1) Angel proclaims that HE IS RISEN FROM THE DEAD... to Mary Magdalene, Mary, mother of Joses and others.

Probable Time & Date: **Sunday very early A.M., April 9, AD 30**

Messianic Prophecy fulfilled: PSALMS 16:8-11,

References: MATTHEW 28:5-7, MARK 16:5-7 LUKE 24:4-8,

(2) The women hasten to notify the Disciples

References: MATTHEW 28:8, MARK 16:8, LUKE 24:9-11, JOHN 20:2

(3) Peter and John examine the empty tomb

References: LUKE 24:12, JOHN 20:3-9

(4) Mary Magdalene weeps in confusion

Reference: JOHN 20:11

(5) Mary observed two Angels seated in the tomb

Reference: JOHN 20:12-13

O. His Appearances and related Events

(1) Jesus appears to Mary Magdalene

References: MARK 16:9, JOHN 20:14-17

(2) Jesus appears to the other female followers

Reference: MATTHEW 28:9-10

(3) Mary Magdalene and the other women provided details to the Disciples

References: MARK 16:10-11, JOHN 20:18

(4) Roman soldiers reported disappearance to the Jewish leaders and are bribed by members of the Sanhedrin

Reference: MATTHEW 28:11-15

(5) Unexplained mysterious occurrence - Saints came out of their graves after His resurrection, and went into the Holy City, and appeared unto many.

Locality: **Jerusalem**

Probable Date: **Sunday P.M., April 9, AD 30**

Reference: MATTHEW 27:52-53

(6) Jesus appeared to two followers on road to Emmaus

Locality: **Emmaus, four miles south of Jerusalem**

References: MARK 16:12-13, LUKE 24:13-35

(7) Jesus appears to Peter

References: LUKE 24:34, 1 CORINTHIANS 15:5

(8) Two report to Disciples in Jerusalem

Reference: LUKE 24:33-35

(9) Jesus appears to the Disciples, except Thomas

Locality: **Jerusalem**

Interesting Information

Although the writers of the Gospels did not directly comment, it is clear that the body of Christ had assumed certain SUPERNATURAL qualities, for example in JOHN 20:19, He was able to pass through the wall or locked doors, but he was not a spirit or a phantom, as he was able to eat "a piece of a broiled fish and some honeycomb" (LUKE 24:42).

References: MARK 16:4, LUKE 24:36-45, JOHN 20:19-24

(10) Disciples report to Thomas

Probable Date: **Sunday P.M., April 16, 30 AD**

Reference: JOHN 20:25

(11) Jesus appears to the Disciples, including Thomas

Probable Date: **late April or early May, 30 A.D.**

References: MARK 16:14, JOHN 20:26-29

(12) Jesus appears to seven Disciples

Locality: **Sea of Tiberias aka Sea of Galilee** (JOHN 6:1)

References: MATTHEW 28:16-17, JOHN 21:1-2; 4-5; 14

(13) Miracle - Jesus provides a miraculous catch of fish

Locality: **Sea of Galilee**

Reference: JOHN 21:3-13

(14) Jesus questioned Peter three times, which equals the number of his Denials

Reference: JOHN 21:15-19

(15) Jesus appeared to over 500 People

Reference: 1 CORINTHIANS 15:6

(16) Appeared to James, brother of Jesus, then to all Apostles

Reference: 1 CORINTHIANS 15:6

(17) His final Appearance

Probable Date: **May, 30 AD**

(18) Jesus by providing the Great Commission authorized and commanded His current Disciples and all future followers to continue and expand His Work

Locality: **Mount of Olives**

References: MATTHEW 28:16-20, MARK 16:15-16

(19) Jesus promised His Apostles Divine Support and Assistance

References: MARK 16:17-18, LUKE 24:46-49, ACTS 1:4-8

P. His Ascension to His Father

Jesus led them to Bethany, lifted his hands, blessed them and then ascended into Heaven and began His rule at the right hand of God, the Father

(1) Miracle, His last, while on earth, was the Ascension

Messianic Prophecies fulfilled: PSALMS 68:18, PSALMS 110:1

References: MARK 16:19-20, LUKE 24:50-53, ACTS 1:9-12

Q. Many actions and sayings of Jesus not recorded

(1) Testimony of the Great Apostle John

Key Passages JOHN 20: 30-31, JOHN 21: 24-25

R. From His Ascension to Pentecost

(1) Soon after his Ascension, a company of approximately 120, including His Apostles, Disciples, mother and brethren left the Mount of Olives and returned to Jerusalem.

This Band of Brothers and Sisters, reassembled in the upper room, which is believed to have served as the abode for several followers and others.

Reference: ACTS 1:12-13

(2) Peter called for a replacement for Judas, to be a witness of His resurrection, after a prayer and the casting of lots, Matthias became an Apostle.

Reference: ACTS 1:15-26

(3) They all continued with one accord in prayers and supplication

Reference: ACTS 1:14

(4) His disciples remained in Jerusalem as instructed

Reference: ACTS 1:4-5

S. Divine Involvement and Appearances since His Ascension

(1) Delivered the Holy Spirit on Day of Pentecost

Reference: ACTS 2:1-11

(2) Directed and watched over the dawning of His Church

Reference: ACTS 2:14-40

(3) Added members to His Church

Reference: ACTS 2:41-47

(4) Appeared to Saul near Damascus

Key Passage: ACTS 22:6-16

Additional references: ACTS 9:1-19, ACTS 26:12-18, 1 CORINTHIANS 15:8

(5) Appeared to the Great Apostle John, while he was in exile on the isle of Patmos

Reference: REVELATION 1:9-20

T. Yesterday, today, until He comes again and forever Lord Jesus or the Word of God is God and High Priest

(1) Lord Jesus rules over every Realm of His Creation and His Kingdom or Church.

He adds new members of His Church to the Book of Life, maintains the universe and controls all other aspects of His Kingdom or Church.

(2) As High Priest, Jesus serves as Mediator and intercedes between God, the Father and His flock of faithful followers or Christians, who have submitted fully to His Will and are continuously cleansed of sin by His Precious Blood.

Lord Jesus, as God is far superior to any human priest from the tribe of Levi, since His High Priesthood is after the order of Melchizedek (HEBREWS 6:20) **and will last forever.**

Reference:

[b] Bible History Online **http://www.bible-history.com/geography/ancient-israel/new-testament-cities.htm**

Jesus suffered a horrendous death in order to provide full remission of sin, redemption and everlasting life to all, who would accept these Blessings under the terms of His Divine offer.... Heaven Awaits!

Chapter X

Christ, our ultimate Pattern

Chapter Contents

A. Introduction

B. Christians are to be formed, conformed and transformed

C. Jesus Christ is the complete living Word of God

D. Importance of Fellowship with likeminded Christians

E. Examples of the Teachings of Christ

F. Examples of the Teachings of His Disciples

A. Introduction

(1) He who is the Way shows us the manner of living that enables us to learn to share His Love and enhance our understanding of His Teachings and those of His Disciples.

JOHN 14:6
Jesus saith unto him; I am the way, **the truth, and the life: no man cometh unto the Father, but by me.**

(a) An almost universally accepted vision of Christ is His attitude of meekness or humility and His complete subjection to his Father in Heaven.

Philippians 2:8
And being found in fashion as a man, **he humbled himself,** and became obedient unto death, even the death of the cross.

(2) On the other hand, we must always remember that man we know, as Jesus is also the Supreme Almighty Deity that created all things, including our massive universe.

References: EPHESIANS 3:9, COLOSSIANS 1:16, REVELATION 4:11, REVELATION 10:6

(3) Gaining an understanding of the Message of Christ and the resolution to that sometimes intense longing deep in our being is usually accompanied with a feeling of resentment to the necessity of humbling ourselves in order to accept the gift of salvation. This is a normal reaction.

(a) Salvation is free, but possibly the most difficult requirement is developing a willingness to follow the example of Christ and TRULY HUMBLE ourselves, but we must!

References: JAMES 4:6, JAMES 4:10, 1 PETER 5:5

(b) We accomplish this by simply overcoming our pride, which can be a major stumbling block, just as our Lord did for us.

MATTHEW 11:29
Take my yoke upon you, and learn of me; for I am meek and lowly in heart: and ye shall find rest unto your souls.

"Take my yoke upon you" is a gentle request that we willingly submit to the Will of God.

"Learn of me" means to study His Behavior, His Teachings and how He interacted with others.

We secure the Promise of "rest unto our souls" by becoming His Disciple and the imitation of his Example, Pattern and Teachings, which leads to righteousness and eternal joyfulness in Heaven.

ISAIAH 32:17
And the work of righteousness shall be peace; and the effect of righteousness quietness and assurance forever.

(4) We are called to follow the footsteps of our Master, by far the greatest man in history.

(a) During His time on earth, He demonstrated a willingness to perform every task with cheerfulness.

B. Christians are to be formed, conformed and transformed

(1) The nature or character of Christ must be formed

(a) The Great Apostle Paul pointed out, rather passionately the importance of the nature or character of Christ being formed in the members of the congregation of His Church at Galatia.

GALATIANS 4:19
My little children, of whom I travail in birth again [undergoing birth pains] until Christ be [is] **formed in you,** I desire to be present with you now, and to change my voice; [in order to express his passionate concern] for I stand in doubt [perplexed] of you.

(2) Christians are to be conformed to the image of His Son

ROMANS 8:29
For whom he did foreknow, he also did predestinate **to be conformed to the image of his Son,** that he might be the firstborn among many brethren [brothers and sisters in Christ].

(3) Christians are to be transformed to the image of His Son, by growing in grace, and in the knowledge of our Lord and Savior

2 CORINTHIANS 3:18
But we all, with open face beholding as in a glass the glory of the Lord, **are changed into the same image** from glory to glory, even as by the Spirit of the Lord.

COLOSSIANS 1:10
That ye might walk worthy of the Lord unto all pleasing, **being fruitful in every good work, and increasing in the knowledge of God;**

Reference: 2 PETER 3:17-18

(a) Knowledge is very important, but understanding alone is not enough, as it cannot alone produce a Christ like character.

(b) In order to grow in grace and take on His likeness we must be obedient to that knowledge, which allows ourselves to align with His Pattern.

JOHN 1:17
For the law was given by Moses, **but grace and truth came by Jesus Christ.**

EPHESIANS 4:15
But speaking the truth in love, may grow up into him in all things, which is the head, even Christ:

JOHN 15:10
If ye keep my commandments, ye shall abide in my love; even as I have kept my Father's commandments, and abide in his love

(4) The natural result of gaining knowledge and obeying our Lord and Savior is that His Will increases in importance, while our concerns with worldly affairs become increasingly less significant.

(a) As a result, we yield increasingly greater control of our lives to Him. Just as John the Baptist learned, accomplished and revealed about 2000 years ago.

JOHN 3:30
He [Christ] must increase, but I must decrease.

(b) As a Christian grows to reflect more of the qualities of Christ and less of human nature, he or she is complying with the instruction of Christ to take up their cross daily.

(5) Our Lord desires us to disregard the fleeting pleasures of our old life, in order to focus our entire attention on His Word and obedience to His Divine Will.

LUKE 9:23-24
And he said to them all, If any man will come after me, let him deny himself, and take up his cross daily, and follow me. For whosoever will save his life shall lose it: but whosoever will lose his life for my sake, the same shall save it.

C. Jesus Christ is the complete living Word of God

(1) The Holy Bible is a somewhat limited version of the Word of God in a written form.

JOHN 1:1
In the beginning was the Word, and the Word was with God, and the Word was God.

JOHN 20:30-31
And many other signs truly did Jesus in the presence of his disciples, which are not written in this book: But these are written, that ye might believe that Jesus is the Christ, the Son of God; and that believing ye might have life through his name.

Additional reference: JOHN 21:24-25

(a) The Holy Scriptures, which will be the Standard by which we judged or evaluated on Judgment Day, are sufficient for all our needs.

ROMANS 2:16
In the day when **God shall judge the secrets of men by Jesus Christ according to my gospel**.

2 TIMOTHY 3:15
And that from a child thou hast known the holy Scriptures, **which are able to make thee wise unto salvation through faith which is in Christ Jesus.**

D. Importance of Fellowship with likeminded Christians

One of Christ's specific reasons for providing the Pattern for His Church was to **create an environment where the members would always watch over each other in love.**

(1) Only in such an atmosphere can true personal spiritual growth be accomplished, which is the result of personal effort in conjunction with loving and nurturing fellowship.

(a) Growing in the knowledge and grace or becoming Christ like is not an independent endeavor, but rather it is a way of life that can only be sustained within a fellowship of likeminded faithful Christians.

1 JOHN 1:7
But if we walk in the light, as he is in the light, **we have fellowship one with another,** and the blood of Jesus Christ his Son cleanseth us from all sin.

E. Examples of the Teachings of Christ

(1) Being Humble or Meek

MATTHEW 18:4
Whosoever therefore shall **humble himself as this little child, the same is greatest in the kingdom of heaven.**

MATTHEW 23:12
And whosoever shall exalt himself shall be abased; and **he that shall humble himself shall be exalted.**

(2) Being Faithful

REVELATION 2:10
Fear none of those things which thou shalt suffer: behold, the devil shall cast some of you into prison, that ye may be tried; and ye shall have tribulation ten days; **be thou faithful unto death, and I will give thee a crown of life.**

(3) Being Forgiving

LUKE 23:34
Then said Jesus, *Father, forgive them;* for they know not what they do. And they parted his raiment, and cast lots.

(4) Being not of this world

JOHN 17:14-17
I have given them thy word; and the world hath hated them, because they [His Disciples then and now] are not of the world, even as I am not of the world. I pray not that thou shouldest take them out of the world, but that thou shouldest keep them from the evil. **They are not of the world, even as I am not of the world. Sanctify them through thy truth: thy word is truth.**

(5) Being Just

JOHN 5:30
I can of mine own self do nothing: as I hear, I judge: and *my judgment is just;* because I seek not mine own will, but the will of the Father which hath sent me.

(6) Love

JOHN 13:34
A new commandment I give unto you, **That ye love one another; as I have loved you, that ye also love one another**.

JOHN 15:13
Greater love hath no man than this, that a man lay down his life for his friends.

(7) Merciful

MATTHEW 5:7
Blessed are the merciful: for they shall obtain mercy.

LUKE 6:36
Be ye therefore merciful, as your Father also is merciful.

(8) Obedience

LUKE 22:42
Saying, Father, if thou be willing, remove this cup from me: **nevertheless not my will, but thine, be done.**

(9) Prayer

MATTHEW 21:22
And all things, **whatsoever ye shall ask in prayer, believing, ye shall receive.**

(10) Pure in heart

MATTHEW 5:8
Blessed are the pure in heart: for they shall see God.

(11) Watchful

LUKE 12:37
Blessed are those servants, *whom the lord when he cometh shall find watching:* verily I say unto you, that he shall gird himself, and make them to sit down to meat, and will come forth and serve them.

REVELATION 16:15
Behold, I come as a thief. *Blessed is he that watcheth,* and keepeth his garments, lest he walk naked, and they see his shame.

F. Examples of the Teachings of His Disciples

(1) Charity

1 TIMOTHY 4:12
Let no man despise thy youth; but be thou an example of the believers, in word, in conversation, in *charity*, in spirit, in faith, in purity.

1 PETER 4:8
And above all things have fervent charity among yourselves: *for charity shall cover the multitude of sins.*

(2) Faithful

1 TIMOTHY 6:2
And they that have believing masters, let them not despise them, because they are brethren; but rather do them service, because they are *faithful* and beloved, partakers of the benefit. These things teach and exhort.

HEBREWS 10:23
Let us *hold fast the profession of our faith without wavering;* (for he is faithful that promised)

Additional reference: REVELATION 17:14

(3) Fear God

ACTS 10:2
A devout man, and one that <u>feared God</u> with all his house, which gave much alms to the people, and prayed to God always.

HEBREWS 12:28
Wherefore we receiving a kingdom which cannot be moved, let us have grace, whereby we may serve God acceptably with reverence and **godly fear**:

(4) Godly

2 TIMOTHY 3:12
Yea, and all that will **live godly** in Christ Jesus shall suffer persecution.

TITUS 2:12
Teaching us that, denying ungodliness and

worldly lusts, we should live soberly, righteously, and **godly,** in this present world;

(5) Good Conscience

1 TIMOTHY 1:5
Now the end of the commandment is charity out of a pure heart, and of a *good conscience,* and of faith unfeigned:

HEBREWS 13:18
Pray for us: for we trust we have a *good conscience,* in all things willing to live honestly.

(6) Goodness

ROMANS 15:14
And I myself also am persuaded of you, my brethren, that ye also are full of *goodness,* filled with all knowledge, able also to admonish one another.

GALATIANS 5:22
But the fruit of the Spirit is love, joy, peace, longsuffering, gentleness, *goodness,* faith

(7) Hope

ROMANS 8:25
But if *we* **hope for that we see not**, then do we with patience wait for it.

ROMANS 12:12
Rejoicing in hope; patient in tribulation; continuing instant in prayer;

(8) Holy

COLOSSIANS 3:12
Put on therefore, as the elect of God, *holy* and beloved, bowels of mercies, kindness, humbleness of mind, meekness, longsuffering;

JUDE 1:20
But ye, beloved, building up yourselves on your most *holy* faith, praying in the Holy Ghost

(9) Humble

COLOSSIANS 3:12
Put on therefore, as the elect of God, holy and beloved, bowels of mercies, kindness, humbleness of mind, meekness, longsuffering;

1 PETER 5:5
Likewise, ye younger, submit yourselves unto the elder. Yea, all of you be subject one to another, and be clothed with humility: for **God resisteth the proud, and giveth grace to the humble.**

1 PETER 5:6
Humble yourselves therefore under the mighty hand of God, **that he may exalt you in due time:**

(10) Just and devout

LUKE 2:25
And, behold, there was a man in Jerusalem, whose name was Simeon; and the same man was *just and devout,* waiting for the consolation of Israel: and the Holy Ghost was upon him.

(11) Kind and Longsuffering

COLOSSIANS 3:12
Put on therefore, as the elect of God, holy and beloved, bowels of mercies, *kindness,* humbleness of mind, meekness, *longsuffering;*

2 CORINTHIANS 6:6
By pureness, by knowledge, by *longsuffering, by kindness,* by the Holy Ghost, by love unfeigned,

Additional references: EPHESIANS 4:2, 2 PETER 1:7

(12) Loving

COLOSSIANS 1:4
Since we heard of your faith in Christ Jesus, and of the love which ye have to all the saints.

1 THESSALONIANS 4:9
But as touching brotherly love ye need not that I write unto you: for ye yourselves are taught of God to love one another.

(13) Meek and quiet spirit

1 PETER 3:4
But let it be the hidden man of the heart, in that which is not corruptible, even the ornament of a **meek and quiet spirit,** which is in the sight of God of great price.

(14) Obedient

1 PETER 1:14
As <u>obedient children</u>, not fashioning yourselves according to the former lusts in your ignorance:

Additional reference: ROMANS 16:19

(15) Patience

2 TIMOTHY 3:10
But thou hast fully known my doctrine, manner of life, purpose, faith, longsuffering, charity, **patience**,

Additional reference: TITUS 2:2

(16) Prayer

JAMES 5:16
Confess your faults one to another, and pray one for another, that ye may be healed. **The effectual fervent prayer of a righteous man availeth much.**

Additional reference: EPHESIANS 6:18

(17) Pure

1 JOHN 3:3
And every man that hath this hope in him purifieth himself, even as he is *pure*.

(18) Righteous

LUKE 1:6
And they were both *righteous* before God, walking in all the commandments and ordinances of the Lord blameless.

Additional references: ROMANS 5:19, 1 PETER 3:12, 1 PETER 4:18

(19) Sincerity

1 CORINTHIANS 5:8
Therefore let us keep the feast, not with old leaven, neither with the leaven of malice and wickedness; but with the unleavened bread of *sincerity* and truth.

Additional references: 2 CORINTHIANS 2:17, 2 CORINTHIANS 8:8

(20) Spirit led

ROMANS 8:14
For as many as are <u>led</u> by the Spirit of God, they are the sons of God.

(21) Steadfast

COLOSSIANS 2:5
For though I be absent in the flesh, yet am I with you in the spirit, joying and beholding your order, and <u>the steadfastness of your faith in Christ.</u>

Additional reference: ACTS 2:42

(22) Without guile

1 PETER 2:1
Wherefore **laying aside** all malice, and all **guile,** and hypocrisies, and envies, and all evil speakings,

Additional references`: 1 THESSALONIANS 2:3, 1 PETER 3:10:

(23) Zealous of good works

TITUS 2:14
Who gave himself for us, that he might redeem us from all iniquity, and purify unto himself a peculiar people, **zealous of good works.**

TITUS 2:7
In all things showing thyself a **pattern of good works:** in doctrine showing uncorruptness, gravity, sincerity

The objective of living a Christian life could be summarized as our being formed, conformed, and transformed into the image of Jesus Christ, by developing understanding and making careful application of His complete Will in our lives....

Heaven Awaits!

Chapter XI

Simplified overview of the Old Testament

Chapter Contents

A. Introduction

B. Three major topics

C. Results of these Promises and His Covenant

D. Books of the Old Testament

A. Introduction

(1) Inspired Word of God

Only an all powerful Supreme Being could have accomplished the feat of assembling this book over 1500 years using numerous writers, who spoke different languages, during different time frames and in different geographic locations.

This is an overview of the inspired Word of God, commonly known as the Bible, which is actually 66 separate books, bounded into one large volume divided into two major sections, the Old and New Testaments.

The Old Testament contains the history of the world and of the Jewish Nation during the period from the creation of the world until about 400 years before the birth of Christ.

(2) A comprehensive study of the Bible reveals a unity of thought, which clearly indicates that it was inspired by one unique supernatural mind.

God preserved the ancient manuscripts and watched over numerous translators, scribes and copyists involved in passing on the Word to future generations.

And finally, God stirred men to invent the printing press and at about the same time to undertake the massive task of translating the Bible from the ancient tongues into English and other languages.

The Old Testament was written primarily in the ancient Hebrew language, which when translated into English provides passages of a colorful, lively and picturesque nature or a combination that result in fascinating descriptions.

This Divine book has been provided to mankind, exactly as God intended without error, through the absolute Power of His Will.

Considering how it was developed, most would agree that it represents a Miracle of the Ages.

(a) It is one of only two links to Lord God Almighty, the other being prayer.

Without doubt the most important volume ever written as it contains Divine guidance as to how to receive the hope and promise of a heavenly everlasting joyous life, **the greatest gift of all.**

(3) Before the Beginning of the World

The Bible contains little information regarding Eternity Past, before the formation of the world. The following Biblical references refer to the time before creation:

PSALMS 90:2
Before the mountains were brought forth, or ever thou hadst formed the earth and the world, even from everlasting to everlasting, thou art God.

JOHN 1:1
In the beginning was the Word, and the Word was with God, and the Word was God.

1CORINTHIANS 2:7
But we speak the wisdom of God in a mystery, even the hidden wisdom, *which God ordained before the world unto our glory.*

TITUS 1:2
In hope of eternal life, which God, that cannot lie, *promised before the world began.*

1 PETER 1:20
Who verily was foreordained before the

foundation of the world, but was manifest in these last times for you.

B. Three major topics

(1) Promises of God to Abraham

That through Abraham's seed or family line, that all Nations would be blessed. God founded the Hebrew Nation, as the Messianic Nation to the World.

The Nation through which the Gift of the Messiah and the New Covenant, would come from God, for the benefit of all peoples until the end of time on earth or the second coming.

Many Bible scholars suggest that God's ultimate objective in founding the Hebrew Nation was to bring Jesus Christ into the world.

(2) Covenant of God with the Hebrew Nation

Simply stated God promised the Hebrew Nation, if they would faithfully Serve Him and only Him that they would enjoy great prosperity as a Nation.

If they did not faithfully serve Him and worshipped Idols, they would be destroyed.

At that time in history, most Nations worshipped Idols; their Idols included gods of sun, gods of the sky, gods of the moon etc.

The story of the Old Testament includes God's efforts to discount the existence of these so-called gods and to introduce the concept of the One and only True Living God.

(3) Promise of God to David

God promised David that his seed would Reign over God's People for all Eternity! That out of his family would come, in the far future, one Great King, the King of kings, who would live and rule over God's People forever.

C. Results of these Promises and His Covenant

(1) The population of the world was blessed through the formation of the Hebrew Nation, which was the Messianic Nation.

(2) Through the Hebrew Nation came the lineage of Jesus through the Family of David.

(3) The Family of David brought blessings on the whole world through the birth of One Great King, the King of kings, The Christ, The Anointed One or Messiah; Who suffered and died to make atonement before God for the sins of all humanity, as Divine Justice requires that all sins be punished.

Jesus took an active part in the Creation, is the God of Abraham, Isaac and Jacob and he came to earth to live as a man. JOHN 1:1 confirms that in the beginning was the Word and the Word was with God and the Word was God. He was with God in the beginning.

John 1:14 substantiates that the Word became flesh and made his dwelling among us. His life served as a living example of how God, the Father expects people to conduct themselves.

D. Books of the Old Testament

(1) The Old Testament contains 39 Books, which have been classified, into three groups:

(a) Historical, the rise and fall of the Hebrew Nation, a total of 17 books. The first book, Genesis covers approximately one half of all human history. The first five books are also known as the Law of Moses.

(b) Poetical, stories of the of the rise or golden age of the Hebrew Nation, a total of 5 books, including Job, Psalms, Proverbs, Ecclesiastes and the Song of Songs or Song of Solomon.

(c) Prophetic, stories of the fall or the dark age of the Hebrew Nation, total of 17 Books, written by a total of 16 Prophets (Jeremiah wrote two, Jeremiah and Lamentations). Bible scholars have divided

the Prophets in major and minor. Those considered Major Prophets are Isaiah, Jeremiah, Ezekiel and Daniel, the balance are classified as Minor Prophets.

(2) The Historical Books

(a) Genesis First Book of the Law of Moses

Written by Moses, possibly during the 40 years of wanderings in the wilderness, **this single book covers approximately fifty percent of human history**

Biblical scholars have estimated the world was created between 6000 and 7700 years ago.

Creation story - 1:1 to 2:3

Estimated timeline: 4000 - 5700 BC

Story of Adam & Eve - 2:15 to 3:24

Cain & Abel - 4:1-16

Noah and the Great Flood - 6:9-9:17

Tower of Babel - 11:1-9

Covenant between God & Abram - 12:1-9; 17:1-8

God changed Abram's name to Abraham and promised that all nations on the earth would be blessed through him. The second promise to Abraham was fulfilled in Jesus. He blessed all nations by offering salvation and remission of sins to all who would come to Him.

Three Holy Visitors - 18:1-15

Estimated timeline 2000 BC

The story of Lot - 19:1-14 (Lot's wife was turned to a pillar of salt - 19:26)

Two Angels visited Sodom, they went to Lot's house, the men of Sodom surrounded Lot's house, demanded that Lot bring out the Angels "that we may know them", Lot offered them his two virgin daughters instead, the men attempted to break in, Lot was pulled into the house by the Angels, who blinded the men who were attempting to enter.

Destruction of Sodom & Gomorrah - 19:15-29

Hagar & Ishmael - 21:8-21

Abraham & Isaac - 22:1-19

Isaac & Rebekah - 24:1-67

Jacob & Esau - 24:1-67

Isaac's blessing on Jacob - 27:1-40

Dream (Vision of the Ladder) - of Jacob at Bethel 28:10-22

Jacob marries the daughters of - Leban (Leah & Rachel) 29:14-30

Joseph, his coat of many colors and his brothers - 37:1-36

The cupbearer and baker - 40:1-23

Dreams of Pharaoh - 41:1-57

Brothers of Joseph journey to Egypt - 42:1-38 to 45:28

Estimated timeline 1700 BC

(b) Exodus - Second Book of the Law of Moses

The Exodus or "going out" of the children of Israel leaving bondage in Egypt and pilgrimage to the Promised Land. The Ten Commandments, recorded in Chapter 20, became the basis of the moral codes of the civilized world.

Birth of Moses - 1:8 to 2-10

Estimated timeline 1515 BC

Moses talked with God - Burning Bush - 3:1-12

God revealed Name to Moses - 3:13-15

Rod of Aaron became a snake and swallowed the snakes of Egyptian magicians - 7:8-13

Ten plagues of Egypt - 7:14 to 11:10

Passover - 12:1-51

Estimated timeline 1494 BC

Pillar of Fire & parting of the Sea - 13:17 to 14:31

Estimated timeline 1492 BC, based upon 1 Kings 6:1, fourth year of Solomon (1012 BC), was in the 480th year after the Exodus.

God provides water & food in the wilderness - 15:22 to 17:7

Song of Moses & Miriam - 15:1-21

Moses on Mount Sinai received the Ten Commandments - 19:1 to 20:26

Golden Calf, a grave sin of Aaron and the Jewish people - 32:1-35

Ark of Covenant - 25:10-22, 37:1-9

Tabernacle and cloud of the Lord - 40:1-38

(c) Leviticus - third Book of the Law of Moses

Leviticus is derived from Levi, who was one of Jacob's 12 sons.

This Book, written by Moses, provides the rituals and ceremonies of the tabernacle services and the duties of the priests, including making sacrifices and teaching the Law of Moses. In LEVITICUS 19:18 the Lord commanded the people to love their neighbors for the first time.

Law of Sacrifice - 1:1 to 7:38

Ordination of the Priests 8:1–36

Holiness Code - 16:1-26:46

(d) Numbers - fourth Book of the Law of Moses

Name based upon the numbering of the children of Israel. Book continues the story of the journey of the people to the Promised Land.

The Census - 1:1 to 4:49

Regulations - 5:1-10:10

Journey to Canaan - 10:11-11:35

Exploration of Canaan - 13:1 to 14:12

Water from the rock - 20:1-12

Years of wandering - 15:1-19:22

Balaam & his donkey - 22:21-38

(e) Deuteronomy - final Book of the Law of Moses

Deuteronomy is defined as the second giving of the law, which was given for the benefit of the generation born in the wilderness.

The format of this book follows the general structure of ancient near eastern treaties, which were made, between greater and lesser powers. Israel, the lesser power, had been freed from bondage in Egypt and was now voluntarily becoming the servants of Yahweh.

Therefore, the book of Deuteronomy is a treaty or contract between God and Israel.

Joshua succeeds Moses - 31:1-8

Death of Moses - 34:1-12

Estimated timeline - 1400 BC

(f) Joshua

Story of Joshua leading the Israelites, across the river Jordan, into Promised Land and the conquering of Canaan.

The first five Books of the Bible or the Law of Moses were carried with the people.

The last part is Joshua's instructions to honor God and live to high personal standards.

Crossing the Jordon River - 3:1-17

Walls of Jericho fall - 5:13 to 6:27

Sun stands still - 10:1-15

Listing of kings defeated - 12:1-24

(g) Judges

Beginning of Theocracy in which God ruled directly through Judges.

Story of Deborah - 4:1 to 5:31

Gideon questions and tests God 6:1-40

Gideon defeats the Midianites - 7:1-25

Exploits of Samson - 15:1-20

Samson & Delilah - 16:1-31

Estimated timeline ABOUT 1380 BC

(h) Ruth

A love story, **the passage 1:16-17** "And Ruth said, Intreat me not to leave thee, or to return from following after thee: for whither thou goest, I will go; and where thou lodgest, I will lodge: thy people shall be my people, and thy God my God: Where thou diest, will I die, and there will I be buried: the Lord do so to me, and more also, if ought but death part thee and me." **is considered to be one of the most beautiful passages in all of literature.** Ruth was the great-grandmother of David, therefore in the human lineage of Jesus.

Ruth & Naomi - 1:1-22

Estimated timeline 1150 BC

Ruth gleans in the field - 2:1-21

Genealogy of David - 4:13-22

(i) First and Second Samuel

Final days of the Theocracy, with the Israelites rejecting Jehovah and calling for the rule of an earthly king - the first was Saul, who was a mighty warrior, but was not after God's own heart - after death of Saul, God's choice, David became the King. These Books cover the lives of Saul, David and Samuel, the last of the Judges.

First Samuel

God called Samuel - 3:1-21

Children of Israel beg for a king - 8:1-23

Samuel anointed Saul 9:1 to 10:27 - estimated timeline about 1043 BC

Samuel anointed David - 16:1-13

David in service of Saul - 16:14-23

David defeated Goliath - 17:1-58

Saul attempted to kill David - 19:1-24

David spared Saul - 24:1 to 26:25

Saul & the witch of Endor - 28:4-25

Death of Saul -.31:1-6

Second Samuel

God promises David an Eternal Throne. The promise was that one day the House of David would bless the world through the birth of the King of kings, who would himself live forever and reign over a Kingdom of endless duration.

David became king of Israel - 5:1-12

Estimated timeline 1048 BC

Sins of David and Bathsheba - 11:1-27

Nathan admonished King David - 12:1-15

Death of Absalom - 18:1-33

(j) First and Second Kings

First Kings opens with the Hebrew Nation in its golden age. Second Kings ends with the nation in ruins. Covers the reign of King Solomon, the Temple, the splendor of Solomon Court, the division and decline of the Kingdom, as well as the saga of Elijah

First Kings

Adonijah appointed himself king - 1:1-10

David appointed Solomon king of Israel - 1:11-40

Estimated timeline 1008 BC

Solomon made a wise decision - 3:16-28

Solomon built the Temple - 6:1-38

Solomon's Pray of Dedication - 8:22-61

Queen of Sheba visited the king - 10:1-13

The splendor of Solomon - 10:14-29

Wives of Solomon - 11:1-13

Death of Solomon - 11:41-43

The son of Solomon, Rehoboam became king, Israel rebelled - 12:1-24

A Kingdom Divided - 1 Kings 12:1 to 2 Kings 16:20

Elijah cared for by ravens - 17:1-6

Widow of Zarephath - (miracle of Elisha) 17:7-27

Lord appears to Elijah and the prophets of Baal on mount Camel - 18:16-46

Vineyard of Naboth - 19:1-21

Second Kings

Elijah taken by a whirlwind into Heaven - 2:1-11

Miracles of Elijah - 2:13-25

Naaman healed of Leprosy - 5:1-27

Seven year old king - 11:1-21

The Kingdoms Fall - 17:1-25:30

Book of the Law found - 22:1 to 23:3

(k) First and Second Chronicles

In the main, duplicate the writings of the Books of Samuel and Kings. Emphasize genealogies, the history of Judah and Temple worship.

First Chronicles

Genealogies - 1:1-9:44

Acts of David - 10:1-29:30

Second Chronicles

Acts of Solomon 1:1-9:31

Acts of the Kings of Judah 10:1-36:23

(l) Ezra

An account of the beginning of the return from captivity in Babylon and the rebuilding of the Temple

Cyrus Permits the Jews to Return 1:1-11

List of Those Who Returned 2:1-70

Altar and Temple Foundations Established 3:1-13

Opposition 4:1-24

Renewal of Construction Work on the Temple 5:1-6:22

Ezra enforced the Law 7:1-8:36

Problems associated with mixed marriages with idolatrous neighbors, which God had forbidden and the cure 9:1-10:44

(m) Nehemiah

The Wall of Jerusalem rebuilt. Many parts of the Book written in the first person or as a personal history

Mission of Nehemiah - 1:1-7:73a

Ezra Reads the Law - 7:73b-8:18

(n) Esther

Esther is the story of the deliverance of the Jews from extermination. A beautiful example of the Providence of God and how He cares for His true followers

Estimated timeline about 525 BC

Note: The Books of Old Testament are grouped by type and not by the date events occurred

Queen Vashi rebelled and was deposed - 1:1-22

Search for replacement - Esther became the Queen of Persia - 2:1-18

The Jews and Their Enemies - 8:7-9:17

Triumph of the Jews - Deliverance! - Feast of Purism instituted. - 9:18-10:3

(3) The Poetical Books of the Old Testament - Stories of the Golden Age of the Hebrew Nation

(a) Job

The story of a righteous man who suddenly had his children and possessions destroyed. Job was then plunged into great personal suffering.

A philosophical Book, which is thought by many Bible scholars to be one of the oldest pieces of literature in existence - his prosperity was restored - Chapter 42.

Introduction - 1:1-5

Speeches - 1:6-42:6

Conclusion - 42:7-17

(b) Psalms

Book is composed of 150 Psalms, of which approximately fifty percent have been ascribed to King David, some of which are quite lyrical with beautiful imagery and expression, including 1, 19, 22, 23, 90, 100 and 103.

It served as the national hymnbook or the "Book of Praises" of the Jews and as the basis of many modern Christian songs.

Considered by many scholars to be the most Glorious Accomplishment of Israel's Golden Age - most quoted Book in the New Testament.

Identified Authors

Moses - Psalm 90

Heman the Ezrahite - Psalm 88

Ethan the Ezrahite - Psalm 89

Solomon Psalms - 72, 127

David (Total of 73 Psalms) 3-9; 11-32; 34-41; 51-65; 68-70; 86; 103; 108-110; 122; 124; 131; 133; 138-145 - The New Testament credits two of the anonymous psalms (2 & 95) to David (Acts 4:25 & Hebrews 4:7)

Asaph (Total of 12 Psalms) 50; 73-83

Sons of Korah (Total of 9 Psalms) 42; 44-45; 47-49; 84-85; 87

The Septuagint (LXX) provided additional authorship identifications as follows:

Jeremiah - Psalm 137

Haggai and Zechariah Psalms - 146-147

Ezra Psalm - 119

Hezekiah (Total of 15 Psalms) 120-134

Anonymous Authorship (Total of 28 psalms)

(c) Proverbs

Written by King Solomon with contributions by Agur (Chapter 30) and by Bathsheba, his mother (Chapter 31) - Please note that "King Lemuel" may have been another name for Solomon.

A proverb is a brief statement regarding a single moral truth in a pointed, pithy, direct fashion.

An ancient oriental method of instruction that was understood by the masses - The basic underlying concept of the Book is that all Wisdom is a gift of God.

A Book for all ages, as practical today as the time in which it was written - should be required reading for all young people as well as their elders.

Proverbs, which provide Wisdom particularly for young men 1:1 to 9:18

Key verse "The fear of God is the beginning of all knowledge" 1:7

Proverbs, which provide Wisdom for and are directed to all people 10:1-24:34

Proverbs, which provide Wisdom for and are directed to leaders 25:1-31:31

The Book of Proverbs contains so many gems of useful knowledge that it should be carefully studied. The following are a few samples of what the reader will find:

Proverbs chapter 1

Objective of the Book; to promote Wisdom, Instruction, Understanding, Righteousness, Justice, Equity, Prudence, Knowledge, Discretion, Learning and Sound Counsels

That the beginning point is the Fear of God - Instructions to follow parental directives and a strong warning against bad companions

Proverbs chapter 2

Wisdom must be sought after. God's Word is the primary source. Warnings about "strange women" that are repeated numerous times in the Book.

Interesting in light of the fact that Solomon was involved with no less than 1000 women

Proverbs chapter 8

Wisdom, personified as a female and its rewards.

Proverbs chapter 9

Warns that "Stolen waters are sweet" and the reward for partaker is Hell.

Proverbs chapter 12

A worthy woman is the glory of her husband.

Proverbs chapter 15

A soft answer turns away wrath.

Proverbs chapter 22

A good name is to be chosen over great riches.

Proverbs chapter 28

He that hides his eyes from the poor shall have many a curse.

(d) Ecclesiastes

Written by Solomon in his old age in an effort to spare future readers the bitterness of his personal experiences and the meaninglessness of an earthly life apart from God - After having everything the world could offer he came to the conclusion that all is "vanity" or regardless of its beauty or value as it would pass away. **All that is really important is the Hope of Heaven or Immortality.**

This conclusion is expressed clearly in ECCLESIASTES 12:13-14 "Let us hear the conclusion of the whole matter: Fear God, and keep his commandments: for this is the whole duty of man. For God shall bring every work into judgment, with every secret thing, whether it be good or whether it be evil."

Personal experience - 1:1 to 2:26

Observations of Solomon - 3:1 to 5:20

His counsel - 6:1-8:17

Conclusions - 9:1-12:14

(e) Song of Solomon or Song of Songs

A glorification of wedded love written by Solomon in the form of a love song with springtime in full blossom, which exhibits Solomon's attraction to nature, orchards, gardens, meadows, vineyards and animals. May have been written to celebrate his marriage to his favorite wife or to symbolize the great love of God for His followers - can be difficult to understand in the King James Version - Is somewhat less difficult in modern translations, such as the New King James Version.

First Poem - 1:2-2:7 (wedding day)
Second Poem - 2:8-3:5 (courtship memories)
Third Poem - 3:6-5:1 (engagement memories)
Fourth Poem - 5:2-6:3 (distressing dream)
Fifth Poem - 6:4-8:7 (In praise of beauty)
Sixth Poem - 8:8-14 (power of love)

(4) The Prophetic Books of the Old Testament - Stories of the Dark Ages of the Hebrew Nation

Major Prophets

The primary mission of the Prophets was to attempt to save the nation from its sins and idolatry. Failing in this, to warn that the nation would be destroyed, but not completely. A small portion would be saved.

Out of this portion would come an influence that would spread over the world and bring all nations to God. That influence would be a Great Man, who would arise from the House of David

The once mighty House of David in the later days had all but disappeared, but would continue and make a comeback when out of family stock would come a sprout so great that it was called "The Branch", referring, of course, to Jesus Christ.

An important prediction is recorded in ISAIAH 7:14 is *"a virgin shall conceive, and bear a son, and shall call his name Immanuel"* (God with us).

(a) Isaiah

This Book was written during the fall of the Hebrew Nation. The masses had generally turned away from God. Isaiah prophesied the captivity of both Israel and Judah, as well as, the return of the exiles and the coming of the Messiah and His Kingdom.

Isaiah was widely quoted in the New Testament.

Key passage: ISAIAH 9:6 *"For unto us a child is born, unto us a son is given: and the government shall be upon his shoulder: and his name shall be called Wonderful, Counselor, The mighty God, The everlasting Father, The Prince of Peace."*

Prophet is appalled by the wickedness of the people of God. Prophecies of condemnation directed to Judah and Israel - Chapters 1 to 8

Estimated timeline 690 BC

Prophecies regarding the coming Messiah & Christian Age - Chapters 9; 11

Singing the praise of God - Chapter 12

Prophecies of condemnation directed to the other nations - Chapters - 10, 13 to 23

Purpose of God in judgment - Chapters 24 to 27

Prophecies of condemnation directed to sinners in Israel - Chapters 28 to 35

Events during reign of Hezekiah and warnings of the threat of Assyria & Babylon - Chapters 36 to 39

Prophecies of relief and the Greatness of God - Chapters 40 to 48

Prophecies of relief and the Grace of God - Chapters 49 to 59

Prophecies of relief and the Glory of God - Chapters 60 to 66

(b) Jeremiah

This Prophet lived in Jerusalem, during the time prior to and during the period the people of the southern kingdom or Judah were held in captivity in Babylon. Through him God made His final attempt to save the City, which failed.

The people refused to obey and were forced to pay the price as foretold. Written with great authority, on the Love of God and the certainty of the final judgment on sinful people

Call of Jeremiah - 1:1-19

General Prophecies to - Judah 2:1 to 45:5

Specific Prediction of captivity for - seventy years

JEREMIAH 25:11-12
And this whole land shall be a desolation, and an astonishment; and these nations **shall serve the king of Babylon seventy years.** And it shall come to pass, when seventy years are accomplished, that I will punish the king of Babylon, and that nation, saith the LORD, for their iniquity, and the land of the Chaldeans, and will make it perpetual desolations.

Specific Prediction of the return of remnant to Jerusalem

JEREMIAH 29:10
For thus saith the LORD, That after seventy years be accomplished at Babylon I will visit you, and perform my good word toward you, **in causing you to return to this place.**

Messages & events before fall of Jerusalem - 34:1 to 38:28

Events during the fall of Jerusalem - 39:1-18

Messages after the fall - 40:1 to 45:5

Prophecies to the Gentiles - 46:1 to 51:46

The fall of Jerusalem - 52:1 to 52:34

Estimated timeline 585 BC (completion of the Book)

(c) Lamentations

This Book is basically a Funeral Dirge over the destruction of Jerusalem. Jeremiah writes of his personal grief over the ruins of Jerusalem and the Temple that he had predicted.

The same theme runs throughout the Book, different wording, but the same general ideas - Horrors of the attack, the ruins which was all due to the sins of the people.

Destruction of the Holy City - 1:1-22

Anger of God - 2:1-22

Cry of despair & for mercy - 3:1-66

Paradise Lost - 4:1-22

Prayer of Remembrance - 5:1-22

(d) Ezekiel

The major theme of the Book is "They Shall Know that I am God". The mission of Ezekiel to explain the reason for God's causing Israel's captivity.

They were Idolaters and the captivity was the cure. Ezekiel was unusual in that he dated most of his writing. He experienced visions and wrote detailed descriptions. This is a complex, but very interesting Book.

Estimated timeline 597 BC

Vision of the glory of God, four Cherubim, wheels, firmament (possibly highly polished gemstones with brilliant refraction) and an image of God - 1:1-28; 10:1-22

Four signs of future Judgment - 4:1-5:17

Visions of coming Judgment - 8:1-11:25

Signs, messages and parables - 12:1-24:27

Parable of the vine - 15:1-8

Parable of the Two Eagles - 17:1-24

Judgment of the Gentiles - 25:1-32:32

Restoration of Israel - 33:1-48:35

Valley of the dry bones - 37:1-14

(e) Daniel

The writer of exciting stories and visions - Carried to captivity while in his youth, later becomes a Hebrew Statesman and Prophet in Babylon.

Had direct contact with Nebuchadnezzar, who built the famous Hanging Gardens.

Very readable history - The Prophet Daniel foresaw the Messiah and recounts his vision in DANIEL 7:13-14, beginning with "I saw in the night visions, and, behold, one like the Son of man."

Jesus often referred to himself as the Son of Man, (MARK 14:61-62, LUKE 22:66-70) because his image had been transformed from His natural state as a spirit to physical form when He came to earth and was born of a woman.

He was given authority, glory and sovereign power; all peoples, nations and men of every language worshipped him. His dominion is an everlasting dominion that will not pass away, and His kingdom is one that will never be destroyed.

Estimated timeline 538 BC

Four men (Shadrach, Meshach, Abed-nego and Son of Man) in the fiery furnace 3:1-30 (Key passage 3:25-26)

Writing on the Wall 5:1-31

Daniel in the lion's den 6:1-24

Visions of Daniel 7:1 to 11:45

Prediction of events at the end of earthly time 12:1-13

Minor Prophets

The Minor Prophets include Hosea, Joel, Amos, Obadiah, Jonah, Micah, Nahum, Habakkuk, Zephaniah, Haggai, Zechariah and Malachi.

Have Sown the Wind; Shall Reap the Whirlwind **HOSEA 8:1-14**

Prediction of a Plague of Locusts **JOEL 1:1-12**

Vision of a Basket of Summer Fruit **AMOS 8:1-14**

Jonah and the Large Fish (referred to by Christ in **MATTHEW 12:38-41**) **JONAH 1:1-17 TO 2:10**

Malachi the last Prophetic Book completed

Estimated timeline 400 BC

Through the Family of David the whole world was blessed by the birth of a Great King, The Christ, The Anointed One or Messiah, Who suffered and died to make <u>atonement</u> before God for the <u>sins</u> of all the many... Heaven Awaits!

Chapter XII

Simplified overview of the New Testament

Chapter Contents

A. Christ is the Heart of the Bible

B. God laid the Groundwork

C. An Account of Jesus Christ and His New Covenant

D. The Four Gospels

E. Acts of the Apostles

F. The Epistles

G. The Revelation of Jesus Christ

A. Christ is the Heart of the Bible

(1) The entire New Testament is focused on the story of the life, death, resurrection and the Divine Teachings of Jesus Christ, our Lord and Savior.

The Old Testament was an account of the Hebrew Nation. In founding the Hebrew Nation, the apparent ultimate objective of God was to bring One Man, His Son Jesus, the promised Messiah and God Himself in human form, into the world.

Jesus provided the instructions and gave His life in order to make it possible for His faithful followers to receive the greatest gift in the Spiritual Realm, which is everlasting life in the Glorious Paradise of the Kingdom of Heaven.

Reference: JOHN 3:16

His arrival was the single most important event in the history of the world, past, current and until He comes again. Christ lived a perfect earthly life, completely free of sin.

He performed numerous miracles and relieved the suffering of many to provide substantiation to His people, the Jews that He was indeed the long awaited Messiah, the Son of the Living God.

Jesus longs for everyone to carefully study, fully understand and follow His Word. He knows your name, understands your situation. His teaching provides humanity with a specific purpose for living, which instructs us to avoid the pleasures of the world and encourages each to live a full Christian life and properly prepare for a place in Heaven, expressing their love for Him by praising our Lord, following His instructions and regular attendance at the services of His Church.

B. God laid the Groundwork

Not only did God maintain the Jewish Nation through its trials and tribulations, but at the same time was preparing the world prior to the arrival of Jesus, by inspiring men to develop roads, governmental services, use common languages and to live in peace.

During the century prior to the birth of Christ several strong Roman leaders emerged including Pompey, Julius Caesar, Anthony, and Octavian.

Approximately 37 years before the birth of Christ, the armies of Octavian and Anthony defeated those lead by the murderers of Caesar, leaving the western part under the control of Octavian, and Anthony holding the eastern part as far as the Euphrates.

Nine years later, Octavian defeated Anthony in the battle of Actium, after which Anthony and Cleopatra took flight to Egypt, where they either were murdered or committed suicide, which left Octavian in the position of holding vast power.

Upon Octavian's return to Rome, the Senate conferred titles, honors and promoted him to supreme commander of the army.

The Roman Empire was born about 27 years before the birth of Jesus, Octavian, now called Caesar Augustus, was crowned its first emperor.

Augustus was a superior leader, securing the borders of the empire and building thousands of miles of high-grade hard surface roads.

These thoroughfares, many of which were used by Jesus and his Disciples, were paved and crowned as they are today or in other words were higher in the middle than on the sides to allow water to run off.

God brought about a time of peace and stability. During which time, Octavian reorganized the provinces to achieve a just administration, instituted tax reform, developed a civil service, and started many public works projects. It was during his reign that Jesus Christ was born.

Augustus' successor was not as capable. Tiberius, though experienced, was not as gifted or as interested in the farewell of his people. However, the period of peace and stability continued. Tiberius spent his last years in a life of debauchery on the island of Capri. Tiberius died in AD 37. One of Tiberius's appointees was the infamous Pontius Pilate.

Three languages were used in the land of Israel during the days of Jesus. Hebrew was the primary language spoken by the Jewish people at that time.

Israel had been under the influence of Greek culture from the time of its conquest by Alexander the Great four hundred years earlier. Latin was also used during the time of Christ. For example, the sign above the cross was written in Hebrew, Latin and Greek. The Romans for matters of military administration generally used Latin.

Civil administration was usually conducted in Greek. The vast majority of inscriptions written by non-Jews, which have been found in Israel, were written in Greek.

This language which possesses numerous commendable traits including a musical and rhythmic, which in poetic form, has an especially noble stateliness of style, combined with an intensity, which makes it an effective for expression of hallowed Truths and was divinely chosen to record the teachings of Christ and His Disciples.

The order and organization that prevailed in the empire, the road system, and the use of common languages were among the factors, which allowed the rapid spread of the Gospel of Jesus Christ.

C. An Account of Jesus Christ and His New Covenant

(1) The New Testament contains a total of 27 books, which have been classified into four groups.

(a) Four Books, commonly called the Four Gospels, contain a narrative of the life of Jesus and the particulars of His teachings

(b) One Book, which begins with the establishment of His Church and the everlasting Reign of Jesus Christ over all peoples and nations. In addition it details a small segment of the overall acts and accomplishments of His Apostles and Disciples.

(c) Twenty-one epistles, which teach, reinforce, clarify and expand upon His doctrine and commandments.

(d) And the Grand Finale, one Book of Revelation, which reveals the ultimate victory of Jesus Christ.

The New Testament begins just before the birth of Jesus. It is basically the story of His life, death, resurrection, and the terms of the New Covenant

Upon the death of Jesus on the cross, the Old Law or Covenant contained in the Old Testament passed away and was replaced with the New Covenant or New Testament.

The purpose of this chapter is to provide the user a general overview of the 27 books that make up the New Testament

D. The Four Gospels

Collectively, the first four books of the New Testament are called the gospels or the good news. Each gospel was written by a different individual and therefore is from a slightly different perspective. Many events in the life of Jesus are recounted in two or more Gospels, while other events or teachings are only covered in one.

(1) Matthew

Believed to have been written by Matthew, one of the Twelve, addressed directly to the Jewish Nation. Matthew presented Jesus as the promised Messiah from the Old Testament. Written prior to the fall of Jerusalem in AD 70

The Birth (**Probable Date: September, 5 BC**) and Preparation of the King 1:1 to 4:16

Vision of Joseph 1:20-24

Visit of the Magi 2:1-12

Flight to Egypt 2:13-15

Massacre of the children 2:16-18

Presentation of the Kingdom, Teachings, Miracles and conflict 4:17 to 25:46

Great Confession 16:13-20

Transfiguration 17:1-2

The Sacrifice 26:1 to 27:66

Probable Time & Date: 3 P.M., Friday, April 7, AD 30

Demise of Judas 27:3-10

Other resurrections 27:52

His Resurrection 28:1-20

Probable Time & Date: Sunday very early A.M., April 9, AD 30

Bribery of the tomb guards 28:11-15

Acknowledged that all Power or Authority in Heaven and Earth had been given to Him 28:18

Emphasis on baptism in the Great Commission 28:19-20

(2) Mark

Written by John Mark, a close companion of Peter, Paul and Barnabas emphasized the Deeds, Authority and Power of Jesus Christ, to the Romans, about 60 AD.

Introduction 1:1-13

Parable of the growing seeds 4:26-29

Early Galilean Ministry 1:14 to 7:23

Tyre and Sidon 7:24-30

Northern Galilee 7:3 to 9:50

Miracle, healing of deaf man 7:31-37

Miracle, sight restored in Bethsaida 8:22-26

Perea and the Journey to Jerusalem 10:1-52

Execution and Resurrection 11:1 to 16:8

Appeared to Mary Magdalene and others 16:9-14

Gives Great Commission, two choices and instructions 16:15-18

Ascension 16:19 (**Probable Date: May, 30 AD**)

(3) Luke

Luke, who wrote this Gospel and the Book of Acts, was an educated Greek physician. He traveled with Paul during his second missionary journey. Written to the Greeks, presents Jesus as a perfect man, who far surpassed the highest ideals of the Greeks.

Prologue 1:1-4

Significant events leading up to the births of Jesus and John, the Baptist 1:5-80

Childhood of Jesus 2:1-52

Beginning of Jesus' Ministry 3:1 to 4:13

The attest of John, the Baptist 3:19-20

Galilean Ministry 4:14 to 9:6

Jesus rejected in His hometown 4:16-30

Miraculous catch of fish 5:1-11

Miracle, son of widow raised from the dead 7:11-17

Sinful woman anoints Jesus 7:36-50

Women traveling with Jesus 8:1-3

Departure from Galilee 9:7-50

Miracles, Teachings and events in the months leading up to His Death 10:1 to 18-14

Judean and Perean Ministry 9:51 to 18:43

Encountered Zacchaeus, Parable of the Ten Servants 19:1-27

End of Public Ministry 19:29-21:37

Events leading up to His Death 22:1-23:56

Trial of Jesus before Herod 23:6-12

Resurrection 24:1-43

Final Words of Jesus 24:44-49

Ascension 24:50-51

(4) John

Written by John many years after the first three Gospels were finished, in order to complete the Message. While Matthew, Mark and Luke present general views of the Life and Teachings of Jesus, John deals with the deeper questions of living the Christian Life in a simple, direct style.

Prologue 1:1-18

Declares the Deity of Christ 1:1-2

Significant summary 1:3-18

Public Ministry of John, the Baptist, who proclaims Jesus as the Messiah 1:19-34

Presentation of the Son of God 1:35 to 4:54

First miracle, water converted to wine 2:1-10

First Cleansing of the Temple 2:13-25

Key Teaching: must be born again 3:1-21

Key Teaching: God is a Spirit and must be worshipped in Spirit and in Truth 4:23-24

Opposition to the Son of God 5:1-12-50

Only in the book of John are the "I am" statements recorded, which refer back to Exodus 3:14

I am the bread of life 6:35

I am the light of the world 8:12

Before Abraham was, I am 8:58

I am the door of the sheep 10:7

I am the good shepherd 10:11

I am the way, the truth and the life 14:6

I am the vine 15:5

Preparation of His Disciples 13:1 to 17:26

Trials, Crucifixion, Resurrection & Appearances 18:1 to 21:23

Epilogue 21:24-25

E. Acts of the Apostles

Written by Luke, the book of Acts covers the actions and power of the Apostles. Includes the rapid growth during the first years of the Church and teaches all were offered the Grace of God through Jesus Christ.

Salutation by Luke to Theophilus 1:1

Confirmation of the Resurrection of Jesus Christ 1:2-3

Ascension 1:9

Two men in white robes immediately appeared and told the amazed Apostles that one day He will return in the same manner. 1:10-11

Meeting of faithful in upper room 1:12-15

Review of betrayal of Judas, Peter quotes Psalms 69:25 & 109:8, which predicted the death of Judas, selection of his replacement 1:16-20

Prayer & casting of lots used in selection of the new Apostle Matthias 1:21-26

Holy Spirit arrives with the sound of a mighty wind in tongues of fire 2:1-3

Disciples begin to speak in other languages, so all could understand 2:4

Peter boldly preached one of the Greatest Sermons of all time. 2:12-40

His Church began with a membership of about 3000 souls. 2:41

The Lord added saved to His Church 2:47

Peter healed a crippled beggar 3:2-10

Deception and death of Ananias & Sapphira 5:1-11

Appointment of the seven 6:5-7

Stephen performed miracles and wonders 6:8

Stephen addresses the Sanhedrin 7:1-53

Martyrdom of Stephen 7:54-60

Saul attempts to destroy His Church 8:1-3

Public ministry of Philip in Samara and to the Ethiopian 8:4-40

The vendetta of Saul against His Church 9:1-2

Saul is blinded, converted, filled with the Holy Spirit and Preaches in Damascus and Jerusalem 9:3-31

Peter healed Aeneas at Lydda 9:32-35

Peter raised Tabitha (Dorcas) from the dead at Joppa 9:36-43

Peter teaches Cornelius at Caesarea 10:1 to 11:18

Death of James by order of King Herod Agrippa 12:1-2

Peter freed from prison by an Angel 12:3-11

An Angel of God struck King Herod with fatal illness for his blasphemy 12:23

First missionary journey 12:25 to 14:28

Jews oppose, Gentiles accept the Word 13:46-48

Jerusalem Council 15:1-35

Second missionary journey 15:36 to 18:22

Selection of Timothy 16:1-5

Macedonian Call 16:6-10

Conversion of Lydia 16:11-15

Paul frees slave girl of a demon 16:16-18

Paul and Silas imprisoned 16:19-25

God frees prisoners with an earthquake 16:26

Conversion of the jailer 6:31-33

Third missionary journey 18:23 to 21:14

Re-baptism of some baptized by John, the Baptist 19:1-5

Final missionary journey to Rome 21:15 to 28:31

F. The Epistles

The Epistles, which make up the largest part of the New Testament, were penned principally by Paul. These letters were written to individual Christians, local congregations, or to several local congregations in an area. These letters were written to answer questions, give guidance as to how Christians must live, what the Church should and should not be, as well as, warnings regarding sin and false teachers.

(1) Romans

Book covers two major topics, justification by faith and addresses a controversy between the Jews and the Gentiles.

Some of the Jews felt they should have a higher status than the Gentiles, since they had been the chosen nation under the Old Covenant. The author Paul points out that all have sinned, that there are no preferences in the eyes of God.

Introduction 1:1–17

Universal Condemnation 1:18–3:20

Justification 3:21–5:21

Sanctification 6:1–8:39

Provisions for Israel 9:1–11:36

Ethics of the people of God 12:1–15:16

Discussion of Personal Matters 15:17–16:16

Conclusion 16:17–27

(2) First Corinthians

Written to Corinthians from Ephesus, by Paul, shortly after the establishment of the Church at Corinth, which was a major city with few moral restraints. Naturally, it was difficult to organize a Church and keep it pure during this period. The purpose of the letter was to direct the Church away from error and disorder and to answer specific questions.

Introduction 1:1–9.

Turmoil and division reported to the apostle Paul 1:10–6:20

Issues and questions raised by the membership 7:1–10:33

Additional concerns 11:1–15:58

Conclusion 16:10–24

(3) Second Corinthians

Paul had learned from Titus that his first letter had resulted in causing a large number of the members to repent. Paul also was advised of certain false teachers, who were denouncing his authority. He wrote expressing pleasure regarding the reported repentance, to warn against false teachings and to defend his spiritual position.

Introduction and Greeting 1:1–11

Ministry of Reconciliation 1:12 to 7:16

The Apostolic Ministry of Paul 2:12 to 6:10

Exhorts followers to avoid sin 6:11 to 7:1

Paul teaches from the Word 7:2 to 9:15

Paul defends Apostolic Authority 10:1 to 12:13

Calls for restoration of order in His Church at Corinth 12:14 to 13:10

Conclusion 13:11-14

(4) Galatians

The Church at Galatia was established during Paul's first missionary journey. Some years later, he received word that many members were being led away into Jewish traditions. His letter warns against false teachings and focuses on justification by faith.

Introduction 1:1–9

Gospel received from God 1:10–12

Evidence substantiating this claim 1:13–2:21

Failure of legalism 3:1–4:31

Liberty in Christ 5:1–6:10

Conclusion 6:11–18

(5) Ephesians

Paul's restatement of the basic message: Christ is the Center and that the Church is united in Him.

Introduction 1:1-2

Believers chosen by God 1:3–6

Wisdom of God in providing redemption through Jesus Christ 1:7–10

The Assurance of the Holy Spirit 1:11–14

Thanksgiving and Prayer 1:15–23

Salvation and developing an understanding of the Love of God 2:1–3:21

Old and new life 4:17–5:21

Christian home 5:22–6:9

Spiritual warfare 6:10–20

Conclusion 6:20–24

(6) Philippians

The first Church established in what is now Europe. Paul provided warnings, discussed personal conduct and the joys of Christian life.

Introduction 1:1-2

Prayer of Thanksgiving on behalf of the Philippians 1:3-11

Discussion of the personal situation of Paul in Rome 1:12-26

Exhortation of Paul to membership 1:27 to 2:4

Supreme Example 2:5-18

Introduction of messengers 2:19-30

Warning regarding legalism 3:1-14

Final Admonitions 3:15-4:1-9

Paul expressed appreciation for gifts 4:10-20

Conclusion 4:21-23

(7) Colossians

Written to His Church at Colossae, a city in Phrygia, a province of Asia Minor, in which false doctrines were being taught. Paul writes that Christ is everything and real joy can only be obtained by truly living a Christian life.

Introduction 1:1-2

Prayer for the Colossians 1:3-14

Divine nature and work of Christ 1:15-23

Role of the Apostle Paul 1:24 to 2:5

Warnings of false teaching 2:6-15

Threat of heresy 2:16 to 3:4

New person in Christ 3:5-17

Practical Instructions 3:18 to 4:6

Commendation and Closing Salutations 4:7–17

Conclusion 4:18

(8) First Thessalonians

Written to His Church at Thessalonica, which had been organized during the second missionary journey of the apostle Paul

One of his early epistles, which primarily addressed the Second Coming of Christ

Personal testimony 1:1–3:13

An appeal 4:1–5:22

Conclusion 5:23–28

(9) Second Thessalonians

Written a few months after his first letter by the apostle Paul, in order to address certain misunderstandings concerning the tribulation prior to the Second Coming of Christ

Introduction 1:1-2

Benefits of prayer 1:3-12

Concerning the Day of the Lord 2:1-2

Sons of perdition 2:3-12

Exhortation to believers 2:13-17

Faithfulness 3:1-15

Conclusion 3:16-18

(10) First Timothy

Written to Timothy, an individual of Greek and Jewish heritage, who had served as a missionary companion of Paul

During this period, Timothy served as minister of His Church at Ephesus. Paul wrote to instruct him in spiritual matters and proper behavior.

Introduction 1:1-2

Ministry 1:3-20

Worship 2:1-15

Prayer 2:1-8

Modesty 2:9-15

Qualifications of Elders and Deacons 3:1-13

Purpose of letter 3:14-16

Error and correction 4:1-16

Treatment of widows and others 5:1-6:2

False teacher compared with a teacher of the Truth 6:3-21

(11) Second Timothy

Introduction 1:1-5

Source of strength during periods of persecution 1:6-2:7

False teachings 2:8-3:9

An example to follow 3:10-17

Final exhortation 4:1-5

Personal situation of Paul 4:6-18

Final Greetings 4:19–21

Conclusion 4:22

(12) Titus

Written by Paul to Titus, a Gentile serving as minister at His Church at Crete, which was in a state of general disorder and Paul wrote words of encouragement and guidance.

Introduction 1:1-4

Qualifications and responsibilities of Elders 1:5-9

Heresy 1:10-16

Appropriate Christian Behavior 2:1-10

Motivation for remaining faithful 2:11-3:2

Final Admonitions 3:3-15

(13) Philemon

Philemon was a wealthy member of the Church at Colossae. Onesimus, one of his slaves, had stolen from Philemon, his master and fled to Rome. Onesimus had been converted by Paul. He wrote to Philemon requesting that he forgive Onesimus and acknowledge him as a brother in Christ.

Introduction 1:1-3

Praise for Philemon 1:4-7

Plea for Onesimus 1:8-16

Pledge and Assurance 1:17-22

Conclusion 1:23-25

(a) Philemon contains an outstanding example of Christian love

Seeks to find the best in others 1:4

Concern for the welfare of others 1:10

Honest in approach to tribulations 1:12

Happily shares the burdens of others 1:18

Assumes the best in others 1:21

(14) Hebrews

The writer points out that Christ is greater than Moses, Joshua, and all the Prophets. That in time past; God had spoken through all of these men, but that now He speaks only through His Son, Jesus Christ. The believers were encouraged to maintain the Faith. Written to a group of Jewish Christians, who were being persecuted, were in a state of despair and were tempted to return to the practice of Judaism

Prologue 1:1–4

Christ superior to angels 1:5-14

Warning: heed the Words of Jesus 2:1-4

The Son of God came to earth in human form 2:5-18

Christ is superior to Moses 3:1-6

Warning: harden not your heart 3:7–4:13

Jesus is now our High Priest, who is substantially superior to the Old Testament priesthood 4:14-16 to 5:1-10

Warning: do not fall away 5:11 to 6:12

Certainty of the Promise of God 6:13-20

Example of Melchizedek 7:1-28

Christ as High Priest of the enhanced Covenant 8:1-13

Worship under Old Covenant 9:1-10

The Blood of Christ was the perfect offering for sin 9:11-28 to 10-18

Faith is required 10:19-25

Warning: do not willfully sin 10:26-31

Faith and Perseverance 10:32–39 to 11:6

Examples of great faith 11:7-40

Living as a reflection of Christ 12:1 to 13:17

Epilogue 13:18-25

(15) James

This book, as well as Peter, John and Jude are considered general epistles. James focuses on morals, ethics and that works and faith are equally important. An early letter, probably written prior to AD 50

Greeting 1:1

Patience in trials and temptation 1:2-18

Personal conduct 1:19-27

Authentic faith 2:1-26

Impartiality 2:1-13

Importance of good works 2:14-26

Control your tongue 3:1-12

Wisdom from Heaven contrasted with false wisdom 3:13-18

Worldly activities & concerns condemned 4:1-5

Humble yourself before God and draw near to Him 4:6-10

Worldly actions condemned 4:11-12

Trust your God in future planning (If the Lord wills) 4:13-15

Avoid boasting, do good 4:16-17

Warning to those rich in worldly possessions 5:1-6

Patience while in distress 5:7-11

Do not swear 5:12

Instructions regarding prayer 5:13-18

Brotherly concern 5:19-20

(16) First Peter

In this general epistle Christians were encouraged to hold fast to their faith, even under persecution.

Greeting 1:1-2

Hope and promise of eternal life 1:3-12

Called for conformity to a Holy lifestyle 1:13-25

Remaining faithful 2:1-25

Advice to husbands and wives 3:1-7

Walking in faith 3:8-22 to 4:6

Love one another in the midst of suffering 4:7-19

Advice to Elders 5:1-4

Victory of faith 5:5-11

Final comments 5:12-14

(17) Second Peter

Another general epistle in which Peter warns of false teachers, exhorts new Christians to grow in faith and knowledge of Jesus. Provided a brief description of the Second Coming of Christ

Introduction 1:1

Advice to new Christians 1:2-21

Warning of false teachings 2:1-22

Avoiding doubt 3:1-7

Cling to the Promises 3:8

Living in the Light 3:11-18

Epistles of John

The first two letters are general epistles. The first is a discourse on doctrine, written to correct errors and to glory in the qualities of the Christian life. The second was written for Christian women, in order to emphasize the Truth of the Gospel and includes warnings of false teachers. The third, which is addressed to Gaius, commends him for treatment of other Christians.

(18) First John

Confirms that Jesus is the Son of God 1:1-4

Walking in the Light and Cleansing Blood of Christ 1:5-8

Confess your sins and He will forgive 1:9-10 to 2:6

Warning: hate not your brother (or sister) 2:7-11

Warning: love not this world 2:12-17

Warning: antichrists or false teachers 2:18-23

Abide in the Truth 2:24-29 to 3:10

Love one another 3:11-24

Differentiate the Truth from false teachings 4:1-6

God is the source of all Love 4:7-21

God is the source of all Life 5:1-20

Final warning 5:21

(19) Second John

Greeting 1:1-4

Beware of false teachers 1:5-9

Warning: Support of false teachers is sinful 1:10-11

Final comments 1:12-13

(20) Third John

Greeting 1:1-2

Praise of Gaius 1:3-8

Denunciation of Diotrephes 1:9-10

Avoid evil 1:11

Praise of Demetrius 1:12

Closing comments 1:13-14

(21) Jude

Greeting 1:1-2

Exhortation to earnestly contend for the Faith 1:3

Beware of false teachers 1:4-20

Keep the Faith 1:21-24

Salutation to our Lord and Savior 1:25

G. The Revelation of Jesus Christ
(The Apocalypse)

Introduction 1:1-3

Greeting 1:4-6

The Promise of the Second Coming of Christ 1:7

Opening comment of the Lord 1:8

Vision of the Glorified Christ 1:9-17a

Declaration, Command and Explanation of the Lord 1:17b-20

Messages to His Churches 2:1-7 to 3:14–22

Worship of God in Heaven 4:1-11

Scroll and the Lamb of God 5:1-10

Worship of the Lamb 5:11-14

Six of the Seven Seals broken 6:1-17

The 144,000 sealed by God 7:1-8

Vast multitude of the Faithful 7:9-17

The Seventh Seal 8-1:5

Six of Seven Trumpets sounded 8:6 to 9:21

Angel with small Scroll 10:1-11

Two Witnesses 11:1:14

Seventh Trumpet 11:15-19

The Woman and Dragon 12:1-17

Two beasts 13:1-18

The Lamb and the 144,000 14:1-5

Three Angels 14:6-13

Harvest of the earth 14:14-20

Bowls of Wrath 15:1-16:21

Judgment of apostate religion 17:1-18

Judgment of Babylon 18:1-24

Marriage of the Lamb 19:1-10

Triumph of the Christ 19:11-16

Demise of the beast 19:17-21

1000 years 20:1-6

The destruction of Satan 20:7-10

The final Judgment at the great White Throne 20:11-15

The new earth 21:1–7

Eternal punishment 21:8

New Jerusalem 21:9–26

Book of Life 21:27

The river of Life 22:1-6

The Promise of Jesus to return 22:7-17

Injunction against adding to or taking away from the Word 22:18-19

Coming soon 22:20

Closing Blessing 22:21

Jesus gave His precious life in order to make it possible for His faithful followers to receive the greatest gift in the Spiritual Realm, which is everlasting life in the Glorious Paradise of the Kingdom of God... Heaven Awaits!

Appendix 1
Quick Start Guide to Glorious Immortality

Appendix Contents

A. Introduction

B. The Importance of understanding Truth

C. Divine Authority is Mandatory

D. Divine Patterns of the Faith

E. Determining the Identify of His Church

F. His Divine Pattern or Plan of Salvation.

G. Closing Comments

H. Now, make your commitment to your Lord and Savior PERSONAL!

A. Introduction

(1) The purpose of this appendix is to provide a guide to assist the searcher of Truth in determining:

(a) The modern name of His Church

(b) How to carefully follow His Divine Pattern (Plan) of Salvation.

This appendix has been written for those living a fast paced lifestyle and all others who wish to learn the Truth quickly.

This is encouraged, because time is definitely of the essence, when a person is seriously considering becoming a Christian.

No man knows the time of his departure from this life, so it is only prudent to act as quick as possible once the Truth is known and understood.

This material is presented in an outline form with verse references only, to provide the individual with the opportunity and advantage of uncovering and confirming the specific Divine Will of God using his or her personal Bible or Biblical computer program.

B. Importance of understanding Truth

The great apostle Peter confirms this declaration in 2 PETER 3:9, "The Lord is not slack concerning his promise, as some men count slackness; but is longsuffering to us-ward, not willing that any should perish, *but that all should come to repentance."*

Jesus requires that we understand the **Truth or the specific Divine Will of God,** and promises that through obedience we will be made free from fear and an ever increasing burden of sin.

Key Passage: JOHN 8:31-32

God has expressed His desire that everyone in the world would follow His Plan of Salvation and then remain faithful; "Who will have all men to be saved, and to come unto the knowledge of the truth."

Reference: 1 TIMOTHY 2:4

What is the meaning of the words know, knowledge and truth, referred to in these passages?

In this context, the words know and knowledge means comprehension or understanding, and the Truth is interchangeable with and comparable to the specific Divine Will of God.

The source of all Truth is the Scriptures, which is defined in JOHN 17:17; "Sanctify them by your truth, your word is truth."

The phrase "Your Word is Truth" is a direct reference to the Scriptures. Christians must seek to be guided in their beliefs and practices solely from the inspired Word of God, **as it is our only source of Biblical Authority.**

The great apostle Paul provides additional assurance, in 2 TIMOTHY 3:16-17; that the scriptures are sufficient for all our needs.

C. Divine Authority is Mandatory

(1) We must have Biblical Authority or support for every belief and practice

(a) Our personal beliefs must be based upon clearly defined convictions or standards.

These convictions or standards must be based solely upon the Word of God, as it is our only source of Divine Authority

This set of convictions or standards must embrace His total counsel, while including only the Patterns, Commandments, Instructions and Examples provided by Jesus, and His Disciples

EPHESIANS 5:10-11
Proving what is acceptable unto the Lord. And have no fellowship with the unfruitful works of darkness, but rather reprove them.

Additional references: 1 THESSALONIANS 5:21, 2 TIMOTHY 1:13

(b) The Apostle Paul commanded that Christians hold fast to only the traditions they had been taught

Reference: 2 THESSALONIANS 2:15

(2) We must understand the everlasting consequences of unauthorized beliefs or practices.

Key Passage: MATTHEW 7:21-23

(3) We must understand that it is sinful to condone unauthorized or condemned beliefs or practices.

Key Passage: 2 JOHN 1:9-11

D. Divine Patterns of the Faith

The Greek word **"tupos"** means a model for imitation, a pattern, form or exact replication. Each time a pattern [tupos] is duplicated certain characteristics and distinctiveness will always be present and identifiable.

Consider why the modern fast food franchises are successful. The developers of these franchises created successful and profitable methods of operations and then expanded by selling exact duplications to individuals seeking to purchase a successful business, making great gains in the process.

In doing so, these developers use the same methods that were employed in the Old Testament and the first century.

(1) The Patterns of the Faith are distinctive

The following examples confirm that the concept of those Patterns is an integrated element of God's Plan

The Greek word **"pistis"** translates as religious truth, or the truthfulness of God, especially reliance upon Christ for salvation, abstractly, the system of religious (Gospel) truth itself: assurance, belief, faith or fidelity.

The Apostle Paul, in EPHESIANS 4:4-6 *clearly states there is only one faith*

EPHESIANS 4:4-6
There is one body, [His Church] and one Spirit, even as ye are called in one hope of your calling; One Lord, one faith, [pistis] one baptism, One God and Father of all, who is above all, and through all, and in you all.

Jude used the same Greek word [pistis] to denote the Faith.

JUDE 1:3
Beloved, when I gave all diligence to write unto you of the common salvation, it was needful for me to write unto you, and exhort you that ye should earnestly contend for the **faith [pistis]** which was once delivered unto the saints.

(2) The Faith consists of a distinctive unchanging Body of Truth.

Jesus and His Disciples originally taught the Faith (also known as, the Message of Christ, the Truth and the specific Divine Will of God) in order to develop belief, faith, trust in Jesus Christ and to explain His Divine Directives

Note: An overview of the Patterns and related elements of Message of Christ has been provided in Appendix 6:

Summary of selected Elements of the Divine Mosaic.

Almost immediately after the very beginning of His Church, this precious Body of Truth, His Gospel was being altered or misrepresented.

Unfortunately, even today generally the full Gospel of Christ, either is **not** being taught or is seriously distorted by the vast majority of teachers.

E. Determining the Identify of His Church

Anyone, who is willing to make the effort, is able to identify and locate His Church by the process of elimination or by simply comparing beliefs, practices and structure of each religious group against the words of the New Testament.

His Church is the largest and most conservative of the five groups that came into being as a result of **Restoration Movement** that occurred during the Second Great Awakening in the early years of the nineteenth century in the eastern and southern regions of the United States.

The basic objective of the Restoration pioneers was to eliminate all unsupported non-Biblical components in worship service and restore the purity of the Church by a complete return to the primitive or the original Church of the first century.

Members of His Church in the United States generally mark the beginning of the Restoration in the United States on August 7, 1801 or the opening day of the famous revival held at Cane Creek, Kentucky, which was attended by tens of thousands seeking to find the Truth.

For over one hundred years, the various factions of the Restoration worked to attain unity and finally agree upon common doctrine, based solely upon the Word of God.

Unfortunately, these efforts failed and in1906 the separate entities of the Restoration split and formed independent Churches.

The reader may find the Appendixes 2, 3, 4, 5, and 6, one or more of the "Suggested Outside References" listed near the end of this guide or internet key-word searches, useful in making this all important determination

If for any reason, after making your best efforts, you are unable to determine the identity of the Church of our Lord, forward an e-mail to luckylynde@gmx.com or drop a note to my attention, 131 W. Foley #1445, Eufaula, Oklahoma 74432. Upon receipt, the author will provide the names and addresses of congregations in your area, of the only church he is aware of that matches the Divine Pattern.

Once His Church is identified, it is recommended that the user request the assistance of the minister or leaders of the local congregation in your area. Then follow carefully, His Pattern or Plan of Salvation; be baptized, for the complete remission or forgiveness of all your sins.

(1) Divine Pattern of His Church

The Greek word for His Church is **"Ekklesia"**, which means "the called out assembly" and people called from one realm (this world) to another (His spiritual Kingdom or His Church.)

This term was first applied to Christianity by Jesus in MATTHEW 16:18. This term applies to both worldwide and universal assembly, headquartered in Heaven, composed of saved believers who are in fellowship with Lord Jesus and one another. This is known as the Body of Christ or His Church, as well as local congregations of His Church throughout the world.

(2) Jesus founded His Church and provided the Divine pattern

Mankind is directed to strictly follow that form of teaching or "the Faith" which was originally delivered or taught orally.

A distinctive unchanging body of **"Truth"**, *which will set you free from fear* and an *ever-increasing burden of sin*, so you may be acceptable *in the sight of God*

References: MATTHEW 16:18, ROMANS 6:17-18, 2 TIMOTHY 1:13, JOHN 8:31-32

Note: The word Truth in JOHN 8:31-32 simply means to carefully follow the Patterns, Commandments, Instructions and Examples set forth in the Word of God. The term "Truth" is interchangeable with and comparable to the term the "Will of God".

(3) Jesus Christ purchased His Church with His shed blood

Reference: ACTS 20:28

(4) Jesus Christ has all Power (Authority) over His Church

Members of His Church submit respectfully to the supreme Power and Authority of Christ. The acknowledgement of the Authority of Christ is one of the distinguishing traits of His Church.

References: MATTHEW 28:18, COLOSSIANS 3:1

(5) Jesus Christ is the Head of His Church, which is His body

Reference: EPHESIANS 1:22-23

(6) Place and Date of the beginning of His Church

His Church was established on the Day of Pentecost, a Sunday, ten days following the Ascension of Christ to the right hand of God, the Father in approximately AD 30, with a beginning membership of about three thousand souls in Jerusalem

The Apostle Peter preached the first and one of the Greatest Sermon of all time proclaiming Salvation through the remission of sin.

References: ACTS 2:41, ACTS 2:14

(7) Only the Lord may add members to His Church

Individuals who have conformed themselves to His Commandments are added to His Church by the Lord.

No man or woman has ever been added to His Church through a vote of the congregation or any other method created by man.

Reference: ACTS 2:47

(a) Only one Church is the true Church of our Lord. His Church has no earthly organization as its headquarters are in Heaven.

References: EPHESIANS 4:4-6, COLOSSIANS 3:1

(8) Jesus Christ pleaded for religious unity in one Faith and that His Church would not be divided.

References: JOHN 17:11, JOHN 17:20-21

(9) Jesus Christ loves and will save the faithful disciples of His Church from the horrors of Hell.

References: EPHESIANS 5:23, EPHESIANS 5:25

(10) The Apostle Paul appealed for religious unity in one Faith.

References: 1 CORINTHIANS 1:10, EPHESIAN 4:4-6

(11) The Apostle Paul predicted Denominationalism.

Reference: ACTS 20:29-31

(12) The modern name of His Church is scriptural

Numerous descriptive expressions for His Church or the Faith appear upon the pages of the New Testament. However, no formal name for His Church or "The Faith" was provided in the first century, as it is unnecessary since there is only one.

Many of the moons of the other planets have names, but our moon has remained unnamed. Why? *Because there is only one!*

God provided a pattern to follow. The use of any name, which is mentioned in the Word of God, would be scriptural. However, the acceptability of other church names, which are not in accord with the Scriptures or that glorify a human name, would be questionable.

(13) The modern name of His Church glorifies His Holy Name.

His Church has about 40 different designations in the Bible, which usually relate to or glorify Christ or God, but no official name. Christ has clearly indicated that Christians are to glorify Him and His name.

While only one church existed in the first century, during the restoration, in the early nineteenth century, hundreds, if not thousands of churches were in existence. The restorers obeyed His Commandment, followed the Biblical Pattern and re-established His Church with a scriptural modern name in tribute to the magnificence of our Lord and Savior.

References: JOHN 13:32, JOHN 17:1

(14) Members of His Church wear the name of Christ.

Isaiah prophesied that the Lord would give the children of God a new everlasting name. For this reason the members of His Church wear the name of Christians only, in Honor of Christ and to His Glory.

References: ISAIAH 56:5, ISAIAH 62:2, ACTS 11:26, 1 PETER 4:16

(15) Divine Pattern of Scriptural Worship

The Authority, Commandment, Pattern or Example for each act of Worship is based solely on inspired Scriptures of the New Testament. The leadership and members of His Church actively seek to be guided in all they do by the Word of God.

The Great Apostle Paul assures us in 2 TIMOTHY 3:15-17 that the Scriptures are by inspiration of God and meet all our needs.

(a) God, the Father revealed to the world through his Son, in the first century, precisely how Christians are to worship Him each Lord's Day.

Reference: JOHN 12:49-50

(b) The purpose of worship is the Glorification and Worship of God

References: PSALMS 100:1-5, 1 PETER 2:9, 1 PETER 4:11

(c) Worship of God is to be truly in Spirit and in Truth

References: JOHN 4:24, 1 CORINTHIANS 14:15

Briefly, to be in the Spirit, one must approach worship or prayer with an attitude of humility, obedience and trust. In Truth is synonymous with the Will of God.

Therefore in this context, in Truth, means to Worship in the prescribed manner provided in the Scriptures or strictly in accord with the Will of God as follows:

(d) Meets on Sunday, the first day of the week

Reference: ACTS 20:7

(e) Several Prayers are offered to God during each Service.

Prayer is a central component of all worship services.

References: MATTHEW 6:7-13, JAMES 5:16, ACTS 2:42, 1 TIMOTHY 2:1, 1 THESSALONIANS 5:17

(f) Vocal singing and making melody in their hearts, without instrumental accompaniment, is an important component of worship.

References: EPHESIANS 5:19, COLOSSIANS 3:16, ACTS 16:25

The use of musical instruments is not mentioned or Commanded in the Holy Scriptures; therefore it can only be considered an unauthorized and illegitimate addition to the worship service.

Hence, it would be a violation of the unyielding Biblical Injunction against "adding to" in REVELATION 22:18-19 and could result in each individual who affirms its use to be eternally lost.

It is true that in the Old Testament, God Commanded and was Worshipped with harps and other instruments.

Reference: 2 CHRONICLES 29:25

However, the New Testament contains no such directive related to the use of any type of musical instrument, as well as, several other patterns Commanded under the Old Law (Testament), such as animal sacrifices in the Worship of God.

(g) Teaching and preaching of the Word to one another each time we gather for Worship.

The Bible is the exclusive basis of all teachings in classes and from the pulpit.

References: MATTHEW 24:14, ROMANS 10:15, 1 CORINTHIANS 9:14, COLOSSIANS 1:28, 2 TIMOTHY 4:2

(h) The Lord's Supper is observed on Sunday, the first day of each and every week

References: MATTHEW 26:26-28, ACTS 20:7, ACTS 2:42, 1 CORINTHIANS 11:23-26

(i) Cheerfully give of our means.

Each week, members are given the opportunity to support the work of the Church by returning to the Lord a portion of the amount they have been prospered.

References: 1 CORINTHIANS 16:2, 2 CORINTHIANS 9:6-8

(16) Throughout the Worship services of His Church, four principles govern all elements:

(a) Glorification and Worship of God

References: 1 PETER 2:9, 1 PETER 4:11

(b) Worship the Father in spirit and in truth

References: JOHN 4:24, 1 CORINTHIANS 14:15

(c) All things are done for edification (instruction)

Reference: 1 CORINTHIANS 14:25-26

(d) All things are to be done decently and in order

Reference: 1 CORINTHIANS 14:40

(17) Divine Pattern - Organizational Structure of Congregations

(a) Jesus Christ is the Head of His Church, which is His Body.

Reference: EPHESIANS 1:22-23

(b) Each mature Congregation or local Church had Elders, who oversaw and tended to the flock.

A group of two or more Elders, who oversaw and tended to the Spiritual needs of its members, governed each congregation of the early church. Elders ordained at that location independently ruled each congregation or local church. Thus each congregation or local church had complete autonomy and was bound to other local churches or congregations, only through Jesus as the Head of His Church and their shared Faith. Biblical scholars assume this type of church government was employed to circumvent widespread apostasy.

References: 1 TIMOTHY 5:17, ACTS 14:23, 1 PETER 5:2

There is misconception regarding the Scriptural government of the Church. Since the people of the United States and several other countries live in a democracy, many believe that the congregation should vote upon issues that affect the majority.

This idea is erroneous, because the church is not a democracy, but a monarchy and <u>Jesus Christ</u> is the everlasting King.

References: 1 TIMOTHY 6:14-15, COLOSSIANS 1:18, JAMES 4:12

(c) Today, Elders of each congregation, who are subject only to the King, oversee their congregation and must meet certain qualifications.

Reference: 1 TIMOTHY 3:1-7

In addition, churches in these last days conform to all other aspects of the first century church government, which includes;

(d) That each local Church has two or more Deacons, who are subject to the Elders, actively serve the church and must meet certain qualifications.

Reference: 1 TIMOTHY 3:8-13

(e) That each local Church has Evangelists, Ministers, Preachers or Teachers who teach or proclaim the gospel

Reference: EPHESIANS 4:11-12

(f) That each local Church has Members, who love the Lord and each other

References: PHILIPPIANS 2:1-3, 1 JOHN 5:1-2

(g) Members of His Church collectively esteem Jesus Christ as Lord and have the highest regard for His Authority.

Reference: MATTHEW 28:18

(h) Adding to, or subtracting from, the simple instructions of Jesus is forbidden and indicates a failure to respect Him as Lord.

Reference: REVELATION 22:18-19

Therefore, congregations of His Church have no governing councils, earthly headquarters or denominational governmental associations, as none such are authorized in the Bible. These societies, which have been created by men, serve only to compete with the Authority of Christ. Such organizations bind human traditions and commandments upon others, which was condemned by Jesus.

Reference: MATTHEW 15:9

F. His Divine Pattern or Plan of Salvation

(1) Counting the Cost of becoming a Christian

Salvation, which is free to all, was purchased with the blood of Christ, upon which an earthly value cannot be placed. Jesus taught that just one soul has a greater value than the entire wealth of the world.

Reference: MATTHEW 16:26

Other elements that could be considered a part of the cost are, the time involved, the monetary requirements and the elimination of many of the pleasures of this world, in order to become a living sacrifice.

Reference: ROMANS 12:1-2

Christ indicated one should carefully consider the cost of following Him

Reference: LUKE 14:28

On the other hand, Jesus offers a crown of life to His faithful followers.

Reference: REVELATION 2:10

Which will you choose?

(2) While on earth, Jesus Christ and His Apostles commanded seven things; we must do, in order to become a child of God.

(a) The new convert must acknowledge, in his or her heart that in light of God's word, that he or she is a sinner. (ROMANS 3:23, ROMANS 5:12, ROMANS 6:23, LUKE 18:13)

(b) The new convert must hear or study the Word of God. (JOHN 5:24, ROMANS 10:17)

(c) The new convert must have faith or trust and be obedient. (HEBREWS 11:6, ROMANS 16:26, ROMANS 16:19, 2 CORINTHIANS 10:5, GALATIANS 3:26)

(d) The new convert must sincerely believe that Jesus is the Son of God (MARK 16:15-16, JOHN 3:16, JOHN 8:24, ACTS 16:31, JOHN 3:36, JOHN 17:21, ACTS 8:37, 1 JOHN 5:13)

(e) The new convert must truly repent of his or her sins and then turn away from sin. (LUKE 13:3, ACTS 3:19, ROMANS 2:4, 2 CORINTHIANS 7:10, ACTS 17:30, ACTS 20:21, 2 PETER 3:9)

(f) The new convert must confess that Jesus is his or her Lord and the Son of God. (MATTHEW 10:32-33, LUKE 12:8, ROMANS 10:9-10, 1 JOHN 4:15)

(g) The new convert must be baptized into Christ, by total immersion, for the remission of sins in the name of the Father, the Son and the Holy Ghost [Spirit] (MATTHEW 28:19, ACTS 2:38, MARK 16:16, JOHN 3:3-5, ACTS 10:47, ACTS 22:16, ROMANS 6:3, HEBREWS 10:22, GALATIANS 3:27)

(3) Additional important factors to fully understand and appreciate

(a) Baptism is a burial by immersion. (MATTHEW 3:16-17, ACTS 8:38-39)

(b) Baptism is a resurrection. (COLOSSIANS 2:12, ROMANS 6:3-6)

(c) When an individual is baptized, he or she goes into the water a sinner, is buried in the water and raised sinless through the blood of Christ (1 JOHN 1:7, REVELATION 1:5)

(4) At that very moment:

(a) The new convert is saved from his or her sins. (1 PETER 3:21)

(b) The new convert has gained Justification (1 CORINTHIANS 6:11)

(c) The new convert has gained entrance into the Kingdom or His Church (JOHN 3:5)

One will be added to His Church, after following His Pattern of Salvation or has been saved, at which time the name of the new convert is added to the membership rolls, in Heaven, by our Lord God Almighty. (PHILIPPIANS 4:3, REVELATION 20:15, REVELATION 3:5, ACTS 2:41, ACTS 2:47, COLOSSIANS 3:1)

(d) The new convert has put on Christ and has become a child of God. (GALATIANS 3:26-27)

(e) The new convert has been born again (JOHN 3:3, 1 PETER 1:23)

(5) After an individual has been baptized, he or she is commanded by the Master to Remain Faithful

One must walk in newness of life (having put away the previous life filled with sin) and continue in faithful obedience. (ROMANS 6:3-4, REVELATION 2:10)

Note: Detailed guidance regarding the very important requirement to remain faithful is provided in Chapter VI, Chapter VII, Section I and Appendix 6

G. Closing Comments

There are seven requirements to be saved.

The number seven is a divine number, which denotes entirety or completeness

These seven things do not constitute simple "church ordinances". When we obey these seven things we do not merely comply with "church doctrines"

These are seven things Commanded by our Lord and Savior, Jesus Christ and His Disciples. In submitting to these things we obey our King.

Jesus is the One who died to set us free and we obey Him in order to accept the freedom that is found only in Him!

If we fail to submit to these Commands, we reject the Authority of the One who died for us... the only One who can set us free! Such rejection will only result in eternal damnation! (2 THESSALONIANS 1:8)

H. Now, make your commitment to your Lord and Savior PERSONAL!

(Your name) will be mine" says the Lord God Almighty, "in the day when I gather my treasured possessions." (MALACHI 3:17 – Updated)

In order to be invited to spend Eternity in the Glorious Paradise of God and to discover its wonders, we must cautiously and carefully follow the Narrow Way... Heaven Awaits!

Appendix 2

Checklist to determine if a religious group is His Church

Appendix Contents

A. Introduction

B. Fundamental Considerations

C. Beliefs regarding Jesus Christ

D. Scriptural Names

E. Scriptural Worship

F. His Divine Pattern or Plan of Salvation

A. Introduction

The purpose of this checklist is to assist the user in determining if any church or faith under his or her personal review conforms precisely to the Scriptural Patterns provided in the New Testament.

This is a very important determination, since, in order to be saved, Christians are directed to conform, organize and harmonize their Worship of God in precise accord with the Patterns, Examples, Commandments and Instructions of Jesus and His Disciples without unauthorized additions or creative enhancements.

The Scriptural correct answer, without exception, to each and every question is yes.

B: Fundamental Considerations

Did this church or faith come into being or commence at the time in history and in the geographical location as recorded in the book of Acts?

Yes ___ No ___

His Church was established, in Jerusalem, on the Day of Pentecost, a Sunday ten days after ascension to the right hand of God in Heaven in about AD 30.

Any church that was established at a different time in history or at a different place cannot be the Church that Christ built. This includes all man-made denominations of today.

Reference: Act 2:1-47

Substantial Biblical support is provided in. Chapter V

Do the members of this church or faith *actively plead* for religious unity, in one faith?

Yes ___ No ___

References: EPHESIANS 4:4-6, JOHN 17:20-21

Is the Holy Bible, *accepted unconditionally,* by the members of this church or faith, as the Inspired Word of God?

Yes ___ No ___

References: 1 PETER 1:22-25, 2 TIMOTHY 3:16-17

Do the members of this church or faith *unconditionally reject* the use of creeds, catechisms or any other directive or document created by any uninspired man or woman used in the Worship of God?

Yes ___ No ___

References: REVELATION 22:18-19, MATTHEW 15:9

Do the members of this church or faith *unconditionally reject* use of any items in the worship of God not specifically referred to in the Scriptures such as, idols (likeness of Mary etc.) musical instruments, candles, incense, religious titles or ranks or choirs?

Yes ___ No ___

References: REVELATION 22:18-19, MATTHEW 15:9

Do members of this church or faith *believe that Salvation can be lost?*

Yes ___ No ___

References: JAMES 5:19-20, 2 PETER 3:17-18

Do members of this church or faith believe that *a member who has fallen away may return to His Church?*

Yes ___ No ___

References: ACT 8:22, JAMES 5:16

C. Beliefs regarding Jesus Christ

Do the members of this Church or faith believe that *Jesus Christ founded His Church?*

Yes ___ No ___

Reference: MATTHEW 16:18

Do the members of this church or faith believe that *Christ is the Head of His Church, which is His Body?*

Yes ___ No ___

Reference: EPHESIANS 1:22-23

Do the members of this church or faith believe that only *one Church is the true Church of our Lord?*

Yes ___ No ___

Reference: EPHESIANS 4:4-6

Do the members of this church or faith believe that *Jesus purchased His Church, with His blood?*

Yes ___ No ___

Reference: ACTS 20:28

Do the members of this church or faith believe that *our Lord is the Savior of the Body, which is His Church?*

Yes ___ No ___

Reference: EPHESIANS 5:23

Do the members of this church or faith submit *respectfully to the supreme Power and Authority of Jesus Christ?*

Yes ___ No ___

References: COLOSSIANS 3:1, MATTHEW 28:18

D. Scriptural Names

A Scriptural name is defined as any appropriate name recorded in the pages of the New Testament.

Does this church or faith *make use of a Scriptural name?*

Yes ___ No ___

Does that name *glorify the name of God the Father or Jesus Christ?*

Yes ___ No ___

Are members of this church or faith *called by a Scriptural name?*

Yes ___ No ___

Does the name by which members are called *glorify the name of God the Father or Jesus Christ?*

Yes ___ No ___

References: JOHN 13:32, JOHN 17:1, ACTS 11:26, 1 PETER 4:16, ISAIAH 56:5, ISAIAH 62:2

E. Scriptural Worship

Do the members of this church or faith *Worship in Spirit and in Truth?*

Yes ___ No ___

References: JOHN 4:24, 1 CORINTHIANS 14:15

"In Spirit" is a matter of the proper attitude and appropriately focusing our minds on spiritual concerns, while consciously attempting to eliminate worldly issues from the active part of our mind during worship services or at times of prayer. "In Truth" is defined in two steps. (1) "In Truth" is interchangeable with and comparable to the term the "Will of God". (2) Christians are directed to conform, organize and harmonize their worship of God in precise accord with the examples, commandments and instructions of Jesus and His disciples without unauthorized additions or creative enhancements.

Do the members of this church or faith believe that *regular attendance to Worship services of His Church is essential to Salvation?*

Yes ___ No ___

References: ACTS 2:42, HEBREWS 10:24-25, ACTS 20:7

Is the purpose of worship in this church or faith the *Glorification and Worship of God?*

Yes ___ No ___

References: PSALMS 100:1-5, 1 PETER 2:9, 1 PETER 4:11

Do the members of this church or faith *meet for Worship services on Sunday, the first day of each week?*

Yes ___ No ___

Reference: ACTS 20:7

Are several prayers offered to God during each Worship service?

Yes ___ No ___

References: JAMES 5:16, ACTS 2:42, 1 TIMOTHY 2:1, 1 THESSALONIANS 5:17, MATTHEW 6:7-13

Do the members of this church or faith *sing and make melody in their hearts, without instrumental accompaniment, during each Worship service?*

Yes ___ No ___

References: EPHESIANS 5:19, COLOSSIANS 3:16, ACTS 16:25

In view of the fact that there is no Scriptural support for use of musical Instruments, would the use of such violate Biblical injunction against adding to Worship?

Yes ___ No ___

Reference: REVELATION 22:18-19

Is the Teaching and/or Preaching of the Word of God, an important part of each Worship service?

Yes ___ No ___

References: MATTHEW 24:14, ROMANS 10:15, 1 CORINTHIANS 9:14, COLOSSIANS 1:28, 2 TIMOTHY 4:2

Is the Lord's Supper observed on each Sunday, the first day of each and every week?

Yes ___ No ___

References: MATTHEW 26:26-28, ACTS 20:7, ACTS 2:42, 1 CORINTHIANS 11:23-26

F. His Divine Pattern or Plan of Salvation

Do members of this church or faith believe that in order to obtain salvation, *one must Acknowledge, in his or her heart, that in the light of God's Word that he or she is a sinner?*

Yes ___ No ___

References: ROMANS 3:23, ROMANS 5:12, ROMANS 6:23, LUKE 18:13

Do members of this church or faith believe that in order to obtain salvation, *one must first hear or carefully study the Word of God?*

Yes ___ No ___

References: JOHN 5:24, ROMANS 10:17

Do members of this church or faith believe that *Salvation is gained by faith, but not by faith only?*

Yes ___ No ___

References: HEBREWS 11:6, JAMES 2:17-18; 20

Do members of this church or faith believe that *one must sincerely Believe that Jesus is the Son of God?*

Yes ___ No ___

References: MARK 16:15-16, JOHN 3:16

Do members of this church or faith believe that *one must earnestly Repent of his or her sins and then make an honest effort to turn away from our sins of the past?*

Yes ___ No ___

References: LUKE 13:3, ROMANS 6:1-2

Do members of this church or faith believe that *one must honestly Confess that Jesus is the Son of God and our Lord?*

Yes ___ No ___

Reference: MATTHEW 10:32-33

Do members of this church or faith believe that *one must be Baptized by total immersion?*

Yes ___ No ___

References: MATTHEW 3:16-17, ACTS 8:38-39

Do members of this church or faith believe that *one must be baptized for the remission of sins?*

Yes ___ No ___

Reference: ACTS 2:38

Do members of this church or faith believe that *one must be baptized in the name of the Father, and of the Son, and of the Holy Ghost (Spirit)?*

Yes ___ No ___

Reference: MATTHEW 28:19

Do members of this church or faith believe that *when an individual is Baptized, he or she goes into the water a sinner, is buried in the water and raised sinless through the Blood of Christ?*

Yes ___ No ___

References: 1 JOHN 1:7, REVELATION 1:5

Do members of this church or faith believe at *that very moment he or she is saved from their sins?*

Yes ___ No ___

Reference: PETER 3:21

Do members of this church or faith believe *that one may only enter His Church after completely following His Pattern of Salvation or has been saved, at which time his or her name is added to the membership rolls or Book of Life, in Heaven, by our Lord God Almighty?*

Yes ___ No ___

References: PHILIPPIANS 4:3, REVELATION 20:15, REVELATION 3:5, ACTS 2:41, ACTS 2:47, COLOSSIANS 3:1,

Do members of this church or faith believe *that after an individual has been baptized, he or she is commanded to Remain Faithful unto death?*

Yes ___ No ___

Reference: REVELATION 2:10

Important Note

Appendix 2 & 3 are similar, but have been designed for two different purposes. Appendix 2 is designed to test any church or faith, while Appendix 3 was developed to assist an individual in comparing the tenets of his or her personal church or faith against the Divine Pattern and includes the reasoning behind each conviction.

One must use the highest level of care to worship precisely in accord with the Patterns provided in the Word of God. Scriptural Worship is not the creation of man, but was ordained by God. ... Heaven Awaits!

Appendix 3

Comparative Analysis - Do you attend His Church?

Appendix Contents

A. Do you attend His Church?

B. Comparative Analysis

C. Jesus warned His followers to beware of false teachers

D. Two questions to seriously consider

A. Do you attend His Church?

This is a question that every individual who loves our Lord Jesus should carefully and critically consider!

In the first century, there was only one Church, but as a result of Satan encouraging men to add their own ideas and traditions to worship, we have the religious divisions of today, which leads to this question.

This significant question immediately leads to two other related questions, which are also of great importance.

Are the members of my church or faith walking the Narrow Way that leads to eternal life?

Reference: MATTHEW 7:13-14

Do the members of my church or faith Worship God in Spirit and in Truth?

Reference: JOHN 4:23-24

In light of the serious warning issued in MATTHEW 7:13-14, it is strongly recommended that every follower of Christ compare and evaluate the beliefs, practices and traditions of their church or faith in comparison with the Commandments, Instructions and Examples, depicted in the Church of the first century by Jesus and His Disciples, exclusively from the pages of the New Testament.

To help make an examination and determination, a series of yes or no and fill in the blank questions have been developed for each user's personal consideration.

The question is followed by a Commentary, which provides support or opposition based solely on the Word of God with verse support or references. In clear-cut instances, the correct Biblical answer will be provided. The following is an example.

Does your church or faith believe in Heaven and Hell?

YES ____ NO ____

Commentary based upon the Word of God

Every individual who has ever lived will come before Jesus on Judgment Day (HEBREWS 9:27) to be judged according to his or her deeds. After the decision of Christ is pronounced he or she will spend eternity either in Heaven or Hell. The correct Biblical answer is YES.

Jesus promised in REVELATION 2:7 "To him that overcometh will I give to eat of the tree of life, which is in the midst of the paradise of God."

The only way to experience Heaven is to be among the Souls that have been saved from everlasting damnation.

Unfortunately, the majority will hear Jesus say, "Depart from me, ye cursed, into everlasting fire, prepared for the devil and his angels:" (MATTHEW 25:41)

Before we begin, it is essential that we review the meaning of the terms "in Spirit" and "in Truth".

The term "in Spirit" is an abstract concept, like beauty, it cannot be defined, only described. People usually know when they move into a Spiritual state, which only occurs when an individual is in the proper frame of mind.

The Spiritual plane is higher than the realm of reality, in which we normally function. We will usually rapidly reach this higher plane when reaching out to God in sincere and humble prayer. It is a mental activity that requires the proper attitude and willingness to focus our minds on Spiritual concerns, while consciously attempting to eliminate all unnecessary worldly issues from the active part of our mind during Worship services or at times of Prayer.

God requires that we Worship with all our Heart, Mind and Soul that was created in His image. (GENESIS 1:26) We all have the ability, but it requires effort and a willingness to conform to His Commandments, in order to offer the Spiritual form of Worship that is; sincere, humble, holy and pure, which corresponds with the Spiritual disposition of God. It is believed the majority of Worshippers fulfill this part of His Commandment.

On the other hand, "in Truth" is a term that can be defined, in two steps. The word Truth in this context simply means to carefully follow the Commandments and Instructions that are written in the Word of God. The term "in Truth" is interchangeable with and comparable to the term the "Will of God"

Now that we understand the Biblical meaning of Truth, the second step is to conform, organize and harmonize the Worship of God, just as He directs in His Word, without any unauthorized additions, subtractions or creative enhancements.

However, in order to walk the Narrow Way and be saved one must also Worship and attend a church that is structured and functions in accordance with the Will of God or "in Truth".

B. Comparative Analysis

The following is a list of questions, designed to assist the user in completing his or her personal serious consideration and to create a comparative analysis of the beliefs, practices and traditions of their church or faith as contrasted with the Will of God or the Commandments, Instructions and Examples of Jesus or His Disciples, as presented in the New Testament. In addition, the absence of Authority will be noted, as required. The correct Biblical answer is provided, if feasible. The following is partial listing of issues to be considered in determining, if an individual is currently walking the Narrow Way that leads to eternal life.

What is the name of your church or faith?

_____

Do you personally believe that it DOES NOT make any difference, which church an individual attends or the faith he or she follows, provided that they believe and have faith in God?

YES ____ NO ____

Do you personally believe that God is forgiving, long-suffering, loving and DOES NOT require strict observance of His Commandments?

YES ____ NO ____

Commentary based upon the Word of God

If you answered yes to either or both questions, please consider the following;

"Attend the Church of your Choice" is a cruel myth that has been restated in the media so many times it has become an accepted truth among the vast majority of the populace. While it is true that in the United States, everyone has the absolute right to attend the church of his or her choice, not every individual residing outside America has that free choice.

The statement "Attend the Church of your Choice" has a much greater meaning than simply free choice, but also indicates that it makes no difference how an individual Worships his or her God. Nothing could be further from the Biblical Truth. For example, In JOHN 4:23-24 Jesus commands His followers to Worship God in Spirit and in Truth. ("In Truth" is defined as "in accordance with the Will of God") The correct Biblical answer is NO to both questions

The implications of this passage were explained fully above, but just consider the following question: How can thousands of different churches and sects, each with its own dogma, many of which claim to be the church that Jesus built, all be worshiping God in Spirit and in Truth?

Unfortunately, many mistakenly believe that the form of Worship makes no difference. Paul reports serious concerns regarding this issue in 1 TIMOTHY 4:1-2 "Now the Spirit speaketh expressly, that in the latter times some shall depart from the faith, giving heed to deceiving spirits and doctrines of demons, speaking lies in hypocrisy, having their own conscience seared with a hot iron,"

Paul continues in 2 TIMOTHY 4:3-4 "For the time will come when they will not endure sound doctrine; but after their own lusts shall they heap to themselves teachers, having itching ears, And they shall turn away their ears from the truth, and shall be turned unto fables."

In 2 CORINTHIANS 11:13-15 Paul issues a further warning "For such are false apostles, deceitful workers, transforming themselves into the apostles of Christ. And no marvel; for Satan himself is transformed into an angel of light. Therefore it is no great thing if his ministers also be transformed as the ministers of righteousness; whose end shall be according to their works"

Is the name of your church or faith found in the New Testament?

YES _____ NO _____

For whom or what was your church or faith named?

_____

What name identifies members?

_____

Does that Name glorify Jesus Christ?

YES _____ NO _____

Were followers of Jesus, ever called this name in the Bible?

YES _____ NO _____

Is the name that identifies members found in the New Testament?

YES _____ NO _____

Commentary based upon the Word of God

The members of His Church are followers of Christ and wear the name of Christians only, in His Honor and to His Glory. (ACTS 11:26) These followers do not carry worldly labels such as Catholics, Mormons, Lutherans, Baptists or the thousands of other names individuals call themselves to identify their religious affiliation, as these are not mentioned in the Word of God.

Approximately 40 descriptive expressions for His Church appear upon the pages of the New Testament including, but not limited to; "house of God" (1 TIMOTHY 3:15), "the church" or "kingdom" (MATTHEW 16:18-19; ACTS 2:47; COLOSSIANS 1:13), "temple of God" (1 CORINTHIANS 3:16) and others.

The use of any name, which is mentioned in the Word of God, is Scriptural. God provided a Pattern to follow. Therefore, all other church names are not in accord with the Scriptures and their acceptability is questionable.

Who was founder of your church or faith?

_____

Commentary based upon the Word of God

The founder of His Church was Jesus Christ, Who from His throne in Heaven, directed the establishment of His Church in Jerusalem, on Sunday, the Day of Pentecost, ten days after His Ascension, in approximately 30 AD, with an opening membership of three thousand souls (ACTS 2:1-47)

What is the specific time and place your church or faith was founded?

_____

Logical Conclusion

Any church or faith that was established at a different time in history or at a different place cannot be the One True Church that Christ built. This includes all man-made denominations of today. Therefore, those who are not a part of His True Church we read about in the Bible, but are a part of a substitute, a man-made organization **have no promise of salvation**.

Does your church or faith observe the Lord's Supper each and every Sunday?

YES _____ NO _____

Commentary based upon the Word of God

It is expected that every member of His Church will assemble for worship on each Lord's Day. A central part of the worship service is the Lord's Supper. The correct Biblical answer is YES.

ACTS 20:7
And upon the first day of the week, when the disciples came together to break bread, Paul preached unto them, ready to depart on the morrow; and continued his speech until midnight.

Does your church or faith encourage each member to support the work of the church, by returning to the Lord a portion of that which they have been prospered and have purposed in their hearts each week?

YES _____ NO _____

Commentary based upon the Word of God

The following passages reveal and make it clear that we are commanded to "lay by in store" as we are prospered and have determined in our hearts. The correct Biblical answer is YES

References: 1 CORINTHIANS 16:2, 2 CORINTHIANS 9:6-8

Does your church or faith believe that each new convert must sincerely REPENT of his or her of sins, in preparation for Baptism?

YES _____ NO _____

Commentary based upon the Word of God

Repentance is required of all men and women, since the only sinless individual to ever walk the earth was Jesus Christ. True repentance is a change of heart in our attitude. The Greek word for repentance is "metanoeo" which means to change your mind or purpose, forsaking evil and following righteousness.

A change of heart desires to do that which is right and is sorrowful when its does something that is wrong. The correct Biblical answer is YES

References: ROMANS 3:23, LUKE 13:5, LUKE 15:10, 2 CORINTHIANS 7:10, ACTS 2:38, 2 PETER 3:9

Does your church or faith believe that each new convert must CONFESS his or her belief in Jesus, as the Son of God, before men, in preparation for Baptism?

YES _____ NO _____

Commentary based upon the Word of God

All must *confess* their Belief in Jesus, as the Son of God, before men.

This is a simple Confession of Faith, which is made just before Baptism. The correct Biblical answer is YES

References: ACTS 8:37, ROMANS 10:10, MATTHEW 10:32-33, 1 JOHN 1:9

Does your church or faith Baptize new converts BY TOTAL IMMERSION ONLY?

YES _____ NO _____

Commentary based upon the Word of God

The word used in the New Testament for baptize is from the Greek word "baptizo", which literally means, "to immerse, submerge or to plunge."

In addition to the literal meaning of the word, immersion was the practice of the Church in apostolic times. Immersion conforms to the description of baptisms performed by the Apostle Paul in ROMANS 6:3-6 in which, he describes a burial and resurrection. Since we must carefully follow the instructions in order to be saved, it is clear that we must *be baptized by total immersion only*. The correct Biblical answer is YES

References: ROMANS 6:3-6, ACTS 8:38, JOHN 3:5, COLOSSIANS 2:12

Does your church or faith Baptize new converts, into Christ, by total immersion, for the remission of sins in the name of the Father, the Son and the Holy Ghost [Spirit]?

YES _____ NO _____

Commentary based upon the Word of God

When a person is *Baptized*, he or she goes into the water a sinner, is buried in the water and raised sinless through the blood of Christ. The correct Biblical answer is YES

References: MATTHEW 28:19, ACTS 2:38, GALATIANS 3:27

Does your church or faith believe in the Virgin Birth of Jesus?

YES _____ NO _____

Commentary based upon the Word of God

The statement in ISAIAH 7:14 is a prophecy of the Virgin Birth of Christ. New Testament passages such as MATTHEW 1:20-25, and LUKE 1:26-31 are accepted as a declaration of the Miracle of His Virgin Birth. The correct Biblical answer is YES

Does your church or faith vote upon the acceptance of either potential new members or converts as members of the congregation?

YES _____ NO _____

Commentary based upon the Word of God

This practice is the creation of men, with absolutely no basis or reference in the Bible. The correct Biblical answer is NO. In view of the fact that this practice is in direct opposition to the following;

ACTS 2:47
Praising God, and having favour with all the people. And the Lord added to the church daily such as should be saved.

Does your church or faith enhance their worship by the addition of objects, or functions not specifically authorized in the New Testament? (Leaders wearing robes or other forms of special attire, candles, incense, choirs, musical instruments, idols, such as the likeliness of Mary or so-called saints, religious flags and banners, Christmas or Easter pageants etc)

YES _____ NO _____

Commentary based upon the Word of God

Adding to Worship is condemned, in both the Old and New Testaments. In DEUTERONOMY 4:2 "Ye shall not add unto the word which I command you, neither shall ye diminish ought from it, that ye may keep the commandments of the Lord your God which I command you." Further in PROVERBS 30:6 "Add thou not unto his words, lest he reprove thee, and thou be found a liar."

The deadly results of adding to Worship is found in LEVITICUS 10:1-2 "And Nadab and Abihu, the sons of Aaron, took either of them his censer, and put fire therein, and put incense thereon, and offered strange fire before the LORD, which he commanded them not. And there went out fire from the LORD, and devoured them, and they died before the LORD."

In 1 CORINTHIANS 4:6, early Christians are advised, "that ye might learn in us not to think of men above that which is written". John clearly states in 2 JOHN 1:9 "Whosoever transgresseth, and abideth not in the doctrine of Christ, hath not God. He that abideth in the doctrine of Christ, he hath both the Father and the Son."

The Biblical Injunction against adding to Worship is clearly stated in REVELATION 22:18-19 we are further warned "For I testify unto every man that heareth the words of the prophecy of this book, if any man shall add unto these things, God shall add unto him the plagues that are written in this book: And if any man shall take away from the words of the book of this prophecy, God shall take away his part out of the book of life, and out of the holy city, and from the things which are written in this book" The correct Biblical answer is NO.

Does your church or faith believe that ALL that is required to be saved is a strong Belief and Faith in God?

YES _____ NO _____

Commentary based upon the Word of God

"Faith Only" is another concept created by men, without any scriptural support. Men have written thousands of pages in a vain effort to support this theory, but to no avail. The correct Biblical answer is NO. This concept is in direct opposition to the following;

MATTHEW 16:27
For the Son of man shall come in the glory of his Father with his angels; and then he shall reward every man according to his works.

JAMES 2:24
Ye see then how that by works a man is justified, and not by faith only.

Additional references: JAMES 2:14-17, JAMES 2:18, ROMANS 2:5-6

Does your church or faith believe that the sinner's prayer or the prayer of salvation, which has been delivered in a sincere and humble manner, will result in the forgiveness of sins?

YES _____ NO _____

Commentary based upon the Word of God

People are saved by carefully following the commandments and instructions of Jesus and His Apostles, not by any prayer or ritual created by man.

Belief that the so-called Prayer of Salvation or Sinner's Prayer will somehow result in forgiveness of sin has absolutely no scriptural support. Therefore, all those who have attempted to use this method of cleansing their sins have failed and continue to be seen as sinners in the eyes of God.

The Bible makes it clear that God does not hear or answer the prayers of sinners, regardless of what they are praying for or about. This does not assume that God cannot hear. God is omnipresent and hears everything. However, the following verses references indicate that God does not hear all prayers in the sense of answering or regarding them. The correct Biblical answer is NO.

1 PETER 3:12
For the eyes of the Lord are over the righteous, and his ears are open unto their prayers: but the face of the Lord is against them that do evil.

A logical question regarding these prayers and the teachings in 1 PETER 3:12:

How can one expect to be a member of the righteous, if they have not carefully followed His Pattern of Salvation?

Additional reference: JOHN 9:31

Does your church or faith believe that once an individual is "saved" he or she is always "saved", regardless of personal conduct, which is known as "once saved, always saved" or the "perseverance of the saints"?

YES _____ NO _____

Commentary based upon the Word of God

This concept means that once a person has been saved, that it is impossible for that person to fall from grace, regardless of how they conduct their lives thereafter. The correct Biblical answer is NO. The fact is that the Bible makes it quite clear that salvation is conditional and an individual may be lost.

References: ROMANS 11:22, 2 PETER 3:17, 2 PETER 2:20-22

Does your church or faith believe that God selects those people who will be saved and they will be saved regardless of their individual spiritual condition, which is known as "Predestination" or "Unconditional Election"

YES _____ NO _____

Commentary based upon the Word of God

The concept of Predestination is that God selected those people who will be saved, regardless of their individual spiritual condition. It is true that God can foresee those who will remain faithful to the end and will be saved, but God desires that all men be saved (1 TIMOTHY 2:4). Man has been given free will or freedom of choice. God wants each individual to make the decision to become a faithful Christian.

The statement of the apostle Peter, "Of a truth I perceive that God is no respecter of persons, but in every nation he that feareth him and worketh righteousness is acceptable unto him" (ACTS 10:34-35) is evidence that God did not predestine individuals to be eternally saved or lost, but allows each man or woman to determine his own destiny. The correct Biblical answer is NO.

Predestination is another religious initiative without any scriptural support and in direct opposition to the words of the great apostle Paul

1 CORINTHIANS 9:27
But I keep under my body, and bring it into subjection: lest that by any means, when I have preached to others, I myself should be a castaway.

Does your church or faith encourage female members to take an active leadership role in your Worship Services? (Fulfilling roles such as serving as a Minister, Teaching an Adult Bible Class, attended by male members, Leading Public Prayers in Worship Services, Serving the Lord's Supper)

YES _____ NO _____

Commentary based upon the Word of God

Many women have abilities equal to any man who is a preacher or elder, however that does not alter the fact that God's Word calls for all women to be submissive in marriage and in the public worship of the Church. Therefore, it is not acceptable to God for any woman to assume the role of a minister or in any leadership role as is confirmed by the following referenced verses. The correct Biblical answer is NO.

References: 1 TIMOTHY 2:11-14, 1 CORINTHIANS 14:34-35

C. Jesus warned His followers to beware of false teachers

In MATTHEW 7:15, Jesus stated the following in regards to false teachings and teachers "Beware of false prophets, which come to you in sheep's clothing, but inwardly they are ravening wolves." In MATTHEW 7:16, Jesus further explains "Ye shall know them by their fruits."

In this context "Fruits" includes the physical worship and practices of the church, which must be compared directly with the Bible and no other source of information. Jesus issued several other warnings including those found in MATTHEW 24:11, MATTHEW 24:24 and MARK 13:22. The Bible, the inspired Word of God, makes it crystal clear that many types of worship are simply unacceptable. (LEVITICUS 10:1-2)

Unfortunately, many people blindly accept any religious teaching without any thought as to whether it is based upon Biblical Truth or the twisted doctrine of man. Following this path can very possibly result in a faithful, deeply religious individual being unacceptable to God in the end. Unfortunately, millions have died believing their souls were in Christ and were actually in great danger.

Jesus stated it plainly in MATTHEW 15:9 "But in vain they do worship me, teaching for doctrines the commandments of men."

Satan has inspired men, since the birth of Christ to become teachers of false doctrines and practices as a snare for the believers who are unwilling to learn or who have simply failed to seek the **Truth.** Others have either failed to search the Scriptures, (JOHN 5:39) in order to test the doctrine of the Faith they attend or simply failed to understand the Word of God. (ROMANS 1:31)

In the first century there was only **one church.** The evil demonic prince of the world has caused the original church built by the hands of Jesus Christ, to be divided into the thousands of religious sects of today.

D. Two questions to seriously consider

Now is the time to truthfully respond to the important questions that you were asked to carefully consider;

Are the members of my church or faith walking the narrow way that leads to eternal life?

YES _____ NO _____

Reference: MATTHEW 7:13-14

Do the members of my church or faith worship God in Spirit and in Truth?

YES _____ NO _____

Reference: JOHN 4:23-24

If you are still uncertain, please carefully reflect on the following;

Do your beliefs, practices and traditions have the power and authority of the Word of God behind them?

Can you take the doctrines of your religion or denomination, beginning with its name and point to a passage in the Bible, in clear support of each belief, practice or tradition?

Millions of sincere deeply religious individuals, who believe that they are living a Christian life and are looking forward to spending eternity with the Lord, are actually in serious danger of not being acceptable to God.

Why? Because they have failed to diligently seek the Truth and have blindly accepted the teachings of men and therefore, **have not worshipped Him "in Spirit" and "in Truth".**

God never promised that it would be easy and expects people to meticulously study and search the scriptures, which can be very gratifying.

Each individual is responsible for his or her own personal salvation.

In 2 Corinthians 11:13-14, the Great Apostle Paul issued a grave warning

"For such are false apostles, deceitful workers, transforming themselves into the apostles of Christ and no marvel; for Satan himself is transformed into an angel of light." Do not allow yourself to be misled…. Heaven Awaits!

Appendix 4

Examples of unsupported Religious Teachings

Appendix Contents

A. Introduction

B. Recommendations

C. Examples of False Teachings

A. Introduction

The purpose of this appendix is to point out examples of teachings or practices of major churches, **which have no scriptural support or are in direct opposition to the teaching of the Bible.**

It remains the sole objective of the author to uncover and highlight the Truth and not to offend, in any way, any person or religious organization.

In this section, we will delineate the various tactics Satan has used to twist the precious Words of the Lord Christ and the eternal effects that inappropriate worship may have on the unsuspecting.

Millions of faithful believers, who love and serve the Lord, may be worshipping in vain. Regardless of the level of their faith, purity, righteousness and other Christ-like characteristics, they have, are all in danger of being eternally lost, if they do not take immediate steps to correct their fatal flaws.

What flaws could possibly affect so many of the best members of the human race? They have fallen in the **trap of the false teachings** that Jesus warned of, in the New Testament. Jesus stated clearly "And in vain they worship Me, Teaching as doctrines the commandments of men." (MATTHEW 15:9)

In addition, they have either **failed to search the Scriptures,** (JOHN 5:39) in order **to test the doctrine of the faith followed or simply fail to understand the Word of God.** (ROMANS 1:31)

Some mistakenly believe that the form of worship makes no difference

Paul reports serious concerns regarding *the form of worship issue* in 1 TIMOTHY 4:1-2 "Now the Spirit expressly says that in latter times **some will depart from the faith,** giving heed to deceiving spirits and doctrines of demons, speaking lies in hypocrisy, having their own conscience seared with a hot iron,"

Paul continues in 2 TIMOTHY 4:3-4 "For the time will come when they will not endure sound doctrine, but according to their own desires, because they have itching ears, they will heap up for themselves teachers; and **they will turn their ears away from the truth, and be turned aside to fables."**

Jesus warned in regards to false teachers *"ye shall know them by their fruits."* (MATTHEW 7:16)

In the first century there was only one Church. Satan, the evil demonic prince of the world, has inspired men, during the time since the birth of Christ, to become teachers of false doctrines and practices as a snare for unsuspecting Christians. Thus causing the original church built by the hands of Jesus Christ to be divided into the thousands of religious sects of today

B. Recommendations

Take control of your spiritual life, do not allow yourself to be a part of the millions of sincere individuals, who believe that they are living a Christian life and looking forward to spending eternity in the Kingdom of Heaven, but have been deceived into accepting false doctrines.

Reject any and all uninspired documents written by men in regard to our Worship of God or any other religious practices, which DO NOT absolutely conform to His Word.

C. Examples of False Teachings

The following is a brief overview of some of these practices, which have no Biblical support or are in direct opposition to the teaching of the Bible, therefore are False Teachings:

(1) Denominations

Jesus prayed that His Church would not be divided in JOHN 17:11 "Holy Father, keep through Your name those whom You have given Me, that they may be one as We are." and in JOHN 17:20-21 "I do not pray for these alone, but also for those who will believe in Me through their word; that they all may be one, as You, Father, are in Me, and I in You; that they also may be one in Us, that the world may believe that You sent Me."

Paul pleads in 1 CORINTHIANS 1:10 "Now I plead with you, brethren, by the name of our Lord Jesus Christ, *that you all speak the same thing, and that there be no divisions among you,* but that you be perfectly joined together in the same mind and in the same judgment".

Paul appealed again in EPHESIAN 4:4-6 *"There is one body and one Spirit, just as you were called in one hope of your calling; one Lord, one faith, one baptism; one God and Father of all,* who is above all, and through all, and in you all."

Denominationalism was predicted in ACTS 20:29-31, when Paul stated clearly *"For I know this, that after my departure savage wolves will come in among you, not sparing the flock Also from among yourselves men will rise up, speaking perverse things, to draw away the disciples after themselves* Therefore watch, and remember, that for three years I did not cease to warn everyone night and day with tears."

It is clear that Divisions or Denominations are **not** acceptable to the Lord and therefore, **millions of their current members are in danger of eternal punishment.**

(2) Once Saved, Always Saved (Also known as Perseverance of the Saints)

This concept is that once a person has been saved, that it is impossible for that person to fall from Grace, regardless of how they conduct their lives thereafter. The fact is that the Bible makes it quite clear that **salvation is conditional** and an individual may be lost, as follows;

ROMANS 11:22
Behold therefore the goodness and severity of God: on them which fell, severity; but toward thee, goodness, if thou continue in his goodness: otherwise thou also shalt be cut off.

1 CORINTHIANS 10:12
Wherefore let him that thinketh he standeth take heed lest he fall.

Note: Read 1 CORINTHIANS 10:1-11 for details leading up to this warning by the Great Apostle Paul.

Additional references 2 PETER 1:10, 2 PETER 2:21-22, 2 PETER 3:17

(3) Baptisms not mentioned in the Bible

Since it is clearly stated that there is one baptism in EPHESIANS 4:5 *"One Lord, one faith, one baptism",* which is by **total immersion** (MATTHEW 3:16-17, MARK 1:9-10, ACTS 8:38-39) **is essential to salvation** (MARK 16:15-16, ACTS 2:38, ROMANS 6:3-4) and other examples of that baptism such as COLOSSIANS 2:12 "*Buried with him in baptism*, wherein also ye are risen with him through the faith of the operation of God, who hath raised him from the dead."

But *no scriptures* related to Infant Baptism, Sprinkling, Pouring or any other forms of "baptism" are recorded in the Bible.

(4) Faith Only

Another concept without any scriptural support and in direct opposition to the following;

MATTHEW 16:27
For the Son of man shall come in the glory of his Father with his angels; and *then he shall reward every man according to his works.*

JAMES 2:24
Ye see then how **that by works a man is justified, and not by faith only**.

JAMES 2:14-17
What doth it profit, my brethren, though a man say he hath faith, and have not works? can faith save him? If a brother or sister be naked, and destitute of daily food, And one of you say unto them, Depart in peace, be ye warmed and filled; notwithstanding ye give them not those things which are needful to the body; what doth it profit? **Even so faith, if it hath not works, is dead, being alone.**

JAMES 2:18
Yea, a man may say, Thou hast faith, and I have works: **shew me thy faith without thy works, and I will shew thee my faith by my works**.

ROMANS 2:5-6
But after thy hardness and impenitent heart treasurest up unto thyself wrath against the day of wrath and revelation of the righteous judgment of God; *Who will render to every man according to his deeds*

(5) Closely related to the doctrine of Faith Only is the "Roman Road", which is also known as "The Highway to a Relationship with God" or "The Gospel of Grace".

The Roman Road is not a discussion of the Roman thoroughfare system, built in the first century, but is an erroneous interruption of God's Plan of Salvation, using passages from Paul's letter to the Romans. These are common and wide spread false teachings. Almost any religious concept can be "proven" by taking individual verses out of context or by misapplication. Denominations use a collection of verses building a false systematic approach to the application of the gospel.

This improper approach to the pattern of salvation makes use of the following collection of passages; ROMANS 3:23, ROMANS 5:8, ROMANS 6:23, ROMANS 10:9-10, ROMANS 10:13 AND ROMANS 11:36.

The individual is then directed to read the following "Sinner's Prayer."

Father, I know that I have broken your laws and my sins have separated me from you. I am truly sorry, and now I want to turn away from my past sinful life toward you. Please forgive me, and help me avoid sinning again. I believe that your son, Jesus Christ died for my sins, was resurrected from the dead, is alive, and hears my prayer. I invite Jesus to become the Lord of my life, to rule and reign in my heart from this day forward. Please send your Holy Spirit to help me obey you, and to do your will for the rest of my life. In Jesus' name I pray, Amen.

After which, the individual is told they have been "born again" and given a list similar to the following of general suggestions:

Welcome to God's family. Now, as a way to grow closer to Him, the Bible tells us to follow up on our commitment.

Get baptized as commanded by Christ.

Tell someone else about your new faith in Christ.

Spend time with God each day. It does not have to be a long period of time. Just develop the daily habit of praying to Him and reading His Word.

Ask God to increase your faith and your understanding of the Bible

Seek fellowship with other followers of Jesus.

Develop a group of believing friends to answer your questions and support you.

Find a local church where you can worship God.

(6) Another example of an erroneous approach to the Plan of Salvation is known as the "Prayer of Salvation"

It Begins With Faith in God (HEBREWS 11:6)

We acknowledge that Jesus Christ is God; and that He came to earth as a man in order to live the sinless life that we cannot live; that He died in our place, so that we would not have to pay the penalty we deserve.

Confess your Sins (ROMANS 3:23, 2 CORINTHIANS 5:21)

We confess our past life of sin – living for ourselves and not obeying God.

Profess Faith in Christ as Savior and Lord (JOHN 1:1-3, 3-16)

The individual is then directed to read the a prayer similar to Sinner's Prayer

Note: Research indicates that both the Sinner's Prayer and Prayer of Salvation are offered in various other forms, including, but not limited to, the four following examples:

"Dear God, have mercy on me and save my soul, for Jesus' sake, amen."

"Dear God, please forgive me of my sins and come into my heart. Amen."

"Heavenly Father, I know that I am a sinner and that I deserve to go to hell. I believe that Jesus died on the cross for my sins. I do now receive Him as my personal Lord and Savior. I Promise to serve you the best I can. Please save me. In Jesus' name, amen."

"Dear Jesus, I am sorry for my sins. Please forgive me and give me a new heart. Amen."

(a) Scriptural Problems with these approaches to gaining salvation

(1) References to these types of prayers are not found in the Bible.

(2) Jesus, nor any of His Apostles, ever instructed anyone to pray for salvation

(3) No person was ever recorded, in the Bible, as being saved by praying the Sinner's Prayer, the Prayer of Salvation or any other prayer.

(b) People are saved by carefully following the Commandments, Examples and Instructions of Jesus and His Disciples, NOT by any prayer or ritual created by man.

If there was ever an excellent candidate for an individual being forgiven of his sins by praying or saying the "sinner's prayer" or "the prayer of salvation" it would have been Saul, who had been praying for some time, according to:

ACTS 9:10-11
And there was a certain disciple at Damascus named Ananias; and to him said the Lord in a vision, Ananias. And he said, Behold, I am here, Lord. And the Lord said unto him, Arise, and go into the street which is called Straight, and enquire in the house of Judas for one called **Saul, of Tarsus: for, behold, he prayeth,**

(c) Prayers did not restore his sight or provide for the remission of sins for Saul and prayer absolutely will NOT provide forgiveness for sinners today.

Ananias provided the answer for Saul, which is recorded in ACTS 22:16, when he said **"And now why tarriest thou? Arise, and be baptized, and wash away thy sins, calling on the name of the Lord."**

(d) The Bible makes it clear that God does not hear or answer the prayers of sinners, regardless of the nature of the prayer.

This does not assume that God cannot hear. God is omnipresent and hears everything. However, the following verses make it clear that He does not hear all prayers in the sense of answering or having any regard for them.

JOHN 9:31
Now we know that God heareth not sinners: but if any man be a worshipper of God, and doeth his will, him he heareth.

1 PETER 3:12
For the eyes of the Lord [are] over the righteous, and his ears [are open] unto their prayers: but the face of the Lord [is] against them that do evil.

ISAIAH 59:1-2
Behold, the LORD'S hand is not shortened, that it cannot save; neither his ear heavy,

that it cannot hear: But your iniquities have separated between you and your God, and your sins have hid [his] face from you, that he will not hear.

(e) How can one expect to be a member of the righteous, if they have not obeyed the His Pattern of Salvation, by completing each of the required elements?

The book of Acts provides several examples of the conversion of individuals or groups. The number of required steps ranged from one to five, with a combination of six steps. The remaining step is that the new convert must *acknowledge,* in his or her heart that in light of God's word, *that he or she is a sinner.* (ROMANS 3:23, ROMANS 5:12, ROMANS 6:23, LUKE 18:13)

In the first example of conversion, in the book of Acts at the very beginning of the Church, on the Day of Pentecost, about three thousand individuals were converted. (ACTS 2:14-47) Note that five of the required steps were delineated. (Hear, Faith, Believe, Repent and Baptism)

In third example of conversion, in the book of Acts, the Ethiopian Eunuch (ACTS 8:26-40) Note that five of the required steps were delineated. (Hear the Gospel, Faith, Believe, Confess and Baptism)

The composite of the first and third examples of conversions in the book of Acts, establishes clearly the general Pattern or Plan of Salvation (Hear the Gospel, Faith, Believe, Repent, Confess and Baptism for the forgiveness of sins.)

(7) Predestination (Also known as Unconditional Election)

This religious concept is that no Christian has any control over his final destination, be it Heaven or Hell. This idea is absolutely false doctrine. It is true that God can foresee those who will remain faithful to the end and will be saved, but God desires that all men be saved (1 Timothy 2:4).

Man has been given free will or freedom of choice and God wants each to make the decision to become a faithful Christian.

(a) The concept of Predestination is that God selected those people who will be saved and they will be saved regardless of their individual spiritual condition.

Yet another religious idea without any scriptural support and in direct opposition to the following;

1 CORINTHIANS 9:27
But I keep under my body, and bring it into subjection: lest that by any means, when I have preached to others, I myself should be a castaway.

1 TIMOTHY 2:3-4
For this is good and acceptable in the sight of God our Saviour; who will have all men to be saved, and to come unto the knowledge of the truth

JOHN 5:24
Verily, verily, I say unto you, He that heareth my word, and believeth on him that sent me, hath everlasting life, and shall not come into condemnation; but is passed from death unto life.

REVELATION 22:17
And the Spirit and the bride say, Come. And let him that heareth say, Come. And let him that is athirst come. And whosoever will, let him take the water of life freely.

MARK 16:15
And he said unto them, Go ye into all the world, and preach the gospel to every creature

(8) Women in Leadership Roles

Many women have abilities equal to any man who is a minister or elder, however that does not alter the fact that God's Word calls for all women to be submissive in marriage and in the public worship of the Church. Therefore, it is not acceptable to God for any woman to assume the role of a Preacher or in any other position of leadership, which is confirmed by the following verses.

1 TIMOTHY 2:11-14
Let the woman learn in silence with all subjection. But I suffer not a woman to teach, nor to usurp authority over the man,

but to be in silence. For Adam was first formed, then Eve. Adam was not deceived, but the woman being deceived was in transgression.

1 CORINTHIANS 14:34-35
Let your women keep silence in the churches: for it is not permitted unto them to speak; but they are commanded to be under obedience, as also saith the law. And if they will learn anything, let them ask their husbands at home: for it is a shame for women to speak in the church.

COLOSSIANS 3:18
Wives, submit yourselves unto your own husbands, as it is fit in the Lord.

(9) Centralized Church Government

Most denominations and religious sects have some form of centralized church government, with various titles or ranks for their leaders.

There is absolutely NO biblical authorization for such entities, titles or ranks.

The only authorized leaders of the Church are called Elders. In order to be selected as an Elder, a man must meet certain qualifications.

The Bible also authorizes Deacons, also a man, who also must meet certain qualifications.

Each Church is authorized to have its own Elders and is bound only to other like congregations through Jesus, who is the Head of His Church and a shared faith. The following Bible verses support this position:

ACTS 14:23
And when they had ordained them elders in every church, and had prayed with fasting, they commended them to the Lord, on whom they believed.

Additional reference: TITUS 1:5

(10) Annihilationism (also known as Conditionalism and conditional immortality)

This false teaching claims that the inmates of Hell will be subjected to time-limited punishment, and then will be exterminated in what is referred to as "the second death" Following that, no part of them; body, soul, mind or spirit will continue to exist in any form.

This belief is based upon a portion of Matthew 10:28, which states, God: "is able to destroy both soul and body in hell."

Please note: The following verse **does not state** that God **will destroy**, but rather that **He has the ability and power to destroy.**

MATTHEW 10:28
And fear not them which kill the body, but are not able to kill the soul: but rather fear him which is able to destroy both soul and body in hell.

While it is true that the second death refers to punishment and a separation from God, the following verses clearly indicate that the separation and punishment will be everlasting.

REVELATION 20:10
And the devil that deceived them was cast into the lake of fire and brimstone, where the beast and the false prophet are, and shall be tormented day and night forever and ever.

Additional references: MATTHEW 25:41, 2 THESSALONIANS 1:9

In addition to personally following the Narrow Way, by studying the Word, prayer and good works each of us must regularly attend a Church that is structured and functions in precise accord with the Will of God or "in Truth"... Heaven Awaits!

Appendix 5

Comparative Analysis of selected religious organizations

Appendix Contents

A. The Divine Pattern – His Church

B. Baptist Church

C. Catholic Church

D. Episcopal Church

E. Lutheran Church

F. Presbyterian Church

G. Methodist Church

H. Christian Church/Disciples of Christ

I. Church of Jesus Christ of Latter Day Saints

J. Jehovah's Witnesses

K. Seventh-Day Adventists

L. Make your own Comparative Analysis Forms

A. The Divine Pattern - His Church

The purpose of this analysis is to compare the teachings of His Church with several other well-known churches

(1) Church: His Church, which is based exclusively upon His Divine Pattern.

(2) Date begun: ~AD 30 - According to Acts Chapter 2, His Church began on the Day of Pentecost with a membership of about three thousand Souls, in the city of Jerusalem

(3) Founder: Jesus Christ

MATTHEW 16:18
And I say also unto thee, That thou art Peter, and upon this rock I will build my church; and the gates of hell shall not prevail against it.

(4) Baptism of believers only: Yes

MARK 16:16
He that believeth and is baptized shall be saved; but he that believeth not shall be damned.

(5) Baptism by immersion only: Yes

ROMANS 6:4
Therefore we are buried with him by baptism into death: that like as Christ was raised up from the dead by the glory of the Father, even so we also should walk in newness of life.

Additional reference: COLOSSIANS 2:12

(6) Baptism for remission of sins: Yes

ACTS 2:38
Then Peter said unto them, Repent, and be baptized every one of you in the name of Jesus Christ for the remission of sins, and ye shall receive the gift of the Holy Ghost.

(7) Baptized in the name of the Father, the Son and the Holy Ghost (Spirit): Yes

MATTHEW 28:19
Go ye therefore, and teach all nations, baptizing them in the name of the Father, and of the Son, and of the Holy Ghost:

(8) Lord's Supper each and every first day of the week: Yes

ACTS 20:7
And upon the first day of the week, when the disciples came together to break bread, Paul preached unto them, ready to depart on the morrow; and continued his speech until midnight.

Additional reference: 1 CORINTHIANS 11:26

(9) Worship in Spirit and in Truth: Yes

JOHN 4:24
God [is] a Spirit: and they that worship him must worship [him] in spirit and in truth

The term "in Spirit" is an abstract concept, like beauty it cannot be defined, only described. People usually know when they move into a spiritual state, which only occurs when an individual is in the proper frame of mind.

The spiritual plane is higher than the realm of reality, in which we normally function. We will usually rapidly reach this higher plane, when reaching out to God, in sincere and humble prayer.

It is a mental activity, which requires the proper attitude and willingness to focus our minds on spiritual concerns, while consciously attempting to eliminate all unnecessary worldly issues from the active part of our mind during worship services or at times of prayer.

God requires that we worship with all our heart, mind and soul, which were created in His image. (GENESIS 1:26) We all have the ability, but it requires effort and a willingness to conform to His Commandments in order to offer the spiritual form of worship that is sincere, humble, holy, and pure, which corresponds with the spiritual disposition of God.

The term "in Truth" is interchangeable with and comparable to the term the "Will of God". The Truth or the Will of God simply means to carefully follow the Patterns, Commandments and Examples or Instructions, which are recorded in the Word of God.

(10) Believe salvation can be lost: Yes

JAMES 5:19-20
Brethren, if any of you do err from the truth, and one convert him; Let him know, that he which converteth the sinner from the error of his way shall save a soul from death, and shall hide a multitude of sins.

Additional reference: 2 PETER 3:17-18

(11) Autonomy of local church: Yes

ACTS 14:23
And when they had ordained them elders in every church, and had prayed with fasting, they commended them to the Lord, on whom they believed.

Additional reference: 1 PETER 5:1-2

B. Baptist Church

(1) Religious organization: **Baptist Church**

(2) Date Begun: **~1607** [1]

(3) Founder: **John Smyth** [1]

(4) Baptism of believers only: **Yes** [1] (MARK 16:16)

(5) Baptism by immersion only: **Yes** [1] (ROMANS 6:4; COLOSSIANS 2:12)

(6) Baptism for Remission of Sins: **No** [1] (ACTS 2:38)

(7) Baptized in the name of the Father, the Son and the Holy Ghost (Spirit): **Unable to determine** (MATTHEW 28:19)

(8) Lord's Supper each and every first day of week: **No** [1] (ACTS 20:7; 1 CORINTHIANS 11:26)

(9) Worship in spirit and in truth: **No** [1] (JOHN 4:24)

(10) Believe salvation can be lost: **No** [1] (JAMES 5:19-20; 2 PETER 3:17-18)

(11) Autonomy of local congregation: **No** [1] (ACTS 14:23; 1 PETER 5:1-2)

C. Catholic Church

(1) Religious organization: **Catholic Church**

(2) Date Begun: **~325** [1]

(3) Founder: **Constantine** [1]

(4) Baptism of believers only: **No** [1] (MARK 16:16)

(5) Baptism by immersion only: **No** [1] (ROMANS 6:4; COLOSSIANS 2:12)

(6) Baptism for Remission of Sins: **No** [1] (ACTS 2:38)

(7) Baptized in the name of the Father, the Son and the Holy Ghost (Spirit): **Unable to determine** (MATTHEW 28:19)

(8) Lord's Supper each and every first day of week: **No** [7] (ACTS 20:7; 1 CORINTHIANS 11:26)

(9) Worship in spirit and in truth: **No** [1] (JOHN 4:24)

(10) Believe Salvation Can Be Lost: **Yes** [5] (JAMES 5:19-20; 2 PETER 3:17-18)

(11) Autonomy of local Congregation: **No** [1]
(ACTS 14:23; 1 PETER 5:1-2)

D. Episcopal Church

(1) Religious organization: **Episcopal Church**

(2) Date Begun: **~1535** [1]

(3) Founder: **Henry VIII** [1]

(4) Baptism of believers only: **No** [1]
(MARK 16:16)

(5) Baptism by immersion only: **No** [1]
(ROMANS 6:4; COLOSSIANS 2:12)

(6) Baptism for Remission of Sins: **Yes** [1]
(ACTS 2:38)

(7) Baptized in the name of the Father, the Son and the Holy Ghost (Spirit): **Unable to determine** (MATTHEW 28:19)

(8) Lord's Supper each and every first day of week: **Unable to determine**
(ACTS 20:7; 1 CORINTHIANS 11:26)

(9) Worship in spirit and in truth: **No** [1]
(JOHN 4:24)

(10) Believe Salvation Can Be Lost: **No** [2]
(JAMES 5:19-20; 2 PETER 3:17-18)

(11) Autonomy of local Congregation: **No** [1]
(ACTS 14:23; 1 PETER 5:1-2)

E. Lutheran Church

(1) Religious organization: **Lutheran Church**

(2) Date Begun: **~1517** [1]

(3) Founder: **Martin Luther** [1]

(4) Baptism of believers only: **No** [1]
(MARK 16:16)

(5) Baptism by immersion only: **No** [1]
(ROMANS 6:4; COLOSSIANS 2:12)

(6) Baptism for Remission of Sins: **No** [1]
(ACTS 2:38)

(7) Baptized in the name of the Father, the Son and the Holy Ghost (Spirit): **Unable to determine** (MATTHEW 28:19)

(8) Lord's Supper each and every first day of week: **No** [8]
(ACTS 20:7; 1 CORINTHIANS 11:26)

(9) Worship in spirit and in truth: **No** [1]
(JOHN 4:24)

(10) Believe Salvation Can Be Lost: **Unable to determine**
(JAMES 5:19-20; 2 PETER 3:17-18)

(11) Autonomy of local Congregation: **No** [1]
(ACTS 14:23; 1 PETER 5:1-2)

F. Presbyterian Church

(1) Religious organization: **Presbyterian Church**

(2) Date Begun: **~1590** [1]

(3) Founders: **Calvin/Knox** [1]

(4) Baptism of believers only: **No** [1]
(MARK 16:16)

(5) Baptism by immersion only: **No** [1]
(ROMANS 6:4; COLOSSIANS 2:12)

(6) Baptism for Remission of Sins: **No** [1]
(ACTS 2:38)

(7) Baptized in the name of the Father, the Son and the Holy Ghost (Spirit): **Unable to determine** (MATTHEW 28:19)

(8) Lord's Supper each and every first day of week: **No** [1]
(ACTS 20:7; 1 CORINTHIANS 11:26)

(9) Worship in spirit and in truth: **No** [1]
(JOHN 4:24)

(10) Believe Salvation Can Be Lost: **No** [1]
(JAMES 5:19-20; 2 PETER 3:17-18)

(11) Autonomy of local Congregation: **No** [1]
(ACTS 14:23; 1 PETER 5:1-2)

G. Methodist Church

(1) Religious organization: **Methodist Church**

(2) Date Begun: **~1729** [1]

(3) Founder: **John Wesley** [1]

tices(4) Baptism of believers only: **No** [1]
(MARK 16:16)

(5) Baptism by immersion only: **No** [1]
(ROMANS 6:4; COLOSSIANS 2:12)

(6) Baptism for Remission of Sins: **No** [1]
(ACTS 2:38)

(7) Baptized in the name of the Father, the Son and the Holy Ghost (Spirit): **Unable to determine** (MATTHEW 28:19)

(8) Lord's Supper each and every first day of week: **No** [1]
(ACTS 20:7; 1 CORINTHIANS 11:26)

(9) Worship in spirit and in truth: **No** [1]
(JOHN 4:24)

(10) Believe Salvation Can Be Lost: **Yes** [2]
(JAMES 5:19-20; 2 PETER 3:17-18)

(11) Autonomy of local Congregation: **No** [1]
(ACTS 14:23; 1 PETER 5:1-2)

H. Christian Church/Disciples of Christ

(1) Religious organization: **Christian Church/Disciples of Christ**

(2) Date Begun: **~1832** [2]

(3) Founders: **Stone/Campbell** [1]

(4) Baptism of believers only: **Yes** [2]
(MARK 16:16)

(5) Baptism by immersion only: **Yes** [2]
(ROMANS 6:4; COLOSSIANS 2:12)

(6) Baptism for Remission of Sins: **No** [2]
(ACTS 2:38)

(7) Baptized in the name of the Father, the Son and the Holy Ghost (Spirit): **Unable to determine** (MATTHEW 28:19)

(8) Lord's Supper each and every first day of week: **Yes** [2]
(ACTS 20:7; 1 CORINTHIANS 11:26)

(9) Worship in spirit and in truth: **No** [2]
(JOHN 4:24)

(10) Believe Salvation Can Be Lost: **No** [2]
(JAMES 5:19-20; 2 PETER 3:17-18)

(11) Autonomy of local Congregation: **No** [2]
(ACTS 14:23; 1 PETER 5:1-2)

I. Church of Jesus Christ of Latter Day Saints

(1) Religious organization: **Church of Jesus Christ of Latter Day Saints**

(2) Date Begun: **~1830** [3]

(3) Founder: **Joseph Smith** [3]

(4) Baptism of believers only: **No** [6]
(MARK 16:16)

(5) Baptism by immersion only: **Yes** [6]
(ROMANS 6:4; COLOSSIANS 2:12)

(6) Baptism for Remission of Sins: **Yes** [5]
(ACTS 2:38)

(7) Baptized in the name of the Father, the Son and the Holy Ghost (Spirit): **Unable to determine** (MATTHEW 28:19)

(8) Lord's Supper each and every first day of week: **No** [7]
(ACTS 20:7; 1 CORINTHIANS 11:26)

(9) Worship in spirit and in truth: **No** [6]
(JOHN 4:24)

(10) Believe Salvation Can Be Lost: **Unable to determine**
(JAMES 5:19-20; 2 PETER 3:17-18)

(11) Autonomy of local Congregation: **No** [5]
(ACTS 14:23; 1 PETER 5:1-2)

J. Jehovah's Witnesses

(1) Religious organization: **Jehovah's Witnesses**

(2) Date Begun: **~1879** [2]

(3) Founders: **Russell/Rutherford** [3]

(4) Baptism of believers only: **Yes** [6]
(MARK 16:16)

(5) Baptism by immersion only: **Yes** [6]
(ROMANS 6:4; COLOSSIANS 2:12)

(6) Baptism for Remission of Sins: **Yes** [5]
(ACTS 2:38)

(7) Baptized in the name of the Father, the Son and the Holy Ghost (Spirit): **Unable to determine** (MATTHEW 28:19)

(8) Lord's Supper each and every first day of week: **No** [1]
(ACTS 20:7; 1 CORINTHIANS 11:26)

(9) Worship in spirit and in truth: **No** [1]
(JOHN 4:24)

(10) Believe Salvation Can Be Lost: **No** [3]
(JAMES 5:19-20; 2 PETER 3:17-18)

(11) Autonomy of local Congregation: **No** [1]
(Acts 14:23; 1 Peter 5:1-2)

K. Seventh-Day Adventists

(1) Religious organization: **Seventh-Day Adventists**

(2) Date Begun: **~1843** [2]

(3) Founders: **Miller/White** [2]

(4) Baptism of believers only: **Yes** [2]
(MARK 16:16)

(5) Baptism by immersion only: **Yes** [2]
(ROMANS 6:4; COLOSSIANS 2:12)

(6) Baptism for Remission of Sins: **No** [4]
(ACTS 2:38)

(7) Baptized in the name of the Father, the Son and the Holy Ghost (Spirit): **Unable to determine** (MATTHEW 28:19)

(8) Lord's Supper each and every first day of week: **No** [1]
(ACTS 20:7; 1 CORINTHIANS 11:26)

(9) Worship in spirit and in truth: **No** [1]
(JOHN 4:24)

(10) Believe Salvation Can Be Lost: **No** [2]
(JAMES 5:19-20; 2 PETER 3:17-18)

(11) Autonomy of local Congregation: **No** [2]
(ACTS 14:23; 1 PETER 5:1-2)

L. Make your own Comparative Analysis Forms

Church or Faith #1

(1) Religious organization:

(2) Date Begun:

(3) Founders:

(4) Baptism of believers only:
(MARK 16:16)

l(5) Baptism by immersion only:
(ROMANS 6:4; COLOSSIANS 2:12)

(6) Baptism for Remission of Sins:
(ACTS 2:38)

(7) Baptized in the name of the Father, the Son and the Holy Ghost (Spirit):
(MATTHEW 28:19)

(8) Lord's Supper each and every first day of week:
(ACTS 20:7; 1 CORINTHIANS 11:26)

(9) Worship in spirit and in truth:
(JOHN 4:24)

(10) Believe Salvation Can Be Lost:
(JAMES 5:19-20; 2 PETER 3:17-18)

(11) Autonomy of local Congregation:
(Acts 14:23; 1 Peter 5:1-2)

Church or Faith #2

(1) Religious organization:

(2) Date Begun:

(3) Founders:

(4) Baptism of believers only:
(MARK 16:16)

(5) Baptism by immersion only:
(ROMANS 6:4; COLOSSIANS 2:12)

(6) Baptism for Remission of Sins:
(ACTS 2:38)

(7) Baptized in the name of the Father, the Son and the Holy Ghost (Spirit):
(MATTHEW 28:19)

(8) Lord's Supper each and every first day of week:
(ACTS 20:7; 1 CORINTHIANS 11:26)

(9) Worship in spirit and in truth:
(JOHN 4:24)

(10) Believe Salvation Can Be Lost:
(JAMES 5:19-20; 2 PETER 3:17-18)

(11) Autonomy of local Congregation:
(Acts 14:23; 1 Peter 5:1-2)

Church or Faith #3

(1) Religious organization:

(2) Date Begun:

(3) Founders:

(4) Baptism of believers only:
(MARK 16:16)

I(5) Baptism by immersion only:
(ROMANS 6:4; COLOSSIANS 2:12)

(6) Baptism for Remission of Sins:
(ACTS 2:38)

(7) Baptized in the name of the Father, the Son and the Holy Ghost (Spirit):
(MATTHEW 28:19)

(8) Lord's Supper each and every first day of week:
(ACTS 20:7; 1 CORINTHIANS 11:26)

(9) Worship in spirit and in truth:
(JOHN 4:24)

(10) Believe Salvation Can Be Lost:
(JAMES 5:19-20; 2 PETER 3:17-18)

(11) Autonomy of local Congregation:
(Acts 14:23; 1 Peter 5:1-2)

References

[1] Jennings, Alvin, **Traditions of Men versus The Word of God,** Fort Worth, TX: Star Bible Publications, 1973.

[2] Steig, Shelly, **Finding the Right Church: A Guide to Denomination Beliefs**, Grand Rapids, MI: Word Publishing, 1997

[3] Cochrane, Mike, **Christianity, Cults & Religions,** Torrance, CA: Rose Publishing, 1994

[4] Stewart, John David, **A Study of Minor Religious Beliefs in America,** Austin, TX: R.B. Sweet Co., 1962

[5] Stewart, John David, **A Study of Major Religious Beliefs in America,** Austin, TX: R.B. Sweet Co., 1962.

[6] Algermissen, Konrad, **Christian Sects,** New York: Hawthorn Books, 1962

[7] Mead, Frank S. **Handbook of Denominations in the United States,** Nashville: Abingdon Press, 1975.

[8] Tomlinson, L.G. **Churches of Today in the Light of Scripture,** Nashville: Gospel Advocate Company, 1962.

In order to successfully follow the Narrow Way, His followers must develop a set of Convictions based solely upon the Word of God, embracing His total Counsel, while including Only the Patterns, Commandments, Instructions and Examples provided by Jesus, His Apostles and Disciples ... Heaven Awaits!

Appendix 6

Summary of selected Elements of the Divine Mosaic
(Partial Listing)

Appendix Contents

A. Introduction

B. Examples of what Lord Jesus really wants from His followers

C. Examples of the Keystones of the Faith

D. Cornerstones of the Faith

E. Generally accepted Biblical facts regarding Lord Jesus and His Church

F. Examples of general elements of the Divine Mosaic

G. Elements of the Message of Christ

H. Worship according to the Divine Pattern

I. Divine Pattern of Congregational, Organizational Structure

J. Divine Pattern of the work of His Church

K. Date and Place of the Establishment of His Church

L. His Divine Pattern or Plan of Salvation

M. Examples of how Christians exhibit faithfulness

N. The Cleansing Power of the Blood of Christ

O. Christ, our ultimate Pattern

A Introduction

A significant reason the vast majority has difficulty in understanding the Message of Christ is that it is presented to mankind in the form of a **Divine Format,** which the author has chosen to label as the Divine Mosaic.

The comprehension of this single fact is a major step toward a greater understanding and the ability to discern the specific Divine Will of God. In addition, this summary in outline form also provides an *additional method of comparing the doctrines of religious organizations* with the elements, specifics or facts, which make up the Divine Mosaic.

(1) The information provided in this Appendix is a partial listing of the elements of the Message of Christ and His Disciples.

The first four books of the New Testament or the Gospels (Matthew, Mark, Luke and John) are devoted to an account of the Life of Jesus, from four points of view

Woven within these four inspired Books also is the **Message of Christ,** which includes His Patterns, Teachings, Instructions or Examples and Commandments, which are clarified and supplemented, by His inspired Disciples in the remaining books of the New Testament. The **Message of Christ is also known as the Faith, the Truth and the specific Divine Will of God.**

An important objective of the author is to assist the user in developing his or her ability to search out the Divine Will of God and identify false or erroneous religious teachings. (Chapter II, Section C)

After the user has gained a solid understanding of the information provided in this manual, he or she will be empowered to come to their own **independent logical conclusions** and **make informed decisions regarding spiritual issues**

B. Examples of what Lord Jesus really wants from His followers

Source: Chapter I

(1) Lord Jesus requires complete obedience to His Words in the New Testament. (MATTHEW 23:23, MARK 13:31, JOHN 14:23, JOHN 15:7)

Simply, that you live your life in **obedience** to the specifics of His Divine Message, which includes strict compliance to the Commandments.

(2) Our Lord requires strict Obedience to His Commandments, which generally fall into three classes

(a) The first type relates to His Divine Patterns

(Pattern of Salvation, forms of Worship in His Church, Prayer etc.), which are fully explained in this manual

These Commandments should present no real difficulty in obeying as they are simply, to be <u>carefully followed.</u>

(b) The second type relate to personal behavior.

For example, the <u>most</u> important Commands are to Love your God and neighbor. (MARK 12:30-31)

The Commandments of the Master were further illuminated, augmented and supplemented by His Apostles in the remaining books of the New Testament.

Paul confirms this role of the Apostles in 1 CORINTHIANS 14:37 "If any man think himself to be a prophet, or spiritual, let him acknowledge that the things that I write unto you are the **Commandments of the Lord.**"

(c) The third type is of a general nature. . .

For example we must believe in His existence (HEBREWS 11:6)

(3) Christians are directed to circumvent and avoid Sinfulness

(a) Jesus provided a comprehensive list (REVELATION 21:8)

(b) The Great Apostle Paul provided two detailed summaries (ROMANS 1:23-31 and 1 CORINTHIANS 6:9-11).

(4) Jesus requires that His followers make their own personal determination of how to find and follow the Narrow Way by searching the Holy Scriptures (JOHN 5:39, ACTS 17:11)

It is the firm belief of the author that the *answer to each and every question and dilemma of life* is provided in His Word.

Therefore, the only way to overcome this dilemma is to turn to the Bible, which contains the *only Divine message* that has ever been supplied to mankind and *is to be our sole source of spiritual information*

Reminder: The *purpose of this manual is to assist the user in completing their personal search,* which includes the determination of the precise requirements to be among the few, who by their individual efforts will have properly prepared for their place in Heaven.

(5) His followers are required to make use of the complete counsel of God. (ACTS 20:27)

(a) There are <u>no</u> unimportant Patterns, Instructions, Examples or Commands

(6) Adding to or taking away from the Holy Scriptures are condemned, in both the Old and New Testaments. (DEUTERONOMY 4:2, PROVERBS 30:6, 2 JOHN 1:9)

(a) Each follower must also seriously consider and keep in mind the stern New Testament injunction against adding to or taking away from the Word of God.

(b) And finally in the closing verses of the last book of the New Testament the meaning of this Commandment is made absolutely crystal clear. (REVELATION 22:18-19)

(c) In addition, (REVELATION 22:18-19) clearly indicates that God has not and will not provide mankind with any revelations other than those, which are included in the His Holy Word.

(7) Christians are directed to shun and reject False Teachers and Teachings (2 TIMOTHY 4:3-4 MATTHEW 24:11, MATTHEW 24:24, ACTS 20:29-30, 2 CORINTHIANS 11:13-15)

C. Keystones of the Divine Mosaic

Keystone Teachings of Lord Jesus

(1) Seek first the Kingdom of God (MATTHEW 6:33)

In order to be acceptable and be saved from the terrors of Hell, Jesus has made it clear that **our Creator** must be made **first** in our lives.

This is the reason why the discussion of our God is presented in Chapter I.

(2) Love your God, with all your Heart, Soul and Mind (MATTHEW 22:37-38, LUKE 10:27, MARK 12:30, JOSHUA 22:5, DEUTERONOMY 6:5; 10:12; 11:13;13:3; 30:6)

(3) Love all members of humanity or your neighbors as yourself (MATTHEW 22:39, MARK 12:31, MARK 12:33, JOHN 13:34)

(4) The Worship of God is to be in Spirit and in Truth (JOHN 4:24)

(5) Search the Scriptures (JOHN 5:39)

(6) Do unto others, as they would have them do unto them. (MATTHEW 7:12, LUKE 6:31)

(7) Biblical Injunction against adding to or taking away from His Word (REVELATION 22:18-19)

(8) All mankind will be judged by the Words of Lord Jesus and His Apostles as presented in the Holy Scriptures (JOHN 12:48, 1 CORINTHIANS 14:37)

Keystone Teachings of His Apostles

(1) Commandments of Apostles are binding (1 CORINTHIANS 14:37)

(2) Save yourself first and then all those who will hear you (1 TIMOTHY 4:16)

(3) Study the Word and consider the entire Counsel of God (2 TIMOTHY 2:15, ACTS 20:27

(4) A child of God who continues in sin has fallen away and can be lost. (GALATIANS 5:4, 1 CORINTHIANS 10:12, HEBREWS 3:12-19, 2 PETER 2:20-22)

(5) A believer who falls away and repents may return to His Church. (ACTS 8:22, JAMES 5:16)

(6) Walk by Faith, not by sight. (2 CORINTHIANS 5:7)

(7) Be prepared to provide others with the Biblical basis of your convictions or beliefs (1 PETER 3:15)

D. Cornerstones of the Faith

Sources: Chapter II and Chapter V

(1) Christian Fellowship (ACTS 2:42, 1 CORINTHIANS 1:9, 2 CORINTHIANS 8:4, 1 JOHN 1:31 JOHN 1:7)

(2) Good Works (2 CORINTHIANS 9:8, EPHESIANS 2:10, JAMES 3:17, EPHESIANS 6:8, COLOSSIANS 1:10, 1 TIMOTHY 2:10, 1 THESSALONIANS 5:15, 2 THESSALONIANS 2:17, 1 TIMOTHY 1:5, 1 TIMOTHY 6:18, 2 TIMOTHY 2:21, 2 TIMOTHY 3:17, TITUS 2:14, TITUS 3:1, TITUS 3:8, TITUS 3:14, HEBREWS 10:24, HEBREWS 13:16, HEBREWS 13:21, , 1 PETER 2:12, 3 JOHN 1:11)

(3) Forgiveness (MATTHEW 6:14-15, LUKE 17:3, LUKE 23:34, MATTHEW 6:12, , LUKE 6:37, MARK 11:25-26

(4) Mercy (LUKE 6:36, MATTHEW 5:7)

(5) Kindness (2 CORINTHIANS 6:6, COLOSSIANS 3:12, 2 PETER 1:7, EPHESIANS 2:7, TITUS 3:4)

E. Generally accepted Biblical facts regarding Lord Jesus and His Church

Source: Chapter II

(1) Jesus has all power [authority] in Heaven and on Earth. Believers submit respectfully to the supreme power and authority of Christ. (COLOSSIANS 3:1, MATTHEW 28:18)

(2) Believers acknowledge that Jesus Christ founded His Church. (MATTHEW 16:18)

(3) Believers acknowledge that Christ is the Head of His Church, which is His Body. (EPHESIANS 1:22-23)

(4) Our Lord is the Savior of the Body, which is His Church. (EPHESIANS 5:23)

(5) Jesus pleaded for religious unity in one Faith. (JOHN 17:20-21)

(6) Jesus Christ shed his blood for His Church. (ACTS 20:28)

(7) Only the Lord can add saved people to His Church. (ACTS 2:47)

(8) Jesus Christ loves His Church. (EPHESIANS 5:25)

(9) His followers proudly wear the name of Christ. (ACTS 4:12, ACTS 11:26, 1 PETER 4:16)

(10) His followers are to be faithful to Christ (REVELATIONS 2:10)

(11) Lord Jesus requires complete obedience to His Words in the New Testament. (MATTHEW 23:23, MARK 13:31, JOHN 14:23, JOHN 15:7)

F. Examples of general elements of the Divine Mosaic

The following are basic elements that stand-alone and simply must be accepted.

(1) Members of His Church are guided by the same Message as was originally delivered to the first century Christians, which is accepted unconditionally, as the complete Inspired Word of God. (2 TIMOTHY 3:15-17, 1 PETER 1:22-25)

(2) Paul pleaded for religious unity in one Faith and confirmed that only one Church is the true Church of our Lord. (EPHESIANS 4:4-6, 1 TIMOTHY 3:15, COLOSSIANS 1:18, EPHESIANS 1: 22)

(3) His Church has no earthly organization as its headquarters are in Heaven. (ACTS 2:47, COLOSSIANS 3:1)

(4) His faithful followers recognize the distinctions between the Old and New Testaments. (COLOSSIANS 2:14, JEREMIAH 31:31-34, HEBREWS 8:7-13, HEBREWS 8:6, HEBREWS 9:15-24, JOHN 1:17, 1 PETER 1:10-12, 2 TIMOTHY 3:16, ROMANS 15:4).

(5) Worship, according to the teachings or commandments of men is prohibited. (MATTHEW 15:9)

(6) Words spoken by Jesus were not spoken on His own Authority, but He spoke only what God instructed Him to speak. (JOHN 12:49-50)

(7) There is only one Pattern (Plan) of Salvation. (EPHESIANS 4:4-6)

(8) His Church was not built by the Apostle Paul or by any other human or group. (MATTHEW 16:16-18, 1 CORINTHIANS 1:13-15)

G. Elements of the Message of Christ

Source: Chapter III

Elements of the Message of Christ include;

(a) Patterns to be observed
(b) Truths to be believed
(c) Commands to be obeyed
(d) Instructions or Examples to be followed
(e) Warnings to be heeded
(f) Assurances to be anticipated

(1) Patterns to be observed

The Message of Christ in part, is an organized system of Divine Patterns.

(a) Divine Pattern or Plan of Salvation

(See Section L)

Detailed information: Chapter VI - His Divine Pattern or Plan of Salvation

(b) Divine Pattern of Prayer
Full information: Chapter VI - Pattern of Prayer, our access to God

(c) Divine Pattern of Worship

(See Section H)

Comprehensive information: Chapter V

(d) His Divine Pattern of the Organizational Structure of His Church

(See Section I)

In depth information: Chapter V

(e) His Divine Pattern of the Work of the Congregation

(See Section J)

Complete information: Chapter V

(2) Examples of Truths to be believed

(a) God exists (HEBREWS 11:6)

(b) God is a Spirit (JOHN 4:24)

(c) Jesus is All Powerful (MATTHEW 28:18)

(d) Jesus is the Resurrection and the Life (JOHN 11:25)

(e) Jesus is Our Savior (JOHN 4:42)

(f) God is Love (JOHN 3:16)

(g) Jesus is the only Way to God, the Father (JOHN 14:6)

(3) Examples of Commands to be obeyed

(a) Love your God, with all your Heart, Soul, and Mind and thy neighbor (LUKE 10:27-28)

(b) Seek first the Kingdom of God (MATTHEW 6:33)

(c) Worship God in Spirit and in Truth (JOHN 4:24)

(d) Search and study the Scriptures (JOHN 5:39, 2 TIMOTHY 2:15)

(e) Old Testament Commandments, which were affirmed or ratified by Christ (MARK 10:19, ROMANS 13:9, MATTHEW 6:33, MATTHEW 6:24, MATTHEW 5:33-37, MATTHEW 5:21, MATTHEW 5:27-28, MATTHEW 15:4, MATTHEW 19:18, MATTHEW 19:18, LUKE 12:15)

(f) Commandments were further clarified, amplified and added to by His Apostles in the remaining books. (1 CORINTHIANS 14:37)

(g) Consider the entire Counsel of God (ACTS 20:27)

(h) Save yourself first and then all those who will hear you (1 TIMOTHY 4:16)

(4) Examples of Instructions or Examples to be followed

(a) His faithful followers are to assemble for Worship on the first day of each and every week (ACTS 20:7)

(b) His faithful followers are to observe the Lord's Supper on the first day of each and every week (MATTHEW 26:26-28, ACTS 20:7, 1 CORINTHIANS 11:23-26)

(c) His faithful followers are to cheerfully give of their means on Sunday, the first day of each and every week. (1 CORINTHIANS 16:2, 2 CORINTHIANS 9 6-7)

(5) Examples of Warnings to be heeded

(a) Stern warnings were issued to all those who refuse to obey (2 THESSALONIANS 1:8, 1 PETER 4:17)

(b) Severe warnings to those who fail to gain a clear understanding of the Message of Christ. (ROMANS 1:31)

(c) We must have Biblical Authority or support for every belief & practice (EPHESIANS 5:10-11)

(d) Strict Biblical Injunction against adding to or taking away from His Word (REVELATION 22:18-19)

(e) Warnings of false teachers and teaching (MATTHEW 24:11, MATTHEW 24:24, ACTS 20:29-30, 2 CORINTHIANS 11:13-15)

In MATTHEW 7:16, Jesus further explains "Ye shall know them by their fruits."

In this context "Fruits" includes the beliefs, physical worship and practices of the religion, which must be compared directly with the Bible and no other source of information

(6) Examples of Assurances to be anticipated

(a) Lord Jesus Assures His faithful servants a Glorious Heavenly home (MATTHEW 16:27, MATTHEW 25:34, MATTHEW 5:11-12, MATTHEW 13:43, MATTHEW 25:21, JOHN 4:36, JOHN 14:3, REVELATION 2:7, REVELATION 2:10-11, REVELATION 2:26-28, REVELATION 3:5, REVELATION 3:20-21, REVELATION 22:14)

(b) Lord Jesus Assures us He will confess all who Confess Him before men (MATTHEW 10:32, LUKE 12:8)

(c) Lord Jesus Assures us an abundant, life on earth (JOHN 10:10, JOHN 16:23-24, MATTHEW 6:6, MATTHEW 6:33, MATTHEW 21:22, MARK 9:23, MARK 10:28-30, MARK 11:24, LUKE 6:38, JOHN 15:7, JOHN 15:10-11)

(d) Lord Jesus Assures us that He will always be with us (MATTHEW 18:20, MATTHEW 28:20).

(e) Lord Jesus Assures us that He will come again (MATTHEW 24:30-31, LUKE 21:27-28, MATTHEW 24:27, MATTHEW 25:31)

(f) Another Assurance that Lord Jesus has made is that there will definitely be a Judgment Day, which we all must attend. (JOHN 5:26-29)

H. Worship according to the Divine Pattern

Source: Chapter V

(1) Purpose of Worship is the Glorification and Worship of God (PSALMS 100:1-5, 1 PETER 2:9, 1 PETER 4:11)

(2) Worship of God must be in Spirit and in Truth (JOHN 4:24, 1 CORINTHIANS 14:15)

(3) Each congregation meets for worship, on the first day of each week. (ACTS 20:7)

(4) Several prayers are offered to God during each worship service. (JAMES 5:16, ACTS 2:42, 1 TIMOTHY 2:1, 1 THESSALONIANS 5:17, MATTHEW 6:7-13)

(5) Vocal or a cappella singing and making melody in their hearts, without instrumental accompaniment, is an essential component of worship. (EPHESIANS 5:19, COLOSSIANS 3:16, HEBREWS 2:12, 1 CORINTHIANS 14:15, ACTS 16:25)

(6) The Bible is the exclusive basis of teachings in classes and from the pulpit. (MATTHEW 24:14, ROMANS 10:15, 1 CORINTHIANS 9:14, COLOSSIANS 1:28, 2 TIMOTHY 4:2)

(7) The Lord's Supper is observed, every Sunday, the first day of each week. (MATTHEW 26:26-28, ACTS 20:7, ACTS 2:42, 1 CORINTHIANS 11:23-26)

(8) Each week, followers are given the opportunity, to support the work of the Church, by cheerfully giving of their means. (1 CORINTHIANS 16:1-2, 2 CORINTHIANS 9:6-8)

(9) His followers are commanded to regularly attend Services of His Church (ACTS 2:42, ACTS 20:7, HEBREWS 10:24-25)

I. Divine Pattern of Congregational Organizational Structure

Source: Chapter V

Following the example of first century Congregations of His Church, congregations of His Church, today make use of the congregational type of church government.

(1) Jesus Christ is the Head of His Church, which is His Body. (EPHESIANS 1:22-23)

There is a misconception regarding the Scriptural government of the Church. Since the people of the United States and several other countries live in a democracy, many believe that the congregation should vote upon issues that affect the majority. This concept is erroneous, because His Church is *not a democracy, but a monarchy and Jesus Christ is the everlasting King.*

(2) Governing each mature congregation of the early church was a group of two or more ordained Elders, who oversaw and tended to the spiritual needs of its members.
(1 TIMOTHY 5:17, ACTS 14:23, 1 PETER 5:2)

The required traits of an Elder are listed and explained (1 TIMOTHY 3:1-7).

(3) That each local Church has two or more Deacons, who actively serve the church.

The required traits of a Deacon are listed and explained (1 TIMOTHY 3:8-13).

(4) That each local Church has teachers (evangelists, ministers, preachers) who teach or proclaim the gospel (EPHESIANS 4:11-12)

(5) That each local Church has Members, who love the Lord and each other (PHILIPPIANS 2:1-4, 1 JOHN 5:1-2)

(6) Members of His Church collectively esteem Jesus Christ as Lord and have the highest regard for His Authority. (MATTHEW 28:18)

(7) Adding to, or subtracting from, the simple instructions of Jesus is strictly forbidden (REVELATION 22:18-19) and is failing to respect Him as Lord.

J. Divine Pattern of the work of His Church

Source: Chapter V

(1) Benevolence (1 TIMOTHY 6:18-19, 2 CORINTHIANS 1:3-5, TITUS 3:8, TITUS 3:14, HEBREWS 10:24)

(2) Evangelism (MARK 16:15-16, ROMANS 1:16, MATTHEW 28:19-20)

(3) Edification & Spiritual Growth (GALATIANS 6:1, EPHESIANS 4:11-16, HEBREWS 10:24-25, ACTS 9:31)

K. Establishment of His Church

Additional Information: Chapter V

On that glorious day of Pentecost, when His Church began in Jerusalem, the renowned Apostle Peter delivered one of the most monumental and significant sermons of all time, on the Life, Death, Burial, and the Resurrection of Jesus Christ, which also marked the beginning of the preaching of the Message of Christ, which proclaimed Salvation through obedience and the remission of sins (ACTS 2:14, ACTS 2:38, LUKE 24:47)

(1) Peter's words prompted three thousand Souls to follow the simple Commandments of the Lord and thus formed, in approximately AD 30 (Bible scholars differ on the actual year, estimates range from AD 29 to AD 33), the first congregation of His Church in the City of Jerusalem.

Based solely upon the Word of God, we know when and where the Church or Kingdom of our Lord began.

L. His Divine Pattern or Plan of Salvation

Source: Chapter VI

While on earth, Jesus Christ and His Apostles commanded seven things; we must do, in order to become a child of God.

(1) The new convert must acknowledge, in his or her heart that in light of God's word, that he or she is a sinner. (ROMANS 3:23, ROMANS 5:12, ROMANS 6:23, LUKE 18:13)

(2) The new convert must hear or study the Word of God. (JOHN 5:24, ROMANS 10:17)

(3) The new convert must have faith or trust and be obedient. (HEBREWS 11:6,

ROMANS 16:26, ROMANS 16:19, 2 CORINTHIANS 10:5, GALATIANS 3:26)

(4) The new convert must sincerely believe that Jesus is the Son of God (MARK 16:15-16, JOHN 3:16, JOHN 8:24, ACTS 16:31, JOHN 3:36, JOHN 17:21, ACTS 8:37, 1 JOHN 5:13)

(5) The new convert must truly repent of your sins and turn away from sin. (LUKE 13:3, ACTS 3:19, ROMANS 2:4, 2 CORINTHIANS 7:10, ACTS 17:30, ACTS 20:21, 2 PETER 3:9)

(6) The new convert must confess that Jesus is Lord and the Son of God. (MATTHEW 10:32-33, LUKE 12:8, ROMANS 10:9-10, 1 JOHN 4:15)

(7) The new convert must be baptized into Christ, by total immersion, for the remission of sins in the name of the Father, the Son and the Holy Ghost [Spirit] (MATTHEW 28:19, ACTS 2:38, MARK 16:16, JOHN 3:3-5, ACTS 10:47, ACTS 22:16, ROMANS 6:3, HEBREWS 10:22, GALATIANS 3:27)

(a) Baptism is a burial by immersion. (MATTHEW 3:16-17, ACTS 8:38-39)

(b) Baptism is a resurrection. (COLOSSIANS 2:12, ROMANS 6:3-6)

(c) When an individual is baptized, he or she goes into the water a sinner, is buried in the water and raised sinless through the blood of Christ (1 JOHN 1:7, REVELATION 1:5)

At that very moment:

(d) The new convert is saved from his or her sins. (1 PETER 3:21)

(e) The new convert has put on Christ and has become a child of God. (GALATIANS 3:26-27)

(f) The new convert has been born again. (JOHN 3:3, 1 PETER 1:23)

(g) The name of the new convert is added to the Book of Life or membership rolls, in Heaven, by our Lord God almighty. (PHILIPPIANS 4:3, REVELATION 20:15, REVELATION 3:5, ACTS 2:41, ACTS 2:47, COLOSSIANS 3:1)

After an individual has been baptized, he or she is commanded to Remain Faithful. (ROMANS 6:3-4, REVELATION 2:10)

M. Examples of how Christians exhibit faithfulness

Source: Chapter VI

(1) Our most important Mission is sharing the "Good News" of Christ with others (MATTHEW 28:19, ROMANS 1:16)

(2) Worshipping God in spirit and in truth (JOHN 4:23-24)

(3) Obeying the Commandments (JOHN 14:23, TITUS 2:12-13)

(4) Seeking to actively serve the Lord (JAMES 2:24, JAMES 1:25, JAMES 1:27 COLOSSIANS 1:10, 1 CORINTHIANS 15:58**)**

(5) Caring for our Brethren in Christ and others in need

(a) Christians must be willing to assist our Brethren in their spiritual growth or who are discouraged or have been overcome by sin or fallen away. (GALATIANS 6:1-2, EPHESIANS 4:11-15)

(b) Christians must be considerate, accommodating and have a willingness to share worldly wealth, with those who are less fortunate, feeble, ailing or in distress (GALATIANS 2:10, JAMES 1:27)

(6) Actively avoiding sin and temptation (MATTHEW 26:41, JAMES 1:12, JOHN 3:6, 1 THESSALONIANS 5:22, REVELATION 3:5)

(7) Living a Simple Life (MATTHEW 6:19-34, 1 TIMOTHY 6:10, ROMANS 13:8, HEBREWS 13:5)

(8) Regularly Studying your Bible (1 PETER 2:2, JAMES 1:21, JOHN 5:39, ACTS 17:11, 2 TIMOTHY 2:15, 2 PETER 3:18)

(9) Regularly going to your Heavenly Father in Prayer (PHILIPPIANS 4:6-7, COLOSSIANS 4:2, HEBREWS 4:16, EPHESIANS 6:18, 1 PETER 3:12)

(10) Controlling your tongue, emotions and thoughts (MATTHEW 12:36-37, JAMES 1:26 JAMES 5:12, EPHESIANS 4:24-27, EPHESIANS 5:4, 2 CORINTHIANS 10:5)

(11) Avoid False Doctrine

(a) The Doctrine of the Church, built by the hands of Jesus Christ, is pure and simple.

(b) The only way to know exactly what God desires is to put your trust in His Words rather than the convictions of man.

(c) Christ and His Apostles have warned us to avoid false teachers and their false doctrine. (2 TIMOTHY 4:3-4 MATTHEW 24:11, MATTHEW 24:24, ACTS 20:29-30, 2 CORINTHIANS 11:13-15)

(12) Faith and Obedience (HEBREWS 11:1, HEBREWS 11:6, ROMANS 1:5, ROMANS 6:16, ROMANS 16:26, 2 CORINTHIANS 7:15, 2 CORINTHIANS 10:5, GALATIANS 3:26)

(13) Confession of Sins (JAMES 5:16, 1 JOHN 1:9)

(14) Repentance of Sins (ACTS 17:30-31, LUKE 13:3, ROMANS 2:4, 2 PETER 3:9, 2 CORINTHIANS 7:10)

(15) Holiness (2 PETER 3:11-14).

(16) Watchfulness (MARK 13:33)

N. The Cleansing Power of the Blood of Christ

Source: Chapter VI

The Blood of Christ is a reoccurring theme in the New Testament, a significant element of the Divine Mosaic

(1) Our God understands the problem of sin and provided a solution in the first century. (1 JOHN 1:7)

(2) God will forgive, if we truly repent and respectfully ask Him to forgive us. "If we confess our sins, He is faithful and just to forgive us our sins and to cleanse [katharizo] us from all unrighteousness." (1 JOHN 1:9)

(a) The original Greek word "katharizo" that is translated "cleanse" in this verse actually means continual cleansing.

O. Christ, our ultimate Pattern

Source: Chapter X

(1) Christians are to be formed, conformed and transformed

(a) The nature or character of Christ must be formed (GALATIANS 4:19)

(b) Christians are to be conformed to the image of His Son (ROMANS 8:29)

(c) Christians are to be transformed to the image of His Son, by growing in grace, and in the knowledge of our Lord and Savior (2 CORINTHIANS 3:18, 2 PETER 3:17-18, COLOSSIANS 1:10)

(2) Knowledge is very important, but understanding alone is not enough, as it cannot alone produce a Christ like character.

(a) In order to grow in grace and take on His likeness we must be obedient to that knowledge, which allows ourselves to align with His Pattern. (JOHN 1:17, EPHESIANS 4:15, JOHN 15:10)

The natural result of gaining knowledge and obeying our Lord and Savior is that *His Will increases in importance, while our concerns with worldly affairs become increasingly less significant.*

(b) As a result, we yield increasingly greater control of our lives to Him. Just as John the Baptist learned, accomplished and revealed about 2000 years ago. (JOHN 3:30)

As a Christian grows to reflect more of the qualities of Christ and less of human nature, *he or she is complying with the instruction of Christ to take up their cross daily.*

(c) Our Lord desires us to disregard the fleeting pleasures of our old life, in order to focus our entire attention on His Word and

obedience to His Divine Will. (LUKE 9:23-24)

(3) Jesus Christ is the complete living Word of God

(a) *The Holy Bible is a somewhat limited version of the Word of God in a written form.* (JOHN 1:1, JOHN 20:30-31, JOHN 21:24-25)

(b) The Holy Scriptures, which will be the Standard by which we are judged or evaluated on Judgment Day, are sufficient for all our needs. (ROMANS 2:16, 2 TIMOTHY 3:15)

(4) Importance of Fellowship with likeminded Christians

One of Christ's specific reasons for providing the Pattern for His Church was to create *an environment where the members would always watch over each other in love.*

Only in such an atmosphere can true personal spiritual growth be accomplished, which is the result of personal effort in conjunction with loving and nurturing fellowship.

(a) Growing in the knowledge and grace or becoming Christ like is not an independent endeavor, but rather it is a way of life that can only be sustained within a fellowship of likeminded faithful Christians. (1 JOHN 1:7)

(5) Examples of the Teachings of Christ

(a) **Being Humble or Meek** (MATTHEW 18:4, MATTHEW 23:12)
(b) **Being Faithful** (REVELATION 2:10)
(c) **Being Forgiving** (LUKE 23:34).
(d) **Being not of this world** (JOHN 17:14-17)
(e) **Being Just** (JOHN 5:30)
(f) **Love** (JOHN 13:34, JOHN 15:13).
(g) **Being Merciful** (MATTHEW 5:7, LUKE 6:36)
(h) **Being Obedient** (LUKE 22:42)
(i) **Prayer** (MATTHEW 21:22)
(j) **Pure in heart** (MATTHEW 5:8)
(k) **Being Watchful** (LUKE 12:37, REVELATION 16:15).

(6) Examples of the Teachings of His Disciples

(a) **Charity** (1 TIMOTHY 4:12, 1 PETER 4:8)
(b) **Faithful** (1 TIMOTHY 6:2, HEBREWS 10:23, REVELATION 17:14)
(c) **Fear God** (ACTS 10:2, HEBREWS 12:28)
(d) **Godly** (2 TIMOTHY 3:12, TITUS 2:12)
(e) **Good Conscience** (1 TIMOTHY 1:5, HEBREWS 13:18)
(f) **Goodness** (ROMANS 15:14, GALATIANS 5:22)
(g) **Hope** (ROMANS 8:25, ROMANS 12:12)
(h) **Holy** (COLOSSIANS 3:12, JUDE 1:20)
(i) **Humble** (COLOSSIANS 3:12 , 1 PETER 5:5, 1 PETER 5:6)
(j) **Just and devout** (LUKE 2:25, .
(k) **Kind and Longsuffering** (COLOSSIANS 3:12, 2 CORINTHIANS 6:6, EPHESIANS 4:2, 2 PETER 1:7)
(l) **Loving** (COLOSSIANS 1:4, 1 THESSALONIANS 4:9)
(m) **Meek and quiet spirit** (1 PETER 3:4)
(n) **Obedient** (1 PETER 1:14, ROMANS 16:19)
(o) **Patience** (2 TIMOTHY 3:10, TITUS 2:2)
(p) **Prayer** (JAMES 5:16, EPHESIANS 6:18)
(q) **Pure** (1 JOHN 3:3)
(r) **Righteous** (LUKE 1:6, ROMANS 5:19, 1 PETER 3:12, 1 PETER 4:18)
(s) **Sincerity** (1 CORINTHIANS 5:8, 2 CORINTHIANS 2:17, 2 CORINTHIANS 8:8)
(t) **Spirit led** (ROMANS 8:14)
(u) **Steadfast** (COLOSSIANS 2:5, ACTS 2:42)
(v) **Without guile or cunning** (1 PETER 2:1, 1 THESSALONIANS 2:3, 1 PETER 3:10)
(w) **Zealous of good works** (TITUS 2:14, TITUS 2:7)

Follow Jesus ... Heaven Awaits!

Appendix 7

Words of Jesus, His Apostles and Disciples
with significant quotes from the Old Testament
(Partial Listing)

Appendix Contents

A. Introduction

B. Scriptural references by topic

A. Introduction

Those familiar with the Bible know that it contains passages that address a whole host of topics ranging from Angels to Words of Jesus regarding Marriage and Divorce or for finding solace when facing the trials and tribulations of this life.

The purpose of this guide is to quickly assist those who are not familiar with the Word of God and wish to tap into the ageless fund of knowledge provided by their Heavenly Father.

This is a *sampling* of the hundreds, possibly thousands of pearls of knowledge, found in the Scriptures which will aid both men and women in living a more fulfilling bountiful life.

Regular study of the Bible is a secret of many successful people.

B. Scriptural references by topic

Abide in Christ
New Testament References: JOHN 15:4-7, 2 CORINTHIANS 3:18, PHILIPPIANS 3:20-21, 1 JOHN 3:2

Ability, Increase in
Old Testament References: PROVERBS 3:26, ZECHARIAH 4:6

New Testament References: ROMANS 8:31, PHILIPPIANS 4:13

Adversity
Old Testament References: PSALMS 34:1, PSALMS 37:24, PSALMS 37:39

New Testament References: LUKE 6:22, JOHN 16:33, ROMANS 8:18, 2 CORINTHIANS 4:17, 1 PETER 1:7, 1 PETER 4:13; 4:14

Angels
Old Testament References: GENESIS 19:1, GENESIS 19:15, GENESIS 28:12, GENESIS 32:1, JOB 4:18, PSALMS 8:5,

New Testament References: MATTHEW 4:6, MATTHEW 4:11, MATTHEW 13:39, MATTHEW 13:41, MATTHEW 13:49, MARK 1:13, MARK 8:38, MARK 12:25, MARK 13:27, MARK 13:32, LUKE 2:15, LUKE 4:10, LUKE 9:26, LUKE 12:8, LUKE 12:9, LUKE 15:10, LUKE 16:22, LUKE 20:36, LUKE 24:23, JOHN 1:51, JOHN 20:12, ACTS 7:53, ROMANS 8:38, 1 2:18, 2 THESSALONIANS 1:7, 1 TIMOTHY 3:16, 1 TIMOTHY 5:21, HEBREWS 1:4, HEBREWS 1:5, HEBREWS 12:22, HEBREWS 13:2, 1 PETER 1:12, 1 PETER 3:22, 2 PETER 2:4, 2 PETER 2:11, JUDE 1:6, REVELATION 1:20, 15:8, REVELATION 16:1, REVELATION 17:1, REVELATION 21:9, REVELATION 21:12

Anger
Old Testament References: LEVITICUS 19:17-18, PROVERBS 14:17, PROVERBS 14:29, PROVERBS 15:1, PROVERBS 15:18, PROVERBS 15:28, PROVERBS 16:32, PROVERBS 22:24-25, PROVERBS 25:28, PROVERBS 29:11, PROVERBS 29:20

New Testament References: ROMANS 12:19, PHILIPPIANS 2:14, COLOSSIANS 3:8, COLOSSIANS 3:21, JAMES 1:19-20

Anger, Control your
Old Testament References: PROVERBS 15:1

New Testament References: MATTHEW 5:22, EPHESIANS 4:26, EPHESIANS 4:31 JAMES 1:19-20

Apostasy
Old Testament Reference: EZEKIEL 18:24

New Testament References: ROMANS 8:12-13, GALATIANS 1:6-9, COLOSSIANS 1:23, COLOSSIANS 2:8, 1 TIMOTHY 1:19, 1 TIMOTHY 4:1, HEBREWS 2:1-3, HEBREWS 3:12-14, HEBREWS 10:23, HEBREWS 13:9, JAMES 5:19-20, 1 JOHN 2:4-6, REVELATION 3:1-5

Apostles
New Testament References: MATTHEW 10:1-4, MARK 6:30, ACTS 1:2, ACTS 1:26, ACTS 2:43, ACTS 4:33, 2 CORINTHIANS 12:12, 2 PETER 3:2

Apostles, False
New Testament References: 2 CORINTHIANS 11:13, REVELATION 2:2

Ashamed, Be not
New Testament References: ROMANS 1:16, ROMANS 5:5, ROMANS 9:33, ROMANS 10:11, PHILIPPIANS 1:20, 2 TIMOTHY 2:15, HEBREWS 11:16, 1 PETER 4:16

Assurance
New Testament References: 2 TIMOTHY 1:12, HEBREWS 6:11, HEBREWS 10:22, 2 PETER 1:10

Attendance, Church Services
New Testament References: MATTHEW 6:33, ACTS 2:42, HEBREWS 10:25, ACTS 20:7

Authority of Bible
Old Testament References: DEUTERONOMY 4:2, DEUTERONOMY 18:20, PROVERBS 14:12

New Testament References: ROMANS 1:16, 1 CORINTHIANS 2:7-13, 1 CORINTHIANS 14:37, GALATIANS 1:8-9, 1 THESSALONIANS 2:13, 1 TIMOTHY 1:3, 2 TIMOTHY 1:13, 2 TIMOTHY 2:15, 2 PETER 1:20-21, 2 PETER 3:15, REVELATION 22:18-19

Authority of Jesus
New Testament References: MATTHEW 28:18, JOHN 12:48, COLOSSIANS 3:17

Baptism
New Testament References: MATTHEW 3:16-17, MATTHEW 28:19-20, MARK 1:9-10, MARK 16:15-16, JOHN 3:23, ACTS 2:38, ACTS 8:36-38, ACTS 10:47-48, ACTS 22:16, ROMANS 6:3-4, GALATIANS 3:27, EPHESIANS 4:5, COLOSSIANS 2:12, TITUS 3:5, 1 PETER 3:20-21

Baptism - Burial by total immersion
New Testament References: MATTHEW 3:16-17, MARK 1:9-10, ACTS 8:38-39, ROMANS 6:4, COLOSSIANS 2:12

Baptism essential for Salvation
New Testament References: MARK 16:15-16, ACTS 2:38, ROMANS 6:3-4

Benevolence of Church
New Testament References: ACTS 11:27-30, ROMANS 15:25-27, 2 CORINTHIANS 1:3-5

Benevolence, Personal
New Testament References: LUKE 10:25-37, JOHN 19:26-27, ACTS 20:34-35, JAMES 1:27, JAMES 2:15-16, GALATIANS 6:10, 1 JOHN 3:17, EPHESIANS 4:28, 1 TIMOTHY 6:18-19

Belief
New Testament References: MARK 9:23, MARK 11:24, MARK 16:17-18, JOHN 1:12, JOHN 3:16, JOHN 3:36, JOHN 6:47, ROMANS 10:9-10, EPHESIANS 1:19, 1 THESSALONIANS 2:13, 1 JOHN 5:13

Believe
New Testament References: MARK 16:16 JOHN 3:16-18, JOHN 3:36, JOHN 6:29, JOHN 6:40; 47, JOHN 8:24-26, JOHN 14:1, JOHN 17:20-21, JOHN 20:31, ACTS 8:34-38, ACTS 10:43, ACTS 16:31, ACTS 18:8, ROMANS 1:16

Bible - Complete revelation of the Will of God
New Testament References: 2 TIMOTHY 3:16-17; JOHN 14:26; ACTS 20:20, 27

Bible - Condemns use of human (false) authority
Old Testament References: PROVERBS 3:5-6, PROVERBS 14:12, JEREMIAH 10:23

New Testament References: MATTHEW 15:9, MATTHEW 15:13, GALATIANS 1:8-9,1 TIMOTHY 1:3, 2 JOHN 9-11, REVELATION 22:18-19

Bible - Final Revelation of God
New Testament References: GALATIANS 1:8-9, JOHN 16:13, 2 PETER 1:3

Bible - Holy Spirit revealed all Truth (Will of God) to the human writers of the Scriptures
New Testament References: JOHN 16:12-13, 1 CORINTHIANS 2:6-12, EPHESIANS 3:1-5, 2 PETER 1:20-21,

Bible - Infallible in original autographs
New Testament References: JOHN 17:17; TITUS 1:2-3; REVELATION 19:9, 21:5

Bible - Inspired Word of God
Old Testament References: DEUTERONOMY 18:18, 2 SAMUEL 23:2, JEREMIAH 1:4-9, JEREMIAH 30:1-4

New Testament References: MATTHEW 10:19-20, JOHN 16:13, 1 CORINTHIANS 2:4, 1 CORINTHIANS 2:10-13, 2 TIMOTHY 3:16-17, 2 PETER 1:19-21

Blame
Old Testament References: GENESIS 3:9-13; EXODUS 32:21-24, 1 SAMUEL 15:3, 9, 13-15

Blessed
New Testament References: MATTHEW 25:34, LUKE 11:28, LUKE 12:37, JOHN 20:29, ACTS 20:35, TITUS 2:13

Blessings in Christ
New Testament References: ACTS 17:25, 2 CORINTHIANS 5:17, GALATIANS 3:27, TITUS 1:2, HEBREWS 5:9

Blessings of God
Old Testament References: GENESIS 22:17, NUMBERS 6:24-26, DEUTERONOMY 28:8, PSALMS 1:1-2, PSALMS 103:2-3, ISAIAH 44:3, JEREMIAH 17:7, MALACHI 3:10

New Testament References: JAMES 1:17, 1 PETER 3:9

Book of Life
New Testament References: PHILIPPIANS 4:3, REVELATION 3:5, REVELATION 13:8, REVELATION 17:8, REVELATION 20:12, REVELATION 20:15, REVELATION 21:27, REVELATION 22:19

Book of Remembrance
Old Testament Reference: MALACHI 3:16

Born Again
New Testament References: JOHN 3:3, JOHN 3:7, 1 PETER 1:23

Charity
New Testament References: MATTHEW 6:3-4, MATTHEW 19:21, 1 CORINTHIANS 13:1-4, 1 CORINTHIANS 13:8, 1 CORINTHIANS 13:13, 1 CORINTHIANS 14:1, 1 CORINTHIANS 16:14, COLOSSIANS 3:14, 1 TIMOTHY 4:12, 2 TIMOTHY 2:22, 2 TIMOTHY 3:10, TITUS 2:2, 1 PETER 4:8, 2 PETER 1:7, 3 JOHN 1:6, REVELATION 2:19

Chastening
New Testament References: HEBREWS 12:6-8, REVELATION 3:19

Childbearing
New Testament Reference: 1 TIMOTHY 2:15

Children
Old Testament References: DEUTERONOMY 6:7, PROVERBS 17:6, PROVERBS 20:7, PROVERBS 22:6, PROVERBS 29:17, ISAIAH 54:13

New Testament References: MATTHEW 18:10, MATTHEW 19:14, ACTS 2:39, EPHESIANS 6:1-4

Children of God
New Testament References: LUKE 18:17, JOHN 1:12, GALATIANS 3:26-29, 1 JOHN 3:2

Christ, Jesus
New Testament References: MATTHEW 3:16-17, MATTHEW 14:33, MATTHEW 16:16, MATTHEW 17:5, MATTHEW 28:18, MARK 1:1, JOHN 1:1-4, JOHN 1:12-14, JOHN 1:16-18, JOHN 6:35, JOHN 8:58, JOHN 10:30, JOHN 11:25, JOHN 14:6, JOHN 14:9, JOHN 21:25

Church, His
New Testament References: MATTHEW 16:18, ACTS 20:28

Church is the Body of Christ
New Testament References: Ephesians 1:22-23, Ephesians 5:23-27, Colossians 1:18, 24

Only one Body of Christ
New Testament Reference: EPHESIANS 4:4-6

Clean Living
New Testament References: 2 CORINTHIANS 7:1, JAMES 4:8, 1 JOHN 1:9

Comfort
Old Testament References: PSALMS 18:2, PSALMS 23:4, PSALMS 27:14, PSALMS 37:24, PSALMS 37:39, PSALMS 46:1-3, PSALMS 55:22, NAHUM 1:7

New Testament References: MATTHEW 11:28, JOHN 16:33

Comfort in times of suffering or sorrow
New Testament References: ROMANS 8:18, ROMANS 8:26-28, 2 CORINTHIANS 1:3-5, 2 CORINTHIANS 12:8-10, PHILIPPIANS 1:29

Commandments of Jesus
New Testament References: MATTHEW 19:18, MATTHEW 28:19-20, MATTHEW 22:36-40, MARK 10:19

Commitment
Old Testament References: PSALMS 37:5, PROVERBS 16:3, JEREMIAH 32:38-39

New Testament References: ROMANS 12:11, CORINTHIANS 7:35

Compassion
Old Testament References: PSALMS 78:38, PSALMS 86:15, PSALMS 111:4, PSALMS 112:4, PSALMS 145:8, LAMENTATIONS 3:22-23

New Testament References: MARK 6:34, 1 PETER 3:8, 1 JOHN 3:17, JUDE 1:21-22

Condemned, Unjustly
New Testament References: MATTHEW 5:11, MATTHEW 5:44, LUKE 6:35

Confess
New Testament References: MATTHEW 10:32-33, MATTHEW 16:15-16, LUKE 12:8, ROMANS

10:9-10, PHILIPPIANS 2:11, JAMES 5:16, 1 JOHN 1:9

Confession
Old Testament References: EZRA 10:11, DANIEL 9:4

New Testament References: ROMANS 10:10, 1 TIMOTHY 6:12, HEBREWS 3:1, HEBREWS 4:14, HEBREWS 10:23

Confession that Jesus is His Son, by God the Father
New Testament References: MATTHEW 3:17, MATTHEW 17:5, MARK 1:11, MARK 9:7, LUKE 3:21-22, LUKE 9:35

Conscience
New Testament References: ACTS 24:16, 1 TIMOTHY 1:5, 1 TIMOTHY 4:1-2

Contentment
Old Testament References: JOB 5:17, PSALMS 37:7, PSALMS 116:7, PSALMS 128:2

New Testament References: MATTHEW 11:29-30, PHILIPPIANS 4:11, 1 TIMOTHY 6:6, HEBREWS 4:10-11, HEBREWS 13:5

Control, Tongue, Emotions, Thoughts
New Testament References: MATTHEW 12:36-37, 2 CORINTHIANS 10:5, EPHESIANS 4:24-27, EPHESIANS 5:4, JAMES 1:26, JAMES 5:12

Conversion
New Testament References: MATTHEW 18:3, JAMES 5:20

Examples of New Testament Conversions:
(Day of Pentecost about A.D.30) ACTS 2:37-41, (Samarians) ACTS 8:5-13, (Ethiopian eunuch) ACTS 8:26-39, (Saul, later known as Paul) ACTS 9:1-20, (Retold by Paul) ACTS 22:6-16, (Cornelius, first Gentile) ACTS 10:1-8, 24-48 (Lydia and her Household) ACTS 16:14-15, (Jailer) ACTS 16:25-34, (Crispus, his family and many Corinthians) ACTS 18:5-8 (About 12 men at Ephesus, who had previously been baptized by John the Baptist, were baptized for the remission of sins) ACTS 19:1-7

Correction, God's
Old Testament References: PSALMS 94:12-13, PROVERBS 3:12

New Testament Reference: HEBREWS 12:10-11

Counsel
Old Testament References: PROVERBS 1:5, PROVERBS 9:9, PROVERBS 12:15, PROVERBS 15:22, PROVERBS 19:20, PROVERBS 27:9

Church, Members added to
New Testament Reference: ACTS 2:41

Courage
Old Testament References: JOSHUA 1:9, PSALMS 27:14, PSALMS 31:24, PROVERBS 14:26, PROVERBS 28:1, ISAIAH 41:10

New Testament References: EPHESIANS 3:12, EPHESIANS 6:10-18, 2 TIMOTHY 1:7, HEBREWS 10:19, HEBREWS 13:6

Covetousness
New Testament References: LUKE 12:15, 1 TIMOTHY 6:6; 10

Cross, The
New Testament References: 1 CORINTHIANS 2:2, GALATIANS 6:14

Danger and Distress
Old Testament References: PSALMS 23:1-6, PSALMS 91:1-16, PSALMS 121:1-8

Death
Old Testament References: PROVERBS 14:32, ISAIAH 25:8

New Testament References: JOHN 8:51, ROMANS 6:23, ROMANS 8:38-39, 1 CORINTHIANS 15:26; 53-58, HEBREWS 9:27, REVELATION 14:13

Depression, Overcoming
Old Testament References: PSALM 30:5, PSALM 33:20, PSALM 42:11, PSALM 121:8, PSALM 147:3

Diligence
Old Testament References: PROVERBS 4:23, PROVERBS 21:5

New Testament References: ROMANS 12:8, 1 CORINTHIANS 15:58, 2 CORINTHIANS 8:7, GALATIANS 6:9, 2 PETER 1:5-10, 2 PETER 3:14.

Discernment
New Testament References: 1 CORINTHIANS 11:29, EPHESIANS 4:14, 2 TIMOTHY 2:7, 1 JOHN 4:6

Discipline, Family
Old Testament References: PROVERBS 20:11, PROVERBS 22:15, PROVERBS 23:13-14, PROVERBS 29:15

New Testament Reference: EPHESIANS 6:4

Divorce
New Testament References: MATTHEW 5:32, MATTHEW 19:3-9

Dominion
Old Testament Reference: PSALMS 119:133

New Testament Reference: ROMANS 6:14

Doubt
New Testament References: MATTHEW 21:21, MARK 11:23

Duty
Old Testament References: DEUTERONOMY 4:40, JOB 36:11, PROVERBS 16:7, ISAIAH 1:19

New Testament Reference: MATTHEW 10:22

Encouragement
Old Testament References: PSALMS 43:5, PSALMS 55:22, ISAIAH 41:10

New Testament References: 2 CORINTHIANS 4:16, 2 CORINTHIANS 13:4, GALATIANS 6:2, PHILIPPIANS 4:13, 1 THESSALONIANS 5:11, HEBREWS 3:13, HEBREWS 10:24

Enemies
Old Testament References: DEUTERONOMY 20:4, PSALMS 37:40, PSALMS 138:7, PROVERBS 16:7

New Testament References: LUKE 1:74, ROMANS 12:14, ROMANS 12:20-21

Envy
New Testament Reference: JAMES 3:14-15

Eternal (Everlasting) Life
New Testament References: JOHN 3:16, JOHN 3:36, JOHN 5:24, JOHN 6:47, JOHN 10:27-28, JOHN 11:25-26, ROMANS 6:23, ROMANS 8:11, GALATIANS 6:8, 2 TIMOTHY 1:10, 1 JOHN 2:25, 1 JOHN 5:13

Eternal Life, Facts of
Old Testament Reference: ECCLESIASTES 12:13-14,

New Testament References: HEBREWS 9:27, JOHN 12:48, JOHN 5:22, ACTS 17:30-31, MATTHEW 25:31-33, MATTHEW 25:46

Evil
New Testament References: JOHN 3:19-20, ROMANS 12:9, 1 CORINTHIANS 10:6, 1 THESSALONIANS 5:22, TITUS 3:2

Faith (also see Trust)
Old Testament Reference: DEUTERONOMY 7:9

New Testament References: MARK 9:23, MARK 11:22, JOHN 20:29, ACTS 15:8-9, ACTS 26:18, ROMANS 1:17, ROMANS 4:16, ROMANS 5:2, 1 CORINTHIANS 2:5, 1 CORINTHIANS 2:4-5, 1 CORINTHIANS 16:13, 2 CORINTHIANS 5:7, GALATIANS 2:20, GALATIANS 3:26, EPHESIANS 2:8, EPHESIANS 3:17, EPHESIANS 6:16, PHILIPPIANS 3:9, TITUS 1:2, HEBREWS 10:23, HEBREWS 10:38, HEBREWS 11:1, HEBREWS 11:6, 1 PETER 1:5-7

Faith - saved by faith, but not by faith only
New Testament References: JAMES 2:20, JAMES 2:24, JAMES 2:26

Faithful, Remaining
New Testament References: MATTHEW 25:21, 1 TIMOTHY 6:2, TITUS 1:9, HEBREWS 2:17, 1 PETER 5:8, 2 PETER 1:10, REVELATION 2:10

Faithfulness of God
Old Testament References: PSALMS 9:10, ISAIAH 25:1, ISAIAH 54:10

New Testament References: 1 CORINTHIANS 1:9, 1 CORINTHIANS 10:13, 1 THESSALONIANS 5:24, 2 THESSALONIANS 3:3, HEBREWS 10:23, 1 JOHN 1:9

Falling Away
New Testament References: LUKE 8:13, 1 CORINTHIANS 10:12, GALATIANS 5:4, HEBREWS 6:6, 2 PETER 3:17

False Teachings (Teachers)
New Testament References: ACTS 20:29-30, 1 CORINTHIANS 4:6, 2 CORINTHIANS 11:13-15, COLOSSIANS 2:8, 2 THESSALONIANS 2:3-10, 1 TIMOTHY 4:1-4, 2 TIMOTHY 4:3-4, HEBREWS 13:9, 2 PETER 2:1, 2 PETER 3:17, 1 JOHN 4:1, 2 JOHN 1:9,

Fear
Old Testament References: DEUTERONOMY 31:6, PSALMS 46:1, PSALMS 118:6, PROVERBS 3:24-26, ISAIAH 12:2, ISAIAH 14:3, ISAIAH 41:10, ISAIAH 41:13, ISAIAH 54:14

New Testament References: LUKE 12:32, ROMANS 8:15, 2 TIMOTHY 1:7

Fearful
New Testament References: MATTHEW 8:26, MARK 4:40, REVELATION 21:8

Fear of God
Old Testament References: DEUTERONOMY 28:58, 2 SAMUEL 23:3, 2 CHRONICLES 19:9, JOB 28:28, PSALMS 19:9, PROVERBS 8:13, PROVERBS 10:27, PROVERBS 22:4, ECCLESIASTES 12:13

New Testament References: LUKE 1:50, LUKE 12:5, ACTS 9:31, 2 CORINTHIANS 7:1,

PHILIPPIANS 2:12, HEBREWS 10:31, HEBREWS 12:28-29

Finances
Old Testament References: PSALMS 112:3, PROVERBS 3:16, PROVERBS 8:18, PROVERBS 13:11, PROVERBS 13:22, PROVERBS 22:1, ECCLESIASTES 5:19,

New Testament Reference: 3 JOHN 1:2

Flesh and Spirit
New Testament References: ROMANS 8:6, ROMANS 8:13, GALATIANS 6:8

Forever
Old Testament References: EXODUS 15:18, PSALMS 23:6, PSALMS 146:10, PROVERBS 29:14, ISAIAH 26:4, ISAIAH 40:8, ISAIAH 51:6, DANIEL 7:18, DANIEL 12:3

New Testament References: MATTHEW 6:13, LUKE 1:33, JOHN 6:51, JOHN 6:58, TIMOTHY 1:17, HEBREWS 10:12, 1 PETER 1:25, 1 JOHN 2:17, JUDE 1:13, REVELATION 1:6, REVELATION 7:12, REVELATION 10:6, REVELATION 11:15, REVELATION 14:11, REVELATION 19:3,REVELATION 20:10, REVELATION 22:5

Forgiveness
Old Testament References: ISAIAH 1:18, PROVERBS 19:11, PROVERBS 20:22

New Testament References: MATTHEW 5:7, MATTHEW 5:44-45, MATTHEW 6:12; 14-15, MATTHEW 18:15-18, MARK 11:25, LUKE 6:37, LUKE 17:3-4, EPHESIANS 4:32, COLOSSIANS 3:13, 1 PETER 3:9

Friendship
Old Testament Reference: ECCLESIASTES 4:9-10

New Testament References: JOHN 15:13

Generosity
Old Testament References: DEUTERONOMY 15:11, DEUTERONOMY 16:17, PSALMS 41:1-2, PROVERBS 3:27-28

New Testament References: LUKE 6:38, 2 CORINTHIANS 8:9, 2 CORINTHIANS 9:7, JAMES 2:15-16

Gentleness
New Testament References: GALATIANS 5:22, 2 TIMOTHY 2:24, JAMES 3:17

Glorify God
New Testament References: ROMANS 15:6, 1 CORINTHIANS 6:20, 1 CORINTHIANS 10:31, 1 PETER 2:12, 1 PETER 4:11

Godhead, One God in three Persons
Old Testament Reference: DEUTERONOMY 6:4

New Testament References: MATTHEW 28:19, 1 JOHN 5:7

Godliness
New Testament References: 1 CORINTHIANS 3:16-17, 2 CORINTHIANS 3:18, PHILIPPIANS 3:20-21, 1 TIMOTHY 4:7-8, 1 TIMOTHY 6:6, HEBREWS 12:14-15, 1 PETER 1:5-6, 1 PETER 1:15-16, 2 PETER 1:1-11, 2 PETER 3:11, 1 JOHN 3:2

God, the Father
Old Testament References: PSALMS 68:5, PSALMS 89:26

New Testament References: JOHN 6:27, GALATIANS 1:1, GALATIANS 1:3, EPHESIANS 6:23, PHILIPPIANS 2:11, 1 THESSALONIANS 1:1, 2 TIMOTHY 1:2, TITUS 1:4, 1 PETER 1:2, 2 PETER 1:17, 2 JOHN 1:3, JUDE 1:1

God, the Holy Spirit or Ghost
Old Testament References: PSALMS 51:11, ISAIAH 63:10, ISAIAH 63:11, EZEKIEL 36:27

New Testament References: LUKE 1:35, LUKE 11:13, JOHN 14:16-17, ACTS 2:33, ACTS 4:31, ACTS 5:32, ACTS 7:55, ACTS 10:38, ACTS 15:8, ACTS 20:28, ROMANS 5:5, ROMANS 14:17, ROMANS 15:13, ROMANS 15:16, 1 CORINTHIANS 2:12, 1 CORINTHIANS 6:19, 1 CORINTHIANS 12:3, 2 CORINTHIANS 13:14, GALATIANS 3:14, EPHESIANS 1:13, EPHESIANS 4:30, 1 THESSALONIANS 4:8, HEBREWS 2:4, 2 PETER 1:21

God, the Son
Old Testament Reference: DANIEL 3:25

New Testament References: MATTHEW 1:23, MATTHEW 4:6, MATTHEW 8:29, MATTHEW 14:33, MATTHEW 16:16, MATTHEW 26:63, MATTHEW 27:43, MATTHEW 27:54, MARK 1:1, LUKE 1:35, JOHN 1:34, JOHN 1:49, JOHN 5:25, JOHN 6:69, JOHN 9:35, 2 JOHN 1:3, REVELATION 2:18

God, Word of (Jesus Christ is the Word of God)
New Testament References: JOHN 1:1, JOHN 1:14, JOHN 2:22, JOHN 5:24, JOHN 14:24, JOHN 15:3, JOHN 17:14, JOHN 17:17, JOHN 17:20, EPHESIANS 6:17, HEBREWS 4:12, REVELATION 19:13

God, The Word of
Old Testament Reference: PROVERBS 30:5

New Testament References: MATTHEW 4:4, MATTHEW 24:35, MARK 4:14, LUKE 4:4, LUKE 8:11, LUKE 8:21, LUKE 11:28, JOHN 8:31, JOHN 12:48, JOHN 14:23, JOHN 15:7, ACTS 6:4, ACTS 20:32, ROMANS 1:16, ROMANS 10:17, HEBREWS 4:12, EPHESIANS 6:17, 2 TIMOTHY 3:15-17, HEBREWS 4:12, HEBREWS 11:3, 1 PETER 1:23, REVELATION 1:1-2

Gospel, The
New Testament References: MARK 16:15, ROMANS 1:16, GALATIANS 1:8, 1 TIMOTHY 1:11

Gossip
Old Testament References: LEVITICUS 19:16, PSALMS 34:13, PROVERBS 11:13, PROVERBS 18:8, PROVERBS 20:19

Grace
New Testament References: JOHN 1:14, ACTS 20:32, ROMANS 5:1-2, 1 CORINTHIANS 15:10, 2 CORINTHIANS 9:8, EPHESIANS 1:6-7, EPHESIANS 2:4-8, COLOSSIANS 4:5-6, TITUS 3:7, HEBREWS 4:16, JAMES 4:6, 1 PETER 1:13, 1 PETER 4:10, 1 PETER 5:5, 2 PETER 3:18

Grace, Grow in
New Testament References: ACTS 20:32, 2 PETER 3:18, COLOSSIANS 3:16, 1 CORINTHIANS 15:10

Gratitude
Old Testament References: PSALM 9:1-2, PSALMS 26:7, PSALMS 30:11-12, PSALMS 68:19, PSALM 92:1-2, PSALM 136:1, ISAIAH 63:7

New Testament References: EPHESIANS 5:20, 1 THESSALONIANS 5:18

Guidance
Old Testament References: 2 SAMUEL 22:29, PSALMS 32:8, PSALMS 37:23, PSALMS 48:14, PSALMS 73:23-24, PROVERBS 3:5-6, PROVERBS 16:9, ISAIAH 28:26, ISAIAH 42:16

New Testament References: ROMANS 8:14, ROMANS 14:1-23, JAMES 1:5-6

Healing
Old Testament References: EXODUS 23:25-26, PSALMS 91:10, PSALMS 103:2-3, PSALMS 107:20, ISAIAH 53:4-5

New Testament References: MATTHEW 8:16-17, 1 PETER 2:24

Hear the Word
New Testament References: MATTHEW 7:24-27, MATTHEW 11:15, MATTHEW 17:5, JOHN 8:32, ACTS 2:37, ACTS 4:4, ACTS 19:5, ROMANS 5:8, ROMANS 10:17, REVELATION 2:7

Heart, The
Old Testament References: 1 SAMUEL 16:7, PROVERBS 3:5

New Testament References: MATTHEW 5:8, MATTHEW 6:21, JOHN 14:1, EPHESIANS 3:17, COLOSSIANS 3:15

Heaven
New Testament References: JOHN 14:2-3, 1 THESSALONIANS 4:16, HEBREWS 12:22-23, 1 PETER 1:4, HEBREWS 9:24, 1 JOHN 5:7, REVELATION 3:12, REVELATION 4:1-2, REVELATION 7:9, REVELATION 7:16-17, REVELATION 21:1-2, REVELATION 21:10, REVELATION 22:1-5

Heaven, beyond our understanding
New Testament Reference: 1 CORINTHIANS 2:9

Hell
New Testament References: MATTHEW 23:33, MATTHEW 25:41, LUKE 12:5, LUKE 16:23, 2PETER 2:4, REVELATION 20:13, REVELATION 20:14, REVELATION 21:8

Holiness
New Testament References: 1 CORINTHIANS 3:16-17, HEBREWS 12:14, 1 PETER 1:15-16, 2 PETER 3:11

Honesty
Old Testament References: LEVITICUS 19:35-36, PSALMS 24:4

New Testament References: MATTHEW 7:12, LUKE 8:15, ACTS 24:16, ROMANS 12:17, ROMANS 13:8, ROMANS 13:13-14, 2 CORINTHIANS 8:21, COLOSSIANS 3:9-10, 1 THESSALONIANS 4:12

Hope
Old Testament References: PSALMS 31:24, PSALMS 42:11, PSALMS 71:5

New Testament References: ROMANS 5:5, ROMANS 15:13, COLOSSIANS 1:27, TITUS 1:2, HEBREWS 6:11, 1 PETER 1:3, 1 PETER 1:13, 1 PETER 1:21, 1 JOHN 3:3

Hospitality
New Testament References: MARK 9:41, ACTS 20:35, ROMANS 12:13, HEBREWS 13:2, 1 PETER 4:9-10, 1 JOHN 3:17

Humility
Old Testament References: 2 CHRONICLES 7:14, PROVERBS 15:33, PROVERBS 22:4,

New Testament References: MATTHEW 18:4, MATTHEW 23:12, JAMES 4:6, JAMES 4:10, 1 PETER 5:6

Indifference, Overcoming
New Testament References: HEBREWS 10:26-31

Integrity
Old Testament References: 1 KINGS 9:4, JOB 31:6, PSALMS 7:8, PSALMS 25:21, PSALMS 26:1, PROVERBS 11:3, PROVERBS 19:1, PROVERBS 20:7

Intercession
Old Testament References: ISAIAH 53:12,

New Testament References: ROMANS 8:26, ROMANS 8:34, HEBREWS 7:25

Joy
Old Testament References: JOB 22:26, PSALMS 32:11, PSALMS 33:21, PSALMS 71:23, PROVERBS 17:22, ISAIAH 51:11-12, HABAKKUK 3:18

New Testament References: JOHN 15:11, JOHN 16:22

Justice
Old Testament References: EXODUS 23:1-2, PROVERBS 17:15, ISAIAH 1:17, ISAIAH 56:1, LAMENTATIONS 3:35-36

New Testament References: MATTHEW 12:7, JOHN 7:24

Kindness
New Testament References: MATTHEW 19:21, 1 CORINTHIANS 13:4; 13, EPHESIANS 4:32, COLOSSIANS 3:12, JAMES 1:27

Knowledge
Old Testament References: EXODUS 31:3, EXODUS 35:31, 2 CHRONICLES 1:12, PSALMS 119:66, PROVERBS 1:7, PROVERBS 2:3, PROVERBS 2:6 PROVERBS 2:10, PROVERBS 9:10, PROVERBS 14:18, ISAIAH 11:2

New Testament References: ROMANS 11:33, 1 CORINTHIANS 13:2, COLOSSIANS 1:9-10, 1 TIMOTHY 2:4, 2 PETER 1:5, 2 PETER 1:8

Labor
Old Testament References: PSALMS 128:2, PROVERBS 2:11, PROVERBS 12:24, PROVERBS 13:11, PROVERBS 20:13, ECCLESIASTES 3:13

New Testament References: EPHESIANS 4:28, 1 TIMOTHY 5:8

Language, Watch your (Tongue)
Old Testament References: GENESIS 10:5, EXODUS 20:7, JOB 5:21, JOB 15:5, JOB 27:4, PSALMS 10:7, PSALMS 12:3, PSALMS 34:13, PSALMS 35:28, PSALMS 37:30, PSALMS 39:1, PSALMS 50:19, PSALMS 51:14, PSALMS 52:2, PSALMS 52:4, PSALMS 71:24, PSALMS 73:9, PSALMS 109:2, PSALMS 119:172 PSALMS 120:2, PSALMS 126:2, PROVERBS 6:17, PROVERBS 6:24, PROVERBS 10:20, PROVERBS 12:19, PROVERBS 15:2, PROVERBS 15:4, PROVERBS 17:20, PROVERBS 18:21, PROVERBS 21:6, PROVERBS 21:23, ISAIAH 59:3, JEREMIAH 9:5, JEREMIAH 9:8, MICAH 6:12, ZEPHANIAH 3:13

New Testament Reference: MATTHEW 12:32, MATTHEW 12:36-37, JAMES 1:26, JAMES 3:5, JAMES 3:6, JAMES 3:8, 1 PETER 3:10, 1 JOHN 3:18

Laziness
Old Testament References: PROVERBS 10:4, PROVERBS 12:24, PROVERBS 13:4, PROVERBS 15:19, PROVERBS 21:5, PROVERBS 28:19

New Testament References: ROMANS 12:11, 2 TIMOTHY 2:6

Leadership
Old Testament References: 1 SAMUEL 16:7, PROVERBS 23:7

New Testament References: MARK 10:44, ACTS 20:28, GALATIANS 6:7, PHILIPPIANS 2:3-5, 1 TIMOTHY 6:11-12

Liberty
Old Testament Reference: PSALMS 119:45

New Testament References: LUKE 4:18, 2 CORINTHIANS 3:17, GALATIANS 5:1, GALATIANS 5:13, JAMES 1:25, JAMES 2:12, 1 PETER 2:16

Life
New Testament References: COLOSSIANS 3:4, JOHN 14:6, JOHN 1:4, ROMANS 6:4, ROMANS 8:6, JAMES 1:12, REVELATION 2:10, REVELATION 2:7, REVELATION 22:14

Life, Long
Old Testament References: DEUTERONOMY 5:16, DEUTERONOMY 6:2, DEUTERONOMY 22:6-7, 1 KINGS 3:14, PROVERBS 3:16, PROVERBS 28:16

New Testament Reference: EPHESIANS 6:2-3

Life, More Abundant
New Testament Reference: JOHN 10:10

Light
New Testament References: JOHN 8:12, 2 CORINTHIANS 4:4, 1 JOHN 1:5

Live Blamelessly
New Testament References: LUKE 1:6, PHILIPPIANS 2:15, PHILIPPIANS 2:15, 1 THESSALONIANS 5:23

Live for the Lord
New Testament References: MATTHEW 6:19-33, PHILIPPIANS 2:15

Live Peaceably
New Testament Reference: ROMANS 12:17-18

Loneliness
Old Testament Reference: ISAIAH 41:10

New Testament Reference: HEBREWS 13:5-6

Lord's Supper
New Testament References: MATTHEW 26:26-30, ACTS 20:7, 1 CORINTHIANS 11:24-26

Love of God
Old Testament References: DEUTERONOMY 7:13, PROVERBS 15:9, JEREMIAH 31:3, ZEPHANIAH 3:17

New Testament References: MATTHEW 22:37-38, LUKE 10:27, JOHN 3:16, JOHN 14:23, JOHN 16:27, JOHN 17:23, 2 THESSALONIANS 2:16-17, 1 JOHN 4:10, 1 PETER 1:8, 1 JOHN 4:19, 1 JOHN 5:1-3

Love your God
Old Testament References: DEUTERONOMY 6:5, DEUTERONOMY 10:12, DEUTERONOMY 11:13, DEUTERONOMY 13:3, DEUTERONOMY 30:6, JOSHUA 22:5

New Testament References: MATTHEW 22:37, MARK 12:30, MARK 12:33, LUKE 10:27

Loving God
Old Testament References: DEUTERONOMY 7:9, PSALMS 37:4, PSALMS 91:14, PSALMS 145:20, PROVERBS 8:21

New Testament References: JOHN 14:21, EPHESIANS 6:23

Loving Home
New Testament Reference: Ephesians 5:17-33

Loving Others
New Testament References: JOHN 13:34-35, JOHN 15:9, JOHN 15:13, ROMANS 12:9-10, 1 CORINTHIANS 13:1-13, EPHESIANS 3:17, COLOSSIANS 2:2, 1 PETER 3:8

Lust
New Testament References: GALATIANS 5:24, TITUS 2:11-12, JAMES 1:13, JAMES 4:7-8, 1 PETER 1:14-16, 1 PETER 2:11, 2 PETER 1:4, 1 JOHN 2:16-17

Lying
Old Testament References: EXODUS 23:1, PROVERBS 19:9, ZECHARIAH 8:17

New Testament References: COLOSSIANS 3:9-10, JAMES 3:14

Marriage
New Testament References: 1 CORINTHIANS 7:3, EPHESIANS 5:22, EPHESIANS 5:25, EPHESIANS 5:31, 1 TIMOTHY 5:8, TITUS 2:4-5, 1 PETER 3:7

Meekness
Old Testament References: NUMBERS 12:3, PSALMS 22:26, PSALMS 25:9, PSALMS 147:6

New Testament References: MATTHEW 5:5, MATTHEW 11:29, 1 PETER 3:4

Mercy
Old Testament References: PSALMS 51:1, PSALMS 86:13, PSALMS 147:11, PROVERBS 3:3, PROVERBS 20:28

New Testament References: ROMANS 12:8, TITUS 3:5

Model Wife and Mother
Old Testament Reference: PROVERBS 31:10-31

Obedience
Old Testament References: DEUTERONOMY 6:18, DEUTERONOMY 29:9, JOB 36:11

New Testament References: MATTHEW 7:21, JOHN 14:15, ROMANS 8:28, HEBREWS 5:9, 1 JOHN 3:22

Obey the Teachings of Christ
New Testament References: MATTHEW 7:21, MATTHEW 22:37-39, MATTHEW 28:20, JOHN 14:15, ROMANS 6:16, ROMANS 13:8-10, HEBREWS 5:8-9, REVELATION 22:14

Patience
New Testament References: ROMANS 5:3-4, ROMANS 15:4-5, COLOSSIANS 1:11, 1 THESSALONIANS 5:14, 1 TIMOTHY 6:11, HEBREWS 10:36, HEBREWS 12:1, JAMES 1:3

Peace
Old Testament Reference: ISAIAH 26:3-4

New Testament References: JOHN 16:33, ROMANS 5:1, ROMANS 14:17-19, PHILIPPIANS 4:4-7, JAMES 3:14-18, 1 PETER 3:11

Perseverance
New Testament References: MATTHEW 10:22, EPHESIANS 6:18

Planning, Include God in future
New Testament Reference: JAMES 4:14-15

Poverty
Old Testament References: PROVERBS 13:18, PROVERBS 30:8

New Testament Reference: 2 CORINTHIANS 8:9

Power
Old Testament References: DEUTERONOMY 8:17, 2 SAMUEL 22:33, 1 CHRONICLES 29:11-12, PSALMS 21:13, PROVERBS 18:21, ECCLESIASTES 5:19, ZECHARIAH 4:6

New Testament References: EPHESIANS 3:20, 2 TIMOTHY 1:7

Praise
Old Testament References: JUDGES 5:3, 1 CHRONICLES 23:30, 1 CHRONICLES 29:13, PSALMS 7:17, PSALMS 21:13, PSALMS 42:5

New Testament Reference: 1 PETER 4:11

Prayer
Old Testament References: PSALMS 50:15, PSALMS 145:18-19

New Testament References: MATTHEW 7:7-8, MATTHEW 21:22, JOHN 15:7, JOHN 16:23-24, COLOSSIANS 4:2, EPHESIANS 6:18, PHILIPPIANS 4:6-7, HEBREWS 4:16, 1 PETER 3:12, 1 JOHN 5:14-15

Prayer, Ask for God's help
New Testament References: MATTHEW 6:6-15, PHILIPPIANS 4:4-9, HEBREWS 4:16, 1 PETER 3:12

Prayers of Jesus
New Testament References: MATTHEW 6:9-13, MATTHEW 11:25-26, MARK 15:34, MARK 14:36, LUKE 23:34, LUKE 23:46, JOHN 11:41-43, JOHN 12:27-28, JOHN 17:1-26

Prayers of Jesus, referenced, but not recorded
New Testament References: MARK 1:35, MARK 6:46, LUKE 3:21, LUKE 9:28, LUKE 11:1

Pride
Old Testament References: PROVERBS 8:3, PROVERBS 16:18, PROVERBS 27:2, ISAIAH 5:21

New Testament References: MARK 9:35, GALATIANS 6:3

Promises, Great and Precious
Old Testament Reference: JOSHUA 1:8

New Testament References: MARK 11:24, LUKE 12:28-32, 2 CORINTHIANS 1:20, PHILIPPIANS 4:19, JAMES 1:2-4, 2 PETER 1:4

Prophecy
New Testament References: 2 PETER 1:19, REVELATION 1:3

Protection
Old Testament References: JOB 11:18, PSALM 27:1, PSALMS 91:9-10, PSALMS 112:7, PSALMS 121:7-8, PROVERBS 3:24, PROVERBS 18:10

Refuge, Find
Old Testament References: PSALMS 46:1-3, PSALMS 18:2, PSALMS 55:22, NAHUM 1:7

Repent
New Testament References: LUKE 13:3, LUKE 24:47, ACTS 2:38, ACTS 3:19, ACTS 8:22, ACTS 17:30, ACTS 26:20, ROMANS 2:4, 2 CORINTHIANS 7:10, 2 PETER 3:9

Repentance
New Testament References: ACTS 20:21, ROMANS 2:4, 2 PETER 3:9

Rest, Blessed
New Testament Reference: MATTHEW 11:28-29

Righteousness
Old Testament References: PSALMS 7:17, PSALMS 23:3

New Testament References: LUKE 1:75, ACTS 10:35, ROMANS 1:17, ROMANS 3:26, ROMANS 4:3, ROMANS 6:13, ROMANS 10:10, ROMANS 14:17, 2 CORINTHIANS 9:10, TITUS 2:12, 1 PETER 2:24

Salvation
Old Testament References: GENESIS 49:18, EXODUS 15:2, 1 SAMUEL 2:1, 2 SAMUEL 22:3, 2 SAMUEL 22:47. PSALMS 13:5, PSALMS 27:1

New Testament References: ROMANS 1:16, ROMANS 13:11-12, 2 CORINTHIANS 6:2, EPHESIANS 6:17-18, 2 TIMOTHY 2:10, 1 PETER 1:8-9, REVELATION 12:10

Save Yourself First
New Testament References: PHILIPPIANS 2:12, 1 TIMOTHY 4:16

Second Coming of Christ
New Testament References: MATTHEW 24:27-31, MARK 8:38, JOHN 14:2-4, 1 CORINTHIANS 15:52-55, 1 THESSALONIANS 4:16-17

Seed of the Kingdom
New Testament References: LUKE 8:11, 1 PETER 1:22-23

Seek the Truth
New Testament References: JOHN 8:32, JOHN 17:17, 1 TIMOTHY 2:4, 2 TIMOTHY 2:15

Seeking God
Old Testament References: DEUTERONOMY 4:29, 1 CHRONICLES 28:9, 2 CHRONICLES 15:2, PSALMS 9:10, LAMENTATIONS 3:25, HOSEA 10:12, AMOS 5:4

New Testament References: ACTS 17:27, HEBREWS 11:6

Self-Control
New Testament References: ROMANS 8:13, ROMANS 13:13-14, 1 CORINTHIANS 9:25, 1 CORINTHIANS 9:27, 1 CORINTHIANS 13:4-5, TITUS 2:12, 2 PETER 1:5-6

Self-Denial
New Testament References: MATTHEW 16:24-26, LUKE 18:29-30, ROMANS 8:12-13, GALATIANS 5:24, TITUS 2:11-12

Shame
Old Testament References: PSALMS 25:20, PSALMS 119:6

Sin
New Testament References: ROMANS 1:18-32, ROMANS 3:23, ROMANS 5:12, ROMANS 5:21, ROMANS 6:16, ROMANS 6:23, ROMANS 7:13, ROMANS 8:2, 1 CORINTHIANS 15:56, GALATIANS 5:21, 1 THESSALONIANS 5:22, 1 TIMOTHY 6:9, JAMES 1:15, JAMES 4:17, 1 JOHN 3:4-10, 1 JOHN 5:17

Sin, Sexual
New Testament References: MATTHEW 5:27-28, ROMANS 1:26-27, 1 CORINTHIANS 6:13, 1 CORINTHIANS 6:18-20, 1 CORINTHIANS 10:13, 1 THESSALONIANS 4:3-4, HEBREWS 2:18, HEBREWS 13:4, JAMES 1:12

Sin, Forgiveness of
New Testament References: 1 JOHN 1:7-10, 1 JOHN 2:1-3; 12, 1 JOHN 3:5

Sin, Remission of
Old Testament Reference: EZEKIEL 36:25-26

New Testament References: MATTHEW 26:28, LUKE 1:77, LUKE 24:47, ACTS 2:38, ACTS 10:43, ROMANS 3:25

Singing
New Testament References: COLOSSIANS 3:16, EPHESIANS 5:19

Strength, Source of
Old Testament References: PSALMS 31:24, ISAIAH 40:29

Stubbornness
Old Testament References: 1 SAMUEL 15:23, 2 CHRONICLES 30:8

New Testament Reference: HEBREWS 3:12

Submission to God's Will
New Testament References: MATTHEW 6:33, MATTHEW 7:21, COLOSSIANS 1:9, JAMES 4:7

Temptation
Old Testament Reference: PROVERBS 6:23-32

New Testament References: MATTHEW 6:13, MATTHEW 26:41, LUKE 8:13, LUKE 22:40, 1 CORINTHIANS 10:6-13, GALATIANS 5:19-21, 1 TIMOTHY 6:9, HEBREWS 2:18, HEBREWS 3:8, JAMES 1:12-16, 2 PETER 2:9, REVELATION 3:10

Temptation, Overcoming
New Testament References: MATTHEW 26:41, LUKE 22:40, 1 CORINTHIANS 10:13, 1 THESSALONIANS 5:22, JAMES 1:12, 2 PETER 2:9, REVELATION 3:10

Thanksgiving
New Testament References: COLOSSIANS 2:7, COLOSSIANS 3:15, EPHESIANS 5:20, 1 THESSALONIANS 5:18

Tribulation
New Testament References: ACTS 14:22, ROMANS 5:3, REVELATION 2:9, REVELATION 7:14

Trust
Old Testament References: PSALMS 37:3-5, PROVERBS 3:5, PROVERBS 29:25

New Testament References: LUKE 16:11, 1 THESSALONIANS 2:4, HEBREWS 2:13, HEBREWS 6:16-18

Trust in the Word of God, not your heart (feelings)
Old Testament References: PROVERBS 14:12, PROVERBS 28:26, JEREMIAH 10:23

New Testament References: MATTHEW 4:4, HEBREWS 4:12

Truth
New Testament References: JOHN 1:17, JOHN 17:17, JOHN 8:32, JOHN 14:6

Unity
Old Testament Reference: PSALMS 133:1

New Testament References: ROMANS 12:16, 1 CORINTHIANS 1:10, EPHESIANS 4:3

Violence, Avoid
New Testament References: MATTHEW 26:52, REVELATION 13:10

Vigilance
Old Testament Reference: PROVERBS 8:34

New Testament References: MATTHEW 24:42, MARK 13:37, 1 PETER 5:8

Wisdom
Old Testament References: 2 CHRONICLES 29:30, PSALMS 45:11, PSALMS 66:4, PROVERBS 4:7, PROVERBS 9:10, PROVERBS 3:13-15, ECCLESIASTES 2:26, ECCLESIASTES 7:12, ECCLESIASTES 7:25, DANIEL 12:3

New Testament References: MATTHEW 4:10, 1 CORINTHIANS 2:6-7, EPHESIANS 1:8, EPHESIANS 1:17, COLOSSIANS 2:2-3, COLOSSIANS 3:16, COLOSSIANS 4:5, JAMES 1:5, JAMES 3:17, REVELATION 4:10-11, REVELATION 7:11

Works, Good
New Testament References: GALATIANS 6:10, 1 TIMOTHY 6:18-19, TITUS 2:14, TITUS 3:1; 8, JAMES 2:20

Work for the Lord
Old Testament References: ECCLESIASTES 3:1, HOSEA 8:7

New Testament References: ROMAN 8:28, 2 CORINTHIANS 9:6, GALATIANS 6:7, COLOSSIANS 3:17, COLOSSIANS 4:5, JAMES 1:5-6; 22

Worry
Old Testament References: PSALMS 9:9, PSALMS 32:7, PSALMS 46:1-3, ISAIAH 32:17

New Testament References: MATTHEW 6:25, MATTHEW 6:34, ROMANS 8:28, 2 CORINTHIANS 4:8-9, PHILIPPIANS 4:6-7, PHILIPPIANS 4:19

Worship
Old Testament References: DEUTERONOMY 26:10, PSALMS 95:6, PSALMS 96:9, PSALMS 150:1-6

New Testament Reference: JOHN 4:23-24

Worship, Adding to
Old Testament References: LEVITICUS 10:1-2, DEUTERONOMY 4:2, PROVERBS 30:6

New Testament References: MARK 7:9, 1 CORINTHIANS 4:6, 2 JOHN 1:9, REVELATION 22:18-19

Worship, Vain
New Testament Reference: MATTHEW 15:9

Reject any and all uninspired documents written by men in regard to the Worship of God or any other religious practices, which Do Not absolutely conform to His Holy Word...Heaven Awaits!

Appendix 8

Selected Prayers and related Teachings of Jesus

Appendix Contents

A. Great recorded Prayers of Jesus

B. Prayers of Jesus, referenced, but not recorded

C. Selected Teachings of Jesus regarding Prayer

D. Memorable Quotation

A. Great recorded Prayers of Jesus

(1) The Lord's Prayer

MATTHEW 6:9-13
After this manner therefore pray ye: Our Father which art in heaven, Hallowed be thy name. Thy kingdom come. Thy will be done in earth, as it is in heaven. Give us this day our daily bread.

And forgive us our debts, as we forgive our debtors. And lead us not into temptation, but deliver us from evil: For thine is the kingdom, and the power, and the glory, forever. Amen.

Note: A line by line analysis of this Glorious Example of Prayer is provided under the heading "Pattern of Prayer, our access to God" in Chapter VI.

(2) Prayers of Thanksgiving

JOHN 11:41-43
Then they took away the stone from the place where the dead was laid. And Jesus lifted up his eyes, and said, Father, I thank thee that thou hast heard me. And I knew that thou hearest me always: but because of the people which stand by I said it, that they may believe that thou hast sent me. And when he thus had spoken, he cried with a loud voice, Lazarus, come forth.

LUKE 10:21-25
In that hour Jesus rejoiced in spirit, and said, I thank thee, O Father, Lord of heaven and earth, that thou hast hid these things from the wise and prudent, and hast revealed them unto babes: even so, Father; for so it seemed good in thy sight. All things are delivered to me of my Father: and no man knoweth who the Son is, but the Father; and who the Father is, but the Son, and he to whom the Son will reveal him. And he turned him unto his disciples, and said privately, Blessed are the eyes which see the things that ye see: For I tell you, that many prophets and kings have desired to see those things which ye see, and have not seen them; and to hear those things which ye hear, and have not heard them.

(3) Prayer of Intercession

Please turn to John chapter seventeen in your personal Bible. This chapter consists of 26 verses, all of which are devoted to the longest recorded prayer of our Lord.

Jesus prays for himself in the first 5 verses. He intercedes on behalf of His disciples in verses 6 through 19.

In the final passage our Savior pleads for all His future believers, including you and me.

(4) Prayers of submission in the shadow of the Cross

MARK 14:36
And he said, Abba, Father, all things are possible unto thee; take away this cup from me: nevertheless not what I will, but what thou wilt.

JOHN 12:27-28
Now is my soul troubled; and what shall I say? Father, save me from this hour: but for this cause came I unto this hour. Father, glorify thy name. Then came there a voice from heaven, saying, I have both glorified it, and will glorify it again.

Additional reference: LUKE 22:39-46

(5) Prayers from the Cross

LUKE 23:34
Then said Jesus, Father, forgive them; for they know not what they do. And they parted his raiment, and cast lots.

MARK 15:34
And at the ninth hour Jesus cried with a loud voice, saying, Eloi, Eloi, lama sabachthani? which is, being interpreted, My God, my God, why hast thou forsaken me?

LUKE 23:46
And when Jesus had cried with a loud voice, he said, Father, into thy hands I commend my spirit: and having said thus, he gave up the ghost.

B. Prayers of Jesus, referenced, but not recorded

MATTHEW 14:23
And when he had sent the multitudes away, he went up into a mountain apart to pray: and when the evening was come, he was there alone.

MARK 1:35
And in the morning, rising up a great while before day, he went out, and departed into a solitary place, and there prayed.

MARK 6:46
And when he had sent them away, he departed into a mountain to pray

LUKE 3:21
Now when all the people were baptized, it came to pass, that Jesus also being baptized, and praying, the heaven was opened

LUKE 5:16
And he withdrew himself into the wilderness, and prayed.

Additional references: MATTHEW 26:36, LUKE 6:12, LUKE 9:28

C. Selected Teachings of Jesus regarding Prayer

MATTHEW 5:44
But I say unto you, Love your enemies, bless them that curse you, do good to them that hate you, and pray for them which despitefully use you, and persecute you;

MATTHEW 7:7-8
Ask, and it shall be given you; seek, and ye shall find; knock, and it shall be opened unto you: For every one that asketh receiveth; and he that seeketh findeth; and to him that knocketh it shall be opened.

MATTHEW 26:41
Watch and pray, that ye enter not into temptation: the spirit indeed is willing, but the flesh is weak.

MARK 11:24
Therefore I say unto you, What things soever ye desire, when ye pray, believe that ye receive them, and ye shall have them.

MARK 13:33
Take ye heed, watch and pray: for ye know not when the time is.

Additional references: MATTHEW 6:5-8, MATTHEW 23:14, LUKE 18:1, LUKE 21:36, LUKE 22:40, LUKE 22:46, JOHN 16:26

D. Memorable Quotation

In his famous quote Alfred, Lord Tennyson observed accurately **"More things are wrought by prayer than this world dreams of."**

Resolve today, in your heart to follow the teachings and example of your Lord and Savior in prayer... Heaven Awaits!

Appendix 9

Significant recorded prayers of the Bible

Contents of Appendix

A. Introduction

B. Selected prayers of the Bible

C. Other significant prayers

A. Introduction

Few, if any Christians of today, have the ability to pray with the audacity of Abraham, the courage of Moses, the intensity of David or the passion of Jesus Christ. Most could markedly improve by simply studying their patterns of prayer.

Readers are encouraged to study the passages presented and referenced in order to gain an understanding of the nature of prayers that God has honored and answered.

It is suggested that you take time to address your Heavenly Father with great humility and sincerity before each meal. You may pray at any time or from any place. If necessary, you may pray silently, since He knows all your thoughts.

B. Selected prayers of the Bible

(1) Abraham's Prayer of Intercession for Sodom

GENESIS 18:23-33
And Abraham drew near, and said, Wilt thou also destroy the righteous with the wicked? Peradventure there be fifty righteous within the city: wilt thou also destroy and not spare the place for the fifty righteous that are therein? That be far from thee to do after this manner, to slay the righteous with the wicked: and that the righteous should be as the wicked, that be far from thee: Shall not the Judge of all the earth do right? And the LORD said, If I find in Sodom fifty righteous within the city, then I will spare all the place for their sakes. And Abraham answered and said, Behold now, I have taken upon me to speak unto the Lord, which am but dust and ashes: Peradventure there shall lack five of the fifty righteous: wilt thou destroy all the city for lack of five? And he said, If I find there forty and five, I will not destroy it And he spoke unto him yet again, and said, Peradventure there shall be forty found there. And he said, I will not do it for forty's sake. And he said unto him, Oh let not the Lord be angry, and I will speak: Peradventure there shall thirty be found there. And he said, I will not do it, if I find thirty there. And he said, Behold now, I have taken upon me to speak unto the Lord: Peradventure there shall be twenty found there. And he said, I will not destroy it for twenty's sake. And he said, Oh let not the Lord be angry, and I will speak yet but this once: Peradventure ten shall be found there. And he said, I will not destroy it for ten's sake. And the LORD went his way, as soon as he had left communing with Abraham: and Abraham returned unto his place.

(2) Prayers of Moses on behalf of Israel

EXODUS 32:11-13
And Moses besought the LORD his God, and said, LORD, why doth thy wrath wax hot against thy people, which thou hast brought forth out of the land of Egypt with great power, and with a mighty hand? Wherefore should the Egyptians speak, and say, For mischief did he bring them out, to slay them in the mountains, and to consume them from the face of the earth? Turn from thy fierce wrath, and repent of this evil against thy people. Remember Abraham, Isaac, and Israel, thy servants, to whom thou sworest by thine own self, and saidst unto them, I will multiply your seed as the stars of heaven, and all this land that I have spoken of will I give unto your seed, and they shall inherit it forever.

EXODUS 32:30-33
And it came to pass on the morrow, that Moses said unto the people, Ye have sinned a great sin: and now I will go up unto the LORD; peradventure I shall make an

atonement for your sin. And Moses returned unto the LORD, and said, Oh, this people have sinned a great sin, and have made them gods of gold. Yet now, if thou wilt forgive their sin; and if not, blot me, I pray thee, out of thy book which thou hast written. And the LORD said unto Moses, Whosoever hath sinned against me, him will I blot out of my book. Therefore now go, lead the people unto the place of which I have spoken unto thee: behold, mine Angel shall go before thee: nevertheless in the day when I visit I will visit their sin upon them. And the LORD plagued the people, because they made the calf, which Aaron made.

(3) Prayer of David

PSALMS 23:1-6
A Psalm of David. The LORD is my shepherd; I shall not want. He maketh me to lie down in green pastures: he leadeth me beside the still waters. He restoreth my soul: he leadeth me in the paths of righteousness for his name's sake. Yea, though I walk through the valley of the shadow of death, I will fear no evil: for thou art with me; thy rod and thy staff they comfort me. Thou preparest a table before me in the presence of mine enemies: thou anointest my head with oil; my cup runneth over. Surely goodness and mercy shall follow me all the days of my life: and I will dwell in the house of the LORD forever.

(4) Other significant Prayers of David

David's confession of sin and plead for pardon PSALMS 51:1-19, prayer of praise and for his son Solomon 1 CHRONICLES 29:9-20, prayer of surrender PSALMS 139:1-24

(5) Prayer of Solomon for Wisdom

1 KINGS 3:6-10
And Solomon said, Thou hast showed unto thy servant David my father great mercy, according as he walked before thee in truth, and in righteousness, and in uprightness of heart with thee; and thou hast kept for him this great kindness, that thou hast given him a son to sit on his throne, as it is this day. And now, O LORD my God, thou hast made thy servant king instead of David my father: and I am but a little child: I know not how to go out or come in. And thy servant is in the midst of thy people which thou hast chosen, a great people, that cannot be numbered nor counted for multitude. Give therefore thy servant an understanding heart to judge thy people, that I may discern between good and bad: for who is able to judge this thy so great a people? And the speech pleased the Lord, that Solomon had asked this thing.

C. Other significant prayers

(1) Daniel's prayer of confession on behalf of Israel

Reference: DANIEL 9:4-19

(2) Prayer of Hannah for a child (Samuel) and thanksgiving

References: 1 SAMUEL 1:10-12, 1 SAMUEL 2:1-11

(3) Prayer of Jacob for deliverance from Esau

Reference: GENESIS 32:9-12

(4) Prayer of Elijah at Mount Carmel

Reference: 1 KINGS 18:36-39

(5) Additional Old Testament references:
JUDGES 16:28, 1 KINGS 8:22-62, 2 KINGS 6:15-18, 2 KINGS 19:14-19; 20:1-7

(6) New Testament references:
LUKE 18:13, ACTS 1:24-25, ACTS 4:24-31, ACTS 7:59-60, ACTS 9:6, EPHESIANS 3:14-21, PHILIPPIANS 1:3-11, COLOSSIANS 1:9-12, JUDE 1:24-25

People are saved by carefully following the Patterns, Commandments, Examples and Instructions of Jesus His Apostles and Disciples.... Not by any prayer or ritual created by man.... Heaven Awaits!

Appendix 10

Relief for the anxious or troubled Mind and Spirit

Contents of Appendix

A: Introduction

B. Human beings all have a natural deep-rooted longing for God

C. Jesus and His Disciples were well acquainted with grief and sorrows

D. Blessed Assurance

A. Introduction

The section following is provided for the benefit primarily to those users who have not yet followed His Pattern of Salvation. Once an individual has completely obeyed and continues in the faith that longing will disappear, but many other concerns of life will remain.

The balance of this appendix will discuss the blessed assurances of the Master and His Disciples regarding dealing with a troubled spirit or heart.

HEBREWS 10:22
Let us draw near with a true heart in full assurance of faith, having our hearts sprinkled from an evil conscience, and our bodies washed with pure water.

B. Human beings all have a natural deep-rooted longing for God

God created mankind in such a manner, that He could have an everlasting, fulfilling and gratifying relationship with each of us.

Every man and woman was created with a built-in longing to know and Worship God.

Until we develop a relationship and make peace with our Creator, during our time on this earth, that yearning or very low key constant sense or feeling, that something is missing or a discontentment, we cannot define or quite put our finger on, which only God can fulfill, will continue forever.

PHILIPPIANS 4:7
And the peace of God, which passeth all understanding, shall keep your hearts and minds through Christ Jesus.

C. Jesus and His Disciples were well acquainted with grief and sorrows

(1) The disappointments suffered by Christ were predicted in the Old Testament

ISAIAH 53:3
He is despised and rejected of men; a man of sorrows, and acquainted with grief: and we hid as it were our faces from him; he was despised, and we esteemed him not.

(2) Jesus predicted the excruciating pain he would suffer

MATTHEW 16:21
From that time forth began Jesus to show unto his disciples, how that he must go unto Jerusalem, and suffer many things of the elders and chief priests and scribes, and be killed, and be raised again the third day.

(3) Paul suffered from an unnamed affliction

2 CORINTHIANS 12:7-9
And lest I should be exalted above measure through the abundance of the revelations, there was given to me a thorn in the flesh, the messenger of Satan to buffet me, lest I should be exalted above measure. For this thing I besought the Lord thrice, that it might depart from me. And he said unto me, My grace is sufficient for thee: for my strength is made perfect in weakness. Most gladly therefore will I rather glory in my infirmities, that the power of Christ may rest upon me.

(4) His followers should expect trials and tribulations

1 THESSALONIANS 3:3
That no man should be moved by these afflictions: for yourselves know that we are appointed thereunto.

D. Blessed Assurance

(1) Blessed assurance - Peace beyond understanding

PHILIPPIANS 4:7
And the peace of God, which passeth all understanding, shall keep your hearts and minds through Christ Jesus.

ROMANS 5:1
Therefore being justified by faith, we have peace with God through our Lord Jesus Christ:

Additional reference: JOHN 14:27

(2) Blessed assurance - Love of God

ROMANS 8:35-39
Who shall separate us from the love of Christ? shall tribulation, or distress, or persecution, or famine, or nakedness, or peril, or sword? As it is written, For thy sake we are killed all the day long; we are accounted as sheep for the slaughter. Nay, in all these things we are more than conquerors through him that loved us. For I am persuaded, that neither death, nor life, nor angels, nor principalities, nor powers, nor things present, nor things to come, Nor height, nor depth, nor any other creature, shall be able to separate us from the love of God, which is in Christ Jesus our Lord.

(3) Blessed assurance - Access to God in Prayer

JOHN 14:13-14
And whatsoever ye shall ask in my name, that will I do, that the Father may be glorified in the Son. If ye shall ask any thing in my name, I will do it.

Additional reference: JAMES 5:16

(4) Blessed assurance - our advocate with the Father

1 JOHN 2:1
My little children, these things write I unto you, that ye sin not. And if any man sin, we have an advocate with the Father, Jesus Christ the righteous:

(5) Blessed assurance - Hope the anchor of your soul

HEBREWS 6:19
Which hope we have as an anchor of the soul, both sure and steadfast, and which entereth into that within the veil;

Additional references: **COLOSSIANS 1:27, 1 THESSALONIANS 4:14-18**

(6) Blessed assurance - Faith

JOHN 14:1
Let not your heart be troubled: ye believe in God, believe also in me.

HEBREWS 11:6
But without faith it is impossible to please him : for he that cometh to God must believe that he is, and that he is a rewarder of them that diligently seek him.

(7) Blessed assurance - our eternal reward in Glory

REVELATION 2:10
Fear none of those things which thou shalt suffer: behold, the devil shall cast some of you into prison, that ye may be tried; and ye shall have tribulation ten days; be thou faithful unto death, and I will give thee a crown of life.

JAMES 1:12
Blessed is the man that endureth temptation: for when he is tried, he shall receive the crown of life, which the Lord hath promised to them that love him.

Additional Good News is provided in Appendix 11, under the heading, Blessings in Christ

And the angel said unto them, Fear not: for, behold, I bring you good tidings of great joy, which shall be to all people....

Heaven Awaits!

Appendix 11

Message to new Christians

Contents of Appendix

A. Introduction

B. Blessings in Christ

C. Recommended course of action

A. Introduction

At the very moment following baptism you have been greatly blessed, have taken on the responsibilities and accepted the limitations related to becoming a Christian.

The decision to turn away from a life of sin to become a follower of Christ is just like an earthly marriage, which should never be entered into lightly, but only after serious consideration.

This appendix is intended to provide the user with a basic outline of some of the blessings in Christ, a recommended course of action and suggestions for avoiding sin and temptation.

Questions beyond the scope of this guide should be directed to the minister or a member of the leadership of the local congregation of His Church.

B. Blessings in Christ

At the very moment you arose from the water you were baptized into Christ (GALATIANS 3:27) and gained the related blessing. The following is a partial listing of the significant benefits and freedoms you have gained:

(1) Gained freedom from sin and feelings of guilt

(a) All your sins, regardless of the extent and the associated feelings of guilt have been washed away.

ACTS 22:16
And now why tarriest thou? arise, and be baptized, and wash away thy sins, calling on the name of the Lord.

(2) Gained freedom from the wages of sin and everlasting punishment

ROMANS 6:23
For the wages of sin is death; but the gift of God is eternal life through Jesus Christ our Lord.

Additional reference: REVELATION 21:8

(3) Gained freedom from fear

Due to the many uncertainties of daily life, many individuals suffer in an almost continuous state of silent fear. In his famous quote, "Most men lead lives of quiet desperation and go to the grave with the song still in them." Henry David Thoreau referred to this common problem as quiet desperation.

While Christ did not assure His faithful followers a carefree life, He did promise to be with each of us always. Therefore, regardless of your personal situation or location, be it joyfulness or adversity, He is always with you.

HEBREWS 13:5
Let your conversation be without covetousness; and be content with such things as ye have: for he hath said, I will never leave thee, nor forsake thee.

Additional reference: MATTHEW 28:20

(4) Gained freedom from the fear of death

Faithful Christians need not fear death!

Actually, the Bible teaches that physical death is a blessing, for two important reasons;

(a) The faithful are assured of resurrection to life.

JOHN 5:29
And shall come forth; they that have done good, unto the resurrection of life; and they that have done evil, unto the resurrection of damnation.

Additional references: LUKE 14:14, JOHN 11:25, HEBREWS 13:6, 1 PETER 1:3, 1 PETER 3:21

(b) The faithful may rest from their labors and the record of their good works will follow them

REVELATION 14:13
And I heard a voice from heaven saying unto me, Write, Blessed are the dead which die in the Lord from henceforth: Yea, saith the Spirit, that they may rest from their labors; and their works do follow them.

(5) Gained access to God, the Father

(a) A continuing relationship with God, the Father and forgiveness of sin, through His Son

JOHN 14:6
Jesus saith unto him, I am the way, the truth, and the life: no man cometh unto the Father, but by me.

EPHESIANS 1:7
In whom we have redemption through his blood, the forgiveness of sins, according to the riches of his grace;

(6) Gained a relationship with the children of God

Another blessing that occurs at the moment of baptism; **you become a child of God.** As His follower, you have immediately gained brothers and sisters in Christ from all parts of the globe and have been added to the Book of Life or the membership rolls of His Church in Heaven. (ACTS 2:47, PHILIPPIANS 4:3, REVELATION 20:15, REVELATION 3:5, ACTS 2:41, COLOSSIANS 3:1)

(a) Best of all, the members of the local congregation are all part of your new family from which many meaningful and lasting relationships will likely develop.

1 PETER 1:22
Seeing ye have purified your souls in obeying the truth through the Spirit unto unfeigned love of the brethren, see that ye love one another with a pure heart fervently:

Additional references: JOHN 15:12, MARK 9:50, ROMANS 14:19, 1 CORINTHIANS 12:25, GALATIANS 6:2, EPHESIANS 4:2, JAMES 5:16 1PETER 1:22, 1 JOHN 4:7, HEBREWS 10:23-24, 1 THESSALONIANS 4:18, 1 JOHN 3:17-18

(7) Gained a meaningful purpose for your life

For centuries human beings have searched for the meaning and purpose of their lives. Solomon revealed the answer in ECCLESIASTES 12:13-14.

(a) Only in Christ can people find genuine fulfillment and contentment.

Regardless of the difficulties encountered, your social or financial standings, the life of any follower who remains faithful until death can only be counted as an overwhelming success, for he or she has gained the greatest prize of all, eternal life in the glorious paradise of the Kingdom of God

C. Recommended course of action

(1) Seek First the Kingdom of God

Reference: MATTHEW 6:33

(2) Love the Lord your God

Reference: MATTHEW 22:37

(3) Of course, you have responsibilities to your earthly family, but your greatest loyalty must be to your God.

Reference: MATTHEW 10:37

(4) Study the Word of God Daily

References: JAMES 1:21, 1 PETER 2:2

(5) Be fervent in daily prayer

Approach your God in prayer with an attitude of sincerity, humbleness and thanksgiving for all the blessings you have received. Begin and end your prayer with words of praise.

Then share with Him, in your own words, your wants, hopes, fear and feel free to ask for His help with any problems. He already knows your situation, but desires that you verbalize your requests and concerns. Prayers are always closed in the name of Jesus Christ

References: COLOSSIANS 4:2, HEBREWS 4:14-16, 1 TIMOTHY 2:8, ROMANS 12:12, PHILIPPIANS 4:6-7

(6) Regularly attend Services of His Church

Reference: HEBREWS 10:24-25

(7) Assist in saving others by sharing the Gospel

References: MATTHEW 28:19, MARK 16:15-16

(8) Avoid sin and temptation

Consider carefully the entertainment and activities you enjoy, such as:

(a) Social Drinking

Drinking to excess is specifically condemned in the Bible.

The stern warnings regarding alcohol are also applicable to illegitimate drugs of today, which were unknown in Biblical Times.

Unfortunately, the Bible does not inform us as to how to determine the dividing line between being sober and drunkenness.

An important question to consider; Does social drinking have the potential of leading to other sinful activities?

Those who see little or no harm in a few social drinks point to:

"Drink no longer water, but use a little wine for thy stomach's sake and thine often infirmities." (1 TIMOTHY 5:23)

That Jesus turned water into wine (JOHN 2:1-10).

It should be noted that both references are to wine, which had a much lower alcoholic content in the first century. In that time, wine was cut with 3 or 4 parts water.

Every alcoholic product sold today would be considered strong drink by Biblical standards.

Does this mean that I can never have another drink?

Not necessarily, however it is quite clear that the dangers of alcohol should always be carefully considered.

Alcohol is one of Satan's most powerful weapons, which he uses very effectively against mankind.

The use of alcohol has caused countless social problems, injuries and deaths.

Therefore the consumption of such beverages, if at all, should be extremely limited.

References: GALATIANS 5:21, 1 CORINTHIANS 5:11, 1 CORINTHIANS 6:10 1 PETER 5:8

(b) Gambling

The words gamble, gambling or gaming were not used in the Bible and therefore is not specifically condemned, but is clearly prohibited by the injunction against coveting the property of others. (LUKE 12:15, EPHESIANS 5:3, COLOSSIANS 3:5)

The magnificent, opulent and lavish gambling palaces are devoted to worldly pleasures or lusts of the flesh and are often referred to as the devil's playground.

The followers of Christ are urged to deny themselves such forms of entertainment. (TITUS 2:12)

(c) Dancing

In the opinion of the author, dancing is specifically condemned in the New Testament.

This opinion, however is *not* shared by many God-fearing individuals, who do not consider social dancing to be a sin, which may occur as a result of a misunderstanding or disagreement regarding the meaning of "revellings and such like" in the following passage.

GALATIANS 5:21
Envyings, murders, drunkenness, **revellings, and such like:** of the which I tell you before, as I have also told you in time past, **that they which do such things shall not inherit the kingdom of God.**

Revellings is defined by Liddell and Scott, recognized authorities on New Testament Greek as *"a jovial festivity with music and dancing."* Therefore is an activity that must be avoided (ROMANS 13:12-14)

(d) Indecent Wearing Apparel

Inappropriate wearing apparel or the lack of proper covering is certainly the origin of many impure thoughts, which can lead to sin.

One of the darkest periods in the life of King David began by his viewing of Bathsheba while she bathed. (2 SAMUEL 11:2-4)

God expects men and women to clothe themselves properly, which will assist in preventing unintentional impure thoughts.(1 PETER 2:11)

Improper wearing attire may cause others to sin!

Simply stated, improper wearing apparel will likely cause others to sin.

It is sinful to dress in such a manner that is intended to excite the lustful eye of the opposite sex.

Such conduct and manner of dress is called lasciviousness.(GALATIANS 5:19)

The wearing of such apparel may lead others to commit mental adultery.

Reference: MATTHEW 5:28

When we cause another to stumble, we may be guilty of the sin ourselves.

Christian women are directed to adorn themselves in modest apparel. (1 TIMOTHY 2:9)

In the Old Testament God made His intentions clear. After Adam and Eve realized that they were naked, they made aprons of fig leafs (GENESIS 3:7). God found these garments to be unacceptable and provided coats of animal hides (GENESIS 3:21). The Hebrew word indicates these coats covered from shoulder to knee. Society has substantially reduced its standard of dress, however Christians will be judged by the Divine Pattern.

His requirements for followers to be properly dressed are still in effect.

In order to conform to the Standard of God, which clearly indicate that Christians are to be clothed from the shoulder to the knee.

(9) Please carefully consider the potential for sin in the following:

Motion Pictures, television programs, Internet sites, rock concerts or the like.

Questionable possessions such as books, pictures, videos, music or other items, which have the potential of causing temptation or sin to occur.

1 THESSALONIANS 5:22
Abstain from all appearance of evil

Suggestions

Cast off questionable possessions

Eliminate any activity or form of entertainment, which is condemned or has the potential for evil

Discard any inappropriate items of wearing apparel

Pray to your Heavenly Father God for strength and wisdom in overcoming temptation and sin.

The Great Apostle James directs us in chapter 4, verse 7 to: Submit yourselves therefore to God. Resist the devil, and he will flee from you.

Submit to and have faith in your Lord God Almighty... Heaven Awaits!

Appendix 12
Biblical Myths, Misconceptions and Mysteries

Contents of Appendix

A. Introduction

B. Adam and Eve

C. Noah's Ark

D. The Ark of His Testament or Covenant

E. Jonah and the whale

F. Birth of our Lord

G. Resurrection of our Lord

H. Well Known Expressions Not found in Holy Scriptures

A. Introduction

Over the years, numerous myths, mysteries, misunderstandings, questions and misconceptions have developed regarding the Biblical account of various events.

The purpose of this appendix is to encourage the reader to use the Bible as their primary reference and not to trust the words of men, by providing approximately 40 answers and corrections to many myths, misconceptions, mysteries and questions

B. Adam and Eve

(1) The Lord took one of Adams ribs to create Eve

GENESIS 2:21-22
And the LORD God caused a deep sleep to fall upon Adam, and he slept: and **he took one of his ribs,** and closed up the flesh instead thereof; And the rib, which the LORD God had taken from man, **made he a woman,** and brought her unto the man.

These verses have convinced many to accept the pervasive myth that all human females have an additional rib as a result of Eve being created from Adams rib.

The belief is incorrect. Men and women both have twelve sets of ribs.

The results of wounds or surgery are not passed on to future generations.

(2) Eve disobeyed the Lord

(a) Many people believe that the first couple was expelled from the Garden of Eden because Eve picked an <u>apple</u> from the tree of the knowledge of good and evil and shared it with her husband. This may make a good story, but the type of fruit is not disclosed in the Scriptures.

This misconception may have resulted archaic meaning of the word apple in Middle English, **which was used to refer to all fruits** (except berries) and may have been passed down verbally over the centuries and then became generally assumed to be an element of the original Biblical chronicle.

GENESIS 2:9
And out of the ground made the LORD God to grow every tree that is pleasant to the sight, and good for food; the tree of life also in the midst of the garden, and the tree of knowledge of good and evil.

(b) The Lord could have forgiven Adam and Eve for their sins, but He also had another overriding concern, which is disclosed in the following verses.

GENESIS 3:22-23
And the LORD God said, Behold, the man is become as one of us, to know good and evil: and now, **lest he put forth his hand, and take also of the tree of life, and eat, and live forever:** Therefore the LORD God sent him forth from the garden of Eden, to till the ground from whence he [Adam] was taken

(3) Many believe that Satan assumed the form of a snake and tempted Eve.

While this is very likely, Satan is not named in the Book of Genesis. In fact, Satan is not mentioned until approximately 3000 years later and is only referred to in the four books of the Old Testament including, Job, Psalms, 1 Chronicles, and Zechariah.

A statement made in REVELATION 12:9 is possibly a disclosure that the serpent which seduced Eve was Satan. If so, this information was not revealed until the writing of the book of Revelation, several thousand years after the event occurred.

(a) The serpent was only described as more subtle than any beast of the field

GENESIS 3:1
Now **the serpent was more subtle than any beast of the field** which the LORD God had made. And he said unto the woman, Yea, hath God said, Ye shall not eat of every tree of the garden?

(b) The belief that Satan was the serpent, as well as, many other preconceived notions regarding Adam and Eve may have resulted from the widespread study in our school system of Paradise Lost.

This epic poem was written by John Milton and published in 1667.

The vivid and creative imagination of the author significantly expanded the Genesis story by adding additional characters and details, which are not a part of the Divine account.

For example in Book IX of Paradise Lost, Satan returns to Eden and possesses a serpent, which then tempted Eve. Hence, a misconception is born.

This is just one example of how deeply the misinformation contained in this famous poem has become imbedded in our culture.

(4) Another widespread misconception is the belief that the first couple only produced two offspring, which were named Cain and Abel.

The Scriptures only provide the names of three male children. The third being named Seth. However, the Scriptures clearly indicate that Adam fathered other sons and daughters.

GENESIS 4:25
And Adam knew his wife again; and **she bore a son, and called his name Seth:** For God, said she, hath appointed me another seed instead of Abel, whom Cain slew.

GENESIS 5:3-4
And Adam lived a hundred and thirty years, and begot a son in his own likeness, after his image; and called his name Seth: And the days of Adam after he had begotten Seth were **eight hundred years:** and **he begot sons and daughters:**

(5) A common question is: Where did Cain's wife come from?

In order for the population to expand, it would have been necessary for one or more of the sons of Adam and Eve to take a sister or daughter of Adam and Eve, for their wife.

Since these individuals were living so close to the original faultless creation, genetic problems would have been nonexistent. It was not until the time of Moses, approximately 2500 years later, when the Laws in opposition to the marriage of close relatives were enacted.

Biblical scholars have estimated that beginning with one or two new families, the population could have easily expanded to at least 100,000 over a few hundred years.

We do know the age of Cain when he married or began to build his city. If Cain married young it would have likely been to a sister. If he married late he would have had a choice among almost innumerable relatives.

GENESIS 4:17
And Cain knew his wife; and she conceived, and bore Enoch: and he built a city, and called the name of the city, after the name of his son, Enoch.

C. Noah's Ark

(1) Many were taught that the animals went into the Ark <u>two by two</u>. This element of the famous Sunday school Bible story, does not match the Scriptures.

(a) Noah was commanded to take seven males and females of each type of clean beasts and the fouls of the air.

(b) The unclean beasts were taken into the Ark two by two. Since under Jewish dietary rules, the vast majority of all creatures were considered clean or edible, most animals and all birds actually entered the vessel seven by seven.

GENESIS 7:2-3
Of **every clean beast thou shalt take to thee by sevens,** the male and his female: and of **beasts that are not clean by two,** the male and his female. Of **fowls also of the air by sevens,** the male and the female; to keep seed alive upon the face of all the earth

D. The Ark of His Testament or Covenant

Shortly after completing the Exodus from Egypt in approximately 1500 BC, Lord Jesus provided Moses the Pattern of the Tabernacle and its opponents.

(1) The following is a brief, but interesting overview of the history of the Ark of His Testament or Covenant the most sacred of the opponents of the Tabernacle.

(a) Our Lord even provided Moses with the names of the craftsmen (Bezaleel and Aholiab), whom He willed to handle the construction of the Ark.

Exodus 36:2
And Moses called **Bezaleel and Aholiab,** and every wise hearted man, in whose heart the LORD had put wisdom, even every one whose heart stirred him up to come unto the work to do it:

(b) After its creation, only members of the tribe of Levi carried the Ark during approximately forty years of wandering in the desert.

(c) Whenever the Israelites camped, the sacred tent or Tabernacle was assembled and the Ark was then placed in the Holy of Holies section of this temporary structure.

(2) The Israelites were led into the Promised Land

(a) At the end of the forty years, members of the tribe of Levi transporting the Ark led Joshua and the Israelites to the banks of the Jordan River.

(b) Across that waterway lay the long awaited Promised Land.

JOSHUA 3:3
And they commanded the people, saying, When ye see the ark of the covenant of the LORD your God, and the priests the Levites bearing it, then ye shall remove from your place, and go after it.

Additional reference: JOSHUA 3:6 .

(3) When the priests entered the river the bottom instantly became dry land and remained so until after the entire Jewish Nation had crossed over.

JOSHUA 4:11
And it came to pass, when all the people were clean passed over, that the ark of the LORD passed over, and the priests, in the presence of the people.

Additional references: JOSHUA 3:15-17, JOSHUA 4:18

(4) Two memorial monuments were constructed.

(a) One monument was constructed using twelve stones removed, one by a member of each tribe, from the Jordan River at the place where the members of the tribe of Levi had stood. These stones were carried to the place where the Israelites camped that night and set up.

(b) The other was a built by Joshua using twelve stones in the midst of the Jordan River at the exact spot where the priests had stood.

Reference JOSHUA 4:1-9

Key Passage: JOSHUA 4:8-9
And the children of Israel did so as Joshua commanded, and took up twelve stones out of the midst of Jordan, as the LORD spoke unto Joshua, according to the number of the tribes of the children of Israel, and carried them over with them unto the place where

they lodged, and laid them down there. And Joshua set up twelve stones in the midst of Jordan, in the place where the feet of the priests which bore the Ark of the Covenant stood: and they are there unto this day.

(5) The Battle of Jericho

(a) During the Battle of Jericho, the Ark was transported round the city once a day for six days, heralded by seven priests sounding seven trumpets of rams' horns and protected by the armed warriors. The Israelites were instructed to remain silent until told to shout.

Reference: JOSHUA 6:4-15

(b) On the seventh day, the seven priests sounding the seven trumpets of rams' horns before the Ark circled the city seven times. Upon completion the people were signaled to generate a great <u>shout</u> and then the <u>massive walls of Jericho came crashing down</u>. Thus, allowing the forces of Joshua to take control of the city.

Reference: JOSHUA 6:16-20

Key passages: JOSHUA 6:16-17, 20
And it came to pass at the seventh time, when the priests blew with the trumpets, Joshua said unto the people, Shout; for the LORD hath given you the city. And the city shall be accursed, even it, and all that are therein, to the LORD: only Rahab the harlot shall live, she and all that are with her in the house, because she hid the messengers that we sent.

So the people shouted when the priests blew with the trumpets: and **it came to pass, when the people heard the sound of the trumpet, and the people shouted with a great shout, that the wall fell down flat, so that the people went up into the city, every man straight before him, and they took the city.**

(c) Some time later the Ark was returned to the Tabernacle, which had been installed at Shiloh.

JOSHUA 18:1
And the whole congregation of the children of Israel assembled together at Shiloh, and set up the tabernacle of the congregation there. And the land was subdued before them.

(6) Forgotten for centuries by the vast majority, interest was renewed in the locating this sacred historical object with the release of the imaginary story of Indiana Jones (forces of good) and the Raiders of the Lost Ark (forces of evil) starring Harrison Ford in 1981.

The drama takes time during World War II. The plot of the film pits Indiana Jones (Ford) against a horde of Nazis, who are in search of this holy relic because their leader, Hitler firmly believed that by possessing the Ark of His Testament, his military forces would <u>become invincible</u>.

(7) This was a fictional motion picture, but the original certainty that possession of the Ark would make the members of a military force invincible actually took place over three thousand years ago.

Rather than continuing to trust Almighty God, the army of Israelites shifted their faith to the Ark of His Testament or Covenant, believing that this man made object would make their <u>forces invincible</u>.

(8) The Israelites carried into a fierce battle with their arch adversaries the Philistines, this sacred container, which held:

(a) The Ten Commandments, which was the written record, on two stone tablets, of the agreement between God and His Chosen People.

Exodus 34:1
And the LORD said unto Moses, Hew thee two tables of stone like unto the first: **and I will write upon these tables the words that were in the first tables, which thou didst break.**

DEUTERONOMY 9:10
And the LORD delivered unto me **two tables of stone written with the finger of**

God; and on them was written according to all the words, which the LORD spoke with you in the mount out of the midst of the fire in the day of the assembly.

Additional information: Chapter I, Section R, Subsection 1

(b) A container or pot of MANNA

EXODUS 16:32
And Moses said, This is the thing which the LORD commandeth, Fill an omer of it to be kept for your generations; that they may see the bread wherewith I have fed you in the wilderness, when I brought you forth from the land of Egypt.

(c) AARON'S ROD that budded

Reference: NUMBERS 17:1-11

Key Passage: Numbers 17:8-10
And it came to pass, that on the morrow Moses went into the tabernacle of witness; and, behold, the rod of Aaron for the house of Levi was budded, and brought forth buds, and bloomed blossoms, and yielded almonds. And Moses brought out all the rods from before the LORD unto all the children of Israel: and they looked, and took every man his rod. And the LORD said unto Moses, Bring Aaron's rod again before the testimony, to be kept for a token against the rebels; and thou shalt quite take away their murmurings from me, that they die not

(d) The contents of the Ark of His Testament was confirmed by the writer of Hebrews

HEBREWS 9:4
Which had the golden censer, and the ark of the covenant overlaid round about with gold, **wherein was the golden pot that had manna, and Aaron's rod that budded, and the tables of the covenant;**

(9) A mystery, which may be resolved in an advanced volume, is why a discrepancy exists between the forgoing verse and 1 Kings 8:9

1KINGS 8:9
There was nothing in the ark save the two tables of stone, which Moses put there at Horeb, when the LORD made a covenant with the children of Israel, when they came out of the land of Egypt.

(10) Unfortunately the Israelites suffered an overwhelming crushing defeat and the Philistines took control of the Ark of His Testament.

Reference: 1 SAMUEL 4:1–11

Key Passage 1SAMUEL 4:10-11
And the Philistines fought, and Israel was smitten, and they fled every man into his tent: and there was a very great slaughter; **for there fell of Israel thirty thousand footmen. And the ark of God was taken; and the two sons of Eli, Hophni and Phinehas, were slain**

(11) The Lord struck back with the most effective counter attack of all time.

First the Philistines brought the Ark of His Testament into the city of Ashdod and placed the Ark in the temple of the pagan god dagon. The Lord destroyed their pagan god and left his temple in ruins, slaughtered many and gave the rest a terrible case of emerods (**"emerods" translates as tumors or hemorrhoids**) in their secret parts. The Philistines move the Ark to Gath and the lord destroyed more citizens and gave many of those left alive a dreadful case of emerods. In addition their land was overrun by mice. They tried moving the Ark to Ekron with exactly the same result. The Ark was under the control of the Philistines for seven months.

At this point, the only concern of Philistine leaders was how to properly return the Ark to the Israelites. The leaders consulted their wise men for suggestions.

The wise men recommended that the Ark be returned on a cart to a border town along with gifts of livestock and a trespass offering of five gold emerods and five gold mice, in hopes that the God of the Israelites would lift His heavy hand from them.

The Ark of His Testament, livestock and gifts of gold in a separate container were delivered to the field of Joshua the Beth-shemite. The Beth-shemites offered sacrifices and burnt offerings.

Out of curiosity many men of Beth-sheet gazed into the Ark and as result the Lord destroyed over 50,000 people that day.

The Beth-shemites sent messengers to the inhabitants of Kirjath-jearim with the following message, "The Philistines have brought again the ark of the LORD; come ye down, and fetch it up to you." The Ark of His Testament remained in Kirjath-jearim for 20 years due to the sins of the Israelites.

King David was improperly transporting the Ark to Jerusalem, which resulted in the death of Uzza, in the latter part of his reign.

Additional information: Chapter I, Section U, Subsection 3

Read the full story in 1 Samuel, Chapters 6, 7 and 8. If you liked this summary, you will enjoy the story. Hint: Has a spectacular ending.

(12) During his ministry between about 626 BC and 586 BC the Prophet Jeremiah forewarned the Israelites that shortly, the Ark of His Testament would be taken and seen no more.

Jeremiah 3:16
And it shall come to pass, when ye be multiplied and increased in the land, in those days, saith the LORD, they shall say no more, **The ark of the covenant of the LORD: neither shall it come to mind: neither shall they remember it; neither shall they visit it ; neither shall that be done any more**

(13) For over 30 years, since the release of the film, the actual location of the Ark, for the majority has been an unsolved mystery.

The latest of several reported sightings transpired in June 2009, when the leaders of Ethiopian Orthodox Church announced via an Italian news agency that the Ark had been located in Ethiopia and arrangements for a public display were being considered.

Another news story added that the Ark was being held for safe keeping in the Church of our Lady Mary of Zion in Aksum, a town in northern Ethiopia.

The highly anticipated public showing never occurred, possibly because upon further investigation the leaders of the Ethiopian Orthodox Church realized that the object in question is a replica of the genuine Ark.

This statement is based upon apparently the little known fact that written verification of the location was recorded by the last human being to actually observe the original Ark of His Testament or Covenant in the location where it is now and will be perpetually displayed.

Using the Scriptures and the works of Josephus, the first century Jewish historian, we can determine that the Ark of His Testament or Covenant was installed in the Temple during the latter part of the reign of King Solomon.

In about 587 BC the Temple was destroyed and most of its riches carried to Babylon.

(14) The prediction in Jeremiah 3:16 was fulfilled when the Ark of His Testament or Covenant vanished during the absolute destruction of Jerusalem.

Apparently, God had preordained that His Ark and its contents would not fall under pagan control again, so He simply translated it, just as He did with Enoch to His Celestial Temple in Heaven. Considering the previous fate of the Philistines, King Nebuchadnezzar and his followers were quite fortunate.

(15) This contention is supported by the words of the Great Apostle John, who was translated into a Heavenly setting and given a glimpse into future about 600 years after the Ark of His Testament disappeared. During that visitation, John became the last human witness to have undeniably viewed the Ark of His Testament.

REVELATION 11:19
And the temple of God was opened in heaven, and there was seen in his temple the <u>ark of his testament</u> [diatheke]: *and there were lightnings, and voices, and thunderings, and an earthquake, and great hail.*

The Greek word diatheke can be translated as either testament or covenant. The editors of American Standard Version of the Bible translated the word diatheke as covenant.

E. Jonah and the whale

One of the all time favorite Bible stories is known as Jonah and the whale. Jonah attempted to run away in order to avoid an assignment of the Lord. As a result Jonah was swallowed and for three days and nights was held in the belly of a great fish.

JONAH 1:17
Now the LORD had prepared a great fish to swallow up Jonah. And Jonah was in the belly of the fish three days and three nights.

(1) The misconception is that the great fish was a whale. This is incorrect, since all members of the whale family are mammals and therefore would never be considered or labeled as a fish.

F. Birth of our Lord

Additional information: Chapter IX, Section B, Subsection 1

(1) This celebrated and amazing event is the subject of several misconceptions and variations between popular folk lore and the Scriptures. The following are a few examples of widespread beliefs, which are a mixture of mythology and Biblical Truth.

(a) The typical Sunday school materials depict Mary riding on a donkey. There is no such reference in the Scriptures.

(b) A popular Christmas carol describes the wise men as Oriental Kings

(c) According to the legend, there were three wise men, who followed His Star (Star of Bethlehem) from Babylonia, which was an ancient cultural region in central-southern Mesopotamia (present-day Iraq), riding camels, who visited the infant Jesus, while He was in the manger.

(2) We have no indication of royalty, specifics regarding where the wise men were from, the date they arrived or the type of animals they were riding, if any.

(3) To follow is a recap of details provided in the Scriptures.

(a) It is clear that the wise men were from the east. How far from the east is not disclosed

(b) We know that the wise men followed His Star, which lead them to Jerusalem.

(c) The wise men called on King Herod apparently believing that the newborn King of the Jews would be with other members of the royalty in the palace.

(d) There were at least two wise men; the total number could have been 3, 7, 40 or many more since the number of wise men is not disclosed

Key Passage: MATTHEW 2:1-2 Now when Jesus was born in Bethlehem of Judea in the days of Herod the king, behold, **there came wise men from the east** to Jerusalem, Saying, **Where is he that is born King of the Jews?** for we have seen his star in the east, and are come to worship him.

(e) Herod and the wise men met twice. During the first conversation Herod learned of the birth of Christ from the wise men. After consulting with his advisors, which is covered in subsection (f) and (g) below, Herod inquired when the wise men had first seen His Star and directed the visitors to Bethlehem and requested that when they found Jesus to report His location.

It would appear that the wise men had traveled for sometime following His Star, since Herod demanded the death of all males under the age of two, making it possible that Jesus was up to two years old.

MATTHEW 2:16
Then Herod, when he saw that he was

mocked of the wise men, was exceeding wroth, and sent forth, and slew all the children that were in Bethlehem, and in all the coasts thereof, from **two years old and under, according to the time which he had diligently inquired of the wise men.**

(f) Herod was troubled by the news of a new born King of the Jews and demanded information from the chief priests and scribes.

MATTHEW 2:4
And when he had gathered all the chief priests and scribes of the people together, **he demanded of them where Christ should be born.**

(g) Herod was then quoted the prophecy recorded in Micah Chapter 5, verse 2.

MATTHEW 2:5-6
And they said unto him, In Bethlehem of Judea: for thus it is written by the prophet, And thou Bethlehem, in the land of Judah, art not the least among the princes of Judah: for out of thee shall come a Governor, **that shall rule my people Israel.**

(h) We know that His Star led the wise men to Jesus and that they rejoiced

MATTHEW 2:9-10
When they had heard the king, they departed; and, **lo, the star, which they saw in the east, went before them, till it came and stood over where the young child was.** When they saw the star, they rejoiced with exceeding great joy.

(i) We know that the wise men visited Jesus in a house, not a manger

(j) We know there were three types of gifts. We do not know the total number of gifts received.

Key Passage: MATTHEW 2:11 **And when they were come into the house,** they saw the young child with Mary his mother, and fell down, and worshiped him: and when they had opened their treasures, they presented unto him gifts; **gold, and frankincense, and myrrh.**

(k) We know that the wise men did not report back to Herod, but departed using a different route.

MATTHEW 2:12
And being warned of God in a dream that **they should not return to Herod,** they departed into their own country another way.

G. Resurrection of our Lord

Many believe that God in His written Word ordained the annual celebration of His Resurrection or Easter, which is another widespread misconception.

(1) This holiday is actually rooted in the traditions of the ancient Saxons who celebrated the coming of the season of spring with a frenzied pagan festival in honor of Eastre or Eostre, a goddess of spring and fertility.

The symbol of this ancient pagan goddess was the rabbit.

Prior to A.D. 325, this festival was celebrated on Friday, Saturday, and Sunday. The Council of Nicaea (Catholic Church) was convened by Emperor Constantine in that year. The Council determined that date of this celebration would float and be fixed yearly using a rather complex formula. Basically the feast is celebrated on the first Sunday following the full moon that takes place on or after March 21 (ecclesiastical vernal equinox), which results in the holiday falling between March 22 and April 25.

(2) The earliest known use of the word Easter (possibly in honor of the pagan goddess) in reference to the Resurrection of Christ was about 500 years later in the eighth century.

Easter appears in King James Version only once (Acts 12:4) and is a mistranslation of the Greek word **pascha,** which translates as Passover. Easter is not found in the American Standard Version.

Acts 12:4
And when he [Peter] had apprehended him,

he put him in prison, and delivered him to four quaternions of soldiers to keep him; intending after Easter [should read Passover] to bring him forth to the people.

(3) We are not commanded to celebrate the Resurrection of our Lord annually, nor are such celebrations prohibited in the pages of the New Testament. Therefore, personal or public celebrations of His Resurrection or Easter, which are not included as a part of the Worship services (weekly services during which the Lord's Supper is served) of His Church would be acceptable.

However inclusion of any cerebration or activities related to Easter as a part of the Worship services can only be considered as an unauthorized addition to the Worship service.

Hence, any such cerebration or activities would be a violation of the unyielding Biblical Injunction, against "adding to" in REVELATION 22:18-19 and would likely result in each individual, who affirms its use, to be eternally lost.

(4) We are commanded to remember our Lord and Savior each week before and during the Lord's Supper, until he comes again.

H. Proverbs or Sayings Not found in Holy Scriptures

The following is an overview of well known Proverbs, Adages, Sayings or Expressions, which many believe are quotes from the Bible that are **not** found in the Holy Scriptures.

(1) God works in mysterious ways.

This is one of few non-Biblical Expressions that could actually be supported with the Scriptures.

References: DEUTERONOMY 29:29, ROMANS 8:28

The apparent source of this expression is the old song entitled "God Moves in a Mysterious Way", By William Cowper, which may have been based upon ISAIAH 55:9. William Cowper was born on November 15, 1731, in Herefordshire, England. Cowper became close friends with the Evangelical clergyman John Newton; together they co-authored the *Olney Hymns*, which was first published in 1779 and included Newton's famous hymn "Amazing Grace." Of the 68 hymns Cowper wrote, "Oh for a closer walk with God" and "God moves in a Mysterious Way" are the most renowned. Cowper died in 1800.

(2) Pride comes before the fall

It is unclear why this Proverb was diminished into its popular usage, as the original has a much greater impact.

PROVERBS 16:18
Pride goeth before destruction, and a **haughty spirit before a fall.**

(3) The eye is the window to the Soul

The Scriptures do not refer to the eye being a window to the Soul, but rather as the light of the body

MATTHEW 6:22-23
The light of the body is the eye: if therefore thine eye be single, thy whole body shall be full of light. But if thine eye be evil, thy whole body shall be full of darkness. If therefore the light that is in thee be darkness, how great is that darkness!

Additional reference: LUKE 11:34

(4) Cleanliness is next to Godliness

This Saying is attributed to John Wesley (1703-1791) the founder of Methodism.

Other the discussion of cleanliness in the book of Leviticus, the Bible is silent on the issue of human hygiene. Of much greater concern is the spotlessness of the soul

Key reference: 1 JOHN 1:9

Additional references: Ephesians 5:26-27, John 15:3, 2 Corinthians 7:1, James 4:8

(5) God helps those that help themselves

This is a quote by Benjamin Franklin recorded in the "Poor Richard's Almanac", 1736.

(6) Spare the rod, spoil the child

Contrary to popular belief this quote is not found in the Bible. However, there are verses with a similar meaning.

References: PROVERBS 13:24, PROVERBS 22:15, PROVERBS 23:13-14, PROVERBS 29:15

(7) Do unto others as you would have them do unto you

To the surprise of many this precise adage is not found in the New Testament. Actually it is a modern paraphrase of the Words of our Lord in MATTHEW 7:12 and LUKE 6:31.

(8) Money is the root of all evil.

This is an excellent example of how a couple of words can change the entire meaning of a saying.

The Biblical Teaching is the "**Love of money** is the root of all evil": Money itself is simply a medium of exchange, which may be used for good or evil. An excessive desire for or love of money is the root of many forms of evil.

Reference; 1 TIMOTHY 6:10

(9) To thine own self be true

This expression is from the Shakespearean tragedy Hamlet. This line "This above all things: to thine own self be true "(*Hamlet*, 3.1.81) is spoken by Polonius counselor to King Claudius

(10) Neither a borrower nor a lender be

Another line from Hamlet, spoken by Polonius, which is often mistaken for Scripture (*Hamlet*, 3.1.78)

(11) Seven Deadly Sins

There is no direct reference in the Bible to the following list; Gluttony, Greed, Sloth, Lust, Vanity, Envy, Wrath, which are commonly known as the Seven Deadly Sins.

All sins should be considered "deadly". The closest passage, which lists seven "sins", known to the author is found in PROVERBS 6:16-19, Which states: "These six things doth the LORD hate: yea, seven are an abomination unto him: **A proud look, a lying tongue, and hands that shed innocent blood, A heart that deviseth wicked imaginations, feet that be swift in running to mischief, A false witness that speaketh lies, and he that soweth discord among brethren**"

Other examples include: PROVERBS 11:20, PROVERBS 12:22, PROVERBS 15:8, PROVERBS 15:26, PROVERBS 16:5 PROVERBS 17:15

(12) Other Examples of proverbs or sayings NOT found in Holy Scriptures

(a) Moderation in all things

(b) This too shall pass.

(c) Predestination

(d) Wedding vows

(e) Once saved, always saved.

(f) The Sinner's Prayer

(g) The Prayer of Salvation

(h) The Roman Road

(i) Rapture - coined by Cotton Mather, infamous for his bloody role in the Salem witch-hunts and trials.

Fear God, and keep his commandments: for this is the whole duty of man. For God shall bring every work into judgment, with every secret thing, whether it be good, or whether it be evil... Heaven Awaits!

Finale

Contents of Finale

A. We are all living in the wilderness of sin and transgression

B. A Cry in the Wilderness

C. There is absolutely no escape from the Realm of God

A. We are all living in a wilderness of sin and transgression

The end of the Great War was a time of great joy for our nation. The troops were coming home.

The war machine had created much prosperity among the populace and the vast majority was happy and looking ahead with great expectations.

At that time, the technology of television existed, but was only available in very limited areas. People used their free time to study their Bibles, visit with friends, relatives, and attend church services or a Saturday movie.

Life was much simpler and safer, but many aspects of life were changing. Temptations of the flesh (eye-catching, near nude young ladies to attract attention in print publications) were used occasionally, then employed widely in the marketing of a wide range of products.

The fact that sex sells is all around us, in TV programs, advertising, movies and our daily mail.

It is reflected in many modes of dress and may be related to problems in our schools, shopping malls and in some cases, churches.

(1) In an attempt to improve and modernize America, our state and federal legislatures have created a moral and religious wilderness, which is reflected in Bob Russell's famous prayer of repentance.

In January of 1996, Joe Wright, senior pastor of the 2,500-member Central Christian Church in Wichita, was invited to offer a prayer on the opening day of the Kansas legislature by Representative Anthony Powell, a Wichita Republican who was also a member of Wright's church. .

Accordingly, *Wright prayed a version of a prayer of repentance that was written in 1995 by Bob Russell, pastor of Southeast Christian Church in Louisville, Kentucky, who offered it at the Kentucky Governor's Prayer Breakfast in Frankfort, Kentucky.* [9] at the opening of the legislature on January 23, and departed, unaware of the stir he had created until his church secretary called him on his car phone.

Heavenly Father, we come before you to ask your forgiveness. We seek your direction and your guidance. We know your word says,* "Woe to those who call evil good." But that's what we've done. (*This is a reference to ISAIAH chapter 5, verse 20, "Woe unto them that call evil good, and good evil; that put darkness for light, and light for darkness; that put bitter for sweet, and sweet for bitter!")

- ❖ **We have lost our Spiritual equilibrium and inverted our values.**
- ❖ **We have ridiculed the absolute truth of your Word and called it moral pluralism.**
- ❖ **We have worshipped other gods and called it multiculturalism.**
- ❖ **We have endorsed perversion and called it an alternative lifestyle.**
- ❖ **We have exploited the poor and called it a lottery.**
- ❖ **We have neglected the needy and called it self-preservation.**
- ❖ **We have rewarded laziness and called it welfare.**
- ❖ **We have killed our unborn and called it choice.**

- ❖ We have killed abortionists and called it justifiable.
- ❖ We have neglected to discipline our children and called it building esteem.
- ❖ We have abused power and called it political savvy.
- ❖ We have coveted our neighbor's possessions and called it ambition.
- ❖ We have polluted the air with profanity and pornography and called it freedom of expression.
- ❖ We have ridiculed the time-honored values of our forefathers and called it enlightenment.

Search us, oh, God, and know our hearts today; try us and see if there be some wicked within us; cleanse us from every sin and set us free.

Guide and bless these men and women who have been sent here by the people of the State of Kansas, and that they have been ordained by you to govern this great state

Grant them your wisdom to rule and may their decisions direct us to the center of your Will.

I ask it in the name of Your Son, the Living Savior, Jesus, Amen.

It was reported that one Democrat walked out in protest, three others gave speeches critical of Wright's prayer, and another blasted Wright's "message of intolerance." House Minority Leader Tom Sawyer (D) asserted that the prayer "reflects the extreme, radical views that continue to dominate the House Republican agenda since right-wing extremists seized control of the House Republican caucus last year."

But Representative Powell, who had invited Wright in the first place, claimed that House Democrats were only trying to make political points with their criticism and affirmed that he supported the theme of the prayer.

Wright said afterwards: "I certainly did not mean to be offensive to individuals, but I don't apologize for the truth."

His staff stopped counting the telephone calls that came from every state and many foreign countries after the first 6,500. Wright appeared on dozens of radio shows and was the subject of numerous TV and print news reports.

This prayer stirred up controversy all over again, when the chaplain coordinator in the Nebraska legislature delivered it, the following month.

Wright later explained, "I thought I might get a call from an angry congressman or two, but I was talking to God, not them. The whole point was to say that we all have sins that we need to repent - all of us.

The problem, I guess, is that you're not supposed to get too specific when you're talking about sin."

Reference: JUDE 1:14-15.

(2) After reviewing this prayer in-depth, the author cannot uncover any inconsistency with the Word of God. However, it does bring into sharp focus the distressing current state of our society and just how far it has drifted from religious standards of our forefathers and the Biblical basis upon which our great country was founded.

B. A Cry in the Wilderness

This is a cry in the wilderness for a final "Great Awakening" to carefully follow the commandments of our Lord and Savior, Jesus Christ, His Apostles and Disciples.

This earnest appeal for a final Great Awakening is based upon the serious dilemma faced by the vast majority of mankind, delineated as follows:

(1) Based upon the reality that the evil prince of this world or Satan has deluded millions using various tactics Satan has used men to twist the Words of the precious Lord Christ and the eternal effects that inappropriate worship may have on the unsuspecting.

Based upon a careful review of recent wide-ranging religious research surveys and publications, as well as, an extensive study of the Word of God, the distressing reality clearly indicates that millions of faithful believers, who love and serve the Lord, are worshipping in vain.

Regardless of the level of their faith, purity, righteousness and other Christ-like characteristics, all are in danger of being eternally lost if they do not take immediate steps to correct the fatal flaws in their beliefs and religious practices

It was prophesied early in the history of the church that such would come to pass. It happened then, **but today is occurring on a much larger scale, with the inclusion of worldly entertainment and promises of great monetary gain.**

TIMOTHY 4:3-4
For the time will come when they will not endure sound doctrine; but after their own lusts shall they heap to themselves teachers, having itching ears; **And they shall turn away their ears from the truth, and shall be turned unto fables.**

Additional references: 1 TIMOTHY 4:1-42, 2 PETER 2:1-3

(2) This is a desperate warning to the grave perils facing the majority of the human race and a fervent plea that all God-fearing individuals begin to work toward unity in a common religious faith, based solely upon obedience to the Words of Jesus, His Apostles or "a thus saith the Lord" in the Bible.

In other words, a Great Awakening is needed, for the worldwide restoration of the first century Church and the unification of all God-fearing believers, using only the pure, plain and simple Examples, Instructions, Patterns, and Commandments of Jesus, His Apostles and Disciples.

The reward of obedience is eternal life in Heaven. Permission to enter the Gates of Heaven must be the life goal of every individual endeavoring to walk the narrow path. In MATTHEW 7:13-14, **Jesus warned that narrow is the way, which leads to eternal life and that few will find it.**

It is of uppermost critical importance for each individual to put his or her spiritual affairs in the highest state of flawlessness because:

C. There is absolutely no escape from the Realm of God

From the very beginning Satan and his evil angels have attempted, usually very successfully, to cloud and misdirect the understanding of mankind, but there is absolutely no means of escape from the Realm of God.

In the Beginning God created the Heavens, earth and all things seen and unseen, as well as all living things. God created every aspect of our realm; **hence, He possesses everything and every living thing within that realm.**

No member of the human race has ever brought anything into this life, nor has been able to take anything from this life, regardless of how valuable, into the dominion of the dead.

Reference: GENESIS 14:22

On the sixth day God created the physical body of man and added the spirit or soul, which was created in His Image. God is a Spirit – therefore does not require a physical body or shell – therefore it is not that we look like Him physically, **but our spirit is in His image.**

GENESIS 1:26
And God said, Let us make man in our

image, after our likeness: and let them have dominion over the fish of the sea, and over the fowl of the air, and over the cattle, and over all the earth, and over every creeping thing that creepeth upon the earth.

Therefore, God is the legal Father of the spirit of every individual ever conceived.

The Spirit of God is eternal and in view of the fact that our spirits or soul were created in His Image that part of our being is also immortal and will live on forever.

Please consider carefully the following inexorable fact of life. **Just as there is no way to avoid physical death, likewise there is no escape from the spiritual realm of God.**

There are two realms of existence, the physical realm in which we all currently reside and the Spiritual Realm, in which we will all live forever, either in great joy or anguish, after our individual death or the second coming of Christ, whichever occurs first.

Jesus Christ is our Supreme Ruler and His Will, as defined by His Words, as well as the writings of His Apostles and Disciples, in the Holy Scriptures is the singular, absolute and final Law.

On Judgment Day, in that Realm, each individual will stand alone before the Master and is responsible to Him alone.

The understanding of this reality and the fact they we each have a choice as to where we spend our eternity should be overwhelming reasons for any reasonable individual to carefully consider the options available.

We plan for the future education of our children, a carefree retirement and our final resting place.

Of much greater importance is the planning of where an individual and his loved ones will spend eternity.

Death is not only the end of our mortal lives, but the beginning of our immortal spiritual lives, which will continue forever.

People all have a natural ingrained fear of the unknown. However, as we grow, we learn to overcome, in large part, this and many other forms of fear.

Therefore the fear of death is natural since it is the last great unknown, but logically it is really just the last phase in the natural progression of all living things.

Christ did not fear death, but was assured of being raised again. His words to the thief on the cross are recorded in LUKE 23:43. And Jesus said unto him, Verily I say unto thee, "Today shalt thou be with me in paradise." At the moment of His death Jesus cried with a loud voice, "Father, into thy hands I commend my spirit:" and having said thus, he gave up the ghost. (LUKE 23:46)

Death is simply a part of the earthly cycle of life and is our unavoidable exit from this world. **Our earthly death simply marks the beginning of an eternal existence.**

The unprepared face an everlasting punishment, from which there is NO POSSIBILITY OF ESCAPE.

On the other hand, individuals who have properly prepared, need not fear death, because they are victorious and have finally Attained Glorious Immortality... Heaven Awaits!

Reference:

[9] **Text of Prayer of Repentance and related newspaper reports regarding the opening prayer at a session of the Kansas House of Representatives, January 23, 1996, delivered by Joseph Wright, www.Snopes.com, www.snopes.com/inboxer/outrage/wright.asp,**

Closing Comments

The information provided, which is the case in the vast majority of similar works of men, **is based solely upon the author's personal interpretation and convictions** related to this most significant and important issue

The author has endeavored in the development of this guide to faithfully follow the advice of the Great Apostle Peter, who in 1 PETER 3:15 wrote "But sanctify in your hearts Christ as Lord: *being ready always to give answer to every man that asketh you a reason concerning the hope that is in you, yet with meekness [humbleness] and fear.*"

It is our sincere hope and prayer that you have found this personal guide to finding and following the narrow winding path to the Glorious Kingdom of Heaven useful and beneficial

Considering the ghastly and hideous alternative this search should be the number one ambition of every human being on earth!

Many believe that we are living in the final days of the earth; that soon Christ will return, the world will end and all human beings will face the final Judgment.

The writer would certainly agree that many signs of the end of the world, predicted by Jesus Christ, about 2000 years ago, are all present in the world today.

MATTHEW 24:7
For nation shall rise against nation, and kingdom against kingdom: and there shall be famines, and pestilences, and earthquakes, in divers [various] places.

However, in MATTHEW 24:36, we are told that only God, the Father knows the time and day the world will end.

Other elements of the prophecy of Jesus on this occasion are much clearer. "And many false prophets shall rise, and shall deceive many. And because iniquity shall abound, the love of many shall wax cold. But he that shall endure unto the end, the same shall be saved." (MATTHEW 24:11-13)

Unfortunately, hundreds of thousands of false prophets have arisen and millions of sincere individuals have been mislead.

The moral standards of our modern society have been substantially lowered since the Second World War, which has resulted in widespread sinfulness and as a result, immorality is rapidly proliferating in our culture.

At the same time, recent surveys indicate that Biblical literacy has reached an all-time high, which distressed many religious leaders, who are fully aware of the eternal consequence.

The author firmly believes that humanity is facing the final eminent catastrophe.

Therefore, it is his plea that each reader would carefully consider and then actively follow the teachings of our Lord, His Apostles and Disciples found in the inspired Word of God... and **always remember that...**

Prayer is the uppermost, finest and most rewarding investment of your earthly time... Heaven Awaits!

Suggested Outside References

Handbook of Denominations in the United States, 12th Edition by Craig D. Atwood, Frank S. Mead and Samuel S. Hill

Traditions of Men versus the Word of God, 1973, by Alvin Jennings

Discovering Our Roots, 1988, by Richard T. Hughes and C. Leonard Allen

References

General References:

Unless otherwise noted all Biblical verse references were copied from software provided by **eveningdew.com**. Electronic versions of the King James Bible, EveningDew Software, November 11, 2008. eveningdew-bible-system.findmysoft.com/

B.W. Johnson, **The People's New Testament. Volumes I and II,** Delight, AR: Gospel Light Publishing Company, 1891

B.W. Johnson, **The New Testament. Commentary Volume III - John,** St Louis 3, MO: Christian Board of Publication, 1886

Holy Bible, New International Version, Nashville, TN: Broadman & Holman Publishers, 1995

Life Application Study Bible, version of King James Bible, Wheaton, IL: Tyndale House Publishers, Inc, 1988-1989

Master Study Bible, version of King James Bible, Nashville, TN: Cornerstone Bible Publishers, 2001

Specific References:

Chapter I

[a] **The Names of God in the Old Testament,** Blue Letter Bible, www.blueletterbible.org, April 1 2002.

Chapter IX

[b] Source: Bible History Online www.bible-history.com/geography/ancient-israel/new-testament-cities.html

This site is also an excellent source of color maps and other ancient area information.

Appendix 3

[1] Jennings, Alvin, **Traditions of Men versus The Word of God**, Fort Worth, TX: Star Bible Publications, 1973.

[2] Steig, Shelly, **Finding the Right Church: A Guide to Denomination Beliefs,** Grand Rapids, MI: Word Publishing, 1997

[3] Cochrane, Mike, **Christianity, Cults & Religions,** Torrance, CA: Rose Publishing, 1994

[4] Stewart, John David, **A Study of Minor Religious Beliefs in America,** Austin, TX: R.B. Sweet Co., 1962

[5] Stewart, John David, **A Study of Major Religious Beliefs in America,** Austin, TX: R.B. Sweet Co., 1962.

[6] Algermissen, Konrad, **Christian Sects,** New York: Hawthorn Books, 1962

[7] Mead, Frank S. **Handbook of Denominations in the United States,** Nashville: Abingdon Press, 1975.

[8] Tomlinson, L.G. **Churches of Today in the Light of Scripture,** Nashville: Gospel Advocate Company, 1962.

Finale

[9] **Text of Prayer of Repentance and related newspaper reports regarding the opening prayer at a session of the Kansas House of Representatives, January 23, 1996,** delivered by Joseph Wright, www.Snopes.com, www.snopes.com/inboxer/outrage/wright.asp, October 27, 2008

Be thou faithful unto death, and I will give thee a crown of life:...
Heaven Awaits!

#######

Detailed Outline of Contents

General Prologue — 7

A. Introduction
B. Summary of Objectives
C. Overview of Appendixes
D. Detailed Outline of Contents
E. How to make the best use of this manual
F. The very first day of Eternity
G. Closing Comments

Chapter I: Understanding our God — 25

A. Introduction
B. Seek First the Kingdom Of God
C. Examples of what Lord Jesus really wants from His followers.
D. Support for an Absolute Belief in God
E. Fear of the Lord Is the Basis of All Knowledge, Wisdom and Understanding
F. The Godhead, a Divine Entity
G. Earthly Structures Similar To the Divine Composition
H. Understanding the Nature of the God of Heaven
I. The Interrelationship and Interaction of the Godhead
J. Attributes of the Godhead
K. Examples of the awesome Power and ferocious Wrath of God
L: The Wrath of God
M. The Love of God
N. The Grace of God
O. Patterns of God
P. Our God is a God of Patterns
Q. Examples of the Blueprints or Patterns of God
R. Patterns provided to Moses and the nation of Israel
S. Pattern of the Temple
T. God requires strict obedience to His Patterns and Commandments.
U. Examples of Disobedience to the Patterns of God
V. Final Comments

Chapter II: Guide to the Divine Format of the Bible — 55

A. Introduction
B. Overview of the Divine Mosaic
C. Simple technique of determining the Divine Will of God
D. Keystones of the Faith
E. Cornerstones of the Faith
F. Generally accepted Biblical facts regarding Lord Jesus and His Church.
G. Examples of general elements of the Divine Mosaic
H. Closing Comments

Chapter III: The Message of Christ — 63

A. Introduction
B. Overview Message of Christ
C. Elements of the Message of Christ
D. Lord Jesus did NOT promise

Chapter IV: The Authority of Christ — 71

A. The Divine Authority of Christ
B. True and False Authority

Chapter V: The Church that Jesus Built — 75

A. Introduction
B. Importance of understanding the Message of Christ
C. Divine Authority is Mandatory
D. Divine Patterns of the Faith
E. Jesus Christ established His Church
F. His Divine Pattern of Scriptural Worship
G. His Divine Pattern of Organizational Structure
H. His Divine Pattern of the Work of the Congregation
I. Christianity is much more than a succession of Patterns
J. Role of female members of His Church
K. Christians must be properly attired
L. Eternal future of His Church

Chapter VI: Preparing for your place in Heaven — 89

A. Becoming a Disciple of Christ
B. Counting the Cost of becoming a Christian
C. His Divine Pattern or Plan of Salvation
D. Remaining Faithful
E. Examples of how Christians exhibit faithfulness
F. Cleansing Power of the Blood of Christ
G. Pattern of Prayer, our access to God
H. Developing an appropriate Attitude
I. Common concern and misperception
J. Jesus urged vigilance and opposition to false prophets and teachings
K. Warnings of false teachers and teaching issued by His Apostles
L. Expect to be criticized for basing your beliefs upon the Words of Jesus

Chapter VII: The Way of the Cross — 105

A. Why did our Savior come to earth?
B. Three days that altered the course of world history
C. The universal problem of sin
D. Why was it necessary for Christ to die on the cross?
E. Satan, the evil prince of this world
F. What happens after death?
G. The Second Coming of Christ
H. The Day of Judgment
I. Knowledge of the absolute certainty of the Day of Judgment
J. The final Verdict

K. The Glory of Heaven
L. Who will be given Divine permission to enter the magnificent Realm of God?
M. Final Comments

Chapter VIII: Introduction to the Life of Christ — 123

A. Pre-existence of Jesus
B. Prophecies and predictions of the Messiah
C. Setting the Stage for His Divine Birth

Chapter IX: The Life of Christ — 127

A. Introduction
B. Life of Christ prior to His Ministry
C. Role of John the Baptist
D. Jesus prepares for His Ministry
E. Launches His Ministry in Galilee, Judea and Samaria
F. Great Galilean Ministry
G. Further training of the Twelve
H. Later Judean Ministry
I. Perean Ministry
J. Culmination of His Miracles and Teachings
K. The Final Days of Jesus in Jerusalem
L. His Last Day with His Apostles
M. The Final Day of His earthly Life
N. His Resurrection
O. His Appearances
P. His Ascension to His Father
Q. Many actions and sayings of Jesus not recorded
R. From His Ascension to Pentecost
S. Divine Involvement and Appearances since His Ascension
T. Yesterday, today, until He comes again and forever Lord Jesus or the Word of God is God and High Priest

Chapter X: Christ, our ultimate Pattern — 165

A. Introduction
B. Christians are to be formed, conformed and transformed
C. Jesus Christ is the complete living Word of God
D. Importance of Fellowship with likeminded Christians
E. Examples of the Teachings of Christ
F. Examples of the Teachings of His Disciples

Chapter XI: Simplified Overview of the Old Testament — 171

A. Introduction
B. Three major topics
C. Results of these Promises and His Covenant
D. Books of the Old Testament

Chapter XII: Simplified overview of the New Testament — 181

A. Christ is the Heart of the Bible
B. God laid the Groundwork
C. An Account of Jesus Christ and His New Covenant
D. The Four Gospels
E. Acts of the Apostles
F. The Epistles
G. The Revelation of Jesus Christ

Appendix 1: Quick Start Guide to Glorious Immortality — 191

A. Introduction
B. The Importance of understanding Truth
C. Divine Authority is Mandatory
D. Divine Patterns of the Faith
E. Determining the Identify of His Church
F. His Divine Pattern or Plan of Salvation.
G. Closing Comments
H. Now, make your commitment to your Lord and Savior PERSONAL!

Appendix 2: Checklist to determine if a religious group is His Church — 199

A. Introduction
B. Fundamental Considerations
C. Beliefs regarding Jesus Christ
D. Scriptural Names
E. Scriptural Worship
F. His Divine Pattern or Plan of Salvation

Appendix 3: Comparative Analysis - Do you attend His Church? — 203

A. Do you attend His Church?
B. Comparative Analysis
C. Jesus warned His followers to beware of false teachers
D. Two questions to seriously consider

Appendix 4: Examples of unsupported Religious Teachings — 211

A. Introduction
B. Recommendations
C. Examples of False Teachings

Appendix 5: Comparative Analysis of selected religious organizations — 217

A. The Divine Pattern – His Church
B. Baptist Church
C. Catholic Church
D. Episcopal Church
E. Lutheran Church
F. Presbyterian Church
G. Methodist Church
H. Christian Church/Disciples of Christ
I. Church of Jesus Christ of Latter Day Saints
J. Jehovah's Witnesses
K. Seventh-Day Adventists
L. Make your own Comparative Analysis Forms

Appendix 6: Summary of selected Elements of the Divine Mosaic — 223

A. Introduction
B. Examples of what Lord Jesus really wants from His followers
C. Examples of the Keystones of the Faith
D. Cornerstones of the Faith
E. Generally accepted Biblical facts regarding Lord Jesus and His Church
F. Examples of general elements of the Divine Mosaic
G. Elements of the Message of Christ
H. Worship according to the Divine Pattern
I. Divine Pattern of Congregational Organizational Structure
J. Divine Pattern of the work of His Church
K. Date and Place of the Establishment of His Church
L. His Divine Pattern or Plan of Salvation
M. Examples of how Christians exhibit faithfulness
N. The Cleansing Power of the Blood of Christ
O. Christ, our ultimate Pattern

Appendix 7: Words of Jesus, His Apostles and Disciples (with significant quotes from the Old Testament) — 233

A. Introduction
B: Scriptural references by topic

Appendix 8: Selected Prayers and related Teachings of Jesus — 245

A. Great recorded Prayers of Jesus
B. Prayers of Jesus, referenced, but not recorded
C. Selected Teachings of Jesus regarding Prayer
D. Memorable Quotation

Appendix 9: Significant recorded Prayers of the Bible — 247

A. Introduction
B. Selected prayers of the Bible
C. Other significant prayers

Appendix 10: Relief for the anxious or troubled Mind and Spirit — 249

A. Introduction
B. Human beings all have a natural deep-rooted longing for God
C. Jesus and His Disciples were well acquainted with grief and sorrows
D. Blessed Assurance

Appendix 11: Message to new Christians — 251

A. Introduction
B. Blessings in Christ
C. Recommended course of action

Appendix 12 Biblical Myths, Misconceptions and Mysteries — 255

A. Introduction
B. Adam and Eve
C. Noah's Ark
D. The Ark of His Testament
E. Jonah and the whale
F. Birth of our Lord
G. Resurrection of our Lord
H. Well Known Expressions Not found in Holy Scriptures

Finale — 265

A. We are all living in the wilderness of sin and transgression
B. A Cry in the Wilderness
C. There is absolutely no escape from the Realm of God

Closing Comments — 269

Suggested Outside References — 269

References — 270

Detailed Outline of Contents — 271

Sources of additional information — 274

For the Son of man is come to seek and to save that which was lost ...Heaven Awaits!

Additional works by J. William Goddard coming soon

In His Footsteps: Heaven Awaits!

An all-inclusive guide to successfully Attaining Glorious immortality in the magnificent Kingdom of Heaven

A simplified approach to a complex subject, dedicated to assisting all His faithful followers or Christians, who wish to increase and enhance their understanding of the Message of Christ.

A Scriptural Guide to Sex, Love and Marriage: Heaven Awaits!

A forthright, clear-cut, easy to understand guide based upon the Word of God

All publications will also be available as e-books.

Additional works by J. William Goddard in development

Attaining Glorious Immortality: Heaven Awaits!

A comprehensive reference manual for Ministers, Evangelists and Teachers

Additional volumes covering advanced spiritual concepts will be produced in the same format, if God wills and only through His gracious providence.

Comments, suggestions or corrections

Are always welcomed and appreciated. Please feel free to forward an e-mail message to luckylynde@gmx.com or drop a note to 131 W. Foley #1445, Eufaula, OK 74432.

For further information, please visit the following web sites:

(Web sites are currently under construction, are expected to be available in early 2014)

attain-glorious-immortality.com

and

truth-of-his-word.com

But rather seek ye the kingdom of God; and all these things shall be added unto you: Heaven Awaits!

www.ingramcontent.com/pod-product-compliance
Lightning Source LLC
Chambersburg PA
CBHW080552090426
42735CB00016B/3212